THE NEW SOUTH

"*The New South* represents the work of some of the most outstanding members of a generation of historians whose work is transforming the way we think about the New South. It will be a great asset to scholars and teachers and a fascinating read for all who are interested in southern history and culture."
—Marjorie J. Spruill, author of *New Women of the New South: The Leaders of the Woman Suffrage Movement in the Southern States*

"Broad in scope and use, *The New South* is an invaluable survey of social and political approaches to work on the South in the twentieth century."
—Grace Elizabeth Hale, author of *Making Whiteness: The Culture of Segregation in the South, 1890–1940*

"*The New South* represents a one-volume treasury of important historical research and recent reinterpretation of the South between the Civil War and the civil rights movement."
—Elizabeth H. Turner, co-author of *Galveston and the 1900 Storm: Catastrophe and Catalyst*

"Professor Harris has assembled some of the finest essays available on a wide range of topics, from individual and collective memory to race, gender, the politics of culture, and the origins of the long civil rights movement. Each essay is accessible and interesting in its own right. Tied together in an elegant and informative introduction, these essays indicate that we have indeed moved into a new era of New South scholarship."
—Jennifer Ritterhouse, author of *Growing Up Jim Crow: How Black and White Southern Children Learned Race*

The era that followed Reconstruction and continued through the Civil Rights Movement in the South has been known since the 1880s as the "New South." Historian C. Vann Woodward laid a foundation for future scholarship of this period through his classic work on the political economy of the postwar South, but new voices are now transforming our understanding of the era in a number of important ways.

In *The New South: New histories*, J. William Harris has compiled an accessible and thorough collection of recent studies highlighting several broad trends notable in the work of today's scholars.

J. William Harris is Professor of History at the University of New Hampshire. He is the author of *Plain Folk and Gentry in a Slave Society* and *Deep Souths: Delta, Piedmont, and Sea Island Society in the Age of Segregation*.

REWRITING HISTORIES focuses on historical themes where standard conclusions are facing a major challenge. Each book presents eight to ten papers (edited and annotated where necessary) at the forefront of current research and interpretation, offering students an accessible way to engage with contemporary debates.

Series editor **Jack R. Censer** is Professor of History at George Mason University.

REWRITING HISTORIES
Series editor: Jack R. Censer

THE NEW SOUTH

New histories

Edited by
J. William Harris

Routledge
Taylor & Francis Group

NEW YORK AND LONDON

First published 2008
by Routledge
270 Madison Ave, New York, NY 10016

Simultaneously published in the UK
by Routledge
2 Park Square, Milton Park, Abingdon, Oxon OX14 4RN

*Routledge is an imprint of the Taylor & Francis Group,
an informa business*

Typeset in Palatino by
RefineCatch Limited, Bungay, Suffolk
Printed and bound in the
United States of America on acid-free paper by
Edwards Brothers, Inc.

Library of Congress Cataloging in Publication Data
The new South : new histories / edited by J. William Harris.
p.   cm.—(Rewriting histories)
Includes bibliographical references and index.
ISBN-13: 978–0–415–95730–4 (hardback : alk. paper)
ISBN-10: 0415–95730–3 (hardback : alk. paper)
ISBN-13: 978–0–415–95731–1 (pbk. : alk. paper)
ISBN-10: 0–415–95731–1 (pbk. : alk. paper)   1. Southern States—
History—1865–1951.   2. Southern States—Historiography.   3. Southern
States—Social conditions—1865–1945.   4. Southern States—Race
relations. I. Harris, J. William, 1946– .
F215.N495 2007
306.0975′09034—dc22   2007025718

ISBN 10: 0–415–95730–3 (hbk)
ISBN 10: 0–415–95731–1 (pbk)

ISBN 13: 978–0–415–95730–4 (hbk)
ISBN 13: 978–0–415–95731–1 (pbk)

CONTENTS

CONTENTS

SERIES EDITOR'S PREFACE

Rewriting history, or revisionism, has always followed closely in the wake of history writing. In their efforts to reevaluate the past, professional as well as amateur scholars have followed many approaches, most commonly as empiricists, uncovering new information to challenge earlier accounts. Historians have also revised previous versions by adopting new perspectives, usually fortified by new research, which overturn received views.

Even though rewriting is constantly taking place, historians' attitudes towards using new interpretations have been anything but settled. For most, the validity of revisionism lies in providing a stronger, more convincing account that better captures the objective truth of the matter. Although such historians might agree that we never finally arrive at the "truth," they believe it exists, and that over time it may be better approximated. At the other extreme stand scholars who believe that each generation or even each cultural group or subgroup necessarily regards the past differently, each creating for itself a more usable history. Although these latter scholars do not reject the possibility of demonstrating empirically that some contentions are better than others, they focus upon generating new views based upon different life experiences. Different truths exist for different groups. Surely such an understanding, by emphasizing subjectivity, further encourages rewriting history. Between these two groups are those historians who wish to borrow from both sides. This third group, while accepting that every congeries of individuals sees matters differently, still wishes, somewhat contradictorily, to fashion a broader history that incorporates both of these particular visions. Revisionists who stress empiricism fall into the first of the three camps, while others spread out across the board.

Today the rewriting of history seems to have accelerated to a blinding speed as a consequence of the evolution of revisionism. A variety of approaches has emerged. A major factor in this process has been the enormous increase in the number of researchers. This explosion has reinforced and enabled the retesting of many assertions. Significant ideological shifts have also played a major part in the growth of revisionism. First, the crisis of Marxism, culminating in the events in eastern Europe in 1989, has given rise to doubts about explicitly Marxist accounts. Such doubts have spilled over into the entire field of social history, which has been a dominant subfield of the discipline for several decades. Focussing on society and its class divisions implied that these are the most important elements in historical analysis. Because Marxism was built on the same claim, the whole basis of social history has been questioned, despite the very many studies that directly had little to do with Marxism. Disillusionment with social history simultaneously opened the door to cultural and linguistic approaches largely developed in anthropology and literature. Multiculturalism and feminism further generated revisionism. By claiming that scholars had, wittingly or not, operated from a white European/American male point of view, newer researchers argued that other approaches had been neglected or misunderstood. Not surprisingly, these last historians are the most likely to envision each subgroup rewriting its own usable history, while other scholars incline towards revisionism as part of the search for some stable truth.

Rewriting Histories will make these new approaches available to the student population. Often new scholarly debates take place in the scattered issues of journals that are sometimes difficult to find. Furthermore, in these first interactions, historians tend to address one another, leaving out the evidence that would make their arguments more accessible to the uninitiated. This series of books will collect in one place a strong group of the major articles in selected fields, adding notes and introductions conducive to improved understanding. Editors will select articles containing substantial historical data, so that students—at least those who approach the subject as an objective phenomenon—can advance not only their comprehension of debated points but also their grasp of substantive aspects of the subject.

Conceptualized by Henry Grady rather early in its existence, the New South nonetheless received little historical attention until C. Vann Woodward's classic work, *Origins of the New South* (1951). In this study Woodward argued that an alliance between northern and southern elites introduced capitalism and also suppressed the economic and political desires of the impoverished, both white and black. Until quite recently this synthesis so dominated interpretations that even those who wished to revise it also worked with it. Now, a new wave of scholarship that focuses on gender, race, and local issues has so engulfed the field that no single hypothesis reigns. In fact, Harris points out that the most recent general approach authored by Edward Ayers can be characterized more by its nuances and shadings than by any clear-cut position regarding the character of the New South. In a sense, the situation here reflects the most recent wave of scholarship that, influenced by postmodernism, embraces ambiguities and impressionistic interpretations.

ACKNOWLEDGMENTS

The editor and publishers wish to thank the following for their permission to reproduce copyright material:

Elsa Barkley Brown, "Negotiating and Transforming the Public Sphere: African American Political Life in the Transition from Slavery to Freedom," in *Jumpin' Jim Crow: Southern Politics from Civil War to Civil Rights*, ed. by Jane Dailey, Glenda Elizabeth Gilmore, and Bryant Simon (Princeton: Princeton University Press, 2000), 28–66.

Jane Turner Censer, "A Changing World of Work: North Carolina Elite Women, 1865–1895," *North Carolina Historical Review*, 73 (1996), 28–55.

Stephen Kantrowitz, "Farmers, Dudes, White Negroes, and the Sun-Browned Goddess," from *Ben Tillman & the Reconstruction of White Supremacy* (Chapel Hill: University of North Carolina Press, 2000), 113–122 and 147–55.

J. William Harris, "Etiquette, Lynching, and Racial Boundaries in Southern History: A Mississippi Example," *American Historical Review*, 100 (April 1995), 387–410.

Nancy A. Hewitt, "New Women," from *Southern Discomfort: Women's Activism in Tampa, Florida, 1880s–1920s* (Urbana, Ill., 2001), chapter 8.

Victoria E. Bynum, "Defiance and Domination: 'White Negroes' in the Piney Woods New South," chapter 8 in Bynum, *The Free State of Jones: Mississippi's Longest Civil War* (Chapel Hill: University of North Carolina Press, 2001), 149–76.

Jack E. Davis, "Pilgrimage to the Past: Public History, Women, and the Racial Order," chapter 2 in Davis, *Race Against Time: Culture and Separation in Natchez since 1930* (Baton Rouge: Louisiana State University Press, 2001), 52–54; 60–82.

W. Fitzhugh Brundage, "Le Reveil de la Louisiane: Memory and

Acadian Identity, 1920–1960," in *Where these Memories Grow: History, Memory, and Southern Identity*, ed. by W. Fitzhugh Brundage (Chapel Hill, University of North Carolina Press 2000), 271–98.

Patricia Sullivan, "Southern Seeds of Change, 1931–1938," from *Days of Hope: Race and Democracy in the New Deal Era* (Chapel Hill: University of North Carolina Press, 1996), 69–93, 96–101.

Jacquelyn Dowd Hall, " 'You Must Remember This': Autobiography as Social Critique," *Journal of American History*, 85 (September 1998), 439–65.

Raymond Arsenault, " 'You Don't Have to Ride Jim Crow': CORE and the 1947 Journey of Reconciliation," in *Before* Brown: *Civil Rights and White Backlash in the Modern South*, ed. by Glenn Feldman (Tuscaloosa: University of Alabama Press, 2004), 32–40, 44–65, 67.

Glenn T. Eskew, "Bombingham," excerpted from chapter 2 in Eskew, *But for Birmingham: The Local and National Movements in the Civil Rights Struggle* (Chapel Hill: University of North Carolina Press, 1997), 53–63; 66–83.

Jane Dailey, "Sex, Segregation, and the Sacred after *Brown*," *Journal of American History*, 91 (June 2004), 119–38, 142–44.

Every effort has been made to contact the copyright holders and relevant parties. The publishers would be very grateful for notification of any omissions.

INTRODUCTION

I

This volume collects examples of the "new histories" being written of the "New South." To understand the sense in which they are in fact "new," it will be helpful to begin with the era when "New South" itself was a fresh term. In 1886, speaking before the New England Club of New York City, Atlanta editor Henry Grady proclaimed the arrival of such a "new South." Unlike the old South, which had "rested everything on slavery and agriculture," this new South had created "a hundred farms for every plantation," "established thrift in city and country," "fallen in love with work," and "achieved a fuller independence for the South than that which our fathers sought . . . to compel in the field by their swords." This new South was also "a perfect democracy, the oligarchs leading in the popular movement"; as for "the negro," the record showed that "no section shows a more prosperous laboring population than the negroes of the South, none in fuller sympathy with the employing and land-owning class."[1]

The concept of a "New South" stuck as a way to distinguish the South after the end of Reconstruction from the "Old South" of slavery. And the first historian of the new South accepted Grady's portrait of the region as a place of progress and promise, where enlightened leaders had justifiably eliminated most black voters from the rolls.[2] Yet perhaps the most accurate thing to say about the early historiography of the New South is that it hardly existed. For example, David M. Potter, writing in 1950, pointed out that in the 15 years after its founding in 1935, the premier scholarly journal in the field, *The Journal of Southern History*, included just 35 articles (out of a total of 215) with a chronological focus on the period after Reconstruction.[3] Potter went on to suggest that southern historians "divert more of [their] research to the twentieth century and the last quarter of the nineteenth." Most surprising to today's reader, he noted that not a single article had appeared in the *Journal* on "the social or economic condition of . . . Negroes since

1

1877," nor a single one on "segregation in the schools, the churches, . . . the public conveniences and public conveyances, or other institutions of the South." "Moreover," he added, "our whole approach" to these subjects was "through some other medium, for example, 'Tom Watson and the Negro,' . . . rather than by means of a direct consideration of the Negro himself."[4]

II

The near absence of historical attention to this period, especially on such central topics as African-American life or the rise of segregation, helps to explain the tremendous influence of a work appearing the year following Potter's survey: C. Vann Woodward's *Origins of the New South, 1877–1913.*[5] In his sweeping synthesis, Woodward presented an enduring interpretation of the post-Reconstruction South, one that differed from Grady's description at almost every point. The New South, Woodward argued, was dominated by a ruling group of industrialists and planters, allies of northern businessmen, who had fastened their grip on southern politics and society to the detriment of both blacks and poor whites. They "redeemed" the South from the "carpetbaggers" and "scalawags" of Reconstruction, took control of the Democratic Party in the region, then acquiesced as the South became, economically, a "colonial" dependent of northeastern capital. In the 1890s, they fought off a challenge to their power and policies from poor farmers (and some industrial workers) of both races in the Populist Party. Like the rest of the country, the South went through a period of Progressive reform, albeit reform "for whites only." The final chapter of *Origins* outlined "the return of the South" to national power as an essential element of Democrat Woodrow Wilson's presidency. Woodward's interpretation, based on deep research, was lucid and elegant; it was also morally powerful, as he clearly took the side of those "who were run, who were managed, and maneuvered and pushed around" against that of the wealthy whites who "ran things."[6] The book became, as one scholar noted 35 years later, the "model against which any new interpretation of the South of the late nineteenth century and the Progressive Era would be measured."[7]

Woodward followed *Origins of the New South* with a shorter, but still highly influential book, *The Strange Career of Jim Crow.*[8] Elaborating on his earlier work, Woodward traced the rise of Jim Crow in the South to the need of the southern political elite to fend off the Populist dream of uniting poor white and black southerners in a program of democratic reform. Southern white leaders fashioned a new regime of racial repression in the 1890s, instituting legal segregation and stripping African Americans of the right to vote. In so doing, they ended a period of relative flexibility and openness in race relations, characteristic, according to Woodward, of the 1880s.

In combination, Woodward's books set the agenda for scholarly research on the history of the New South. Many historians took up Woodward's points, deepening our understanding of such topics as Henry Grady's "New South creed," the origins of Populism, the movement to disfranchise black voters, or the sources of southern economic backwardness.[9] These historians modified some of Woodward's specific interpretations, without challenging his fundamental arguments. Others did challenge the key arguments, disputing, for example, whether planters or urban businessmen were allies or enemies, whether the rise of formal segregation in the 1890s merely ratified in law an already-pervasive custom, or whether Tom Watson and other southern Populists had been truly committed to political equality for blacks.[10] Still, the terms of the debates were largely Woodward's, and his questions and sources continued to be the starting points for other historians' research.[11]

III

When Woodward published his influential books, the political and racial regime established in the 1890s was still in place. The Civil Rights revolt of the 1950s and 1960s radically altered the orientation of historians of the South in many ways (as it did for historians of the U.S. more generally), and African-American history became, for the first time, a central preoccupation of the historical profession. Woodward himself was unusual among southern historians in the attention he paid to black history, but his interest was focused mainly on African Americans' place in the South's economic and political systems, rather than on African-American life in itself. (The work of African-American scholars, much of it distinguished, did not enter the professional mainstream before 1950.) By the 1960s, many young historians were attracted to the study of African-American history, and those interested in the South after Reconstruction were attracted especially to the Civil Rights Movement. They produced many important studies: of Martin Luther King and other leaders, of the Student Non-Violent Coordinating Committee and other organizations, and of dramatic confrontations such as the Montgomery bus boycott, the sit-ins, and the Selma campaign.[12]

The combination of Woodward's legacy and the attention to the drama of the Civil Rights Movement created a second kind of historiographical influence: on the chronological boundaries that dominated historians' attention. Thus the writings, on the one hand, of Woodward, his supporters, and his critics, and, on the other hand, of

3

historians of the Civil Rights Movement at its height, formed, in tandem, a set of bookends that tended to focus historians' research primarily on the formation of a New South in the late nineteenth century and on its (partial) destruction in the 1950s and 1960s. Notwithstanding significant work on the intervening years (notably George B. Tindall's *The Emergence of the New South, 1913–1945*[13]) the long period from 1913 to the end of World War II drew the attention of relatively few scholars, and the overall effect was of a history that had fast-forwarded through several decades between two eras of political and racial change.[14]

IV

The imprint of Woodward's books and arguments is still with us, and studies of the Civil Rights Movement have burgeoned. But in the past 25 years, the study of the New South, like historical scholarship more generally, has been transformed by the shift of attention, going back to the 1960s, toward the lives and cultures of ordinary people. Social historians have been especially attracted to the study of groups relatively neglected in earlier studies: African Americans, women, and workers in an industrializing society. In southern history, the new attention to African Americans has already been noted.[15] The appearance of Anne Firor Scott's *The Southern Lady: From Pedestal to Politics, 1830–1930* gave a crucial boost to the study of women, and by the mid-1980s scholarship on southern women had blossomed.[16] Southern industrial workers, too, received new attention.[17] Social history often took the form of in-depth studies of particular communities, where researchers could take advantage of censuses, tax records, and other sources with information on ordinary people. Dozens of New South communities have been the subjects of such intense study. In a related development, historians began to pay far more attention to ethnic groups, such as immigrants and Mexican-Americans, and geographical areas, such as the southern borderlands and highland regions, that fit poorly, or not at all, within the simple dichotomy of "white" and "black" that has shaped much writing on southern history.[18]

Cultural historians, like social historians, turned their attention to ordinary people in studies of race, religion, family, gender, and popular memory.[19] In practice, these subjects are often deeply intertwined. For example, it is impossible to understand the nature of racial violence in the South without understanding also popular conceptions of gender, since white supremacists often justified or excused violence against African Americans as necessary to protect the "purity" of white women.[20] Similarly, historians of the New South have shown how southern whites crafted and popularized historical memories of slavery, the Civil War, and Reconstruction that helped to justify and strengthen an oppressive racial regime of Jim Crow.[21]

V

The essays collected here have been chosen to represent some of these prominent trends in current research: memory; women and gender; the meanings of race at particular moments in particular communities; the diversity of peoples in the South. In many ways their subjects can be seen as natural extensions of concerns evident in Woodward's work, but they also show that historians of the New South have passed into what might be called a "post-Woodward" era of research, in the questions they ask and the methods they use. They also illustrate research that is "post-Woodward" in a more mundane sense, in their focus on the period from World War I to the 1950s. A theme evident in the latter essays is that the South was never static, and that, long before the mid-1950s, we can see manifestations of what historian Jacquelyn Dowd Hall, among others, has called the "long Civil Rights Movement."[22]

Three of the essays here deal explicitly with public memory: Jack E. Davis's analysis of the annual "Natchez Pilgrimage," Jacquelyn Dowd Hall's essay on Katherine Du Pre Lumpkin, and W. Fitzhugh Brundage's study of the "revival" of Acadian identity in Louisiana. The women of the Pilgrimage portrayed the southern past in ways that helped to reinforce white supremacy, but Hall's essay shows how a mid-twentieth-century intellectual used her personal memories to build "a new perspective" that allowed her openly to challenge white supremacy. As Brundage shows, however, those who promoted the preservation of "authentic" Acadian history and culture largely ignored race, slavery, and the Civil War.

Several of the essays—those of Elsa Barkely Brown, Jane Turner Censer, and Nancy A. Hewitt, as well as Hall and Davis—focus explicitly on women—white and black, immigrants and natives, insiders and outsiders, traditionalists and reformers. Several others demonstrate the fruitfulness of gender analysis for understanding the course of southern history. The selections by Victoria E. Bynum, J. William Harris, and Stephen Kantrowitz all show how popular conceptions of masculinity and femininity helped to shape the popular conceptions of racial difference, and vice versa, with consequences in many areas of public life.

Several of the essays included here are based on local studies. Bynum, Harris, Brown, Hewitt, Davis, and Glenn T. Eskew each examine in depth a single city, town, or rural county. Together they show how the specifics of time and place have shaped the meanings of race and class in southern communities, and how those meanings can change over time.

A majority of the essays cover events or developments in the period between the Progressive era and the mid-1950s. Essays by Eskew, Patricia Sullivan, and Raymond Arsenault, in particular, are concerned with the origins of the "long Civil Rights Movement." They show the importance of the activism in the 1930s and 1940s in creating conditions and precedents for the great popular movement of later decades. Finally, Jane Dailey's essay offers an important counterpoint—the deep roots of the *opposition* to desegregation in popular white religious culture.

VI

One result of historians' attention to local settings and to cultural diversity is a far greater sense of complexity in southern history after Reconstruction. A further consequence is that, while southern historians may have gone "beyond" the Woodward interpretation, they have not replaced it with a comparable, overarching synthesis.

This was evident in the appearance of, and reaction to, the most ambitious attempt since *Origins of the New South* to synthesize and explain the 30-year period after Reconstruction in the South: Edward L. Ayers's *The Promise of the New South: Life after Reconstruction*.[23] As Ayers explained, he was especially interested in "everyday life" in the New South. He incorporated many of the voices of ordinary southerners, and he paid much attention to regional and local diversity within the South. His "open" narrative, as he called it, portrayed the South as "a new hybrid society of indeterminate shape." It was a place both "fluid and active"; its history was marked by "contingency and multiplicity," "disjunctions," "continual redefinition and renegotiation," and "unresolved tensions." One reviewer, acknowledging the resulting richness in Ayers's portrayal, nevertheless concluded that "Ayers's diversity and fluidity becomes chaos—no different from that experienced by any other rapidly changing society."[24] In defense of his approach, Ayers argued that he did see the period as united by an overarching theme: that "the currents of industrial capitalism, the national state, and new cultural styles ran deeply throughout the New South," and that, "as a result, there were things going on simultaneously . . . that appeared to have little to do with one another but that in fact spring from a common source: the conflict between the economic, ideological, and cultural legacies of the slave South and those conveyed by the human and material carriers of late nineteenth-century modernity." In the broadest sense, one might describe the New South of Woodward in similar terms, but Ayers concluded that the

South's struggles with modernity made its history more complex than "any of the categories that historians have devised to explain them."[25]

When we consider that Ayers's book covers only the period from 1877 to 1906, when the "New South" had, by most definitions, still almost two generations to live, it is clear that synthesizing the rich explorations of culture and the detailed analyses of complex changes in many different communities and regions—exemplified by the essays in this volume—will be a daunting task for future historians. Perhaps they will conclude, as one has suggested, that the term "New South" itself should be relegated to a more modest function, to name a particular conception of a particular time "that has meaning only by virtue of the claims of its late nineteenth- and early twentieth-century boosters."[26]

The challenges of synthesis and interpretation faced by historians of the New South are common in much historical writing. This is only in part because of the sheer volume of new research. It is also because, as recent historians have emphasized, people in the past, including those marginalized in earlier historical writing, have resisted and sometimes blunted the structures of cultural, political, and economic power that have sought to contain and constrain them. Those who, as C. Vann Woodward put it, "were run, who were managed, and maneuvered and pushed around," at times refused to run, evaded the managers, maneuvered themselves, and pushed back. In so defying and evading the categories in which their contemporaries sought to confine them, they also defy and evade categorization by the historians who seek to understand the history of the South. It is thus the agency of people in the past, as much as any factor, that makes it difficult for historians to construct neat syntheses of their history.

A NOTE ON EDITORIAL PRACTICE

All the essays here have been reduced from their original length, some modestly, others more extensively. Cuts in the texts of essays are indicated with ellipses, and when explanatory comments have been added in the text itself, these are enclosed in brackets []. Editor's explanatory notes, including notes pointing to omitted topics, appear at the bottom of the page. Notes from the original essays appear at the end of each chapter. While few of the authors' original notes have been entirely omitted, many have been cut because of space limitations. In notes, as in the text, omissions are indicated by ellipses.

NOTES

1 The speech is excerpted in Paul D. Escott, et. al. (eds.), *Major Problems in the History of the American South*, Vol. II: *The New South* (2nd ed., Boston, 1999), 91–92.

2 Phillip Alexander Bruce, *The Rise of the New South* (Philadelphia, 1905). It should be pointed out that there is no clear consensus among historians about whether the term "New South" properly designates all of southern history after 1877, as is implied, for example, by the title of Numan V. Bartley, *The New South: 1945–1980* (Baton Rouge 1995), or instead has an endpoint such as WWI, the New Deal, or the 1950s that divides it from a "modern South," as suggested, for example, by the chapter titles of a leading textbook, William J. Cooper, Jr. and Thomas E. Terrill, *The American South*, second edition (New York, 1996). In this volume, essays have been limited to the period after 1877 and before the beginning of the mass phase of the Civil Rights Movement in 1955.

3 David M. Potter, "An Appraisal of Fifteen Years of the *Journal of Southern History*," *Journal of Southern History* [*JSH*], 16 (February 1950), 25–32.

4 Ibid., 31.

5 (Baton Rouge 1951.) Woodward was already known for his biography of a Populist Party leader: *Tom Watson, Agrarian Rebel* (New York, 1938); he was the author of the essay referred to by Potter as one of the few to deal in any way with black southerners: "Tom Watson and the Negro in Agrarian Politics," *JSH*, 4 (February 1938), 14–33.

6 Woodward to Virginia Durr, June 8, 1952, quoted in Morton Sosna, *In Search of the Silent South: Southern Liberals and the Race Issue* (New York, 1977), 11.

7 Richard L. Watson, Jr., "From Populism through the New Deal: southern political history," in *Interpreting Southern History: Historiographical Essays in Honor of Sanford W. Higginbotham*, ed. by John B. Boles and Evelyn Thomas Nolen (Baton Rouge, 1986), 311. See also the issue of *JSH*, 67, 4 (November 2001), which is devoted to the legacy of *Origins of the New South* on the fiftieth anniversary of its publication.

8 (New York, 1955.)

9 Among the most prominent were Paul M. Gaston, The *New South Creed: A Study in Southern Mythmaking* (New York, 1970); Lawrence Goodwyn, *Democratic Promise: The Populist Moment in America* (New York, 1976); Steven Hahn, *The Roots of Southern Populism: Yeoman Farmers and the Transformation of the Georgia Upcountry, 1850–1890* (New York, 1983); J. Morgan Kousser, *The Shaping of Southern Politics: Suffrage Restriction and the Establishment of the One-Party South, 1880–1910* (New Haven, 1974); Roger L. Ransom and Richard Sutch, *One Kind of Freedom: The Economic Consequences of Reconstruction* (Cambridge, Eng., 1977); Gavin Wright, *Old South, New South: Revolutions in the Southern Economy Since the Civil War* (New York, 1986).

10 For examples, see Jonathon M. Wiener, *Social Origins of the New South: Alabama, 1860–1885* (Baton Rouge, 1978); Howard N. Rabinowitz, *Race Relations in the Urban South, 1865–1890* (New York, 1978); Barton Shaw, *The Wool Hat Boys: Georgia's Populist Party* (Baton Rouge, 1984).

11 For surveys of this literature, see the appropriate essays in *Interpreting Southern History*, ed. Boles and Nolen, and in John Boles (ed.), *A Companion to the American South* (Malden, Mass., 2002). For syntheses of the work on Populism and Progressivism in the South, see Robert C. McMath, Jr., *American Populism: A Social History, 1877–1898* (New York, 1993); Dewey W. Grantham, *Southern Progressivism: The Reconciliation of Progress and*

Tradition (Knoxville, 1983); and William A. Link, *The Paradox of Southern Progressivism, 1880–1930* (Chapel Hill, 1992).

12 For an introduction to this large literature, see Charles W. Eagles, "The Civil Rights Movement," in Boles (ed.), *Companion*. Important early exceptions were two works on black leadership in the New South: August Meier, *Negro Thought in America, 1880–1915: Racial Ideologies in the Age of Booker T. Washington* (Urbana, Ill., 1963), and Louis R. Harlan, *Booker T. Washington: The Making of a Leader, 1856–1901* (New York, 1972).

13 (Baton Rouge, 1967.)

14 Most of the exceptions focused on politics and national policy. See the historiographical surveys in Watson, "From Populism through the New Deal," and Pamela Tyler, "The Impact of the New Deal and World War II on the South," in *Companion*, ed. by Boles, 444–60.

15 In addition to work noted below, major studies of African Americans in the New South include Leon F. Litwack, *Trouble in Mind: Black Southerners in the Age of Jim Crow* (New York, 1998); David Levering Lewis, *W.E.B. DuBois: Biography of a Race, 1868–1919* (New York, 1993); John D. Anderson, *The Education of Blacks in the South, 1860–1901* (Chapel Hill, 1998); William E. Montgomery, *Under Their Own Vine and Fig Tree: The African-American Church in the South, 1865–1900* (Baton Rouge, 1993); and Stewart E. Tolnay, *The Bottom Rung: African American Family Life on Southern Farms* (Urbana, Ill., 1999).

16 Scott, *Pedestal to Politics* (Chicago, 1970). The index to *Origins of the New South* includes just four brief mentions of women. For a survey of work to the mid-1980s, see Jacquelyn Dowd Hall and Anne Firor Scott, "Women in the South," in Boles and Nolen (eds.), *Interpreting Southern History*, 454–509; and for more recent work, Elizabeth Hayes Turner, "Women in the Post-Civil War South," in Boles (ed.), *Companion*, 348–68. Among the most influential of the early works were Jacqueline Jones, *Labor of Love, Labor of Sorrow: Black Women, Work, and the Family from Slavery to the Present* (New York, 1985), Jacquelyn Dowd Hall, *Revolt against Chivalry: Jesse Daniel Ames and the Women's Campaign against Lynching* (New York, 1979), and Marjorie Spruill Wheeler, *New Women of the New South: The Leaders of the Woman Suffrage Movement in the Southern States* (New York, 1993).

17 See Daniel Letwin, "Labor Relations in the Industrializing South," in Boles (ed.), *Companion*, 424–43. Examples of influential work on labor include David L. Carlton, *Mill and Town in South Carolina, 1880–1920* (Baton Rouge, 1982); Delores E. Janiewski, *Sisterhood Denied: Race, Gender, and Class in a New South Community* (Philadelphia, 1985); Jacquelyn Dowd Hall, James Leloudis, Robert Korstad, Mary Murphy, Lu Ann Jones, and Christopher Daly, *Like a Family: The Making of a Southern Cotton Mill World* (Chapel Hill, 1987); Eric Arnesen, *Waterfront Workers of New Orleans: Race, Class, and Politics, 1863–1923* (New York, 1991); Michael K. Honey, *Southern Labor and Black Civil Rights: Organizing Memphis Workers* (Urbana, 1993); Bryant Simon, *A Fabric of Defeat: The Politics of South Carolina Millhands, 1910–1948* (Chapel Hill, 1998); and Robert Rodgers Korstad, *Civil Rights Unionism: Tobacco Workers and the Struggle for Democracy in the Mid-Twentieth-Century South* (Chapel Hill, 2003).

18 In addition to a number of works cited above and below, examples of local studies include Earl Lewis, *In Their Own Interests: Race, Class, and Power in Twentieth-Century Norfolk, Virginia* (Berkeley, 1991); James C. Cobb, *The Most Southern Place on Earth: The Mississippi Delta and the Roots of Regional Identity*

(New York, 1992); Mart Stewart, *"What Nature Suffers to Groe"*: *Life, Labor, and Landscape on the Georgia Coast, 1680–1920* (Athens, Ga., 1996); J. William Harris, *Deep Souths: Delta, Piedmont, and Sea Island Society in the Age of Segregation* (Baltimore, 2001). Examples of work on immigrants and borderlands include Nancy A. Hewitt, *Southern Discomfort: Women's Activism in Tampa, Florida, 1880s–1920s* (Urbana, Ill., 2001), and Neil Foley, *The White Scourge: Mexicans, Blacks, and Poor Whites in Texas Cotton Culture* (Berkeley, Calif., 1997). Gerald Sider, *Living Indian Histories: Lumbee and Tuscarora People in North Carolina* (Chapel Hill, 2003), examines the history of an ethnic group that is neither "white" nor "black." For the growing body of work on Appalachia, see John C. Inscoe, "The Discovery of Appalachia: Regional Revisionism as Scholarly Renaissance," in Boles (ed.), *Companion*, 368–86.

19 Examples include Allen Tullos, *Habits of Industry: White Culture and the Transformation of the Carolina Piedmont* (Chapel Hill, 1989); Ted Ownby, *Subduing Satan: Religion, Recreation, and Manhood in the Rural South, 1865–1920* (Chapel Hill, 1990); Evelyn Brooks Higginbotham, *Righteous Discontent: The Women's Movement in the Black Baptist Church, 1880–1920* (Cambridge, Mass., 1993); Nancy MacLean, *Behind the Mask of Chivalry: The Making of the Second Ku Klux Klan* (New York, 1994); LeeAnn Whites, *The Civil War as a Crisis in Gender: Augusta, Georgia, 1860–1890* (Athens, Ga., 1995); Glenda Elizabeth Gilmore, *Gender and Jim Crow: Women and the Politics of White Supremacy in North Carolina, 1896–1920* (Chapel Hill, 1996); Tera W. Hunter, *To 'Joy My Freedom: Southern Black Women's Lives and Labors after the Civil War* (Cambridge, Mass., 1997); Paul Harvey, *Redeeming the South: Religious Cultures and Racial Identities among Southern Baptists, 1865–1925* (Chapel Hill, 1997); Grace Elizabeth Hale, *Making Whiteness: The Culture of Segregation in the South, 1890–1940* (New York, 1998); Jennifer Ritterhouse, *Growing Up Jim Crow: How Black and White Southern Children Learned Race* (Chapel Hill, 2006).

20 On violence and race, see Joel Williamson, *Crucible of Race: Black–White Relations in the American South since Emancipation* (New York, 1984); W. Fitzhugh Brundage, *Lynching in the New South: Georgia and Virginia, 1880–1930* (Urbana, 1993); and Stewart E. Tolnay and E. M. Beck, *A Festival of Violence: An Analysis of Southern Lynchings, 1882–1930* (Urbana, Ill., 1995).

21 Woodward himself briefly addressed the significance of the "cult of the Lost Cause" in *Origins of the New South*, 154–57, and Gaston wrote about the "Old South myth" and its uses in *New South Creed*, 167–86. Among more recent works on southern white memory are Rollin G. Osterweis, *The Myth of the Lost Cause, 1865–1900* (Hamden, Conn., 1973); Charles Reagan Wilson, *Baptized in Blood: The Religion of the Lost Cause, 1865–1920* (Athens, Ga., 1980); Thomas Lawrence Connolly and Barbara L. Bellows, *God and General Longstreet: The Lost Cause and the Southern Mind* (Baton Rouge, 1982); Gaines M. Foster, *Ghosts of the Confederacy: Defeat, the Lost Cause, and the Emergence of the New South* (New York, 1987); W. Fitzhugh Brundage, *The Southern Past: A Clash of Race and Memory* (Cambridge, Mass., 2005); and Whites, *Civil War as a Crisis in Gender*.

22 Jacquelyn Dowd Hall, "The Long Civil Rights Movement and the Political Uses of the Past," *Journal of American History*, 91 (March 2005), 1233–63. For some of the major books on this period since Tindall, *Emergence of the New South*, see Dan T. Carter, *Scottsboro: A Tragedy of the American South* (Baton Rouge, 1969); Sosna, *In Search of the Silent South*; James C. Cobb and Michael V. Namorato (eds.), *The New Deal and the South* (Jackson, 1984); Pete Daniel,

Breaking the Land: The Transformation of Cotton, Tobacco, and Rice Cultures since 1880 (Urbana, 1985); Jack Temple Kirby, *Rural Worlds Lost: The American South, 1920–1960* (Baton Rouge, 1987); Robin D. G. Kelley, *Hammer and Hoe: Alabama Communists during the Great Depression* (Chapel Hill, 1990); John Egerton, *Speak Now against the Day: The Generation before the Civil Rights Movement* (New York, 1994); Neil R. McMillan (ed.), *Remaking Dixie: The Impact of World War II on the American South* (Jackson, 1997).

23 (New York, 1992).
24 Howard N. Rabinowitz, "The origins of a poststructuralist New South: a review of Edward L. Ayers's *The Promise of the New South: Life after Reconstruction*," *JSH*, 59 (August 1993), 509; Edward L. Ayers, "Narrating the New South," *JSH*, 61 (August 1995), 555–65 ("hybrid" quote 560). Ayers's essay is in part a response to Rabinowitz.
25 Ayers, "Narrating the New South," 559.
26 Rabinowitz, "Poststructuralist New South," 514.

1

NEGOTIATING AND TRANSFORMING THE PUBLIC SPHERE

African American political life in the
transition from slavery to freedom

Elsa Barkley Brown

*Historians have dramatically increased our knowledge of black women's lives
in the New South, and especially of black women's reform activities in the
Progressive Era. Elsa Barkley Brown, in her examination of women's political
activity in Richmond from Reconstruction to 1900, expands and deepens this
knowledge. She focuses not on conflicts between blacks and whites, but on
developments within the African-American community.*

*In Reconstruction, she argues, African Americans understood freedom as
something to be "acquired by all of them collectively." Even though they were
denied formal voting power, women were still expected to play a key role in a
democratic politics. The black church provided a "cultural base" and a physical
space for this collective politics.*

*By the end of the century, however, the "black public sphere emerged as
more fractured and perhaps less democratic." Both middle-class women and
working-class men and women "were increasingly disfranchised within the
black community, just as middle-class black men were increasingly disfranchised in the larger society." In the face of developing class differentiation
and new conventions of gender, both men and women justified authority
"along distinctively gendered and class-based lines."*

*Brown concludes with provocative reflections on how these new, gendered
ideas about politics, based on "masculine notions of blackness and race progress," helped to shape an African-American collective memory that was, and
is, "partial, distorted, and dismembered," especially in the way that violence
against women has been given much less emphasis than it deserves in both
historical and contemporary times.*

* * *

On April 15, 1880, Margaret Osborne, Jane Green, Susan Washington, Molly Branch, Susan Gray, Mary A. Soach and "over two hundred other prominent sisters of the church" petitioned the Richmond, Virginia, First African Baptist Church's business meeting to allow women to vote on the pastor:

> We the sisters of the church feeling that we are interested in the welfare of the same and also working hard to finish the house and have been working by night and day ... We know you have adopted a law in the church that the business must be done by the male members. We don't desire to alter that law, nor do we desire to have anything to do with the business of the church, we only ask to have a vote in electing or dismissing him. We whose names are attached to this petition ask you to grant us this privilege.[1]

The circumstances surrounding these women's petition suggest the kinds of changes taking place internally in late-nineteenth- and early-twentieth-century black Richmond and other southern black communities. In the immediate post-Civil War era women had voted in mass meetings and Republican Party conventions held at First African, thus contradicting gender-based assumptions within the larger society about politics, political engagement and appropriate forms of political behavior. Now, women sitting in the same church were petitioning for the right to vote in an internal community institution, couching the petition in terms designed to minimize the request and avoid a challenge to men's authority and position.

Scholars' assumptions of an unbroken line of exclusion of African American women from formal political associations in the late nineteenth century have obscured fundamental changes in the political understandings within African American communities in the transition from slavery to freedom. Women in First African and in other arenas were seeking in the late nineteenth century not a new authority but rather a lost authority, one they now often sought to justify on a distinctively female basis. As these women petitioned for their rights within the church and as other women formed voluntary associations in turn-of-the-century Richmond they were not, as often depicted in the scholarly literature, emerging into the political arena through such actions. Rather, these women were attempting to retain space they traditionally had held in the immediate post-emancipation period. This essay explores the processes of public discourse within Richmond and other southern black communities and the factors that led to increasingly more clearly gendered and class spaces within those communities to understand why women by the 1880s and 1890s needed to create their own pulpits from which to speak—to restore their voices to the community. This exploration suggests how the ideas, process, meanings, and practice of freedom changed within the late-nineteenth-century southern African American communities and what the implications of those changes may be for our visions of freedom and for the possibilities of African American community in the late twentieth century.

After emancipation, African American men, women, and children, as part of black communities throughout the South, struggled to define on their own terms the meaning of freedom and in the process to construct communities of struggle. Much of the literature on Reconstruction portrays freed African Americans as rapidly and readily adopting a gendered private-public dichotomy.[2] Much of the literature on the nineteenth-century public sphere constructs a masculine liberal bourgeois public with female counterpublic.[3] This essay, focusing on the civic geography of post-Civil War black Richmond, suggests the problematic of applying such generalizations to African American life in the late-nineteenth-century South. In the immediate post-emancipation era black Richmonders enacted their understandings of democratic political discourse through mass meetings attended and participated in (including voting) by men, women, and children and through mass participation in Republican Party conventions. They carried these notions of political participation into the state capitol, engaging from the gallery in the debates on the constitutional convention floor.

Central to African Americans' construction of a fully democratic notion of political discourse was the church as a foundation of the black public sphere.[4] In the post-slavery era, church buildings also served as meeting halls and auditoriums as well as educational and recreational facilities, employment and social service bureaus, and bulletin boards. First African, especially, with a seating capacity of nearly four thousand, was the site of large political gatherings. Schools such as Richmond Theological Seminary and Richmond Colored High and Normal School held their annual commencement exercises at First African Baptist, allowing these events to become community celebrations. . . . As a political space occupied by men, women, and children, literate and non-literate, ex-slave and formerly free, church members and nonmembers, the availability and use of First African for mass meetings enabled the construction of political concerns in democratic space. This is not to suggest that official versions and spokespersons were not produced, but these official versions were the product of a fairly egalitarian discourse and, therefore, represented the conditions of black Richmonders of differing classes, ages, and genders. Within black Richmonders' construction of the public sphere, the forms of discourse varied from the prayer to the stump speech to the testimonies regarding outrages against freedpeople to shouted interventions from the galleries into the debates on the legislative floor. By the very nature of their participation—the inclusion of women and children, the engagement through prayer, the disregard of formal rules for speakers and audience, the engagement from the galleries in the formal legislative sessions—Afro-Richmonders challenged liberal bourgeois notions of rational discourse. Many white observers considered their unorthodox political engagements to be signs of their unfamiliarity and perhaps unreadiness for politics.[5]

In the decades following emancipation as black Richmonders struggled to achieve even a measured amount of freedom, the black public sphere emerged as more fractured and perhaps less democratic at the end of the nineteenth century, yet even then it retained strong elements of a democratic agenda. This essay examines the changing constructions of political space and community discourse in the post-emancipation era.

Envisioning freedom

In April 1865, when Union troops marched into Richmond, jubilant African American men, women, and children poured into the streets and crowded into their churches to dance, kiss, hug, pray, sing, and shout. They assembled in First African, Third Street African Methodist, Ebenezer, and Second African not merely because of the need to thank God for their deliverance but also because the churches were the only institutional spaces, and in the case of First African certainly the largest space, owned by African Americans themselves.[6] As the process of reconstruction unfolded, black Richmonders continued to meet regularly in their churches, now not merely to rejoice. If Afro-Richmonders had thought freedom would accompany emancipation, the events of the first few weeks and months of Union occupation quickly disabused them of such ideas. Throughout the summer and fall of 1865 black Richmonders reported numerous violations of their rights. Among them were pass and curfew regulations designed to curtail black mobility and force African American men and women out of the city to labor in the rural areas. Pass and curfew violators (eight hundred in the first week of June) were detained in bullpens—one for women and children, a separate one for men—away from and often unknown to family members. Black Richmonders also detailed numerous incidents of disrespectful treatment, verbal abuse, physical assault, and torture. "Many poor women" told "tales of their frights and robberies"; vendors told of goods destroyed by military police. . . .[7] Many spoke of the sexual abuse of black women: "gobbling up of the most likely looking negro women, thrown into the cells, robbed and ravished at the will of the guard." Men and women in the vicinity of the jail testified "to hearing women scream frightfully almost every night."[8]

15

The regular meetings in the African churches, originally ones of jubilation, quickly became the basis for constructing a discourse about freedom and organizing large-scale mass protest. On June 10, 1865, over three thousand assembled at First African to hear the report of the investigating committee that had conducted hearings and gathered the evidence and depositions necessary to present black Richmonders' case directly to Governor Francis H. Pierpoint and to the "chief head of all authority," the president of the United States. The protest memorial drawn up during the meeting was ratified at meetings in each of the other churches and money was raised through church collections to send six representatives (one from each church in Richmond and one from First Baptist, Manchester) to Washington. On Friday, June 16, these delegates delivered the mass meeting's protest directly to President Andrew Johnson. . . .[9] In their memorial, as in their meetings, black Richmonders recounted not merely the abuses but they also used their individual stories to construct a collective history and to combat the idea of being "idle negroes" unprepared for freedom.[10]

> We represent a population of more than 20,000 colored people . . . more than 6,000 of our people are members in good standing of Christian churches, and nearly our whole population constantly attend divine services. Among us there are at least 2,000 men who are worth $200 to $500; 200 who have property valued at from $1,000 to $5,000, and a number who are worth from $5,000 to $20,000. . . . 3,000 of us can read, and at least 2,000 can read and write, and a large number of us are engaged in useful and profitable employment on our own account.

The community they described was one based in a collective ethos; it was not merely their industry but also their responsibility that was the basis on which they claimed their rights.

> None of our people are in the alms-house, and when we were slaves the aged and infirm who were turned away from the homes of hard masters, who had been enriched by their toil, our benevolent societies supported while they lived, and buried when they died. . . .

They reminded Johnson of the efforts black men and women in Richmond had taken to support the Union forces against the Confederacy.

> During the whole of the Slaveholders' Rebellion we have been true and loyal to the United States Government. . . . We have

been their pilots and their scouts, and have safely conducted them through many perilous adventures.

. . . . And finally they invoked the religious destiny that emancipation had reaffirmed, reminding the president of a "motto once inscribed over the portals of an Egyptian temple, '*Know all ye who exercise power; that God hates injustice!*' "[11] . . . . When local white newspapers refused to publish their account, they had it published in the *New York Tribune*.[12] Throughout 1865 and 1866 black Richmonders continued to meet regularly in mass meetings where men, women, and children collectively participated in constructing and announcing their own story of community and freedom.[13] The story told in those mass meetings, published in northern white newspapers, carried in protest to Union officials, was also carried into the streets as black Richmonders inserted themselves in the pre-existing national political traditions and at the same time widened those traditions. John O'Brien has noted that in the immediate aftermath of emancipation, black Richmonders developed their own political calendar, celebrating four civic holidays: January 1; George Washington's Birthday; April 3 (Emancipation Day); and July 4.[14] White Richmonders were horrified as they watched former slaves claim civic holidays and traditions they believed to be the historical possession of white Americans and occupy spaces, like Capitol Square, which had formerly been reserved for white residents.[15]

The underlying values and assumptions that would pervade much of black people's political struggles in the city were forged in slavery and war and in the weeks following emancipation. Military regulations that limited black mobility and made finding and reunifying family members even more difficult placed the economic interests of white men and women above the material and social interests of African Americans. The . . . raids on black homes, which made all space public and subject to the interests of the state, obliterated any possible distinctions between public and private spheres. Demanding passes and evidence of employment denied black Richmonders the right to act and to be treated not as economic units and/or property but as social beings and family members. The difficulty of finding decent housing at affordable prices further impeded freedpeople's efforts to bring their families together. All of these obstacles to and expectations of family life were part of what Eric Foner speaks of as the " 'politicization' of every day life."[16]

These political issues underpinned Afro-Richmonders' petition to Johnson and would continue to underpin their political struggles in late-nineteenth-century Richmond. Even as they fashioned individual stories into a collective history, black Richmonders could and did differ on the means by which they might secure freedom—vigorously debating issues such as the necessity of confiscation.[17] But they also understood freedom as a collective struggle. When they entered the formal political arena through Republican Party politics in 1867, this understanding was the foundation for their initial engagement with issues of suffrage and democracy. As Julie Saville has observed for South Carolina, freedpeople in Richmond "were not so much converted to the Republican Party as they were prepared to convert the Republican Party to themselves."[18] The post-Civil War southern black public sphere was forged in jubilation and struggle as African American men, women, and children claimed their own history and set forth their own political ideals.

All the resources of black Richmonders became elements in their political struggles. The *Richmond Whig*, intending to ridicule the inappropriateness of freedpeople's behaviors and assumptions, highlighted the politicized nature of all aspects of black life during Reconstruction; the freedpeople's "mass meetings, committee meetings, and meetings of the different societies all have political significance. The superstitions of the colored people are availed on, and religion and Radicalism are all jumbled together. Every night they have meetings and musterings, harangues and sermons, singing and praying-all looking to political results."[19] Similarly the *Richmond Dispatch* reported an 1867 Republican meeting which began with "Harris, colored" offering "the most remarkable" prayer "we have ever heard. It was frequently interrupted by laughter and manifestations of applause":

> Oh, Lord God, bless our enemies—bless President Johnson. We would not even have him sent to hell. Come, oh come, good Lord, and touch his heart even while I am talking with you here to-night. [Amen.] Show him the error of his ways. Have mercy upon our "Moses," [Sarcastic, Great laughter and amens.] who, like Esau, has sold his birthright for a morsel of pottage—took us in the wilderness and left us there. Come down upon him, oh Lord, with thy blessing. God bless us in our meeting to-night, and help us in what we do. . . .[20]

What the *Whig* and the *Dispatch* captured was a political culture in which the wide range of institutional and noninstitutional resources of individuals and the community as a whole became the basis for defining, claiming, and securing freedom in post-emancipation Richmond. The church provided more than physical space, financial resources, and a communication network; it also provided a cultural base that validated emotion and experience as ways of knowing, and drew on a collective call and response, encouraging the active participation of all.[21]

Virginia's rejection of the Fourteenth Amendment brought the state under the Reconstruction Act of 1867; a constitutional convention became prerequisite for full restoration to the Union. Black men, enfranchised for the delegate selection and ratification ballots, were to have their first opportunity to engage in the political parties and legislative chambers of the state. The struggles in which they had engaged in the two years since emancipation influenced the manner of black Richmonders' initial participation in the formal political arena of conventions and voting. On August 1, 1867, the day the Republican state convention opened in Richmond to adopt a platform for the upcoming state constitutional convention, thousands of African American men, women, and children absented themselves from their employment and joined the delegates at the convention site, First African Baptist Church. . . .

This pattern persisted whenever a major issue came before the state and city Republican conventions held during the summer and fall of 1867, or the state constitutional convention that convened in Richmond from December 1867 to March 1868. A *New York Times* reporter estimated that "the entire colored population of Richmond" attended the October 1867 local Republican convention where delegates to the state constitutional convention were nominated. Noting that female domestic servants were a large portion of those in attendance, the correspondent reported: "as is usual on such occasions, families which employ servants were forced to cook their own dinners, or content themselves with a cold lunch. Not only had Sambo gone to the Convention, but Dinah was there also."[22]

These men and women did not absent themselves from work just to be onlookers at the proceedings, but to be active participants. They assumed as equal a right to be present and participate as the delegates themselves, a fact they made abundantly clear at the August 1867 Republican state convention. Having begun to arrive four hours before the opening session, African American men and women had filled the meeting place long before the delegates arrived. Having shown up to speak for themselves, they did not assume delegates had priority in discussion or in seating. Disgusted at the scene, as well as unable to find a seat, the conservative white Republican delegates removed to the Capitol Square to convene an outdoor session. That was quite acceptable to the several thousand additional African American men and women who, unable to squeeze into the church, were now still able to participate in the important discussions and to vote down the proposals of the conservative faction.[23]

Black men, women, and children were also active participants throughout the state constitutional convention. A *New York Times* reporter commented on the tendency for the galleries to be crowded "with the 'unprivileged,' and altogether black." At issue was not just these men's and women's presence but also their behavior. White women, for example, certainly on occasion sat in the convention's gallery as visitors silently observing the proceedings; these African Americans, however, participated from the gallery, loudly engaging in the debates. At points of heated controversy, black delegates turned to the crowds as they made their addresses on the convention floor, obviously soliciting and relying upon mass participation. Outside the convention hours, mass meetings were held to discuss and vote on the major issues. At these gatherings vote was either by voice or rising and men, women, and children voted. These meetings were not mock assemblies; they were important gatherings at which the community made plans for freedom. The most radical black Republican faction argued that the major convention issues should actually be settled at these mass meetings with delegates merely casting the community's vote on the convention floor. Though this did not occur, black delegates were no doubt influenced by both the mass meetings and the African American presence in the galleries, both of which included women.[24]

Black Richmonders were operating in two separate political arenas: an internal one and an external one. While these arenas were related, they each proceeded from different assumptions, had different purposes, and therefore operated according to different rules. Within the internal political process women were enfranchised and participated in all public forums—the parades, rallies, mass meetings, and the conventions themselves.[25]

It was the state constitutional convention, however, that would decide African American women's and men's status in the political process external to the African American community. When the Virginia convention began its deliberation regarding the franchise, Thomas Bayne, a black delegate from Norfolk, argued the inherent link between freedom and suffrage, and contended that those who opposed universal suffrage were actually opposing the freedom of African American people. In rejoinder, E. L. Gibson, a conservative white delegate, enunciated several principles of republican representative government. Contending that "a man might be free and still not have the right to vote," Gibson explained the fallacy of assuming that this civil right was an inherent corollary to freedom: if the right were inherent then it would belong to both sexes and to all from "the first moment of existence" and to foreigners immediately. This was "an absurdity too egregious to be contemplated."[26] And yet, this "absurd" notion of political rights was what was in practice in the Richmond black community— males and females voted without regard to age, the thousands of rural migrants who came into Richmond suffered no waiting period but immediately possessed the full rights of the community. What was

absurd to Gibson and most white men—Republican or Democrat—
was obviously quite rational to many black Richmonders. Two very different conceptions of freedom and public participation in the political
process were in place.

In the end only men obtained the legal franchise. . . . African
American women were by law excluded from the formal political arena
external to their community. Yet this does not mean that they were not
active in that arena; witness Richmond women's participation in the
Republican and the constitutional conventions. Southern black men
and women debated the issue of women's suffrage in both the external
and internal political arenas. In Nansemond County, Virginia, for
example, the mass meetings resolved that women should be granted
the legal franchise; in Richmond, while a number of participants in a
mass meeting supported female suffrage, the majority opinion swung
against it.[27] But the meaning of that decision was not as straightforward
as it may seem. The debate as to whether women should be given the
vote in the external political arena occurred in internal political arena
mass meetings where women participated and voted not just before and
during, *but also after* the negative decision regarding legal enfranchisement. This maintained the status quo in the external community;
ironically enough, the status quo in the internal community was maintained as well—women continued to have the vote. African American
men and women clearly operated within two distinct political systems.

Focusing on formal disfranchisement obscures women's continued
participation in the external political arena. In Richmond and throughout the South exclusion from legal enfranchisement did not prevent
African American women from shaping the vote and the political
decisions. Throughout the late 1860s and 1870s women continued to
participate in political meetings in large numbers and to organize
political societies. Some like the Rising Daughters of Liberty and the
Daughters of the Union Victory in Richmond or the United Daughters
of Liberty organized by coal miners' wives living outside Manchester
had all-female memberships. Others, like the two-thousand-member
National Political Aid Society, the Union League of Richmond, and the
Union Equal Rights League of Manchester had male and female
members. . . .

Women's presence at these meetings was anything but passive. In
the violent political atmosphere of the last years of Reconstruction, they
had an especially important and dangerous role. . . . For those women
and men who lived in outlying areas of Richmond and attended outdoor meetings, political participation was a particularly dangerous
matter, a fact they clearly recognized. Meetings were guarded by
posted sentinels with guns who questioned the intent of any suspicious people, usually white men, coming to the meeting. A reporter for

the *Richmond Daily Dispatch* described one such encounter when he attempted to cover a political meeting of fifty women and twenty-five men.[28]

Women as well as men took election day off from work and went to the polls. Fraud, intimidation, and violence became the order of election days. White newspapers and politicians threatened loss of jobs, homes, and lives. Afro-Richmonders countered with a group presence. Often even those living within the city and short distances from the polling places went early, even the night before, and camped out at the polls, hoping that their early presence would require the acceptance of their vote and that the group presence would provide protection from violence and intimidation. . . . The fact that only men had been granted the vote did not at all mean that only men should exercise the vote. Women throughout the South initiated sanctions against men who voted Democratic; some went along to the polls to insure a properly cast ballot. As increasing white fraud made black men's voting more difficult, early arrival at the polls was partly intended to counter such efforts.

Although election days in Richmond were not as violent as they were elsewhere throughout Virginia and other parts of the South, guns were used to intimidate and defraud. It is also probable that in Richmond, as elsewhere throughout the South, when black men went to camp out overnight at the polls, households feared leaving women and children unprotected at home. Thus the women's presence, just as the group presence of the men, may have been a sign of the need for collective protection. If Richmond women were at all like their sisters in South Carolina and Danville, they may have carried weapons with them-to protect themselves and /or help protect the male voters.[29] Women and children's presence reflects their excitement about the franchise but also their understanding of the dangers involved in voting. The necessity for a group presence at the polls reinforced the sense of collective enfranchisement. . . .

In the dangerous political atmosphere of the late nineteenth century, the vote took on a sacred and collective character. Black men and women in Richmond, as throughout the South, initiated sanctions against those black men perceived as violating the collective good by supporting the conservative forces. Black Democrats were subject to the severest exclusion: disciplined within or quite often expelled from their churches and mutual benefit societies; denied board and lodging with black families. Additionally, mobs jeered, jostled, and sometimes beat black Democrats or rescued those who were arrested for such acts. Women were often reported to be in the forefront of this activity. Similarly, black women were said to have "exercised a positive influence upon some men who were inclined to hesitate or be indifferent" during the early 1880s Readjuster campaigns.[30]

All of this suggests that African American women and men understood the vote as a collective, not an individual, possession; and furthermore, that African American women, unable to cast a separate vote, viewed African American men's vote as equally theirs. They believed that franchise should be cast in the best interest of both. This is not the nineteenth-century patriarchal notion that men voted on behalf of their wives and children. By that assumption women had no individual wills; rather men operated in women's best interest because women were assumed to have no right of input. African American women assumed the political rights that came with being a member of the community even though they were denied the political rights they thought should come with being citizens of the state.

To justify their political participation Richmond and other southern black women in the immediate post-Civil War period did not need to rely on arguments of superior female morality or public motherhood. Their own cultural, economic, and political traditions provided rationale enough. An understanding of collective autonomy was the basis on which African Americans reconstructed families, developed communal institutions, constructed schools, and engaged in formal politics after emancipation. The participation of women and children in the external and internal political arenas was part of a larger political worldview of ex-slaves and free men and women, a worldview fundamentally shaped by an understanding that freedom, in reality, would accrue to each of them individually only when it was acquired by all of them collectively. Such a worldview contrasted sharply with the "possessive individualism" of liberal democracy.[31] This sense of suffrage as a collective, not an individual, possession was the foundation for much of African American women's political activities in the post-Civil War era.[32] Within these understandings the boundary lines between men's and women's political behavior were less clearly drawn and active participation in the political arenas-internal or external-seldom required a retreat into womanhood or manhood as its justification.*

Renegotiating public life

The 1880 First African women's petition followed three contentious church meetings, some lasting until two or three o'clock in the morning, at which the congregants considered dismissing and/or excluding the pastor, the Reverend James H. Holmes. This discussion was initiated at a 5 April meeting where two women were charged with fighting

---

* A paragraph on a female militia unit organized "for ceremonial purposes" has been omitted—ed.

about the pastor. The 6 April meeting considered charges of "unchristian conduct" on the part of Holmes; those men present voted to exclude Holmes. A meeting on 11 April endorsed a protest signed by all but two of the deacons against the earlier proceedings. The protest charged the anti-Holmes faction with trying to "dispose of the deacons, take charge of prayer meetings, the Sunday school and revolutionize things generally." The discussions that ensued over the next two months split the congregation; the May and June church business meetings were "disorderly" and "boisterous." Holmes and the deacons called in the mayor, city court judge, and chief of police to support the pastor and the police to remove or arrest those members of the congregation designated as "rebellious." After the anti-Holmes faction was removed from the church, the June meeting expelled forty-six men for "rebelliously attempting to overthrow and seize upon the church government." It also excluded the two women initially charged, one for fighting and the other for tattling; exonerated Holmes "from all false" accusations; and thanked the civil officers who attended the meeting and restored order. Only after these actions did the church consider the women's petition, which had been presented in the midst of the controversy more than two months earlier.[33]

First African's records do not adequately reveal the nature of gender relations within the church in the late 1860s and 1870s. We do know that the pre-Civil War sex-segregated seating patterns were abandoned by Richmond black Baptist churches immediately after the Civil War and that by the late 1860s women "not only had a voice, but voted in the business meetings" of Ebenezer Baptist Church.[34] Women who voted in political meetings held in First African in the late 1860s and 1870s may have carried this participation over to church business meetings. Often in the immediate post-Civil War period, business and political meetings were not clearly distinguishable.

The petition of the women of First African makes clear, however, that by the early 1880s, while women attended and apparently participated in church meetings, the men had "adopted a law in the church that the business must be done by the male members." Whether Margaret Osborne, Jane Green, and others thought that their voices and interests were being inadequately represented, even ignored, by the deacons, or wanted to add their voices to those, including the deacons, who were struggling to retain Holmes and control of First African, these women understood that they would have to defend their own rights. The women argued their right to decide on the pastor, justifying their petition by both their work on behalf of the church and the importance of their economic support to the church's ongoing activities and to the pastor's salary. Not until after the matter of Holmes's exclusion was settled were the petitioners granted their request. Since

24

they apparently remained within First African, the petitioners' organization probably indicates that they were not among those dissatisfied with Holmes. It does suggest, however, their dissatisfaction with church procedure and the place of women in church polity. Still, the petition was conservative and the women denied any intention to demand full voting rights in church matters. The petition was not taken as a challenge to church authority, as were the actions of the anti-Holmes faction. When brought up for a vote in the June meeting, the women's petition was adopted by a vote of 413 to 16.[35]

The women's petition and the vote in favor of it suggest the tenuous and ambiguous position that women had come to occupy both within First African and within the internal political arena more generally. They participated actively in church meetings but the authority for that participation and the question of limiting women's role resurfaced throughout the late nineteenth century. In the 1890s the women of First African would again have to demand their rights, this time against challenges to their very presence at church meetings, when a deacon sought to prohibit women from even attending First African business meetings. The women protested and the church responded quickly by requiring the deacon to apologize to the women and assure them that they were welcome at the meetings. The degree of women's participation and decision-making powers, however, remained ambiguous.

In 1901–1902 during another crisis period in First African, a number of men sought to blame the problems on women. John Mitchell, Jr., a member of First African and editor of the *Richmond Planet*, cited the active participation of women ("ladies who knew nothing of the machinery at work or the deep laid plans on foot") and children ("Sunday School scholars from 8 years of age upward") in church affairs, suggesting that they did not comprehend the proceedings and had been easily misled or manipulated by male factions. Deacon J. C. Farley cited women's active participation in church meetings as the problem, reminding the congregation that "it was the rule of the church" that women were only allowed to vote on the pastor but had extended their participation far past that. And the new minister, the Reverend W. T. Johnson, admonished the women, saying that "the brethren could almost fight in the church meeting and when they went out they would shake hands and laugh and talk. But the sisters would talk about it going up Broad St. and everybody would know what they had done." First African women rejected these assessments of their church's problems. A significant number walked out rather than have their participation censured; those who remained reportedly refused to be silent but continually "talked out in the meeting." Sister Margaret Hewlett later sought out the editor of the *Richmond Planet* to voice her opposition to the men's denunciation of women's roles and to make clear that the women thought the church's problems lay in the male leadership, saying specifically "the deacons were the cause of all the trouble anyway."[36]

In the early 1890s, the *Virginia Baptist* publicized its belief that women, in exceeding their proper places in the church by attempting to preach, and in the community by their "deplorable" efforts to "exercise the right of suffrage," would lose their "womanliness."[37] The complexity of gender relations within the African American community was such that at the same time First African was debating women's attendance at church meetings and the *Virginia Baptist* was advocating a severely restricted women's role, other women such as Alice Kemp were known throughout the community as the authors of prominent male ministers' sermons and women such as the Reverend Mrs. Carter were establishing their reputations as "soul-stirring" preachers. The *Richmond Planet* reported these women's activities without fanfare, as if they were commonplace. The debate over women's roles also had become commonplace. The Reverend Anthony Binga, pastor of First Baptist (Manchester), noted the debate in his sermon on church polity: Binga supported women teaching Sunday School, participating in prayer-meetings and voting "on any subject pertaining to the interest of the church" including the pastor; but he interpreted the Bible as forbidding women "throwing off that modesty that should adorn her sex, and taking man's place in the pulpit." The subject received community-wide attention in June 1895 when Ebenezer Baptist Church staged a debate between the ministers of Second Baptist (Manchester) and Mount Carmel, judged by other ministers from Fourth Baptist, First African, First Baptist (Manchester) and others on the subject. "Resolved that a woman has every right and privilege that a man has in the Christian church."[38]

The debates within First African and other churches over women's roles were part of a series of political struggles within black Richmond in the late nineteenth and early twentieth centuries. As formal political gains, initially secured, began to recede and economic promise became less certain and less surely tied to political advancement, the political struggles over relationships between the working class and the newly emergent middle class, between men and women, between literate and nonliterate, increasingly became issues among Afro-Richmonders. . . .

The authority of the church in personal and civil matters decreased over the late nineteenth and early twentieth centuries. The church quietly acknowledged these changes without directly confronting the issue of its changed authority. The use of civil authorities to resolve the church dispute, especially since individual members continued to face censure if they relied on civil rather than church sanctions in a dispute with another member, suggests the degree to which First African tried to maintain its traditional authority over its members while acknowledging the limitations of its powers. First African turned outside not only itself but also the black community by inviting the intervention of the mayor, police chief and judge.[39] The decreasing authority of the church, however, accompanied a shrinking sphere of influence and activity for the church and the development of secular institutions and structures to take over, compete for, or share functions traditionally connected to the church as institution and structure. The changing church axis suggests important developments in the structures, nature, and understandings of community in black Richmond.

After the Reverend James Holmes and the deacons of First African survived the 1880 challenge to their leadership, one of their first actions was to establish a regulation that church business meetings be closed to all but members. They had argued that it was outside agitators who had instigated and sustained the disorder and opposition. While this reflects concerns about internal church business, the closing off of the church was reflected in other central ways that potentially had more far-reaching consequences, and suggests the particularization of interests, concerns, and functions of internal community institutions, and the changed nature of internal community politics. Having completed, at considerable expense, their new edifice, First African worried about avoiding damage and excess wear and tear. In November 1882 the church adopted regulations designed to eliminate the crowds of people attending weddings in the church by requiring guest lists and tickets, and to deny entirely the use of the main auditorium with the largest capacity for "programmes, closing of public schools, political meetings or feasts." In February 1883 when the Acme Lyceum requested use of the main auditorium for a lecture by Frederick Douglass, the church, following its new regulations, refused to grant the request, although it did offer as a substitute the use of its smaller lecture room. That same year it denied the use of the church for the Colored High and Normal closing. The paucity of facilities available to black Richmonders meant that these activities now had to be held in much smaller facilities and the possibilities for the large mass meetings that First African had previously hosted were now reduced. Political meetings and other activities moved to other, smaller church sites or to some of the new halls being erected by some of the societies and businessmen. . . . Without the large facility of First African, graduations and school closings could no longer be the traditional community-wide mass celebrations. Denied the use of First African and barred from the Richmond Theatre where the white high school students had their graduation, the 1883 Colored High and Normal graduation class held their exercises in a small classroom where very few could attend.[40]

First African['s] ... actions reinforced the narrower sense of party politics that white Republicans had already tried to enforce. Disturbed at black influence over Republican meetings, beginning in 1870 white Republican officials had taken steps to limit popular participation and influence in party deliberations. First they moved the party conventions from First African to the United States courtroom, a facility that held many fewer people and was removed from the black community; then they closed the gallery, thus allowing none but official delegates to attend and participate. In such a setting they were able to adopt a more conservative platform. Black Republicans had continued, however, to hold mass meetings, often when dissatisfied with the official Republican deliberations. When they were dissatisfied with Republican nominees for municipal office that came from the 1870 closed party convention, for example, black Republicans agreed to convene their own sessions and make their own nominations.[41]

In increasingly delimiting the church's use ... and attempting to reserve the church for what was now designated as the "sacred," First African contributed to the increasing segmentation of black Richmond.[42] With the loss of the largest capacity structure some black Richmonders recognized the need to reestablish a community space. Edward A. Randolph, founder and first editor of the *Richmond Planet*, used Acme Literary Association meetings to argue regularly throughout 1883 and 1884 for the construction of a hall, a public meeting place within the community. His call was reinforced when the Choral Association was denied use of the Richmond Theatre and had to have its production in a small mutual benefit society hall, an inadequate facility for such a production. The construction of a large auditorium on the top floor of the Grand Fountain, United Order of True Reformers' bank and office building when it opened in 1890 was an effort to provide that space. It could hold larger gatherings than the other halls and most churches but still had only a small percentage of the seating capacity of First African.[43] A mass meeting on the scale common in the 1860s and 1870s could be held only outside the community, and the facilities for such were often closed to African Americans. As political meetings moved to private halls rather than church buildings, they became less mass meetings not only in the numerical sense; they also became more gatherings of an exclusive group of party regulars. This signaled not only a change in the role of the church but also a change in the nature of politics in black Richmond. The emerging format gave business and professional men, especially, greater control over the formal political process. First African's prohibitions against mass meetings, school closings, and other programs did not last long; the need and desire of members and other Afro-Richmonders for a space that could truly contain a community-wide activity eventually led members to

ignore their prohibition. But instituting the prohibition had not only significantly affected community activities in the early 1880s; it also meant
that, even after strict enforcement was curtailed, decisions about using
the church for graduation exercises, political meetings, and other activities were now subjects of debate. Afro-Richmonders could no longer
assume the church as a community meeting place; instead they had to
argue such. The church remained an important community institution,
but it increasingly shared power with both civil authorities and other
community institutions such as mutual benefit and fraternal societies.

The efforts by white Republican officials to limit popular decision-
making and the decreased accessibility of First African as a community-
wide meeting place affected a politics that had been based in mass
participation. Mass meetings . . . were now less regular. These changes
were exacerbated by the struggle to retain the vote and office-holding
and the necessity, therefore, to counter various tactics of both white
Republicans and Democrats. The fraudulent tactics employed to eliminate black voters, for example, led some black Republicans, like John
Mitchell, who continued to argue against literacy qualifications for
voting, in the 1890s to encourage nonliterate black men to abstain from
voting. . . . Mitchell thought it important to get those least likely to be
challenged or disqualified, and most capable of correctly marking the
ballots, through the lines first before polls closed on them. While
Mitchell argued for a temporary change in practice—not perspective—
regarding the right of all to vote, his and other prominent black Republicans' prioritizing of the literate voter significantly changed the makeup
of the presumed electorate.

As the divisions between black and white Republicans became
deeper in the 1890s, Mitchell and other black Republicans began to hold
small Republican caucuses in selected homes, in essence attempting to
control ward conventions by predetermining nominees and issues.
The ward conventions themselves were often held in halls rather than
the larger churches. The organization in 1898 of a Central Republican
League, which would oversee black Republican activities through sub-
leagues in all the city's wards, reinforced the narrowing party politics
framework. Republican Party decision-making was now more clearly
limited to Party regulars; the mass of black voters and other election
activists were expected to support these channels of decision-making.[44]
These changes, consistent with democratic politics and republican
representative government as practiced in late-nineteenth-century
United States, served to limit the power and influence of most black
Richmonders in the electoral arena. If many black men abandoned
electoral politics even before formal disfranchisement, it was in large
measure due to the effectiveness of the extralegal disfranchisement
efforts of white men. The exclusion from real decision-making power

within the Republican Party and, in this respect within the community, was also decisive.

The increasingly limited notion of political decision-makers that these changes encouraged is also evident in other ways. In 1896, during a factional dispute among black Republicans, John Mitchell challenged the decisions made in one meeting by noting that a substantial portion of those attending and participating were not even "legal voters," that is, they were women. Although he espoused feminine dress and comportment, Mitchell supported women's rights and championed Dr. Sarah G. Jones's success as a physician as evidence of women's equality. He also endorsed women's suffrage while advising black women to understand the racism of the white women's suffrage movement and not to align themselves with it. Despite these personal convictions, Mitchell could dismiss or minimize opposing factions by a reference to the participation of women, suggesting the ways in which the meanings and understandings of politics, of appropriate political actors, and even of the ownership of the franchise had changed in the late nineteenth century.[45]

Questions of qualifications for participation in the external political arena and internal community institutions were now frequent. During the conflictual 1901 business meeting at First African, for example, John Mitchell, Jr., questioned his opponents' right to participate even though they were all church members by pointing out their unfamiliarity with parliamentary procedure or their inelegant ways of speaking. The women . . . refused to accept these as criteria for their participation and even denigrated what he put forth as his formal qualifications by talking out when he got up to speak, saying derisively, "Don't he look pretty."[46] Questions of formal education had already affected the congregation in fundamental ways, most obviously in the late-nineteenth-century debate over song, a debate that represented a significant change in the basis of collective consciousness.

The antiphonal nature of the traditional church service at First African and many black churches reinforced a sense of community. The services included spontaneous verbal and nonverbal interaction between minister and prayer, speaker, and congregation, thus allowing for the active participation of everyone in the worship service. It was this cultural discourse that was carried over into the political meetings. One important element that bound the congregation together was song; as Lawrence Levine has noted, through their collective song church-goers "meld[ed] individual consciousness into the group consciousness."[47] However, the practice of lining hymns, which was basic to collective song, was one that white visitors often referred to when they described what they perceived as the unrefined black church services. Some black churchgoers saw the elimination of this practice as part of the work of uplifting the religious style and uplifting the race. But with the elimination of this practice, those unable to read and follow the lyrics in a song book were now unable to participate, to be fully a part of the community, the collective. It was the equivalent of being deprived of a voice, all the more significant in an oral culture. . . . The debates about women's roles in the church and in the more formal political arenas, like the debate over lining the hymns, were part of widespread discussions about the nature of community, of participation and of freedom.

The proliferation of scholarly works centered on the flowering of black women's political activity in the late nineteenth and early twentieth centuries[48] has perhaps left the impression that this was the inaugural moment or even height of black women's participation in politics. Overt or not, the suggestion seems to be that black women came to political prominence as (because) black men lost political power.[49] In much of this scholarship the reasons for black women's "emergence" are usually tied to external factors. For example, the development of black women's clubs in the late nineteenth century and their important roles in the political struggles of the twentieth century most often have been seen by historians as the result of the increasing development of such entities in the larger society and as reactions to vitriolic attacks on the morality of black women. Such a perspective explains this important political force solely in terms of external dynamics, but external factors alone cannot account for this development.[50] The internal political arena, which in the immediate post-Civil War era was grounded in the notion of a collective voice that gave men, women, and children a platform and allowed them all participation, came increasingly in the late nineteenth century to be shaped by a narrowing notion of politics and appropriate political behavior.

While mass meetings continued to be held, the more regular forums for political discussions were literary societies, ward meetings, mutual benefit society and fraternal society meetings, women's clubs, labor organizations, newspapers, streetcorners, kitchens, washtubs, and saloons. In the development of literary societies as a primary venue for public discussion, one can see the class and gender assumptions that by the turn of the century came to be central to the political organization of black Richmond. While some, as the Langston Literary Association, had male members only, most of the literary societies founded in the 1880s and 1890s had middle-class and working-class men and women members. Despite the inclusive nature of the membership and often of the officers, the form of discussion that developed privileged middle-class males. Unlike mass meetings where many people might take the floor in planned and unplanned expositions and attendees might freely interrupt or talk back to speakers, thus allowing and building mass participation, literary forums announced discussion topics in advance; charged individual members, apparently almost always male, to prepare a paper on the subject; and designated specific, also male, members to reply.

The discussions that then ensued were open to all present, but the structure privileged those familiar with the conventions of formal debate. Women, who served as officers and attended in large numbers, may have joined in the discussion but their official roles were designated as the cultural arm of the forum—reading poetry, singing songs, often with political content appropriate to the occasion. The questions under consideration at the meetings often betrayed the class bias of the forum. Even when the discussions centered on some aspect of working-class life and behavior, the conversation was conducted by middle-class men. The purpose of the forums, as articulated by the Acme Literary Society, suggested the passive observer/learner position that most were expected to take: to hold "discussions, lectures, and to consider questions of vital importance to our people, so that the masses of them may be drawn out to be entertained, enlightened, and instructed thereby."[51] . . . . In the changing circumstances of the late nineteenth century, working-class men and women and middle-class women were increasingly disfranchised within the black community, just as middle-class black men were increasingly disfranchised in the larger society. Men and women, working-class and middle-class, at the turn of the century were struggling to move back to a political authority they once had—internally and externally. As they did so they each often justified such authority along distinctively gendered and class-based lines.

African American men countered the image of themselves as uncivilized, beastly rapists—an image white southerners used to justify disfranchisement, segregation, and violence—with efforts to demonstrate their own manhood and to define white males as uncivilized and savage.[52] While white Richmonders told stories of black barbarity, John Mitchell, Jr., inverted the tale. The *Richmond Planet*, for example, repeatedly focused on the sexual perversions of white men with cases of rape and incest and spoke of white men in terms designed to suggest their barbarism: "Southern white folks have gone to roasting Negroes, we presume the next step will be to eat them."[53] In the process of unmanning white males, however, Mitchell and others developed a narrative of endangered black women. Urban areas, once sites of opportunity for women, became sexually dangerous places for the unprotected female, easy prey to deceitful and barbarous white males.[54] Black men's political rights were essential so that they could do as men should—protect their communities, homes, families, women. The focus on manhood could, initially, be the venue for discussing domestic violence as well. For example, the Reverend Anthony Binga, sermonizing against physical abuse of one's wife, drew on the discourse of manhood: "I have never seen a man whip his wife. I mean a *man*. Everyone who wears a hat or a coat is not a *man*. I mean a *man*." . . . .[55] Concurrent with the narrative of sexual danger in the city and the larger society was an implied corollary narrative of protection within one's own community. Thus the discourse on manhood could keep the concern with violence against women in the public discussion while at the same time setting the stage for issues of domestic abuse and other forms of intraracial violence, which could be evidence of the uncivility of black men, to be silenced as politically dangerous.

In drawing on the new narrative of endangered women, middle-class black women, increasingly disfranchised by the connections between manhood and citizenship in the new political discourse, turned the focus from themselves and on to the working class, enabling middle-class women to project themselves as the protectors of their less fortunate sisters. In this manner they reinserted themselves into a public political role.[56] Autonomous women's organizations, such as the Richmond Women's League (later the Richmond Mothers' Club), or women's divisions within other organizations, such as the Standing Committee on Domestic Economy of the Hampton Negro Conference, developed to serve these functions. These associations promulgated class-specific ideas of respectability, in part justifying their public role through the need to impart such protective measures to working-class women. Specific constructions of womanhood, as manhood, thus became central to the arguments for political rights. Through discussions of manhood and womanhood, middle-class men and women constructed themselves as respectable and entitled, and sought to use such constructions to throw a mantle of protection over their working-class brothers and sisters. By increasingly claiming sexual violence as a women's issue, middle-class black women claimed a political/public space for themselves but they also contributed to an emerging tendency to divert issues of sexual violence to a lesser plane and to see them as the specific interest of women, not bound up in the general concerns and struggle for freedom. This set the stage for the masculine conception of liberation struggle, which would emerge in the twentieth century.[57]

Collective history/collective memory

In July 1895 three black women—Mary Abernathy, Pokey Barnes, and her mother, Mary Barnes—were convicted in Lunenberg County, Virginia, of murdering a white woman. When the women were moved to the state penitentiary in Richmond their case became a cause celebre in the black community there. For over a year black men and women in Richmond struggled to keep the Lunenberg women from being hanged or returned to Lunenberg County for a retrial, fearing that a return to Lunenberg would mean death, the women lynched at the hands of an angry white mob. The community succeeded and the three women were eventually released. The organization of black Richmonders in defense of these women partly illustrates the increasingly gendered nature of internal community politics. Men and women were portrayed as having decidedly different roles in the defense; one avenue of defense was to draw on ideas of motherhood in defending these three women; and the Lunenberg women's release called forth very particular discussions of respectability and womanhood. John Mitchell, Jr., portrayed himself as the militant defender of the women. Women, led by schoolteacher Rosa Dixon Bowser, organized the Richmond Women's League for the purposes of raising funds for the women's defense, visiting them in jail and supporting their husbands and families. Through her column in the *Woman's Era* and her participation in the National Federation of Afro-American Women, Bowser, as did Mitchell, brought the case to national attention. The front page stories in Mitchell's *Planet* emphasized the Lunenberg women as mothers, especially reporting on Mary Abernathy's pregnancy and the birth of her child in her jail cell. While the pictures and stories during the fourteen-month struggle for their release portrayed the women as simply clad, barefoot, farm women, the announcement of Pokey Barnes's final victory was accompanied by a photograph of her now transformed into a true Victorian woman with an elegant balloon-sleeved dress, a symbol of respectable womanhood. . . . Mitchell emphasized the importance of this transformation: "The picture showing what Pokey Barnes looked like when brought to Richmond the first time and what she appears to-day will be a startling revelation to the public and will fill with amazement the conservative people everywhere when they realize what a terrible blunder the execution of this young woman would have been." He thus suggested that it was her ability to be a respectable woman (signified superficially by a class-based standard dress) that was the justification for his and others' protection of her.[58]

But the year-long discussion of these women's fates . . . occurred alongside stories about lynchings or near lynchings of black men. Importantly, therefore, when black Richmonders spoke of lynching in the late nineteenth century, they had no reason to assume the victim to be male. When a freed Pokey Barnes rode as "mascot" in the 1896 Jackson Ward election rally parade, the idea of Mitchell and other black men as defenders was reinforced. But also affirmed was the underlying understanding that violence, including state repression, was a real threat to African American women as much as men. This meant that the reconstruction of clearly delineated notions of womanhood and manhood as the basis for political activism remained relatively ambiguous in late-nineteenth-century black Richmond. But issues of class and gender were increasingly evident, as when Pokey Barnes and Mitchell accepted public speaking engagements—ones in which she was clearly expected to be the silent symbol of oppression and he the vocal proponent of resistance. Barnes, countering that assumption, set forth her own understandings of her role and qualifications, contradicting the class and gender assumptions of Mitchell and of those who invited them: "she said that she was not an educated lecturer and did not have any D.D.'s or M.D.'s to her name, but she was simply Pokey Barnes, C.S. (common sense)." Her two-hour lecture on her ordeal, while giving credit to Mitchell, established herself not only as victim but also as heroine.[59]

The rescue of the Lunenberg women by black Richmonders brought women's struggles to the fore of black rights and reaffirmed violence against women as part of their collective history and struggle. At the same time black Richmonders struggled to create a new category of womanhood that would be respected and protected, and of middle-class womanhood and manhood that could protect.[60] The plight of the Lunenberg women reaffirmed the collective history of black men and women at the same time as it invigorated increasingly distinct political vehicles for middle-class black men and women.

Just as disfranchisement, segregation, lynching, and other violence denied the privileges of masculinity to African American men; segregation, lynching, sexual violence, and accusations of immorality denied the protections of womanhood to African American women. Increasingly, black women relied on constructing not only a respectable womanhood but, in large measure, an invisible womanhood. Hoping that a desexualized persona might provide the protection to themselves and their communities that seemed otherwise unobtainable, many black women carefully covered up all public suggestions of sexuality, even of sexual abuse. In the process issues specific to black women were increasingly eliminated from public discussion and collective memory.[61] In the late twentieth century therefore many African Americans have come to link a history of repression and racial violence exclusively to challenges to black masculinity and thus to establish a notion of freedom and black liberation that bifurcates public discussion and privileges men's history and experiences. In 1991 when Supreme Court justice nominee Clarence Thomas challenged his questioners by calling the Senate Judiciary Committee hearings a "high-tech lynching," black Americans were divided in their response. Some men and women supported his analysis; others opposed either Thomas's analogy or his right to, in using such, assume the mantle of black manhood that he had so often rejected. Few people, however, questioned the assumption basic to Thomas's analogy that lynching and other forms of violence had historically been a masculine experience. Similarly, when black people across the country responded to the video of Los Angeles policemen's brutal beating of Rodney King, a narrative of state repression against black men followed.[62] The masculine focus is most evident in the widespread public discussion of "endangered" black men. While appropriately focusing attention on the physical, economic, and social violence that surrounds and engulfs many black men in the late-twentieth-century United States, much of this discussion trivializes, or ignores, the violence of many black women's lives—as victims of rape and other forms of sexual abuse, murder, drugs and alcohol, poverty, and the devastation of AIDS. Seldom are discussions of rape and domestic violence included in summits on black-on-black crime. The masculinization of race progress that this implies often has some black leaders looking for ways to improve the lot of men, not only omitting women from the picture but often even accepting the violence against women. . . .

Such is the long-term consequence of political strategies developed in the late nineteenth century to empower black men and black women. Understandable and necessary in their day, they served to maintain a democratic agenda even as black political life became more divided. Eventually, however, the experiences of men were remembered as central to African Americans' struggles but the experiences of women, including the physical violence—lynchings, rapes, sexual and other forms of physical abuse as employees in white homes, domestic abuse— as well as the economic and social violence, which has so permeated the history of black women in the United States, were not as vividly and importantly retained in our memory. We give life and validity to our constructions of race, community, and politics by giving those constructions a history. Those who construct masculine notions of blackness and race progress and who claim only some forms of violence as central to African American liberation struggles are claiming/ remembering a particular history. African American collective memory in the late twentieth century often appears partial, distorted, and dismembered. The definitions and issues of political struggle that can come from that partial memory are limited. Before we can construct truly participatory discussions around a fully democratic agenda where the history and struggles of women and men are raised as issues of general interest necessary to the liberation of all, we have some powerful lot of reremembering to do.[63]

NOTES

1 Petition of Mrs. Margaret Osborne et al. to the deacons and members of the First Baptist Church, April 15, 1880, recorded in First African Baptist Church, Richmond City, Minutes, Book 11, June 27, 1880 (microfilm), Virginia State Library and Archives (hereafter FABC).

2 The idea of the immediate adoption of a gendered public-private dichotomy pervades much of the historical literature on post-Civil War black communities. It is most directly argued by Jacqueline Jones [in] *Labor of Love, Labor of Sorrow: Black Women, Work, and the Family from Slavery to the Present* (New York, 1985), 66 [and] is also an accepted tenet [in] Eric Foner, *Reconstruction: America's Unfinished Revolution 1863–1877* (New York, 1988), esp. 87.

3 Many recent discussions of the public sphere among U.S. scholars have orbited around the work of Jurgen Habermas, [especially] *The Structural Transformation of the Public Sphere: An Inquiry into a Category of Bourgeois Society*, trans. Thomas Burger with assistance of Frederick Lawrence (Cambridge, Mass, 1989). See also Jurgen Habermas, "The Public Sphere: An Encyclopedia Article (1964)," *New German Critique* I (Fall 1974): 49–55. Critics who have emphasized the masculine bias in the liberal bourgeois public sphere and posited a female counterpublic include Nancy Fraser, "Rethinking the Public Sphere: A Contribution to the Critique of Actually Existing Democracy" and Mary Ryan, "Gender and Public Access: Women's Politics in Nineteenth-Century America," both in *Habermas and the Public Sphere*, ed. Craig Calhoun (Cambridge, Mass., 1992), 109–142 and 259–89, respectively. . . .

4 For a study that conceptualizes the history of the black church in relation to Habermas's theory of the public sphere, see Evelyn Brooks Higginbotham, *Righteous Discontent: The Women's Movement in the Black Baptist Church, 1880–1920* (Cambridge, Mass., 1993), esp. 7–13. . . .

5 Similar negotiations and pronouncements occurred in other post-emancipation societies. [See for example] Thomas C. Holt, " 'The Essence of the Contract': The Articulation of Race, Gender, and Political Economy in British Emancipation Policy, 1838–1866," paper presented at . . . University of Chicago, October 1993. . . .

6 The question of ownership was one of the first issues Afro-Richmonders addressed, as antebellum law had required that the titles be in the names of white-male supervising committees. . . . [B]lack churchgoers had by the end of 1866 obtained titles to all of their church buildings. See *New York Tribune,* [NYTr] June 17, 1865; Peter Randolph, *From Slave Cabin to Pulpit* (Boston: Earle, 1893), 94–95; John Thomas O'Brien, Jr., "From Bondage to Citizenship: The Richmond Black Community, 1865–1867" (Ph.D. diss., University of Rochester, 1974), 273–275.

7 Statement of Jenny Scott, wife of Ned Scott, colored, June 6, 1865; Statement of Richard Adams, colored, June 8, 1865; [and others] all in Records of the Assistant Commissioner for the State of Virginia, Bureau of Refugees, Freedmen and Abandoned Lands, 1865–1869, Record Group 105, M1048, reel 59, National Archives, Washington, D.C.; *NYTr*, June 12, 17, August 1, 8, 1865; *Richmond Times*, July 26, 1865; S.E.C. (Sarah Chase) to Mrs. May, May 25, 1865, in Henry L. Swint, ed., *Dear Ones at Home: Letters* from *Contraband Camps* (Nashville, 1966), 159–160; Julia A. Wilbur in *The Pennsylvania Freedman's Bulletin* 1 (August 1865), 52, quoted in John T. O'Brien, "Reconstruction in Richmond: White Restoration and Black Protest,

April–June 1865," *Virginia Magazine of History and Biography* 89 (July 1981): 273–275.

8 *NYTr*, August 1, 8, 1865. One of the most neglected areas of Reconstruction history and of African American history in general, is that of violence against women. This has led to the still prevalent assumption that black women were less likely to be victims of racial violence and the generalization that this reflects the fact that black women were less threatening than black men. . . . Only recently have historians begun to uncover and analyze sexual violence against black women as an integral part of Reconstruction history. See, for example, the dissertation in progress by Hannah Rosen, University of Chicago, which examines the rapes connected with the 1866 Memphis race riot [and] Catherine Clinton, "Reconstructing Freedwomen," *Divided Houses: Gender and the Civil War*, eds. Catherine Clinton and Nina Silber (New York, 1992), chapter 17.

9 *NYTr*, June 12, 17, 1865.

10 The *Richmond Times* (May 24, 1865), in refusing to publish black Richmonders' statements of protest, reasoned that . . . only the "idle negroes" were targets of military restrictions and inspections. Throughout the early months of emancipation both white southerners and white Unionists defined freedpeople's mobility in search of family or better jobs and in expression of their newfound freedom as evidence of an unwillingness to work. Similarly, those who chose to vend goods on city streets rather than signing work contracts with white employers were seen as lazy or idle. See O'Brien, "From Bondage to Citizenship," 117–131; see also various communications among the military command reprinted in U.S. War Department, *The War of the Rebellion*: . . ., Series I, Volume XLV, Part III—*Correspondence, etc.* (Washington, 1894), 835, 932–933, 1005–1006. . . .

11 *NYTr*, June 17, 1865.

12 Black Richmonders were countering the very different image of their community put forth not only by white southerners but also by Union officers. [See for example] Major General H. W. Halleck . . . to Hon. E. M. Stanton, Secretary of War, June 26, 1865, in *The War of the Rebellion*, 1295–1297. . . .

13 O'Brien, "From Bondage to Citizenship," chapters 6–9.

14 Ibid., 326.

15 See, for example, *RE*, February 23, 1866; *Richmond Dispatch* [*RD*], July 6, 1866 . . .

16 Foner, *Reconstruction*, 122.

17 *RD*, April 19, 1867; *New York Times* [*NYTi*], April 19, 1867.

18 Julie Saville, "A Measure of Freedom: From Slave to Wage Laborer in South Carolina, 1860–1868" (Ph.D. diss., Yale University, 1986), 273.

19 *Richmond Whig*, April 1, 1867.

20 *RD*, October 5, 1867.

21 Aldon Morris makes a similar argument regarding the church and the modern civil rights movement, emphasizing the ways in which the church served as a physical, financial, and cultural resource . . . *The Origins* of the *Civil Rights Movement: Black Communities Organizing for Change* (New York, 1984). . . . For an argument that eliminating emotions and aesthetics from acceptable forms of public discourse becomes a means to eliminate particular groups of people from active participation in public life, see Iris Marion Young, "Impartiality and the Civic Public: Some Implications of Feminist Critiques of Moral and Political Theory," in *Feminism as Critique: On the*

Politics of Gender, eds. Seyla Benhabib and Drucilla Cornell (Minneapolis, 1987), 56–76.

22 *RD*, August 1, 2, September 30, October 9, 1867; *NYTi*, August 1, 2, 6, October 18, 1867. My discussion of these events follows closely Peter J. Rachleff, *Black Labor in the South: Richmond, Virginia, 1865–1890* (Philadelphia, 1984), 45–46. . . .

23 *RD*, August 1, 2, 1867; *NYTi*, August 2, 6, 1867; see also Rachleff, *Black Labor in the South*, 45; Richard L. Morton, *The Negro in Virginia Politics, 1865–1902* (Charlottesville, Va., 1919), 40–43.

24 The October 1867 city Republican ward meetings and nominating convention adopted the practice common in the black community's mass meetings: a voice or standing vote which enfranchised men, women, and children. See, for example . . . *RD*, September 20, October 9, 1867; January 2, 4, 14, 23, 24 . . . 1868; *NYTi*, August 6, 1867 . . .; Rachleff, *Black Labor in the South*, 45–49. . . .

25 Compare black women's active participation in Richmond's formal politics—internal and external—in the first decades after the Civil War to Michael McGerr's assessment that nineteenth-century "women were allowed into the male political realm only to play typical feminine roles—to cook, sew, and cheer for men and to symbolize virtue and beauty. Men denied women the central experiences of the popular style: not only the ballot but also the experience of mass mobilization." McGerr's analysis fails to acknowledge the racial basis of his study, i.e., it is an assessment of white women's political participation. Michael McGerr, "Political Style and Women's Power, 1830–1930," *Journal of American History* 77 (December 1990): 864–885, cap. 867. My analysis also differs substantially from Mary P. Ryan, *Women in Public* [who] . . . finds black women's political expression in the Civil War and Reconstruction eras restricted "with particular severity" and "buried beneath the surface of the public sphere," see 146–147, 156, *passim*.

26 *NYTi*, January 11, 22, 1868. The Debates and Proceedings of the Constitutional Convention of the State of Virginia, Assembled at the City of Richmond (Richmond, 1868). 505–507, 524–527.

27 RD, June 18, 1867; Rachleff, *Black Labor in the South*, 48.

28 Rachleff, *Black Labor in the South*, 31–32; *Richmond Daily Dispatch*, May 10, 1867; *New Nation*, November 22, 29, December 6, 1866; Holt, *Black over White*, 3 5; Avary, *Dixie after the War*.

29 . . . *RE*, October 22, 1867; *Richmond Whig*, October 19, 1867; Robert E. Martin, "Negro Disfranchisement in Virginia," *The Howard University Studies in the Social Sciences*, I (Washington, D.C., 1938): 65–79. . . .

30 Howard N. Rabinowitz, *Race Relations in the Urban South, 1865–1880* (New York, 1978), 222: Airutheus Ambush Taylor, *The Negro in the Reconstruction of Virginia* (Washington, D.C., 1926), 181, 269; Michael B. Chesson, "Richmond's Black Councilmen, 1871–96," in *Southern Black Leaders of the Reconstruction Era*, ed. Howard N. Rabinowitz (Urbana, Ill., 1982), 2 1911; Peter J. Rachleff, "Black, White and Gray: Working-class Activism in Richmond, Virginia, 1865–1890" (Ph.D. diss., University of Pittsburgh, 1981), 473, 488n, *RD*, October 25, 26, 1872. . . . .

31 See Thomas C. Holt, " 'An Empire over the Mind': Emancipation, Race, and Ideology in the British West Indies and the American South," in *Religion, Race, and Reconstruction: Essays in Honor of C. Vann Woodward*, ed. J. Morgan Kousser and James M. McPherson (New York, 1982), 283–314. . . .

32 This is not to suggest that African American women did not desire the vote

nor that they did not often disagree with the actions taken by some black men. One should, however, be careful about imposing presentist notions of gender equality on these women. . . .

33 FABC, 11, April 5, 6, 11, May 3, June 27, 1880.

34 First African minutes for 1841–1859 and 1875–1930, are available at First African and on microfilm in Archives, Virginia State Library. . . .

35 FABC, 11, June 27, 1880.

36 FABC, 111, November 7, 20, 1899; *Richmond Planet [RP]*, July 6, 20, August 10, 31, 1901, March 8, 15, 1902. . . . [D]ebates over gender roles within black churches occurred on congregational and denominational levels. For studies which examine these debates at the state and/or national level, see, for example, Higginbotham, *Righteous Discontent*; Glenda Gilmore, "Gender and Jim Crow: Women and the Politics of White Supremacy in North Carolina, 1896–1920" (Ph.D. diss., University of North Carolina at Chapel Hill, 1992). . . .

37 *Virginia Baptist* cited in *Woman's Era* I (September 1894), 8.

38 *RP*, July 26, 1890; June 8, 1895; September 17, 24, November 19, 1898; September 9, 1899; Anthony Binga, Jr., *Sermons on Several Occasions*, I (Richmond, 1889), 97–99. Both Kemp and Carter were Baptist. A few women also conducted services in the Methodist church. . . .

39 In July 1880 a council representing nine Richmond black Baptist churches censured First African for having called the police. "The First African Baptist Church, Richmond, Virginia, to the Messengers & Churches in General Ecclesiastical Council Assembled," in FABC, 11, following April 3, 1881, minutes. . . .

40 FABC, II, June 27, November 6, 1882; February 5, April 2, 1883. . . .

41 Rachleff, "Black, White, and Gray," 307–309.

42 See, for example, the discussion of the reconfiguration of leisure space, including the barring of cakewalks and other dancing from the church, in Elsa Barkley Brown and Gregg D. Kimball, "Mapping the Terrain of Black Richmond," *Journal of Urban History* (forthcoming).

43 *New York Globe*, October 1883–January 1884. . . .

44 For information on the Central Republican League, see *RP*, August–September 1898; *Richmond Evening Leader*, August 6, 16, 24, 27, 30, September 1, 28, October 12, 1898. . . .

45 *RP*, January 26, 1895; October 17, 1896. . . .

46 *RP*, July 6, 1901.

47 Lawrence Levine, *Black Culture and Black Consciousness: Afro-American Folk Thought from Slavery to Freedom* (New York, 1977).

48 The scholarly emphasis on this latter period is not merely a reflection of available sources. It also reflects the conceptual paradigms that have guided the investigation of black women's politics: a focus on the national level, often with minimal attention to different patterns within the North and the South; the acceptance of what Suzanne Lebsock has called the "consensus . . . that for women the standard form of political participation" in the nineteenth century "was the voluntary association"; an emphasis on autonomous women's organizations; and a focus on excavating political (and feminist) texts. . . . Suzanne Lebsock, "Women and American Politics, 1880–1920," in *Woman, Politics, and Change*, eds. Louise A. Tilly and Patricia Gurin (New York, 1990), 36.

49 Seeing the 1880–1920 period as "the greatest political age for women (including black women)," Suzanne Lebsock raises the question "what does

it signify" that such occurred at "the worst" age for black people; "an age of disfranchisement and increasing legal discrimination": "Women and American Politics," 59, 37. Glenda Gilmore . . . contends that black women in North Carolina gained political prominence at the turn of the century as (because) black men vanished from politics—either leaving the state altogether or sequestering themselves in a nonpolitical world, "Gender and Jim Crow," chapter 5. It is an idea, however, that is often unstated but implicit in much literature which imagines black women's turn-of-the-century club movement as their initial emergence into politics. Such a narrative contributes to the fiction that black women were safer in the Jim Crow South than were black men.

50 I am indebted to Stephanie J. Shaw for making the point that it was internal community dynamics more so than external factors which gave rise to the black women's clubs in the late nineteenth century. See Stephanie J. Shaw, "Black Club Women and the Creation of the National Association of Colored Women," *Journal of Women's History* 3 (1991): 10–25. . . .

51 *New York Globe*, 1883 and 1884, *passim*; Acme quote is June 23, 1883; *RP*, July 26, 1890; January 12, 1895; 1890–1895, *passim*.

52 Efforts to demonstrate manhood increasingly took on class and status dimensions. For an example of this, see the discussion of black militias and the military ritual taken on by black fraternal orders such as the Knights of Pythias, in Barkley Brown and Kimball, "Mapping the Terrain."

53 See for example, *RP*, June 11, 1891; February 24, September 22, 1900. . . . [See also] Gail Bederman, "'Civilization,' the Decline of Middle-class Manliness, and Ida B. Well's Antilynching Campaign (1892–94)," *Radical History Review* 52 (winter 1992): 5–30; . . . Hazel V Carby, " 'On the Threshold of Woman's Era': Lynching, Empire, and Sexuality in Black Feminist Theory," *Critical Inquiry* 12 (autumn 1985): 265.

54 The idea of sexual danger had been a part of the Reconstuction era discourse, as evidenced in the mass indignation meetings and testimonies. . . . Now a more clearly gendered discourse developed where violence against men was linked to state repression and the struggle against it to freedom and violence against women became a matter of specific interest, increasingly eliminated from the general discussions.

55 First African also excluded men found to have physically abused their wives. Binga, "Duty of Husband to Wife," in Binga, *Sermons on Several Occasions*, I, 304–305 (emphasis in original); FABC, 11, August 6, September 3, November 5, 1883, April 7, 1884. . . .

56 . . . . Suzanne Lebsock has taken the development of women's clubs with these concerns as possible evidence of the increased instances of exploitation of women: "Women and American Politics," 45. I suggest that the exploitation is not increased or even of greater concern, but that the venues for expressing and acting on that concern and the ideology through which this happens—both the narrative of endangerment and the narrative of protection—are the new, changed phenomenon. While the emphasis on motherhood and womanly virtues which undergirded the ideology of middle-class women as protectors may resonate with much of the work on middleclass white women's political activism in this period, . . . African American women's prior history of inclusion, not exclusion, shaped their discourse of womanhood and their construction of gender roles; they did so not in concert with ideas in the larger society but in opposition. . . .

57 James Oliver Horton and Lois E. Horton suggest that a masculine conception

of liberation, based on violence as an emancipatory tool available princi- pally to men, developed within African American political rhetoric in the North in the antebellum period. "Violence, Protest, and Identity: Black Manhood in Antebellum America," in James Oliver Horton, *Free People of Color: Inside the African American Community* (Washington D. C., 1993), chap. 4.

58 Abernathy's and the Barnes' trials, incarceration, retrials, and eventual releases can be followed in the *RP*, July 1895–October 1896; *Richmond Times*, July 23, 1895; *RD*, September 13–19, October 2,23, November 8, 9, 12, 14, 16, 21, 23, 24, 27, 28, 1895; July 5, 1896. . . . Discussions of the case can be found in Brundage, *Lynching in the New South*; and Samuel N. Pincus, *The Virginia Supreme Court, Blacks and the Law 1870–1902* (New York, 1990), chapter 11 [and Suzanne Lebsock, *Murder in Virginia: Southern Justice on Trial* (New York, 2003)].

59 *RP*, March 6, 1897.

60 The narrative of class and gender, protectors and protected, was not uncontested. For . . . a counternarrative that emphasized the possibilities of urban life not only for the middle class but importantly the possibilities of urban life for single, working-class black women . . . [see] Elsa Barkley Brown, "Womanist Consciousness: Maggie Lena Walker and the Independ- ent Order of Saint Luke," *Signs: Journal of Women in Culture and Society* 14 (spring 1989): 610–633.

61 . . . . Histories that deal with respectability, sexuality, and politics in all its complexity in black women's lives have yet to he written. For beginning discussions see Darlene Clark Hine, "Rape and the Culture of Dissemblance: Preliminary Thoughts on the Inner Lives of Black Midwestern Women," *Signs: Journal of Women in Culture and Society* 14 (summer 1989): 919– 920; Elsa Barkley Brown, " 'What Has Happened Here': The Politics of Difference in Women's History and Feminist Politics," *Feminist Studies* 18 (summer 1992): 295–312; Paula Giddings, "The Last Taboo," in *Race-ing Justice, En- gendering Power: Essays on Anita Hill, Clarence Thomas, and the Construction of Social Reality*, ed. Toni Morrison (New York, 1992), 441–463.

62 Bytches With Problems, "Wanted," is one effort by young black women to democratize the discussion of repressive violence. Focusing on the often sexualized nature of police brutality against black women, they remind us that such is often less likely to be included in statistics or acknowledged in the public discussion. *The Bytches* (Noface Records, 1991).

63 Elsa Barkley Brown, "Imaging Lynching: African American Women, Com- munities of Struggle, and Collective Memory," in *African American Women Speak Out: Responses to Anita Hill-Clarence Thomas*, ed. Geneva Smitherman (Detroit, [1995]).

2

A CHANGING WORLD OF WORK
North Carolina elite women, 1865–1895

Jane Turner Censer

For most white southerners, defeat and occupation were traumatic and life-altering experiences. Censer's essay here focuses on the ways in which white women faced the aftermath of the war. Her careful examination of elite white women in North Carolina shows that they responded differently, and reconstructed their own lives differently, depending on their age.

Drawing on the sociological concept of "generations," she shows that the oldest cohort of women, those born before 1820, found it difficult to adjust to a world without slaves. The next generation proved to be more adaptable, while the youngest generation—those who "came to maturity during either the war or Reconstruction"—resembled their counterparts outside the South in the ways they worked, wrote, and thought. Censer argues that such a generational analysis helps to reconcile apparently conflicting accounts by historians of the fate of white southern women after the war. The essay also illustrates one of the many ways in which diversity, rather than uniformity, characterized social and cultural developments in the New South.

* * *

When the Civil War ended, North Carolinians could see the mark that years of war had left on their state. They could begin to count its toll in the more than forty thousand Tar Heel soldiers who had died and in the thousands of others who returned home physically or psychologically maimed. The conflagration's impact was even more apparent in the shattered southern economy. For many years the altered world that emerged at war's end influenced the decisions that women and men made in their homes and workplaces. At question and of interest are the continuities and changes that North Carolinian women from privileged families faced in the work they undertook both inside and outside the home.

Currently historians disagree about how women from the former planter class adapted to the very different postbellum world. All who study these women build upon the pioneering book, *The Southern Lady*, that Anne Firor Scott published over twenty-five years ago. Arguing that the Civil War began the emancipation of upper-class women, Scott depicts antebellum southern women as severely restricted by expectations that their destiny lay only with home and family. Scott argues that the ravages of war provided women with a widened sphere of influence and interests. Whether the widowed plantation mistress overseeing her lands or the unmarried adult daughter searching for a means of support, the southern woman learned to manage for herself and demonstrated a pluck and resourcefulness that had earlier been stifled. Scott's treatment of the postwar years is brief, for she outlines a century of southern women's activities. More recently, Edward Ayers, in his survey of the South from 1877 to 1906, also notes an expanded sphere for women.[1]

The interpretation that stresses change in the lives of postbellum southern women his received criticism from several different angles. Jonathan Wiener disputed any notion that increased numbers of widows ran plantations by noting that the 1870 manuscript census for black belt Alabama counties reveals no increase in the proportion of women heading plantation households. Other scholars more generally dismiss the possibility of increased choices and autonomy for southern women. In particular, George C. Rable, while arguing for genuine change during the Civil War, believes that change ended with the war—the poverty of postwar society allowing little leisure or latitude for altering gender roles. Similarly Suzanne Lebsock has suggested that women faced increasingly circumscribed options in a postwar world marked by poverty and racial adjustment.[2] Despite these disagreements with Scott's views, relatively few studies have focused on southern females collectively in the late nineteenth century, and none have attempted to map the contours of daily routines of these women.[3]

This essay seeks to reconcile these conflicting scholarly views and remedy past neglect by sketching the activities and attitudes of elite women in North Carolina. The women selected for this study represent forty-four Piedmont and coastal families, the elite status of each woman being based on her family's possession of at least twenty slaves during the 1850s. Diversity exists among the families in the variety of staple crops produced on their plantations, differing levels of personal wealth, their religious affiliation, and residency in either town or countryside. The group constitutes a large enough part of the Carolina elite to ensure broad similarities between the ladies and their neighbors. Surveying the changes and the continuities that prevailed in the concurrent worlds of female work—the domestic activities within the home and paid employment within the community—provides a more revealing interpretation of the women and their society. Although members of a small group, these genteel women demonstrate, in their actions and attitudes, general patterns of southern women's physical and psychological response to postwar challenges. Their multifaceted experiences can be used to produce a typology of shared elite female attitudes and behavior that can be tentatively extended to include other southern women of their class. Extensive reading in the published and unpublished writings of other privileged postwar southern women suggests that the subjects of this article were largely typical for their region as well as their state.[4]

Examining these North Carolina ladies yields no simple, one-dimensional interpretation. The differences in attitudes and behavior between genteel women of various ages become apparent. Despite individual variations and other important factors such as marital status, the evidence suggests that these women can best be understood in three main groups: older women, who were born before 1820; women born before 1845, who in general had been young wives and mothers during the war; and young women who came to maturity during either the war or Reconstruction. Such a division more systematically helps to reveal continuities and alterations over time among these generations of southern women.[5]

Older North Carolina women—mature women who at the outbreak of war in 1861 were forty years of age or already had adult children—may have changed least in their activities and attitudes. In the period immediately after the Civil War, elite matrons found their households newly burdensome without the assistance of slaves. Emancipation was a heavy blow for these women, who, for the first time in their lives, were confronted with a new order that did not include slaves. In 1865 the mood was especially grim, but even two years later an elderly Warrenton matron was "very low" in spirits because she could not "stand the great change, which has been introduced into our social system."[6]

Susan Bullock, a sixty-three-year-old widow living on her plantation in Granville County, tersely chronicled major concerns in her diary (children and grandchildren, religion, weather, and the progress of farm and household work). She also documented her struggles with household help. On January 24, 1867, the family cook left. Within three weeks Bullock had hired a new cook, three plantation workers, and two other servants, whom she referred to as a "housewoman" and "a small waiting maid." The new cook and one of the laborers soon departed, and Susan Bullock grimly recorded, "We are having trouble with the darkies." After her son consulted a "Yankey" (probably an official of the Freedmen's Bureau posted in a neighboring town), Bullock, using the old vocabulary of slavery, reported the result: "[T]he Yankey ordered the return of our runaway servants." She viewed a servant who left "without an excuse" as analogous to the slave who stole him or herself. The language of free labor and contract had not won over this elderly widow who continued, perhaps unconsciously, her antebellum practice of using no surnames for the servants.[7]

Difficulties in adjusting to free labor were no passing problem for the older women. Eliza Jane Lord DeRosset, a Wilmington matron in her fifties at the war's end, provides a revealing case study of how sullenly older women continued to respond over time to the new organization of household service. Eliza DeRosset's story of "servant problems" began in August 1865 as she fumed that John, then her family's only servant, was "very insolent" and stayed only because his wife had not yet returned to Wilmington. By June 1866 she employed four servants, Maumee, Louisa, Maria Swann, and an unidentified yardman, but complained that they were "quite enough to take ill looks from."[8]

Eliza DeRosset's anger, while not dissipating, tended over time to resolve into a frantic pursuit of servants who either were, or resembled in behavior, her lost slaves. In 1867 she mused that Maria Swann "is a great comfort to me, Maumee too, I do not know what I would do without her, and John brought me his second daughter 10 years old and begged I would take her just as tho' she belonged to me." At that point DeRosset rather proudly reported that she had only one "strange" servant (i.e. one who had not been earlier owned by the family), a very efficient dining room "girl." Such a situation—servants who had once been family slaves, an ex-slave bringing his daughter to live in the former master's family—immensely pleased Eliza DeRosset, perhaps because it seemed to show a dependence that recalled the old days of slavery. But the happy state of events lasted only a short time. Six months later when she believed that Maria Swann had stolen some of her china, DeRosset brought in the authorities. Ultimately Maria was fined one dollar and court costs; but this certainly was not the "proper" outcome for patrician Eliza DeRosset, who had hoped that her servant would be sentenced to the workhouse—a punishment recalling the past compulsions of slavery. In this lady's eyes such leniency was akin to levying the punishment on her: "[I]t makes my blood boil to think of the indignities we are obliged to submit to from even our former servants."[9]

Although Eliza DeRosset's relationship with her servants remained rocky, it also remained no less necessary to her, and the saga continued. In May 1868 she decried her "wretched country" and wished herself in England where one of her sons was then living and where she believed poor white people to be virtually enslaved. She pointed out her major problem: "the negroes" in her opinion were "getting past bearing—every day they are worse and worse. I cannot get a cook now."[10]

Not long before her death in 1876, Eliza DeRosset employed—or in her terms—"kept two servants only." Here she explicitly noted that although her widowed daughter-in-law had joined the household, the grandchildren's elderly nurse did not figure in that tally. Over ten years after slavery's demise, Eliza DeRosset still used a possessive vocabulary as she referred to this servant: "Maumee is given to [my daughter-in-law] Jennie—and I am very scrupulous in not calling upon her."[11]

Younger matrons, while having no greater experience than their mothers and aunts with domestic chores, continued to display some dependence on and a similar condescension toward former slaves. However, whether from necessity or by choice, the women of the second generation demonstrated far greater flexibility toward household work and proved more physically and psychologically adept than their predecessors. Thirty-five-year-old Ann Pope accompanied her complaint about the freed people leaving and otherwise "doing very badly here" with a diatribe about her living conditions. "I live in dirt, eat, and sleep in it," she declared, "I want the power of annihilation. I get so mad that I don't know what to do—but I grin and endure it." In the same letter she admonished her teenage niece that "I have got Donum cooking for me, but I intend getting a stove and doing my own cooking so you had better come down and pay me a visit and I will give you some lessons."[12]

The ladies of the second generation carried on with fewer servants, and a small number even learned to live without domestics. Although they had employed nursemaids to care for children, these mothers generally had little difficulty with tasks related to child care; however, housekeeping skills did not come so easily to elite women, who only slowly and painfully expanded their competence. Even six years after the war Catherine "Kate" Douglas DeRosset Meares suffered when she had no servant. She once complained that "for several days we had to do all our cooking & cleaning up—because we could not get a servant, but today we succeeded in getting one. You would have laughed to see Cousin Rosa & me trying to cook some biscuits & make some coffee for breakfast." The following year when Meares was without a servant for over two months, she and her son sometimes had only bread and milk for breakfast, "when we could get the cow milked." Yet she did learn to accomplish heavy household work and later reported that "yesterday I was washing windows & the consequence is, I am so stiff & sore today that I can hardly move."[13]

Younger matrons accepted their new situations but also fondly recalled the prewar period, which they remembered as a time when housekeeping meant overseeing a staff of dependable, properly submissive servants. Although their standards for the well-conducted household, much like their ideal of relations among the races, continued to hearken back to the time of slavery, these younger women did not exhibit the same obsession about procuring servants that seemed to preoccupy the Eliza DeRossets of the first generation. Like Ann Pope, who was learning to cook on a new stove, many elite women tried to manage with fewer servants by using modern technology—new stoves, sewing machines, and washing machines—to replace human work with machine labor.[14] Eventually the second generation made its peace with the new system. By 1885 Kate Meares philosophically remarked to her son about a shortage of servants: "It is too bad things should be in such a condition—but it isn't peculiar to your part of the country."[15]

It was the youngest generation—the young unmarried schoolgirls of the war period and their even younger siblings—that was able to accept domestic chores with relative aplomb. The dislocations of the war introduced the older members of this group to responsibility at an early age. Eliza Lord, as part of a large family whose mother became increasingly incapacitated before her early death, learned about household activities during wartime. In 1863 Eliza began keeping house for her mother, who was enduring a difficult pregnancy. Eliza's grandmother praised the young girl's resourcefulness by declaring, "she is certainly the most practical useful child of her age I ever saw."[16] Such past experience proved beneficial ten years later when Eliza, as a newlywed, did all of her own housework.

Other young women stepped into the breach when servants left. When the family cook resigned in 1875, it was twenty-year-old Annis Meares, not her mother, Mary Exum Meares, who assumed responsibility for managing the kitchen. Later Annis transferred this task to her sister, Esther. As both daughters and wives, this younger group undertook housework with an equanimity never approached by the previous two generations. To be sure, these young women more often merely accepted, rather than enthusiastically embraced, such household chores. Before her marriage Rosa Biddle included churning among her daily duties. Perhaps such past work led her after marriage to comment complacently on her good health "notwithstanding the hard work & cooking." In 1883 one young matron, Mary Cameron, declared that her health was so much better that she could do her own housework. She underscored her point by alluding to the servants she was willingly foregoing: "We have had nine applications from different parties to come live with us, but I do not intend to get anyone, at least yet awhile."[17]

Thus younger southern women, especially those of the third generation, came to play a more physically active role in their households. Although the straitened circumstances of elite families in the postbellum world and the weakening of bonds with the African American community may have compelled some of this adaptation, young women so ably managed with fewer servants and a degree of work that their grandmothers would have considered drudgery that a change in attitude seems apparent. Obviously this new capability also had its elements of irony. As southern women were becoming more adept in domestic arts, they were exchanging the managerial functions of their grandmothers for actual physical labor. Although more skillful than their predecessors, the younger women were also more domesticated. Even larger changes in the conceptions of work for women came from outside the traditional sphere of the home. Here, as elsewhere, differences between generations are clearly apparent.

The general loss of property and land values in the aftermath of war called forth women's efforts beyond their expected household duties. Perhaps the area in which some married women or widows first took responsibility lay in their assumption of plantation business affairs. In the absence of husbands, a number of antebellum widows and politicians' wives managed their plantations—directing the cultivation, harvest, and sale of crops, budgeting finances for the purchase of necessary provisions, etc.—albeit with overseers employed to actually supervise labor. Although never superintending farm affairs, other plantation matrons were at least somewhat acquainted with the managerial needs of their lands.[18] The Civil War increased women's involvement in plantation management, as sons and husbands went to war, many of whom never returned. For example, Jane Caroline "Carey" North Pettigrew (of the wealthy and socially prominent Washington County Pettigrews) supervised and provided for her husband's slaves for several years after they were removed to the family's Cherry Hill plantation in South Carolina in 1862.[19]

After the war a number of elite women found themselves solely responsible for the management of their plantations. As Orville Vernon Burton has suggested, the women who led plantation households tended to be older, often with teenage or young adult sons. North Carolina elite women who shouldered such responsibility were all at least thirty years old; however, it is difficult to ascertain exactly how far the management of such women reached and how long it lasted. In one case, George Little made it clear that his widowed sisters took responsibility for the hiring and firing of their farm workers. In November 1865 he described his widowed, fiftyish sister, Susan Skinner, as experiencing some "difficulties" with her "darkies." The following May, as he sympathized with his widowed niece, Sally Tarry Hamilton, about problems she was encountering with freedmen, he reminded her that "your aunt Mary Mosby and Aunt Susan have been fortunate in retaining such servants as they wanted. They had to discharge a good many and get new ones to work their farms." Other cases suggest that women tended to rely on the assistance of male relatives or to hire managers to supervise their laborers. Drew Gilpin Faust, in a recent examination of one Texas slaveholding woman's experiences during the Civil War, argues that women shrank from slave management because of the violence involved. While managing free labor would not involve the threats and impositions of punishments that had been so essential to plantation slavery, it still meant directing the work of men of both races, often outdoors.[20]

The case of the widowed Susan Bullock vividly illustrates the difficulty of discovering the extent of women's involvement in plantation management. At her husband's death in 1866, Susan Bullock had four adult sons (ranging in age from twenty to thirty-nine) who lived either with or near her. She depended on them, especially twenty-four-year-old Austin and twenty-year-old Walter, to oversee many plantation duties, such as dividing the crops, picking up guano at the nearby town, and going to the sawmill. Yet Bullock clearly perceived herself as responsible for hiring both plantation laborers and household domestic workers. On February 5, 1867, she indicated that two freedmen, Mordecai and John, were burning a plant bed (in preparation for tobacco planting) and noted that "they are the only field hands I have hired yet[.] To M[ordecai]. I give 120 dollars to John 80 dollars." One year later Bullock recorded that she had hired one "Woodson" for ten months for sixty dollars. These notes contrast with an entry six months later that "Walter [her son] hired two boys this morning." Susan Bullock also chronicled work on plantation chores and crops that occurred while her sons were absent. After participating in the decision to buy a new reaper, she recorded two days later that she "commenced cutting wheat this morning with the reaper Austin, Walter & myself bought of Mr. C. Handy." While she most often mentions "the" wheat or "the" tobacco, whose ownership is indefinite, Susan Bullock sometimes clearly differentiated between her crops and those belonging to her sons, when she wrote about "my tobacco" or "my corn."[21]

Despite the active role she played in at least some areas of plantation management, Susan Bullock seems to have considered that responsibility merely to be one part of her life. She was more affected by the death of her husband and loss of his companionship than by the increased authority over plantation work that came with her widowhood. Although she accepted plantation affairs as being within her sphere, she did not seem particularly to savor them. The one change in status that most agitated Susan Bullock was giving up management of her household in 1869, apparently because of poor health. She wrote, "The morning corresponds with my feelings, gloomy and sad, . . . after keeping house 44 years last Nov. I give it up this morning and take a side seat at Walter's table." On one level this was a largely symbolic change for Bullock since her son Walter and his wife had moved in with her more than a year earlier. Yet, the relinquishing of her role as mistress of the household—emphasized by the seating arrangement at the table—seemed of far greater moment to her than any power over plantation management.[22]

While some women assumed control over hiring laborers and appear to have been willing to bargain with the freedmen over wages, others remained aloof from direct supervision of plantation workers. In 1866 a thirty-six-year-old unmarried woman in Franklin County, Jane Hawkins, contracted the management of labor on her lands to Mr. Brownfield Clarke. An agreement for that year with fifteen male freedmen obligated them to work "on the plantation of Miss J. A. Hawkins and in the charge" of Mr. Clarke. The contract specifies monthly wages for each laborer but does not indicate who would pay them. After 1870 the old plantation system moved more into share-cropping and renting; elite women's role in labor management may have changed as the new system of tenant farming reduced the problem of supervising laborers. A typical case was the widowed Ann Downey Davis of Granville County who, by 1885, was having her tobacco grown by a renter.[23]

Women of the younger generations appear to have been less involved with issues of plantation management for several reasons. By the 1870s members of North Carolina's planter elite were beginning their retreat away from unprofitable plantations. Women were at the forefront of this movement since they generally were less comfortable with rural life and agricultural pursuits. Susan Polk Rayner accepted the postwar decision of her husband, Kenneth, to migrate to Memphis, Tennessee, not far from the Mississippi cotton plantations that he had purchased. The venture quickly failed; and by 1868, Mr. Rayner was ill, depressed, and bankrupt. Although Susan Rayner had refused to spend summers on a plantation for almost thirty years, she boldly investigated a number of pieces of land. Without consulting her husband, she used the remainder of her own legacies to buy a farm south of Memphis in Desoto County, Mississippi, where she moved her family in 1869. While managing the smaller farm, the Rayners were able to rebuild their finances. Kenneth Rayner received a government appointment to the Alabama Claims Commission in 1874 and moved his family to Washington, D.C.[24]

Although Susan Rayner chose farm life in Mississippi as a way to support her family, significant numbers of North Carolina women seem to have preferred town or city life. In 1879 Rosa Biddle, who had grown up on a Craven County cotton plantation, expressed her disdain for the agricultural life: "I have no faith in cotton, have all my life been dependent upon it & when I thought of going to Charlotte, it was a relief to me that I would not immediately be connected with it." Many women of the second and third generations not only applauded the movement away from the old plantations, they tried to bring it about. Understandably, some widows sought to disassociate themselves from the responsibilities of their lands, but younger married women also tried to avoid the old plantations. One such woman was Anne Cameron Collins who convinced her husband, George, not to attempt to repurchase any of the lands belonging to Somerset Place, the Collins family plantation. Mr. Collins reluctantly agreed with his wife about the financial risk involved in such a commitment and assured her that he "would be extremely unwilling to do anything in which I would not have your hearty approval & cooperation which I would not have." As her sons tried to rescue the family plantation from debt, Carey Pettigrew wrote about her five daughters, "naturally enough the girls get tired of living down here, the neighborhood is very narrow, the associations common! common!" Many women found the postwar plantation to be extremely confining, a situation worsened by the lack of money to finance visits to town or city.[25]

Many of the women who owned plantations in the aftermath of the Civil War were first generation matrons. Especially mindful of societal strictures against female employment outside the home, few of this group sought paid work other than sewing. These women, most of whom were over age forty, may also have been experiencing a lessening of physical strength and endurance that further reduced the desirability or even possibility of employment. Only the unusual woman, such as Frances "Fanny" Ann Devereux Polk, widow of educator and Confederate general Leonidas Polk, was willing and able to undertake teaching at the advanced age of sixty.[26]

In contrast, the second generation of women—whether single, married, or widowed—searched for ways to aid the family economy. Many undertook traditional women's work, such as taking in boarders or selling handmade items and farm produce, activities that nevertheless had been rare among their social group before the war. Although in poor health, Mary Jones took in ten boarders to support her family, and, while coping with a husband descending into alcoholism and debility, her sister, Sallie Jones Collins, opened a boardinghouse in Hillsborough. Mary Norcott Bryan, who had married just before the war began, made numerous items that she sold to aid her family's finances. The proceeds from her garden paid her husband's expenses when he traveled to New Bern in 1865 to look after their real estate interests there. Mary Bryan took great pride in her contributions. "I made a good deal of money myself of which I was very proud," she proclaimed.[27]

At least a few second generation women found another kind of work that could generally be accomplished within the home—writing, primarily for newspapers and magazines. While a number of antebellum American women had distinguished themselves as writers, this occupation was most common among those women who lived in the Northeast where the large publishing houses were located. Mary Bayard Devereux Clarke's long-standing interest in literature no doubt eased her transition into editing periodicals and writing for pay. In 1853 as a twenty-six-year-old wife and mother, she anonymously edited two volumes of poetry by North Carolinians; and, during the Civil War, she wrote numerous pro-Confederate poems. After the war she served as the assistant editor of *Southern Field and Fireside* and became editor of *Literary Pastime* in 1868. Mary Bayard Clarke continued to produce poetry, but she also wrote remunerative hymns, book reviews, short stories, travel sketches, and reminiscences. In 1879 she assisted her husband, William J. Clarke, in editing the *Signal*, a Republican newspaper in Raleigh. Other second generation women, such as Virginia Durant Covington, produced widely read articles and novels.[28]

Writing was not the only income opportunity available, and a number of second generation women successfully undertook paid employment outside the home. Fanny Pender, widow of Confederate general William D. Pender, became postmistress of Tarboro. In 1874 Ann Biddle Pope, who probably traded on her influence as daughter of a prominent Baptist minister, accepted a position as housekeeper of the Baptist school in Raleigh.[29]

The third generation of women, those who came to maturity during and after the war, continued and extended the employment activities pursued by their predecessors. In 1870 at the age of twenty-four, Frances Christine Fisher published the first of more than thirty novels under the pseudonym of Christian Reid. Fisher, whose father had died in the Civil War, was probably the best known of the third generation authors and wrote prolifically to support herself, her sister, her aunt, and the family homestead, which she ruefully dubbed "Castle Rackrent."[30]

Moreover, clerical work slowly became available to women in the latter half of the nineteenth century. In 1879 Mamie Cain, a young woman from Orange County, was in Raleigh "writing for the legislature." Five years later Carey Pettigrew's twenty-four-year-old daughter, Caroline, explored the possibilities for a clerkship in the federal government in Washington. At first she received little encouragement from North Carolina's congressmen. According to her mother, "several of the delegation entirely opposed her applying for a place on the score of the wickedness and bad reputation of the positions." But Senator Matt W. Ransom promised to do all that he could to help her, and Miss Pettigrew found that her female friends in Baltimore, many of whom were North Carolina expatriates, disputed those officials' low opinion of female workers. One of her friends wrote that "doubtless there were many bad people in the departments, but many ladies against whom there wasn't a whisper." Although Caroline Pettigrew did not receive a governmental job, others of her generation were successful at obtaining federal employment. And a few women of the third generation began to find work that generally was unconventional for females of the postwar era. Twenty-three-year-old Annie Lowrie Alexander, for example, returned from Baltimore in 1887 to practice medicine in Mecklenburg County, and in 1890 a female relative of the Faison family in Duplin County was clerking in a store.[31]

The most common occupation pursued by members of the second and third generations was teaching. No other work seemed to offer as many possibilities with as few drawbacks, and women decided to enter teaching for several different reasons. Teaching permitted many genteel women to utilize the skills that years of education in elite schools had given them. Moreover, teaching could be harmonized with expanded rather than radically altered gender roles. Even the most rigid traditionalists believed that teaching young children was an appropriate female role, but only when practiced by mothers within the home. Furthermore, in the period before the war North Carolinians had become accustomed to a few women, especially northern women, serving as schoolteachers. Moreover, a small number of antebellum North Carolina women had worked in schools that were male-dominated family businesses.[32]

Although teaching could be undertaken either as a salaried job or entrepreneurial enterprise, it generally did not promise a financial bonanza. Numerous historians have pointed out that teaching salaries for men were miserable and that those for women were even lower. The expansion of the number of teaching positions for women in the North had often been touted as an economy because female teachers there received one-half or one-third of the salary paid to their male counterparts. Even schoolteachers who operated their own schools did not necessarily make much money.[33] Nonetheless, teaching in the mid-nineteenth century offered great flexibility, relatively short hours, and little or no manual labor. In comparison to other businesses a day school for students in the primary grades required little capital, and only the larger residential schools necessitated a substantial physical plant. Female teachers could also see expanding possibilities in public education in the South. North Carolina was the only southern state that had instituted a public school system before the Civil War. Remunerative teaching opportunities were available both in the state school system, which was revived and expanded after 1870, and in the numerous private academies and schools for elite young ladies.[34]

During and immediately after the war a number of women of the middle generation turned to teaching. In 1865 when Bettie Quince opened a school with twenty scholars, her relatives praised her "peculiar fitness" for it. Others of the second generation began residential schools that continued for many years. One such case is that of Martha and Mary Mangum, who opened a school for young ladies in 1862 at their Walnut Hall plantation that proved to be a great success.[35]

The experiences of Kate Meares, who had been widowed during the war, demonstrate how some young widows of the middle generation reconciled work and family obligations. Before the war Meares made a conventionally successful and apparently happy marriage and never envisioned a life of independence. The death of her husband in the Battle of Malvern Hill in 1862 left her the responsibility of raising and supporting three young sons. Although she continued to rely on her father for financial advice and her parents wanted her to return to the family home in Wilmington, Kate Meares made her own living and her own life. Over the next fifteen years she moved among a number of different teaching positions—some obviously chosen to be near her sons who were away in school, others to be near her parents.[36]

Although she briefly taught in Granville County and later headed the music department in a school run by a relative in Wilmington, Kate Meares sought a niche for herself that would combine her Episcopalian piety and desire for good works with teaching and a steady income. On land donated by her father, prominent Wilmington physician, Dr. Armand John DeRosset III, Kate Meares was instrumental in founding the St. James Home, which operated as the charitable adjunct of St. James Episcopal Church, one of Wilmington's most elite Episcopal churches. At the home she helped to organize a free school, which had sixty students by October 1872, and to start an infirmary. In 1875 she then moved to Germantown, Pennsylvania, where she taught elocution, French, and music at a girls' school. She returned to North Carolina in 1876 when Aldert Smedes asked her to become the first "lady principal" of St. Mary's Academy in Raleigh—a position she held from 1877 until 1881.[37]

Kate Meares was not the only second generation widow who turned to teaching to support her family. Honoria "Nora" Devereux Cannon, the sister of both Catherine Ann Edmondston and Mary Bayard Clarke, returned from Tennessee to her native North Carolina in 1867 following her husband's death. She relied on the benefice of relatives until she obtained a teaching position at St. Mary's in Raleigh in 1872. Mrs. Cannon's three daughters were permitted to live with their mother on campus and received scholarships to attend classes. After three years at St. Mary's, she moved back to Somerville, Tennessee, where she and her husband had lived during the Civil War. In 1881 at the age of fifty-two she was elected superintendent of Fayette County public schools. Tennessee's first elected female public official, Nora Cannon served as school superintendent for two years and was reelected in 1886.[38]

Teaching played a particularly significant role for women in the third generation. Anne Firor Scott notes numerous references to women teachers of this general age group, and other evidence suggests that many young women at some point undertook teaching. All four of Mary Alves Long's older sisters who came to maturity in the 1870s taught school or were governesses at one point or another. Jane Long, after working as a substitute teacher in the New York City public schools, gained a position teaching English at Peace Institute in Raleigh.[39]

A number of teachers began their careers by instructing their younger siblings or the children of relatives. In the few years prior to her accepting a teaching job at St. Mary's, Nora Cannon had informally instructed her Edmondston nephews and nieces. In 1876 Roberta Lord taught a class of only ten scholars, each of whom paid a $1.50 monthly fee; however, by 1882 she had obtained a position in South Amboy, New Jersey, with which she was "very much pleased."[40]

The early career of Caroline Pettigrew provides a revealing example of the kind of young woman likely to turn to teaching. Born in 1860, she grew up in a respected genteel family whose wealth had been radically reduced by the war. At St. Mary's in Raleigh she proved to be an excellent student who studied hard and tried "to improve all her opportunities." Her mother, Carey, and her uncle, the Reverend William S. Pettigrew, endeavored to continue young Caroline's promising education and managed to gather together enough money for her tuition until early 1878. After an unsuccessful attempt at locating a teaching position, she returned home to teach her two younger sisters. In 1880 she received a two-year scholarship to Peabody Institute in Nashville. This additional training (along with family connections) helped Caroline obtain a teaching post at a public elementary school in New Bern in 1882. The following year she taught at an orphanage in Oxford, North Carolina, and by 1886 she was teaching near New York City and had been offered a position in Morristown, New Jersey.[41]

There is little doubt that the level of commitment to and satisfaction in the teaching profession varied greatly among third generation ladies. Some teachers worked for the income that teaching provided and were content to relinquish their classroom responsibilities within a few years for marriage or other forms of support. Jeannie Meares offered no argument when her suitor told her, "I feel so sorry for you in that hot schoolhouse today, my darling that I am obliged to tell it to you." And even those who felt a greater commitment found some positions more appealing than others as they met the challenge of dealing with numerous children. Lavinia "Lena" Smith was both a teacher and administrator at the Vine Hill Academy in Scotland Neck. Although the school was flourishing, her grandmother noted that Lena's students were "mostly young beginners that it is not much pleasure to teach."[42]

A small number of elite women made teaching a long-term occupation in a way that had not been available to them previously. Mary Lord began teaching in 1868 when she was twenty-three years old, and many of her positions were in either Brooklyn or the environs of New York City. In 1878 a cousin reported that "Mary Lord is so happy at her school." Her teaching continued until she married more than a decade later. Adelaide "Addie" Savage Meares taught over four thousand students in forty-two consecutive years at the same Wilmington school. Although Meares and other lifetime teachers have left relatively little testimony about their commitment to schoolteaching, it is apparent, even early in their lives, how much they emphasized their love of learning and education. As a student in 1875, the young Addie Meares called her school, Wilmington's Tileston Institute, "a splendid school" and added that "so far, I am perfectly delighted with it." Two years later she declared her intention "to study several years longer . . . [for] Father thinks it is a great mistake for girls to stop school and go out into society so soon, and I do also, so I am not anxious to be a young lady."[43]

No matter how long they taught, the teaching profession offered new choices to postwar southern women and formed a solid alternative to the domestic life. In 1877 Esther Meares told her cousin, "I was so sorry your Mother could not get me a [teaching] situation. It would be so much better than cooking, don't you think?" Within three years Esther was teaching in a school with thirty-eight scholars.[44]

Teaching not only removed women from domestic chores at home, it also seems to have offered them the chance to either delay or avoid marriage. Given the large numbers of young men killed in the war, it can be argued that this opportunity was simply demographic determinism at work—an unbalanced sex ratio would necessitate that not all women could marry and many could not marry early. In some cases these young women appear to have preferred their unmarried state to the marital possibilities that confronted them. Mary Lord offers one example of long delays. In 1875 her cousin, believing that Mary would marry a rather dissipated suitor at the end of the month, wrote, "she runs a fearful risk but being 30 years old & after 6 years consideration will put her foot into it." Despite her long deliberation Mary did not put her foot into it, and another fifteen years passed before she did marry.[45]

Esther Meares, who preferred teaching to housework, indicated that she found her suitors to be either unacceptable or unappealing. Even before she received a teaching position, Esther disqualified a number of matrimonial candidates. At age twenty-three, Meares flippantly described to her cousin a Sunday evening that she had spent with one suitor: "He talked a great deal about matrimony; I tried to hush him up by telling him I would never marry anyone unless they were in every way my superior. He said of course I meant in the way of trade, and that he thought he was a good a trader as there was in the country. Some men are so conceited. Don't you think so."[46]

If Esther Meares were in fact waiting for such a "superior," she apparently never found him. Three years later when a Mr. Murdock "courted her again," she rejected his proposal with the blunt pronouncement that "she would not live in Salisbury with any man." Esther's comments display a disdain more for the men who wooed her than for the institution of marriage. Whether she found men as a group unappealing cannot be determined, but it is clear that Meares was dismissive of the possibilities that presented themselves. Her comments also demonstrate a marked lack of concern with her increasing age and offer intriguing suggestions into why she, like some of the other teachers, never married.[47]

To explore fully the appeal of teaching for the third generation, it is important to discuss briefly the world of courtship and marriage for the young ladies coming of age in the postwar period. In the South, as elsewhere in the United States, marriage was still touted as the most appropriate station for women, the goal to which they should aspire. Most young southern women still married, and some scholars dispute the thesis that the proportions of southern women who married changed radically in the decades following the war. However, a number of elite southern women seem to have either ignored or explicitly questioned the importance of marriage.[48]

The apparent lack of overall change may have masked altered attitudes among genteel women toward marriage, which did not seem to receive the same accolades it had in the prewar period. Some women clearly suggested that the constraints of marriage on their autonomy would not be welcomed. Jeannie Meares told her fiance of one week's standing, "yes, it is hard to give up one's name and independence, but I feel confident that mine will be entrusted to a very kind & loving heart." The belief that their suitors were of a lower class or otherwise "unequal" seems to have played a role in motivating the actions of some women, like Annie Pettigrew and Esther Meares, who turned down those men they found socially unacceptable. Equally as important as these critiques was the skepticism that marriage would better a woman's lot in life. In 1877 Carey Pettigrew wrote of her daughter Jane's courtship: "I do not think Jane has quite made up her mind, but he is very devoted, and so highly spoken of by all who know him, that if she marries at all, I doubt any one making her happier." In the prewar period a devoted patrician mother such as Jane Caroline North Pettigrew would barely have entertained the notion about her daughter that she voiced in the doubt "if she marries at all." In this case young Jane did accept the proposal. Other elite women sometimes echoed a similar wistfulness about whether marriage or any man could make them happy.[49]

A large number of these women were increasingly reluctant to leave their parents and siblings. As Jeannie Meares exclaimed to her fiance, "I have been the oldest unmarried daughter for [so] long, that the thought of giving up my place to another and going out from under my Mother's care causes a quick throb of pain sometimes." Rosa Biddle, who married at age thirty-one, found it difficult both to leave her family and to visualize happiness in marriage. She told her fiance, "you can't imagine how sad it makes me to say 'good bye' to my dear old home, . . . I know my dear mother finds it a heavy burden of sadness tho' she esteems you highly & believes as we all do that you will make me happy if it is in the power of man to do so."[50]

For some women who actively delayed or avoided marriage, teaching provided an alternative that interrelated two important goals. These women were able to remain either with or near their families while providing needed financial and physical assistance. At the same time that they were maintaining close ties to their families, they were also achieving a measure of accomplishment and autonomy for themselves. Sometimes it was difficult to reconcile the goals of attachment and self-sufficiency. Mary Lord most fully expressed this conflict and the torment it caused her when she wrote from her teaching job in Brooklyn, "I am so distracted all of the time to go home, and so frantic for fear that I might have to do so." The separation from her motherless younger siblings weighed on the young Miss Lord who stated that "I get perfectly wretched when I think of the children losing their dependence on me, and it is so hard to be separated from them; still I wouldn't go home for anything, and at the same time look forward to it with the greatest eagerness as the end & sum of my desires."[51]

For other women whose jobs lay closer to home, such goals could more easily be put in tandem. Lena Smith supplemented her education at St. Mary's with art studies in New York City and a year at the State Normal College. In 1880 she accepted a position at Vine Hill Academy where she taught until 1899, when she founded her own school in Scotland Neck. Lena lived with her parents for many years and never moved from her native Halifax County. Peter Evans Smith, the noted Confederate engineer and inventor whose postwar career had been unsuccessful, was proud of the initiative Lena and her two sisters took in supporting themselves. In a touching letter inspired by his failing eyesight, he wrote of his daughters, "I am thankful they have sense and energy enough to take care of themselves. If it were otherwise I should sink under my troubles but that thought and the thought of your dear Mother buoys me up to further exertions."[52]

As elite women confronted the postwar period, they displayed divergent responses. The matrons of the first generation clung tightly to their beliefs about the necessity of servants for proper household management and generally pursued their domestic activities as in the years before the war. Yet some among these ladies successfully assumed the reins of plantation management when the occasion arose. The women of the second generation bridged the world of their mothers and daughters—by learning domestic chores, albeit unwillingly; by encouraging the relocation of their families to towns; by sometimes turning to paid work to earn money; and by providing an education for their daughters.

The entrance of southern elite women into paid employment reveals an ethic—new in the South—that promoted a form of economic self-support and independence among the second and third generations. Second generation women saw education as the means of providing their daughters with opportunities. While not necessarily advocating a "career" or a lifetime of work, mothers implicitly wanted their daughters not to feel pressured into marriage, especially unpromising marriages to unacceptable spouses. The efforts of Carey Pettigrew exemplify the goals of second generation mothers. Assisted by her bachelor brother-in-law's generous contribution from his small salary as an Episcopal priest, Mrs. Pettigrew embarked upon a decades-long program to educate her children. Discussing her "dread of debt," Carey Pettigrew declared in 1879, "if I had the opportunity of borrowing the money to educate my children I certainly would, as that would make them independent and able to support themselves." And this ethic was absorbed by her daughters, including the young Caroline who had excelled at St. Mary's and wanted a teaching position because she "was very anxious to do something for herself, to assist in paying off Mr. Smedes and to help with her younger sisters."[53]

In adhering to an ethic that emphasized domestic capability, self-support, family solidarity, and wariness about marriage, the second and third generations could draw from a literature of advice books, popular magazines, and best-selling novels that had been circulating in the North for several decades. In addition, southern-born authors such as Mary Virginia Haws Terhune (who used the pseudonym, Marion Harland) and Augusta Jane Evans created popular images of self-reliant, successful heroines that appealed to southern elite women. Somewhat ironically these notions gained vigor in the South even as they began to wane in the North.[54]

A number of scholars might find peculiar a discussion of choices available in an economically devastated land. With few exceptions the South's wealthy families lost their fortunes and livelihoods as a result of the ravages of war, the emancipation of the slaves, and the reforms of Reconstruction. Would economic necessity not provide sufficient explanation for the changing behavior of elite women? Were not domestic expertise and paid employment outside the home simply the result of circumstances that necessitated few, if any, changes in social outlook and attitudes? The altered economic conditions certainly served as a precondition to the new activities of elite women. Given the choice, the great majority of these ladies would have gladly fore-gone much of the work that was demanded of them. But this is where the generational divide is useful—it stands as a reminder of the diver-sity of attitudes and responses to similar economic conditions that was possible within the confines of southern society. Although the members of the third generation still preferred to have other women undertake household chores, these ladies achieved a capability that did not make servants the obsession that they had been for the matrons of the first generation.

Generally the women of the second and third generations sought employment not so much to avoid starvation but to fund the education of their children or siblings. Some of the women who had been excel-lent students probably saw in teaching a way to continue to live in a world of books, ideas, and gentility, and their actions, even more than their actual words, suggest that work begun out of necessity may have continued out of commitment. The third generation was responding to a hard world, but some of these ladies came to believe that marriage was neither a panacea nor even a social obligation and that other pos-sibilities existed. For these young ladies the call and needs of family sounded like a clarion, so that a Mary Lord was torn between seeing her younger siblings grow up without her and wanting to continue her teaching career in the high-paying North.

This examination of the attitudes and work of elite white women in the postwar South can lead to a new understanding of the historical debate about change. Scholars such as Jonathan Wiener, who have used plantation management as a gauge of women's autonomy, are probably correct that the number of women planters rose little in the decades after the Civil War. Yet many assertive elite women, not to mention enterprising men, would have disputed the operation of a plantation in the postbellum economy as a worthwhile aspiration. Change for these people meant the lure of town life rather than the uncertainty of independent farming. Modem scholars also have cat-egorized schoolteaching, clerking, and secretarial work as "women's fields" and tend not to consider the entrance of women into these occupations as "genuine" change. Such a view overlooks the satisfactions that schoolteaching—with its separate culture and its own sphere of influence—could offer women who did not wish to marry or share in the new domesticity that was invading the South. The unmarried schoolteacher was the "new woman" of the late-nineteenth-century South; that her concerns lay with family, education, piety, and benevolence should not obscure the expanded roles and different lifestyles newly available to southern women following the Civil War.

NOTES

1 Anne Firor Scott, *The Southern Lady: From Pedestal to Politics, 1830–1930* (Chicago, 1970); Edward L. Ayers, *The Promise of the New South: Life After Reconstruction* (New York, 1992).

2 Jonathan Wiener, "Female Planters and Planters' Wives in Civil War and Reconstruction: Alabama, 1850–1870," *Alabama Review* 30 (April 1977): 135–149; George C. Rable, *Civil Wars: Women and the Crisis of Southern Nationalism* (Urbana, Ill., 1989), chapter 13; Suzanne Lebsock, *The Free Women of Petersburg: Status and Culture in a Southern Town, 1784–1860* (New York, 1984). . . .

3 [On] postbellum southern women's efforts at benevolent or moral reform, see LeeAnn Whites, "The Charitable and the Poor: The Emergence of Domestic Politics in Augusta, Georgia, 1860–1880," *Journal of Social History* 17 (summer 1984): 601–613; Marsha Wedell, *Elite Women and the Reform Impulse in Memphis, 1875–1915* (Knoxville, 1991); Anastatia Sims,"The Sword of the Spirit: The W.C.T.U. and Moral Reform in North Carolina, 1883–1933," *North Carolina Historical Review* [*NCHR*] 64 (October 1987): 394–415; and Suzanne Lebsock, *"A Share of Honour": Virginia Women. 1600–1945* (Richmond, 1984); John Carl Ruoffs, "Southern Womanhood, 1865–1920: An Intellectual and Cultural Study" (Ph.D. Diss., University of Illinois, 1976); Anastasia Sims, "Feminism and Femininity in the New South: White Women's Organizations in North Carolina, 1883–1930" (Ph.D. diss., University of North Carolina, 1985); and Florence Elliott Cook, "Growing Up White, Genteel, and Female in a Changing South, 1865–1915" (Ph.D. diss., University of California, Berkeley, 1992). . . .

4 . . . . Among letters; diaries, and memoirs [of postwar southern white women], see especially Virginia Ingraham Burr, ed., *The Secret Eye: The Journal of Ella Gertrude Clanton Thomas, 1848–1889* (Chapel Hill, 1990); Frances Butler Leigh, *Ten Years on a Georgia Plantation since the War, 1866–1876* (1883; reprint, Savannah, 1992); E. Grey Dimond and Herman Hattaway, eds., *Letters from Forest Place: A Plantation Family's Correspondence, 1846–1881* (Jackson, 1993); Belle Kearney, *A Slaveholder's Daughter* (1900; reprint, New York, 1969); Betsy Fleet, ed., *Green Mount after the War: The Correspondence of Maria Louisa Wacker Fleet and Her Family, 1865–1900* (Charlottesville, 1978); Orra Langhorne, *Southern Sketches from Virginia, 1881–1901*, ed. Charles E. Wynes (Charlottesville, 1964); Nancy Chappelear Baird, ed., *Journals of Amanda Virginia Edmonds: Lass of the Mosby Confederacy, 1859–1867* (Delaplane, Va., 1984); Mary D. Robertson, ed., *A Confederate Lady Comes of Age: The Journal of Pauline DeCaradeuc Heyward, 1863–1888* (Columbia, S. C., 1992); Carol Bleser, ed., *The Hammonds of Redcliffe* (New York, 1981). . . .

5 Numerous historians have used generations as a way to look at the different experiences of groups. For a discussion this concept, see Howard Schuman and Jacqueline Scott, "Generations and Collective Memories," *American Sociological Review* 54 (June 1989): 359–381. Other factors must also be taken into account. In *Ladies, Women and Wenches: Choice and Constraint in Antebellum Charleston and Boston* (Chapel Hill, 1990), Jane H. and William H. Pease make a compelling case for the importance of marital status as well as race and class in determining the options open to women.

6 Peter R. Davis to Bettie Amis, March 25, 1867, Elizabeth Amis Cameron (Hooper) Blanchard Papers, Southern Historical Collection, University of North Carolina Library, Chapel Hill [SHC].

7 Susan Bullock Diary, January 24, 30, February 5, 18, 19, 1867, in the John Bullock and Charles E. Hamilton Papers, SHC. . . . The adjustments of elite women to the loss of their household servants in 1865 can be followed in Leon F. Litwack, *Been in the Storm so Long: The Aftermath of Slavery* (New York, 1979), 336–360. . . .

8 Eliza J. DeRosset to Louis H. DeRosset, August 6, 1865, DeRosset Family Papers, SHC.

9 Eliza J. DeRosset to Louis H. DeRosset, June 17, 1866, April 8, November 24, 1867, January 12, 1868, DeRosset Family Papers.

10 Eliza J. DeRosset to Louis H. DeRosset, May 24, 1868, DeRosset Family Papers.

11 Eliza J. DeRosset to Kate Meares, April 9, 1876, Meares and DeRosset Family Papers.

12 Ann J. Pope to Rosa Biddle, n.d., 1865, Samuel S. Biddle Papers, Special Collections, Duke University Library [DU].

13 Kate Meares to L. H. Meares, October 24, 1871, September 9, 1872, Meares-DeRosset Papers. For examples of young matrons doing their own housework, see Sallie Collins to Anne Collins, January 30, 1866, Anne Collins Papers, SHC. . . .

14 For a discussion of an elite woman obtaining household appliances in the postwar period, see Rebecca Anderson to Anne Collins, March 10, 1866, Anne Collins Papers. Ruth Schwartz Cowan, *More Work for Mother: The Ironies of Household Technology from the Open Hearth to the Microwave* (New York, 1983) presents an excellent overview of the growing importance of appliances in the home.

15 Kate Meares to Richard A. Meares, September 2, 1885, Meares-DeRosset Papers.

16 Eliza Lord to Kate Meares, Lossie Myers, and Alice Daves, September 19, 1863, DeRosset Family Papers.

17 Kate Meares to Richard A. Meares, September 2, 1885, Meares-DeRosset Papers; Mary T. Meares to Frederick Meares, March 20, 1875, William B. Meares Papers, SHC; . . . Rosa Biddle to Samuel P. Smith, July 26, 1879, and Rosa Biddle Smith to M. E. Biddle, October 6, 1886, Samuel S. Biddle Papers; Mary Cameron to "My Dear Cam," Bailey Family Papers, Virginia Historical Society, Richmond.

18 Scott, *Southern Lady*, 34–35, 81–82, 106–110; Catherine Clinton, *The Plantation Mistress: Woman's World in the Old South* (New York, 1982), 188–196; Orville Vernon Burton, *In My Father's House Are Many Mansions: Family and Community in Edgefield, South Carolina* (Chapel Hill, 1985), 128–131. This role [had] even older roots. See Laurel Thatcher Ulrich's description of the "deputy husband" in *Good Wives: Image and Reality in the Lives of Women in Northern New England, 1650–1750* (New York, 1982), 36–50.

19 See, for example, Burton, *In My Father's House*, 134–136. Carey Pettigrew's Cherry Hill experiences are chronicled in Wayne K. Durrill, *War of Another Kind: A Southern Community in the Great Rebellion* (New York, 1990), 83–85, 148–149, 153–156, 162–164.

20 Burton, *In My Father's House*, 262–264, 284–287; George Little to Sally Hamilton, November 17, 1865, William Tarry Papers, DU; George Little to Sally Hamilton, May 11, 1866, Bullock-Hamilton Papers (emphasis in original); Drew Gilpin Faust, " 'Trying to Do a Man's Business': Slavery, Violence and Gender in the American Civil War," *Gender and History* 4 (summer 1992); Clinton, *Plantation Mistress*, 187–395.

21 Susan Bullock Diary, January 5, April 11, September 8, 9, February 5, 1867, February 29, August 5, 1868, July 15, 23, 1867, June 17, 19, 1868, Bullock-Hamilton Papers.

22 Susan Bullock Diary, January 1, December 6, 1869, Bullock-Hamilton Papers.

23 "Agreement with Brownfield Clark" [1866], Hawkins Family Papers, SHC; John Downey to Ann Downey Davis, February 9, 1885, Samuel S. Downey Papers, DU. . . .

24 Gregg Cantrell, *Kenneth and John B. Rayner and the Limits of Southern Dissent* (Urbana, Ill., 1993), 49–58, 152–160, 313, explores the Rayners' marriage and the wealth Susan Polk brought to it.

25 Rosa Biddle to S. P. Smith, June 22, 1879, Samuel S. Biddle Papers; George P. Collins to Anne Cameron Collins, February 8, 1874, Anne Collins Papers; Jane Caroline Pettigrew to William S. Pettigrew, June 6, 1880, Pettigrew Family Papers, SHC. Ayers, *Promise of the New South*, 56, 63, also documents this flight from rural districts but ascribes it only to single (unmarried, widowed, or divorced) women's desires. . . . [W]hite widows in Edgefield County, South Carolina, were disproportionately likely to live in towns in the postwar period. See Burton, *In My Father's House*, 303.

26 Beth Gilbert Crabtree and James W. Patton, eds., *"Journal of a Secesh Lady": The Diary of Catherine Ann Devereux Edmondston, 1860–1866* (Raleigh, 1979), xxvi.

27 Anne Cameron to George and Anne Collins, July 29, 1866, Anne Collins Papers; Mary Biddle Norcott Bryan Scrapbook, SHC, 157, 169, 191.

28 *Dictionary of North Carolina Biography*, "Clarke, Mary Bayard Devereux"; Edward T. James et al., eds., *Notable American Women, 1607–1950: A Biographical Dictionary*, 3 vols. (Cambridge, Mass., 1971), 1:342–344; Crabtree and Patton, *"Journal of a Secesh Lady,"* 729, 737–738; Mary T. Tardy, *The Living Female Writers of the South* (Philadelphia, 1872), 442–449, 458.

29 William W. Hassler, ed., *The General to His Lady: The Civil War Letters of William Dorsey Pender to Fanny Pender* (Chapel Hill, 1965), 262; Mary E. Biddle to Rosa Biddle, August 4, 1874, Samuel S. Biddle Papers.

30 For biographical sketches of Frances Christine Fisher Tiernan, see Richard Walser, *Literary North Carolina: A Brief Historical Survey* (Raleigh, 1970), 26–27; Edwin Anderson Alderman et al., eds., *Library of Southern Literature*, 16 vols. (Atlanta, 1908–1913), 12: 5369–5375. . . .

31 Anne Collins to Anne Cameron, January 12, 1879, Anne Collins Papers; J. C. Pettigrew to William S. Pettigrew, February 28, 1884, Pettigrew Family Papers. . . .

32 Edgar Wallace Knight, *Public School Education in North Carolina* (1916; reprint, New York, 1969), 201; Stanley L. Falk, "The Warrenton Female Academy of Jacob Mordecai, 1809–1818," *North Carolina Historical Review* 35 (July 1958), 281–298. Christie Anne Farnham, *The Education of the Southern*

Belle: Higher Education and Student Socialization in the Antebellum South (New York, 1994), depicts the curriculum and social life of the schools in which the older generations of elite women were educated. . . .

33 Keith Melder, "Women's High Calling: The Teaching Profession in America, 1830–1960," *American Studies* 13 (fall 1972): 19–32. George Rable stresses the smallness of the gains that female teachers made and argues, "They set no precedents, inspired few imitators, and unsettled few minds." See, Rable, *Civil Wars*, 274–283, 285.

34 Rable, *Civil Wars*, 274–283; Knight, *Public School Education*, 212–328. See also William A. Link, *A Hard Country and a Lonely Place: Schooling, Society, and Reform in Rural Virginia, 1870–1920* (Chapel Hill, 1986). . . .

35 Rebecca S. Davis to Kate Kennedy, July 29, 1865, DeRosset Family Papers. For information on the Mangum sisters, consult Sandra Lee Kurtinitis, "Sally Alston Mangum Leach, A Profile of the Family of a Plantation Mistress: An Analytical Study of the Correspondence of the Family of Willie P. Mangum" (Ph.D. diss., George Washington University, 1986), 150–156, 205–207, and the Willie Mangum Family Papers, Library of Congress, Washington, D.C. Amory Dwight Mayo furthered the notion that only in the 1880s did the numbers of southern women teachers actually increase over prewar levels; however, the statistics he presents that concern women teaching in public schools are woefully incomplete and can neither show their entrance into tutoring and private schools nor their displacement of the northern women who earlier held such positions. See Amory Dwight Mayo, *Southern Women in the Recent Educational Movement in the South*, ed. Dan T. Carter and Amy Friedlander (1892; reprint, Baton Rouge, 1978), xx–xxi, 167.

36 Eliza J. DeRosset to Louis H. DeRosset, February 4, 1868, DeRosset Family Papers.

37 James Sprunt, *Chronicles of the Cape Fear River, 1660–1906*, 2d ed. (Raleigh, 1916), 612–613; William Lord DeRosset, *One Hundredth Anniversary Commemorating the Building of St. James Church, Wilmington, North Carolina, April 30th and May 1st, 1939: The Two Hundred and Tenth Year of the Parish* (Wilmington, N.C., 1939), 11; Kate Meares to Louis H. Meares, October 24, 1871, October 10, 1872, Kate Meares to Armand and Richard A. Meares, February 4, 1875, Kate Meares to Richard A. Meares, September 25, 1875, Alice Daves to Kate Meares, August 27, 1877, all in the Meares-DeRosset Papers.

38 Crabtree and Patton, "*Journal of a Secesh Lady*," xxxi, xxxiv, 738–739.

39 Scott, *Southern Lady*, 112; Mary Alves Long, *High Time to Tell It: "Ah, Distinctly I Remember"* (Durham, N.C., 1950), 151–160, 217.

40 Kate Meares to Richard A. Meares, October 15, 1875, Eliza DeRosset to Kate Meares, January 16, 1876, Cattie DeRosset to Kate Meares, January 31, 1882, all in Meares-DeRosset Papers; Crabtree and Patton, "*Journal of a Secesh Lady*," xxxi.

41 Jane Caroline Petrigrew to William S. Pettigrew, January 4, 1876, January 27, 1878, ... in Pettigrew Family Papers.

42 W. A. Williams to Jeannie Meares, June 18, 1881, John and William A. Williams Papers, SHC; Grandma to Rebe Smith, August 20, 1882, Peter Evans Smith Papers, SHC. . . .

43 Adelaide Meares to "Dear Miss Mary," ca. October 11, 1875, and Adelaide Meares to "My Dear May," February 14, 1877, both in Adelaide Savage Meares Papers, DU.

44 Essie Meares to Louis H. Meares, November 7, 1877, Meares-DeRosset Papers; Mary T. Meares to Fred Meares, November 20, 1880, William B. Meares Papers.

45 Kate Meares to Richard A. Meares, June 3, 1875, Meares-DeRosset Papers.

46 Essie Meares to Louis H. Meares, March 25, 1877, Meares-DeRosset Papers.... For an examination of never-married women, primarily New England born, see Lee Virginia Chambers-Schiller, *Liberty, a Better Husband. Single Women America: The Generations of 1780–1840* (New Haven, 1984).

47 Mary T. Meares to Fred Meares, November 20, 1882, William B. Meares Papers.

48 Rable, *Civil Wars*, 270–271; Orville Vernon Burton, "On the Confederate Home Front: The Transformation of Values from Community to Nation in Edgefield, South Carolina" (paper presented at the Woodrow Wilson International Center for Scholars, Washington, D.C., May 1989). Interestingly the question of whether there were class differentials in the proportions of never-married women has not been examined by scholars.

49 Jeannie Meares to W. A. Williams, ca. June 1881, John and William A. Williams Papers; Jane Caroline Pettigrew to William S. Pettigrew, July 31, 1877, Pettigrew Family Papers.

50 Jeannie Meares to W. A. Williams, August 26, 1881, John and William A. Williams Papers; Rosa Biddle to S. P. Smith, December 15, 1879, Samuel S. Biddle Papers....

51 Mary Lord to Kate Meares, May 9, 1876, Meares-DeRosset Papers. See also Betsy Devereux Jones to Sophia Turner, November 3, 1878, Josiah Turner Papers, SHC.

52 Typescript newspaper article, July 7, 1879, and Peter E. Smith to Lena Smith, July 13, 1880, both in Peter Evans Smith Papers....

53 Jane Caroline Pettigrew to William S. Pettigrew, July 1, 1879, August 1, 1878, Pettigrew Family Papers....

54 Frances B. Cogan, *All-American Girl: The Ideal of Real Womanhood in Mid-Nineteenth-Century America* (Athens, Ga., 1989) outlines the distinction between "real" and "true" womanhood. "Real" womanhood involved physical health, domestic competency, and industriousness, whether at home or working for wages as opposed to the ideals of "true" womanhood, which emphasized female fragility, timidity, and dependence....

3

FARMERS, DUDES, WHITE NEGROES, AND THE SUN-BROWNED GODDESS

Stephen Kantrowitz

Stephen Kantrowitz's essay, taken from his book on South Carolina politician Benjamin Ryan Tillman, analyzes Tillman's appeal to his rural white constituents. Tillman came from a well-to-do and politically prominent family known for its penchant for violence (one brother served two years in jail for manslaughter, and another served time for assault and was later himself murdered). Born in 1847, Tillman missed service in the Confederate army because a tumor destroyed his left eye just as he reached the age to join. But Tillman, along with other whites, believed his leadership among the vigilante groups that helped to restore white supremacy and the power of the Democratic Party in South Carolina during Reconstruction was as valuable as service during the war. He was a key participant in the 1876 "Hamburg Massacre," when whites provoked a confrontation with black militiamen in the town of Hamburg, killing several, including prisoners executed in cold blood.

After Reconstruction, though, Democrats divided among themselves. Small farmers in the state, suffering from low cotton prices and rising debts, blamed the wealthy "aristocrats" who ran the party and whose policies, they believed, benefited merchants and others who lived off the backs of honest "producers." Some whites who favored financial reforms and debt relief for small farmers were even willing to ally with black voters in the Republican Party, if necessary, to take power in the state. Tillman, too, took up the mantle of reform, but he refused to compromise on white supremacy. He was elected governor, and later Senator; he was also instrumental in the successful movement to disfranchise South Carolina's blacks.

In the selection here, Kantrowitz argues that Tillman's success was in large part based on his ability to articulate the cultural values and express the fears and resentments of South Carolina's poor white farmers. These values and fears were rooted in popular understandings of gender, race, and class. The foundation stones of a good society, Tillman told them, were "independent"

67

*and "manly" producers: especially white male farmers, assisted by white
women and by properly subordinate black laborers. Wealthy merchants and
similar people were not only exploiters but also "effeminate dandies" and
"effete aristocrats," not real men. Tillman's reform measures were much less
substantial than those of the independent challengers of the 1880s or the
Populist Party of the 1890s, but Tillman was successful in convincing white
voters that parties such as the Populists were a threat to white supremacy.
Most of those voters "embraced his alternative, albeit almost purely rhetorical,
vision of reform." For Kantrowitz, Tillman's successes illustrate the power of
culture in uniting whites and bolstering white supremacy.*

* * *

(1) Farmers and others

In the years after his speech [to the state agricultural society] at
Bennettsville [in 1885], Tillman sketched a portrait of conflict between
the farmers and their enemies. This juxtaposition of honest citizens
and contemptible others usually took the form of an attack, and between
1885 and 1887, Tillman's constant skirmishes with state officials brought
him a level of statewide attention that his modest proposals alone
would not have received. Before we turn to his organizational practice,
therefore, we ought to meet him as most South Carolinians did during
this period—as an increasingly skillful rhetorician, deftly playing the
expectations of producerism, patriarchy, and white male solidarity
against the status quo.

Tillman's farmers were producers, employers, husbands, and fathers;
they were "the common people who redeemed the State from Radical
rule," the "real Democrats and white men" in whose hands political
authority properly belonged. White women and African Americans
had legitimate (although quite different) roles to play in this white
man's world, whereas white merchants, lawyers, and other urban men
owed their livelihoods to the men who produced society's real wealth.
As C. Vann Woodward has noted, "[T]he word 'farmer' is laden with
ambiguities that have made it a convenient disguise for a variety of
interests." In tying legitimate authority to race, occupation, and gender, Tillman celebrated white farming men's individual and collective
mastery while attempting to evade or elide questions of class difference among them. This was not always simple. Before the war, Tillman
claimed in an 1886 article, "the land-owning farmers were the salt of
the earth and called no man master." As he wrote those words, he
himself owned over 1600 acres, making him a wealthy farmer by any
standard.[1] His own activism, he later claimed, had begun after "over-
extension" and a few "bad years" in the early 1880s left him in debt
and forced him to sell several hundred acres. But many white male

68

agricultural workers had never been "land-owning farmers," before the war or ever since; as tenants or laborers, they had subsisted at the margins of the planters' and yeomen's worlds. As he refined his vision, Tillman sought to muffle or absorb such tensions.[2]

White men's landlessness and indebtedness did not mean that the ideal was faulty but that something had gone seriously awry. He laid blame for white farmers' growing hardship on their granting black laborers too much authority, becoming indebted to merchants, and thereby falling under the sway of the corporate and financial "money power." Their fundamental mistake, however, was in allowing themselves to be governed by selfish, incompetent, and corrupt aristocrats. When Tillman began speaking to audiences in 1885 and 1886, he painted a grim picture of the economic state of white farming households. Even "without counting negroes," at least half of the vast agricultural majority had to borrow money to plant, which meant resorting to liens or mortgages. But it was easier to get into debt than to get out of it, and farmers grew dependent on agricultural credit, until "like the opium eater; they cannot quit if they would." Every year, farmers slipped deeper and deeper into debt to predatory merchants and finally into a humiliating "hopeless servitude." Tillman told an upcountry crowd that "we want to get from under the lien law, where it forces men to run to the merchants with their hats in their hands and ask, 'Is the Lien Law opened yet?' "* He denounced the "merchants and bankers . . . who have got rich on the poor man." He sought to distinguish between farmers who also acted as merchants and "true" farmers such as himself. Merchants and servants of corporate interests extracted a living from the productive labor of others; they could "make money whether it rains or not." "I had rather a thousand times go down with my brother farmers than fatten at their expense," Tillman declared, allying himself rhetorically with poor white men against other wealthy men.[3]

Tillman's rhetoric notwithstanding, no sharp line separated agricultural and merchant capital: throughout the post-Reconstruction decades, planters became merchants and merchants became planters. During the last decades of the century men committed to mercantile, industrial, and financial development built mills, stores, and banks. Settlements became villages and towns, and their leading citizens competed with one another to attract railroad lines and investment. Whether they had been planters, yeomen, factors, or Yankees, members of this emerging "town class" saw agriculture as only one among many enterprises. Tillman shared certain goals with such men. Like New South visionaries, he urged farmers to produce more food and

---

* Under the lien law, farmers borrowed money from a merchant using the future crop as collateral for the loan.

less cotton, and he owned a few shares of stock in local banks. But Tillman's orientation remained defiantly agricultural, and he professed enormous skepticism about this rising economic order. He feared a New South in which "half our lands will he owned by aliens and the sons of many old slaveholders will have sunk to the level of their former servants . . . hewers of wood and drawers of water for capitalists and merchants."[4]

White men's hardship, and sometimes their ignorance, allowed those "former servants" to contribute to the agricultural crisis. "[W]e have turned our lands over to the negroes to manage," Tillman complained, "the Anglo-Saxon abdicating in favor of the African, brains and energy giving place to muscle and ignorance." In part, white men were playing out the lessons they had learned during slavery valuing labor over land and therefore tolerating their workers' destructive farming practices. It was for this reason that Tillman called slaves and slavery "a curse" on the antebellum South. Now that land, not slaves, had become the source of wealth and value in Southern agriculture, he urged farmers to pay more attention to how their tenants and laborers tilled the soil. Freedmen could not farm intelligently on their own account. "Cuff, freed from the dread of a master, does as little as he can," Tillman explained, offering a familiar post-Reconstruction vision of black indolence and incapacity. A white man who rented to "ignorant lazy negroes" was therefore encouraging the "butchery" of his land. Agricultural renewal would be impossible as long as white landowners and tenants took their orders from cotton-obsessed furnishing merchants and landowners allowed black sharecroppers the day-to-day autonomy they so ardently sought.[5]

Whether or not they considered themselves farmers, black South Carolinians lacked the capacity for citizenship that would make them eligible for inclusion in Tillman's farmers' movement. Although it appears that early on black farmers sometimes successfully sought to participate in local reform movement activities, the fact that blacks constituted a majority of the state's farmers did not interest Tillman. "The farmers" were white men. Indeed, Tillman and other "agricultural reformers" sometimes seemed to yearn for a South emptied of African Americans: "[W]e must get rid of the negroes, who are eating up the whites," Tillman told a county fair audience in 1886. But as a large landowner, Tillman would hardly have agreed with the bitter Edgefield farmer who declared in 1889 that planters "who labor with their own hands are independent of the negro, and if those who presume to be our leaders would not retain hundreds upon their plantations we would not be confronted with the 'Southern Problem.'" Tillman might have employed dozens rather than hundreds of black laborers, but he sought to control them, to master them—not to make them disappear. Black labor largely underwrote his kind of "independence."[6]

But when blacks stepped out of white men's fields, Tillman argued, and especially when they entered politics, they threatened to bring back Reconstruction's "radical misrule." Although the Republicans did not seriously contest statewide elections after 1882, they remained locally active. During the 1880s and early 1890s, African Americans continued to vote and hold office, especially in the lowcountry counties constituting the state's vast, gerrymandered "black seventh" congressional district. Despite challenges by white Democrats, black men such as Robert Smalls and George W. Murray periodically represented South Carolina in Congress. The possibility of a political resurgence by the black majority lingered in every development of the early post-Reconstruction decades, threatening at any moment to undo the revolution of 1876. But Tillman believed that "Negro Domination" would not return without aid from villainous white men. Like a writer to the *Charleston News and Courier*, he saw black voters as "credulous, ignorant and suspicious; just the material to be as plastic as putty in the hands of shrewd and ambitious leaders." By the early 1800s, such leaders' reputations for malefaction had transcended the legendary and become more or less occult. To white Democrats, men like Reconstruction governors Franklin Moses, Robert Scott, and Daniel Chamberlain were no longer simply carpetbaggers and scalawags but "vampires" and "phantasmagorical ghosts," so demonized in defeat that only supernatural language could describe their ghastly doings and the horrors that would follow their return.[7]

Tillman also argued that apportionment schemes favoring the lowcountry continued the antebellum tradition of using the black majority against white farmers. In both the state legislature and Democratic Party conventions, methods of apportionment based on total population allowed the lowcountry's tiny white minorities to speak with a louder voice than that of their more numerous upcountry cousins. The current Democratic leaders profited from the status quo and therefore refused either to reapportion the legislature or to modify the convention system of nominating state officers. Continuing Martin Gary and George Tillman's appeal to upcountry sectionalism, Ben Tillman argued that upcountry white men's overthrow of Reconstruction had earned them the right to greater representation. An Edgefield correspondent pointed to the county's large and overwhelmingly Democratic returns in the years since 1876 and asked whether "the very citadel of the Democracy [is] to be denied . . . [just] representation?" Tillman made the charge more racially pointed. He reckoned that a legislator from Edgefield represented 9,000 people, whereas one from Charleston or Richland represented 5,000 or 6,000 people, "mostly negroes." Complaining further that "[o]ne white man in Spartanburg or Edgefield should certainly be equal to one negro in Charleston or Columbia," Tillman made his white urban opponents invisible and the cities they cherished essentially black. He also argued that the convention system was an affront to democracy and an invitation to rule by "a political aristocracy." They "mak[e] us delegate our power to delegates who delegate somebody else," he complained, "so that by the time they reach Columbia they are nothing but office-seeking politicians."[8]

At the 1886 Democratic convention, however, opponents of primaries and reapportionment unself-consciously made arguments that smacked of patrician superiority. If candidates for state offices had to mount popular campaigns seeking support from individual voters across the state, one delegate suggested, men would "get into office simply upon their capital" or be beholden to railroad companies for free passes. Men "without means" would either be denied office or be subject "to corporation influence." Governor John P. Richardson perceived a more practical drawback. Noting that "[e]very dissatisfied element flocks to [Tillman's] standard at once," he feared the Edgefield upstart might actually win the gubernatorial nomination if the party held a primary.[9]

Tillman's main campaign was not for office, however, but for the establishment of a state college for white farmers. Real "agricultural advancement," Tillman argued, could take place only if the state reconsidered its educational priorities and established a freestanding agricultural college, a place where young men could learn progressive, scientific farming. By training a cadre of young white men each year in the latest agricultural methods, the state could exchange the antebellum pattern of "[c]ut down, wear out, and move West" for scientific agriculture and diversification focused on food crops. He contrasted the potential benefits of such a college with the shortcomings of the state's existing institutions for white men, Columbia's South Carolina College and Charleston's Citadel. These were schools for effeminate dandies and parasites, not manly farmers. Echoing both Gary and the Greenbackers, he portrayed South Carolina College—alma mater of half the state leadership—as elitist and ornamental. "[H]aving been taught that labor is degrading," the "liberally educated" graduates of such schools could easily become "helpless beings, . . . 'too proud to beg, too honest to steal, too lazy to work.' " The college's inadequate agricultural "annex," which received the state's Morrill Act money, was "a child [put] to nurse in the house of its enemies."[10]

Defenders of the existing institutions and foes of the agricultural college suggested that collective solutions could not resolve essentially individual problems: farmers' poverty resulted from laziness or incompetence, and those who worked hard would succeed without the state intervention Tillman championed. "If the legislature granted every request made by the farmers, this *alone*, would not materially better their condition," wrote a Charleston planter, rejecting an overture from a Tillman organizer. "The material interest of any class, can only be improved by the individual efforts of the numbers of that class." He therefore opposed "a Farmer's political party." Another foe of the agricultural college put it more succinctly. "The Farmers' Movement is a good thing," he quipped, "if it's a brisk one between the plowhandles."[11]

Such opponents of his efforts, Tillman charged, were effete aristocrats living off of inherited wealth, a corrupt "ring" embodying "all the evils of aristocracy with none of its benefits." The farmer, Tillman said, looked on as his tax money was wasted, and he himself was "contemptuously pushed aside to make room for men who are really his inferiors in intelligence and honesty, and who are selfish in all their aspirations." Their "absurdities, extravagance and folly" recalled the fiscal excesses of "radical misrule." Even the agricultural college would fail unless "real" farmers controlled it, for it could not be entrusted to the current agricultural leadership of "broken-down politicians and old superannuated Bourbon aristocrats, who are thoroughly incompetent, who worship the past, and are incapable of progress of any sort, but who boldly assume to govern us by divine right." "These men," Tillman explained, "the remnant of the old regime[,] . . . worship the past and are marching backwards when they march at all."[12]

As these attacks suggest, Tillman's understanding of political and economic virtue was sharply gendered, but it was not based on a simple opposition of male independence to female dependence. Rather, it offered a vision of male and female agricultural interdependence, under siege from men whose unproductive and aristocratic ways undercut their claim to leadership and perhaps even to manhood itself. Tillman rooted both masculine and feminine virtue in productive labor. In one of his most provocative attacks, he dubbed the Citadel, a military institution dear to upper-class Charleston, a "military dude factory" and called for its transformation into a college for white women. More than simply derogating the school and its graduates, Tillman implied that such men had less value than the female graduates the new school would produce. But proper education for white women, far more than a slap at urban "dudes," was an essential part of Tillman's vision of a prosperous agricultural commonwealth. A Barnwell newspaper echoed Tillman's analysis when it asserted "that if the funds that have been expended on worthless young men in South Carolina alone since the war had been appropriated to the business education of women, scores of homes would have been spared by mortgages, and ample support made for families who have been dragged down to want." Tillmanite legislators included "schools for our beautiful girls" in the list of changes that would bring "dignity for labor." Tillman spoke in joking but respectful and affectionate terms of his own wife's perspective on his agitation. "[Y]ou don't know how many candle lectures I have received," he told the 1886 farmers' convention, "and I think I will take Mrs. Moses's advice hereafter if I can only get out of this scrimmage without losing my scalp." He claimed that his agitation had initiated conversations between other husbands and wives as well, and "families are split and husbands and wives are in some cases on opposite sides." White farming women clearly had at least a consultative role in the body politic.[13]

By contrast, Tillman suggested, "aristocrats" misunderstood white women's proper roles in predictably haughty ways. The urban Columbia campus of the state university received the state's federal money for agricultural education, but Tillman insisted that although the college subsisted in part on this "stolen 'farmer's money,' " it could never be "a fitting temple for our sun-browned goddess, Agriculture." In its halls, he explained, agriculture occupied "the position of a bond slave . . . only tolerated because of her dower." She was "never . . . made one of the family." Instead of recognizing sun-browned skin as the badge of a white woman's agricultural labor, aristocrats had mistaken her for an African American slave and unfairly appropriated the fruits of her labor. If these men could mistake Ceres for a slave, they could not be relied on to grant white farming women and their labor the respect they deserved.[14]

The rule of the aristocrats had disordered South Carolina's broader "household," for under them the "state has proved a veritable stepmother to her 'agricultural interests,' " Tillman complained, "and they have been neglected or subordinated to everything else." In order to suggest the corrupting influence of "nonproducers" rule, Tillman explained that in the years since Redemption, the Democratic Party, "that interesting old lady," had become somewhat "corpulent" and "slouchy." His farmers' movement, however, had stirred her from her lethargy, causing her to recognize "among the farmers who are here this familiar face and that, which she remembered as among the foremost of those who redeemed the state in '76." Moved by that memory, Tillman went on, she resolved to reward the farmers instead of the undeserving offspring who had up until now claimed precedence. "I know who to depend on, and if these boys are going to move I am going to follow them. I can't depend on your city chaps and lawyers any longer." Determining to "move back to the farm," the party/mother explained that "my health has not been good of late, and I am nearly dead for a piece of home-cured bacon and corn bread." But the return to agricultural ways wrought a miraculous transformation.

Once she rejoined a farming household, the Democratic mother no longer simply craved homemade provisions but could help produce them, declaring that "[t]hese farmers ought to raise more meat and corn, and I am going to show them how to do it." No longer a weakened, inattentive "step-mother," she had become a nurturing household member with an important role in the process of social and economic regeneration.[15]

But masculine virtues differed from feminine virtues in at least one crucial respect: men were supposed to be soldiers, capable of the kind of collective military action that had produced the victory of 1876. Here again, Tillman argued that the Democratic leadership mistakenly emphasized the honor of individual men rather than understanding martial virtues as essentially collective. Individual "dudes" were nothing; an army of white men was everything.

In the 1880s, when most leading Democrats could point to a Confederate war record, the memory and legacy of 1876 served Tillman extremely well. Tillman's Red-shirt service became evidence of his personal courage, but more important, it became evidence of his boundless commitment to white male authority. In confrontations with lowcountry leaders, he boasted of being "one of the Hamburg rioters who dared even the devil to save the State," and he continually lambasted the *Charleston News and Courier* for its initially critical response to that now-legendary massacre. When an opponent suggested that Tillman had shirked his duty as a white man by failing to serve in the Confederate army Tillman not only told the story of the loss of his eye but added that instead of a Civil War record, "I have a little record of 1876, and I know something about Ned Tennant and the Ellenton riots, and have had a little to do with managing elections." Anyone who had been with him at Hamburg, he told an upcountry crowd, "would not say that he, Tillman, could split the Democratic party."[16]

When Tillman attacked individual members of the Democratic leadership, these men often responded as though he had provoked them into an affair of honor. But although Tillman delighted in sparking outrage, he showed no interest in giving or demanding "personal satisfaction." In 1885, he sought to make an alliance with Luther Ransom, Columbia correspondent for the *Augusta Chronicle* and secretary to state agricultural commissioner A. P. Butler. Privately, Tillman all but promised Ransom the secretaryship of a proposed farmers' legislature in exchange for favorable newspaper coverage, and he suggested that Ransom could do this without jeopardizing his "bread and butter." But when Tillman publicly charged Butler's agricultural department with wasting money, Ransom defended his employer and attacked Tillman. Tillman responded by writing publicly that Ransom was "trying perhaps to earn his salary and keep his place," "fighting for potatoes" rather than for principles. He warned Ransom to cease his insinuations and "attack me like a man . . . and then I shall know how to answer him." Ransom took what in an earlier decade would have been the only honorable course. Tillman, he wrote, "lied—l-i-e-d. No insinuation about that, I hope, Benjamin?"[17]

But Tillman had no interest in satisfying his own or anyone else's aggrieved sense of honor. He might declare that he could not "now remain silent without being accused of having fled at the first glint of steel," and he sometimes used words such as "insulting" and "resent" that echoed antebellum preliminaries, but he refused to be goaded into a duel. After Ransom's charge, Tillman reminded readers that dueling was now illegal in South Carolina and that if he issued a challenge using weapons "to put us on an equality, if I killed him it would be murder." "A few years ago, my reply would have been a challenge, but it is no longer either safe or honorable to fight duels in South Carolina, and Major Ransom knows it," he explained. In rejecting nonlethal confrontation, he landed another blow: Ransom was not "physically" his "equal," Tillman claimed, and he "would as soon strike a woman." The issue at stake was collective rights, not individual reputations. Ransom's challenge was the act of a "Hessian," a mercenary in the service of the state leadership, and it demanded a collective rather than a personal response. Tillman's "poverty-stricken, debt-enslaved, tax-ridden farmers are organizing . . . [f]rom the mountains to the sea" to take on the "Columbia Ring" that had set Ransom against him. Tillman was interested not in exchanging pistol shots but in defining and mobilizing white manhood.[18]

Tillman's campaigns for greater respect for farmers, and for the establishment of a new college focused on agriculture, brought him great popularity. Farmers, suffering from low prices and debt, had meanwhile organized themselves in the Farmers' Alliance. The Alliance, whose membership boomed throughout the South and the West (where wheat farmers were also suffering), denounced "monopolies," especially in the financial markets, and campaigned for new national policies that would help the nation's farmers and other "producers." Tillman endorsed most of the Alliance ideas, and the Alliance in South Carolina gave him strong support when he decided to run for governor as a Democrat in 1890. Tillman's opponents dismissed his supporters as "wool-hats" too ignorant to understand their own interests, but he easily won the nomination for governor in the state Democratic Convention. Conservative Democrats were so outraged that they bolted from the party and ran their own candidate, Alexander Haskell, as in independent, even appealing to African Americans to vote for them, and against Tillman, in the general election. Tillman's supporter denounced Haskell and the independents as "white

Negroes"—much as Mississippians in Jones County denounced Newton Knight and his community as "white Negroes." (See the essay by Victoria Bynum in this volume.) Tillman won easily and took office as South Carolina's governor.

However, Tillman was immediately faced with a difficult political issue. When the federal government ignored the demands of the Farmers' Alliance, it's members organized a new third party, the "People's Party" or "Populists." In neighboring states, thousands of white farmers left the Democrats for the Populists, and in South Carolina, members of the Farmers' Alliance expected Tillman to do the same. But Tillman refused, and in South Carolina, unlike Georgia and North Carolina, the Populists had little effect on state politics. In the following section, Stephen Kantrowitz explains why.

(2) Why there was no Populism in South Carolina

The Haskellite bolt further solidified Tillman's identification of himself with anti-aristocratic white unity. But even as Haskellites and their sympathizers fumed in defeat, Tillman faced a serious challenge from another quarter. Because he became governor of South Carolina as part of a national wave of agrarian protest and because he drew support from the Farmers' Alliance, Tillman was often mistaken for a Populist. Local as well as national observers counted him as an Alliance governor, and from the third party's inception in 1891, many Alliancemen expected him to support its challenge to both the Democrats and the republicans.[19]

Tillman refused. Radical Alliance and Populist proposals went far beyond his modest program of reform and college building within a white man's Democratic Party. In particular, he feared the potential for federal control in the Alliance's proposed "subtreasury," a system of government-owned warehouses in which farmers could deposit their crops and receive interest-free loans from the government of up to 80 percent of the crop's market value. The subtreasury's advocates claimed that it would break the crop lien's cycle of credit and debt, turning the federal government into a servant of the producing classes rather than a tool of moneyed interests. As Lawrence Goodwyn has argued, the subtreasury was the heart of the Populist challenge, and struggling white farmers in South Carolina and elsewhere seemed to agree. In many Southern states, white Populist leaders attempted to form political coalitions with black voters, appealing to their common agricultural hardships and offering the subtreasury as an alternative to the crop lien, which oppressed both whites and blacks, owners, renters, and croppers. In nearby states, the leading Democratic insurgents against the Redeemers plunged into these waters, endorsing the subtreasury and seeking alliances with black voters. Georgia's Tom Watson and Alabama's Reuben Kolb stepped across the political color line; in North Carolina, Leonidas Polk seemed ready to do so as well. Yet Tillman demurred. Conservatives accused him of being a Populist, but if "Populism" meant radical economic change through federal intervention, the creation of a third national political party and an interracial political alliance, Tillman was no Populist. . . .[20]

Tillman insisted that the war against the "money power" he seen as a continuation of the wars of secession and Redemption. For him, "reform" meant the collective struggle of independent white men against tyrannous federal authority and African American equality. In his view, the Populists had made the critical error of believing that one could fight the "money power" by forming a coalition with its chief allies, black Republicans and the federal government. The subtreasury, Tillman feared, would "concentrate the business of the people in the hands of a centralized power at Washington." Moreover, it would create "an army of political hirelings," guaranteeing "the perpetuation in power of the party by which it was established." As for black political participation, that could only bring back Reconstruction and its concomitant evils. "Negro domination hangs over us," he warned in 1891, "like the sword of Damocles."[21]

Tillman's stand against the subtreasury temporarily reunited him with conservative leaders. . . . But Tillman's opposition to the subtreasury created a deep rift within his coalition. Although he initially said he would submit to the will of an "informed" majority of Alliancemen with regard to the subtreasury, he opposed the subtreasury "in its details" and suggested that a majority of South Carolina Alliancemen did as well. He proposed a safe, state-level alternative: state-chartered banks that could loan paper money based on the value of farmland. But this did not satisfy those with more expansive visions of "reform." Indeed, it offered relief only to landowners—an even narrower definition of "the farmers" than the white male producerism Tillman had generally promoted.[22]

But radical Alliancemen had counted Tillman's victory in 1890 as their own, and they would not willingly defer to him. In 1891, they invited subtreasury advocates to speak, including Watson, who attracted large and enthusiastic Democratic crowds, and national Alliance lecturer Ben Terrell, a gifted orator from Texas who had taken the state by storm less than two years before. Tillman could avoid confronting the Populist Watson, but he could not avoid debating Terrell, still nominally a Democrat. For once, Tillman got the worst of it. The state Alliance convention rebuked him and endorsed the subtreasury over his objections. Reporting on Tillman's debate with Terrell, the Populist-leaning *Cotton Plant* spoke bluntly: "Gov. Tillman opposes the only measure that promises to break the power of a few men to rob the farmer." In Washington, D.C., the Populist *National Economist* was even harsher, accusing Tillman of seeking the Alliance's "destruction."[23]

Tillman's opposition to the subtreasury threatened to cost him his mantle of leadership. Even allies from the early days of the farmers' movement threatened to break with Tillman over the subtreasury, and some seemed ready to support the third-party movement. A fellow subtreasury opponent warned the governor that it was "unwise for you to make an unnecessary issue with the farmers." Since the subtreasury had been endorsed by Alliances all around the country, this reformer did not "see how you can claim that it will be repudiated by the intelligent farmers of the South." His was one of many warnings to Tillman that he dare not alienate the Alliance.[24]

In the case of the subtreasury, Tillman decided that power mattered more than principle. Frightened by the hostile response of his Alliance supporters and the possibility of losing all leverage with them, he first determined "to remain absolutely silent & let things drift." By the time the 1892 campaign began, he went further, making a good show of capitulating to subtreasury advocates. At the May 1892 Democratic convention, the "Alliance governor" accepted the Alliance's national platform, including the subtreasury proposal, and was present when the state Democratic Party adopted it. He did not become a subtreasury advocate, however, and his more or less tacit consent could be interpreted in many ways. Even after the Democratic convention, many were left wondering "what was exactly [his] position" regarding the Alliance's more radical demands. But the many white Alliancemen who had come to see Tillman as their representative welcomed his apparent reversal as the return of the prodigal son. Tillman, after all, had embodied the farmers' movement since before the arrival of the Alliance, and to many, he remained a credible "Moses." The reputation he had built since the mid-1880s stood him in good stead as he faced down this new challenge. As a county Alliance president reassured him during the difficult days of 1891, "We have some complaints in this Co[unty] but . . . will not come up wanting if do not say too many nice things about those *citadel dudes*."[25]

Tactical capitulation on the subtreasury issue enabled Tillman to prevent state Alliance leaders from taking the far more dangerous step of bolting from the Democratic Party. Tillman implored his more radical allies not to act precipitately. "Above all let: me beg you not to join any Third party move this year,", he wrote to Alliance Democrat and U.S. congressman A. C. Latimer. "After it is clearly shown that no relief can be expected from the Democratic party as now constituted, we may find it necessary to fight for relief under another name, but for the true principles of Jeffersonian Democracy. The name itself is dear." Although he believed that eventually "self interest might force us" to form a new party in coalition with Midwestern farmers, he insisted that for the time being, white Southerners "had to stand together for God, for home, and for native land" against "the Force Bill and negro domination." "You cannot divide without bringing ruin" he told white audiences, for "division in South Carolina means the negro." In the worst case, "the third party divides the whites & both factions appeal to the negroes, & that means in the long run political debauchery & corruption with a final division of offices between the races & a return to the evils of the reconstruction era." At public occasions such as the July 1891 meeting of the Edgefield County Farmers' Alliance, he made his reform allies swear to fight for Alliance demands within the Democratic Party. This, he later claimed, "tied the hands" of potential third-party leaders in South Carolina. As the 1892 political campaign began, though, several upcountry Democratic county conventions nevertheless seemed poised for a third-party bolt.[26]

In the 1892 election, Tillman once again attacked the conservative leadership of his own party and presented himself as a reformist alternative to Populist radicalism. As luck would have it, an appropriate rallying cry for his middle ground was readily available in the form of "free silver." Insisting that the coinage of silver would expand the circulating medium sufficiently to alleviate the credit crisis, Tillman echoed bimetallists throughout the nation. The rhetoric of silver also suited Tillman's style of attack, for proponents of the white metal charged that the Reconstruction-era demonetization of silver (the "Crime of '73") had been part of a Wall Street conspiracy against producers. Silver was also safe: unlike the subtreasury, it required no extension of federal power into local affairs. For some radicals, this made silver a sham, for it provided the appearance of reform without returning financial control to the producers. Perhaps for this reason, free silver provoked little controversy among even the most conservative South Carolina Democrats.[27]

But free silver's enemies included Grover Cleveland, the likely Democratic nominee for president in 1892 and the man to whom the Populists would point in their campaign to woo South Carolina's Democrats. Advocacy of silver would allow Tillman to distinguish himself from Cleveland and to continue to offer at least the appearance of reform to white Democrats poised on the brink of revolt. Attacking gold Democrat Cleveland as a "bag of beef" and threatening to stick a pitchfork in him—the threat that earned him his ever-after-familiar moniker "Pitchfork Ben"—Tillman attempted to remain the champion of the farmers while muffling more radical alternatives. The tactic worked. Although he continued to oppose any bolt from the party, he volunteered to lead the state against Cleveland's renomination. The delegation he led to the 1892 Democratic National Convention voted almost unanimously against Cleveland, but Cleveland's eventual nomination provoked no mass exodus from the party of white supremacy. Once again, Tillman had used violent attacks on an unworthy white man to establish himself as the spokesman of the farmers.[28]

As the November election approached, Tillman proudly contrasted South Carolina's Democratic orthodoxy with the Populists' inroads in neighboring Georgia and North Carolina. He explained to an admirer that "[w]e have had a hot fight & have been 'between the D---l & the deep sea' " which was to say the "Third Party on one hand & Haskellism on the other. But by good generalship we have kept the party together & are in better shape than any other Southern state." Indeed, South Carolina's Populists fared quite poorly by comparison with their regional counterparts. Alone among the former Confederate states, South Carolina was tardy in selecting representatives to the People's Party's National Committee. The *Cotton Plant*'s editor finally announced a state third-party ticket, including presidential electors, just two weeks before the November election.[29] Nationally, the Populist ticket won over a million votes but no Southern electors, and South Carolina was one of the few Southern states where Populism was reduced to insignificance. "You cannot divide without bringing ruin," Tillman had told audiences of white men, and divide they did not—at least not in the casting and counting of ballots.[30]

Tillman was only correct in boasting that "good generalship" had carried the day if that generalship is understood to have been conducted over most of the preceding two decades. Many of Tillman's critical anti-Populist battles had been won not since 1890 but during the 1870s and 1880s, when he helped bring an end to Reconstruction and establish the white-supremacist limits of state-level reform. By the time he became governor, he had already helped shape a state political culture that severely limited white men's room for maneuver on matters of racial hierarchy and federal power. At the same time, he had crafted an explicitly white-supremacist alternative to producerist radicalism, one that limited legitimate collective action not just to white men but also to white male farmers who forswore interracial political activity. His tactical skills served him well in 1892, but they alone would not have sufficed.

In South Carolina, as throughout the South, no Populist coalition could succeed even momentarily unless it could draw on both black and white support. By the 1890s, however, white radicals' own fear and ambivalence about black political participation, rooted in their experience of the past quarter century, made such a call all but unthinkable. Indeed, even the few white Populists of 1892 made no overt move to attract black support. Some white radicals understood the need to pierce the slogans of white supremacy and expose the racial demagoguery of their enemies, but they did not know how to confront the expectations that gave Tillman's message its potency. Even agrarian radicals who proudly declared themselves opposed to monopoly in all its forms found it difficult to describe democratic citizenship in terms that transcended the particular experiences of white men.

White Populists struggled, mostly without success, to reconcile their economic analyses with their historic and daily experiences of white manhood. The most famous "divided mind" of white Southern Populism belonged to Georgia's Tom Watson, whose intellectual and political biography has been a major historiographical battleground for Populism's analysts. But local, less dramatic cases better explain the structural weaknesses of Populism in South Carolina. Take the case of Alliance leader Colonel Ellison S. Keitt and his son Joseph, who along with *Cotton Plant* editor J. W. Bowden became the state's leading third-party activists. The elder Keitt predicted that a coming revolution would pit "the farmers, mechanics, wage workers and laborers, the wealth producers of the nation" against the "money power." Keitt had fought against Reconstruction, and he understood that Redemption still loomed large in the state's politics, so he boldly attempted to shift the meaning of Redemption's struggle from a conflict over race to one over class and section. "Negro domination we hear so much about is a myth," he declared in 1894. "In the worst days of radicalism the negroes did not control. The carpetbaggers, dominated by Grant's bayonets, dominated." In 1876, "we assaulted their lines and drove them . . . from the State." If the fight had always been a struggle among white men and even an enfranchised black majority could not "dominate," then an opening might exist for a Populist movement. But even this limited retreat from white-supremacist orthodoxy was too much for Bowden, who sought to distance his paper from such sentiments. In the aftermath of the devastating 1892 defeat, Bowden offered an explicitly white-supremacist rationale for allowing those who had supported Populist presidential candidate James Weaver to continue to vote as Democrats in state elections. Haskellites, he pointed out, had continued to vote even after their apostasy, and South Carolina Populists at least had not "appeal[ed] to 'Cuffee' to help them defeat the expressed will of the white people."[31]

Other, more universalistic visions also ran up against the limits of white male producerism. Like many radical Alliancemen, white Abbeville farmer Patrick Henry Adams had understood Ben Tillman's 1890 victory as the prelude to a greater contest against the "money power." At an open meeting of his sub-Alliance, Adams made a bold appeal to "Tillmanite or Anti Tillmanite, . . . Democratic, or Republican, or Third-Partyite, . . . White or Colored," suggesting that he was sympathetic to the possibility of a third party and an interracial coalition. But Adams unwittingly expressed the white supremacy inherent in reform in the world Tillman had helped make. In Adams's analysis, the poverty of "our southern farmers" had begun with emancipation, when they set about planting cotton because "they had labor here trained in the cotton fields." His farmers, like Tillman's, were white landowning employers. It did not occur to Adams that a majority of South Carolina's agricultural workers—"Colored" but by his own reckoning no less a part of "the body politic"—might regard themselves as farmers or understand postemancipation agricultural economics rather differently. Adams also urged his audience to continue resisting the efforts of the "Northern capitalist . . . to crush us to death." Giving up that struggle, he explained, would not "comport well with Southern manhood and Southern heroism." In the sectional context of his remarks, these phrases could only suggest arms-bearing white manhood. They would not have been understood to include black men, whose sectional "heroism" had been almost universally in Northern blue; it certainly seems unlikely that he intended to refer to the black Union soldiers who had made their camps on Edgefield plantations [in Tillman's home county] in 1865. Assertive black manhood, far from being understood as "Southern" or "heroic," appeared in white public discourse in the form of the black rapist, the antithesis of white manhood and the enemy of white womanhood. Although Adams's speech was free of overt racial antagonism, when he sought a language of manly resistance adequate to the coming fight, he settled on the idiom of white manhood common to slaveholding, secession, war, and Redemption. Struggling against these self-imposed limits, his envisioned crusade of "our Southern farmers" against the "money power" was doomed to failure.[32]

In winning their struggles from the mid-1870s to 1890, men like Tillman had fatally undermined the possibility of the development of a race-neutral language of manhood and citizenship. What remained was the language of "the farmers," a language common to Democrats and Populists, a language that implied whiteness and masculinity even as it laid claim to universality, a language in which only white men's collective struggle could bring political or economic "redemption." This was not simply a discourse but a powerful political and historical reality, one that overwhelmed the best intentions of those who sought to escape or defeat it. . . .

Tillman's organization and leadership could not have succeeded without the cooperation of thousands of white voters who shared his concerns about the implications of Populist radicalism and embraced his alternative, albeit almost purely rhetorical, vision of reform. Some Southern radicals may indeed have regarded Tillman, in the words of historian Lawrence Goodwyn, as "a transparent charlatan who was far more dedicated to the building of a personal political career than to leading a party revolution," but clearly many of the men those radicals sought as constituents did not agree. After living with slavery, secession, war, Reconstruction, paramilitary terror, and economic hardship, few white men could articulate a critique of the social order that did not prove vulnerable to co-optation by the state's reigning agrarian rebel, a man who successfully cast the Populists as the latest incarnation of "radical misrule," "Bourbon" incompetence, and "Negro domination." To the extent that Tillman could pass himself off as an authentic representative of white farmers, it was because he understood these men's shared history—and because he had helped shape it. Over the course of the 1890s, as Populists throughout the South struggled vainly to create an alternative political culture in which black and white men could cooperate for mutual benefit, white Democrats mobilized white armies against them. But alongside those armies they also mobilized a common understanding of white manhood, a language and history shaped by men like Ben Tillman.[33]

Even a victorious biracial Populism might not have accomplished the radical transformation its proponents sought. Its programs might have failed to bring the relief they promised, and its coalition might have collapsed because of its own internal divisions. But this is not what happened in the 1880s and 1890s. Rather, during its short life, radical biracial agrarian politics struggled against both the long, deep history of racial hierarchy and the sharp, contemporary reality of Democratic violence, fraud, and legal discrimination. That recent history was not . . . virtually "spontaneous." Certainly white-supremacist assumptions and reactions arose unbidden from the minds and hearts of white men. But it took a good deal of strong, often coercive leadership to transform those reactions into collective actions and still more of the same to sustain the project over time. Since Reconstruction, Ben Tillman more and more often had been one of the men providing that leadership, and by 1892, it appeared that he had won. The final victory over the Populists . . . marked yet another defining moment in the reconstruction of white supremacy.

NOTES

1 *Charleston News and Courier* [*CN&C*], 23 Jan. 1890; C. Vann Woodward, *Origins of the New South, 1877–1913* (Baton Rouge, 1951), 192; Benjamin Ryan Tillman [BRT] in *CN&C*, 18 Jan., 30 Apr. 1886, 30 Mar. 1887; Francis Butler Simkins, *Pitchfork Ben Tillman: South Carolinian* (Baton Rouge, 1944), 88–90. . . .

2 BRT deed to Whitney, 1887, Index to Deeds, book 10, p. 33, Edgefield County Archives [ECA].

3 BRT Bennettsville speech, 5 Aug. 1885, clipping in Benjamin Ryan Tillman

Papers, Clemson University [BRTP-CL], pt. 5; *Edgefield Advertiser* [*EA*], 26 Aug. 1886; *Edgefield Chronicle* [*EC*], 21 Oct. 1885; *CN&C*, 9 June 1892, 9 Sept. 1891, 6 Jan., 30 Mar. 1887. . . .

4 BRT in "The Farmers Aroused," *CN&C*, 30 Apr. 1886. On the post-Reconstruction economic transformation of the state, see David L. Carlton, *Mill and Town in South Carolina, 1880–1920* (Baton Rouge, 1982); Lacy K. Ford, Jr., "Rednecks and Merchants: Economic Development and Social Tensions in the South Carolina Upcountry, 1865–1900," *Journal of American History* 71 (Sept. 1984), 294–318; Randolph Dennis Werner, "Hegemony and Conflict: The Political Economy of a Southern Region, Augusta, Georgia, 1865–1895," (Ph.D. diss., University of Virginia, 1977). . . .

5 *CN&C*, 18 Jan. 1886; BRT, speech to the Edgefield Agricultural Society, *EC*, 24 June, 1 July 1885; *EA*, 9 July 1885, clipping in BRTP-CL, pt. 5.

6 *CN&C*, 6, 8 Apr., 22 Mar., 1 Nov. (county fair) 1886; *EC*, 26 June 1889. For comparably dismissive expressions of frustration, see *Cotton Plant*, Mar. 1885.

7 *CN&C*, 18 Dec. 1886; Wolfe to Hemphill, 18 July 1892, Hemphill Family Papers, Perkins Library, Duke University [PL].

8 Editorial against the "Greenville Idea" for reapportionment, *CN&C*, 21 July 1886; *EA*, 22 July 1886; *CN&C*, 5 May 1890. By 1892, however, Tillman had made a complete about-face and adopted Dawson's line on representation. The call for a primary "was designed to break up ring rule," the governor explained to white Alliancemen in 1892; "it was never intended to take any advantage of the brave democrats of the negro counties" (ibid., 25 Mar. 1892). A direct primary, he said, would "destroy the political equilibrium of the State"—not incidentally an equilibrium that favored the incumbent governor (*Columbia Daily Register*, 24 Mar. 1892, clipping in BRTP-CL, pt. 8).

9 *CN&C*, 6 Aug. 1886; Begley, "Governor Richardson Faces the Tillman Challenge," *South Carolina Historical Magazine*, 89 (1988), 119–26.

10 BRT Bennettsville speech, 5 Aug. 1885, clipping in BRTP-CL, pt. 5; *CN&C*, 11 Jan. 1886. On alumni, see William J. Cooper, *The Conservative Regime: South Carolina, 1877–1890* (Baltimore, 1968), table 6, p. 213, and Daniel Walker Hollis, *College to University* (Columbia, 1956).

11 Rivers to Crosland, 19 July 1887, Elias S. Rivers Papers, South Caroliniana Library, University of South Carolina [SCL] (emphasis in original); *EA*, 25 Nov. 1886.

12 BRT in *CN&C*, 5 May 1890, 30 Nov. 1885, 10 Nov. 1886, 3 Dec. 1885.

13 *Barnwell Sentinel*, quoted in *CN&C*, 15 Oct. 1889; BRT to Waddill, 30 May 1892, "Measure for Measure," n.d., Burn Family Papers, SCL; *CN&C*, 30 Apr. 1886; unidentified newspaper, 23 Apr. 1892, clipping in BRTP-CL, pt. 5, vol. 2 ("split").

14 BRT in *CN&C*, 3 Dec. 1885. On farm women as productive laborers in another late-nineteenth-century context, see Michael Goldberg, *An Army of Women: Gender and Politics in Gilded Age Kansas* (Baltimore, 1997), esp. 26–27. . . .

15 *CN&C*, 28, 11 Jan., 30 Apr. 1886.

16 Ibid., 4, 29 Aug., 26 Jan. 1888, 28 June, 12 May 1890; Simkins, *Pitchfork Ben Tillman*, 130.

17 Tillman to Ransom, 11 Aug., 2 Sept., 9 Oct., 11 Nov. 1885, typescript in BRTP-CL. . . . Ransom was present at the April 1886 farmers' convention. See *CN&C*, 30 Apr. 1886. Their falling-out begins in ibid., 16, 20 Sept. 1886.

18 BRT in *CN&C*, 1, 7 Dec. 1885; Howard to BRT, 25 May 1890, BRTP-CL, pt. 3;

BRT to Barnwell, 17, 23 July 1890, BRTP-CL, pt. 2; BRT in *CN&C*, 28 Sept. 1886; Ransom in ibid., 4 Oct. 1886.

19 *National Economist*, 15 Nov. 1890.

20 For the subtreasury proposal, see George Brown Tindall, ed., *A Populist Reader* (New York, 1966), 80–87. For a discussion of its economics, see Lawrence Goodwyn, *Democratic Promise: The Populist Moment in America* (New York, 1976), 571–81.

21 *CN&C*, 25 July 1892 (2d ed.); *Atlanta Journal*, 30 Apr. 1891, quoted in *CN&C*, 5 May 1891.

22 Butler in *CN&C*, 31 July 1891; BRT to Elder, 8 June 1891, BRTP-CL ("details"); BRT interview in *Cotton Plant*, n.d., reprinted in *Spartanburg Herald*, 30 May 1891, clipping in BRTP-CL, pt. 5; BRT to Wilson, 18 June 1891, BRTP-CL; *Atlanta Journal*, 30 Apr. 1891, quoted in *CN&C*, 5 May 1891; ibid., 12 May (BRT's alternative), 9 June (rebuttal noting many defects of proposal) 1891. . . .

23 *National Economist*, 15 Nov. 1890; Wolfe to BRT, 7 July 1891, Governor BRT Letters, South Carolina Department of Archives and History [SCDAH]; *CN&C*, 11 Sept. 1891; Watson to Charles, 11 June 1892, Charles Family Papers, SCL; Edgefield County Farmers' Alliance Minutes, 2 Oct. 1891, SCL; *Cotton Plant*, 11 Apr. 1891; *National Economist*, 1, 8 Aug. 1891.

24 Elder to BRT, 2 June 1891, Pope to BRT, 24 Jan. 1891, Governor BRT Papers, SCDAH; *CN&C*, 12 May, 11, 14 July 1891; Neal to BRT, 15, 24 Apr. 1891, Governor BRT Letters, SCDAH.

25 BRT to Stokes, 30 May 1892, BRT to Crosland, 26 Aug. 1891, BRTP-CL, pt. 1; Irby to Evans, 8 Feb. 1892, John Gary Evans Papers, SCL; *CN&C*, 20 May 1892; Barber to BRT, 4 June 1892, Governor BRT Letters, SCDAH ("position"); BRT to Stokes, 30 May 1892, BRTP-CL, pt. 1; Harvey to BRT, 27 July 1891, Governor BRT Letters, SCDAH ("*dudes*"; emphasis in original).

26 BRT to Latimer, 2 Mar. 1892, BRTP-CL, pt. 1; *CN&C*, 29 Feb. 1892, 9 Sept. 1891, 25 July 1892 (2d ed.); BRT to Cartledge, 17 Sept. 1892, Governor BRT Letterbooks, SCDAH; BRT to *Augusta Chronicle*, 13 Feb. 1893, BRTP-CL; *Cotton Plant*, 19 May 1894; *CN&C*, 28 June 1894; third-party efforts in ibid., 4 (Anderson), 20 (Oconee) May 1892.

27 On silver, see Max Silverman, "A Political and Intellectual History of the Silver Movement in the United States, 1888–1896" (Ph.D. diss., New York University, 1986); and Gretchen Ritter, *Goldbugs and Greenbacks: The Antimonopoly Tradition and the Politics of Finance in America, 1865–1896* (New York, 1997).

28 *CN&C*, 29 Feb. 1892, 27 Dec. 1885 (silver), 27 June 1890, 19 May, 24, 25 June 1892. Tillman had used the figure of the pitchfork before this: e.g., "He didn't object to fair criticism and analysis, but when they attacked him he also attacked them with the pitchfork end." (*CN&C*, 4 Aug. 1889).

29 BRT to Moore, 5 Oct. 1892, Governor BRT Letterbooks, SCDAH; *CN&C*, 5 July 1892; *Columbia State*, PO, Oct. 1892; *CN&C*, 21 Oct. 1892. At the last moment, the party reportedly received and rejected offers of cooperation from the Republican Party, which had mobilized for the federal election. See *CN&C*, 30, 31 Oct. 1892.

30 *CN&C*, 9 Sept. 1891, 25 July 1892 (2d ed.); BRT to Latimer, 2 Mar., 1 Sept. 1892, Tompkins to McLaurin, 1 Nov. 1892, BRTP-CL, pt. 1. Unlike earlier independent movements, the Populists appear to have drawn mainly white voters. Thirty-six percent of the total Populist presidential vote came from two white-majority upcountry counties, Pickens and Oconee. . . .

31 86 *CN&C*, 19 May 1892; list of Populist electors-at-large in *Columbia State*, 20 Oct. 1892; Keitt in *CN&C*, 5 Aug. 1890; *Cotton Plant*, 10 Mar. ("myth"), 26 May, 1 Sept.1894 ("Cuffee"). The debate over the Democratic credentials of onetime Haskell and Weaver voters continued among the members of the state Democratic Executive Committee. See *CN&C*, 8 June 1894. . . . Watson could declare to white and black farmers that "[y]ou are kept apart that you may be separately fleeced of your earnings. You are made to hate each other because upon that hatred is rested the keystone of the arch of financial despotism which enslaves you both" (*Arena* 6 [1892], quoted in C. Vann Woodward, *Tom Watson, Agrarian Rebel* (New York, 1938), 220. But he could also, before a white South Carolina audience, call the Lodge Elections Bill the "Force Bill" and claim that it had been defeated through the efforts of the national Alliance. See *CN&C*, 11 Sept. 1891. For critical perspectives on Watson and Georgia Populists' biracialism, see Charles Crowe, "Tom Watson, Populists, and Blacks Reconsidered," *Journal of Negro History* 55 (1970), 99–116; and Barton C. Shaw, *The Wool-Hat Boys: Georgia's Populist Party* (Baton Rouge, 1984).

32 Untitled manuscript, [1890–92], Patrick Henry Adams Papers, SCL.

33 Goodwyn, *Democratic Promise*, 248.

4

ETIQUETTE, LYNCHING, AND RACIAL BOUNDARIES IN SOUTHERN HISTORY

A Mississippi example

J. William Harris

The following essay is based on a study of two incidents—a tar-and-feathering and a lynching—in Vicksburg, Mississippi, during and immediately after World War I. The essay argues that the "color line," as whites named the boundary between themselves and blacks, was fundamentally a cultural construct, reinforced in day-to-day life with a system of racial etiquette, and, when whites perceived it to be threatened, reinforced with violence.

But this racial boundary was inherently unstable, since whites presumed it to be based on non-existent biological realities. In times of rapid change, such as the World War, the color line as whites perceived it came under severe pressure. Mississippi was one of the most racially repressive of all southern states, but in Vicksburg during the war, demands for manpower, money, and ideological commitment all promoted ideals of citizenship in which race was irrelevant. Some African Americans saw this as an opportunity for more open resistance to white supremacy and its consequences. Many whites, in turn, reacted to this resistance with alarm. Still, whites themselves were sharply divided about how they should respond to breaches in the "color line." In part, as the events in Vicksburg show, this was because not only the practices of white supremacy but also the widely accepted understandings of the role of gender in public life were being challenged.

* * *

On a summer day in Vicksburg, Mississippi in 1918, a car pulled up to the City Hall, followed by a crowd of people. Several men emerged from the car and pulled out after them Dave Cook, his upper body coated with tar and feathers. The men dragged Cook to the top of the stone structure on the front of the building and hung around his neck a sign that read "I am disloyal to the United States government." The sign said, in effect, that Dave Cook, a white man and small farmer who lived on the outskirts of town, was a war slacker of some kind.[1]

As the jeering crowd grew, the car sped off, soon to return with another tarred and feathered victim—this time a prominent physician, John A. Miller. Dave Cook was taken down, and his sign was hung on Dr. Miller. Finally County Sheriff Frank Scott led Miller away to the "protection" of the jail, and Mayor J. J. Hayes sent the crowd, now swollen to 2,000, home with the plea that they "be satisfied with work already accomplished."[2]

Tarring-and-feathering is a folk practice with deep European and American roots. In the antebellum South, it had been, according to Bertram Wyatt-Brown, an integral part of a system of honor. Among its other functions, honor served as one way to divide whites (who had it) from blacks (who did not); ritual shaming with tar and feathers was one way to punish white violators of the code of honor.[3] It is thus understandable why a Vicksburg crowd would use that traditional ritual to humiliate unpatriotic men. More difficult to understand is how Dr. Miller found himself subject to that humiliation. For Dr. Miller, unlike Dave Cook, was a black man.

It is the seeming contradiction in the use of a white man's ritual to punish an African American that marks this event as rich in multiple meanings, as an event that offers us what Cornel West has called a "methodological moment" for the analysis of racism.[4] At the center of this moment lies the "color line" separating white and black in the New South. In Vicksburg, the strains of war had torn apart some of the social fabric of race. By paying close attention to the ways it did so, we can learn something about the ways that the skeins not only of race, but also of class and gender, were entangled in the cultural matrix of the early 20th-century South.

White Southerners then imagined "races" to be primordial—rigidly defined, biologically determined populations; the "color line" was simply the place where the two races met. There was, however, no possibility that a color line could be drawn literally—blacks in the South could not be locked or driven away, because the South's econ-omy was totally dependent on their labor, and no definition rooted in biology could successfully be used to place every individual in his or her proper place. It was not the presence of two races in the South that created a boundary between them, but the presence of a boundary that created two races. Like the levees that held back the Mississippi River, that boundary had to be constructed, but the materials at hand were symbolic, not physical. The line was drawn in law, where African Americans were segregated and denied full citizenship; in speech and gesture; in joke and story; in mocking laughter and brutal violence.[5]

To focus on the symbolic creation of the color line is to highlight the ways in which race was and is a culturally constructed system of meanings, rather than a class relationship or an expression of psychological forces. To write of race in this way is not to deny that class can be important—sometimes very important—in defining its contours.[6] As a hierarchical system under which blacks could be economically exploited, race in the South functioned much like class, so much so that, in some forms of analysis, race *is* class, operating under another name. To be sure, few today endorse the simple form of economic determinism stressed by Oliver C. Cox, who argued that "race prejudice" is "propagated among the public by an exploiting class" to justify its exploitation of the stigmatized group.[7] Many, however, accept the far more nuanced arguments of historians such as Barbara J. Fields, who treat race as an ideology originating in class relationships.[8] Even in these more subtle forms, however, most class analyses of the phenomenon of race, have, in the words of David Roediger, "often been boiled down to the notion that class ... is more real, more fundamental, more basic or more *important* than race, both in political terms and in terms of historical analysis."[9] They are often embarrassed by their attempts to account for the passionate loyalties elicited by racial and ethnic ties, loyalties that may cross class boundaries, that persist in both rich and poor countries throughout the world, and that lead at times to extreme violence.[10]

It is the passions so often evident in racial conflict that have directed other analysts toward its psychological wellsprings. In particular, the sexual obsessions so evident in much racist ideology and behavior have drawn the attention of historians of the South. Both Joel Williamson and Jacquelyn Hall have emphasized the sexual fears that called forth lynchings, and Hall has also stressed the sexual element in the sadistic voyeurism in many lynchings, which frequently involved castration of the victim, and often included the hanging of the nude body, before or after killing, for display.[11] Yet psychological theories of race have their own weaknesses as forms of historical analysis. It is difficult to account for changes in any system that springs from psychological sources. And, as Pierre Van den Berghe notes, while "there is unquestionably a psychopathology of racism ... in racist societies most racists are not 'sick' "[12]

Both class and psychological perspectives on race are valuable, but they remain, even in combination, incomplete. In focusing on the functions and, perhaps, the foundations of racism, both these modes of analysis divert our attention toward what race does and away from what it is. "Race" is a matter of culture; it is part of a system of meanings. With signs and symbols, groups of people divide themselves from "others" according to characteristics they conceive to be primordial and thus unchangeable.[13] Economic advantage and psychological projection are two, but not the only two, contexts in which these cultural conceptions may arise and flourish.[14]

For the South in the Age of Segregation, one crucial context was the aftermath of emancipation. The Civil War and Reconstruction had wiped out the legal and even much of the economic basis for racial subordination. African American political status was radically transformed; the former slaves were not only legally freed, but also made citizens and, in the amended Constitution, guaranteed "equal protection of the law."[15] As racial subordination was re-imposed in the long process of "redeeming" the South, racial boundaries had to be drawn in new ways. A taboo on sexual contact between black men and white women became central to that boundary.[16] Southern whites stripped away voting rights and other public attributes of equal citizenship. Racial subordination also was continually re-created in the routine actions of the everyday world. In that world, racial etiquette and violence served to mark a new color line.[17]

One of the striking and, to many white southerners, disturbing aspects of emancipation had been the breakdown of the etiquette of racial slavery.[18] As one white woman (writing in 1901) recalled about the period immediately following the Civil War, it was only when she discovered that a Negro could be "rude to me and my father not resent it" that she had realized how "the world had indeed turned upside down"[19] After Reconstruction etiquette became central to the marking of racial boundaries. While the laws of etiquette were largely informal and a part of "local knowledge," varying from place to place and time to time, a relatively consistent set of rules governed face-to-face behavior in meetings between blacks and whites throughout the South in the age of segregation.[20]

Racial rules concerning the etiquette of hats embodied the symbolism of racial subordination. A black man always had to remove his hat when speaking to a white. On meeting a white on a sidewalk or roadway, he had at least to touch his hat, and preferably remove it. A white man, by contrast, would never remove his hat because of the presence of a black person. In particular, white men did not tip or remove their hats when speaking with or in the presence of black women, as they should always do for white women.[21]

Other rules of etiquette similarly displayed and reinforced racial hierarchy. In Natchez, Mississippi, in the 1930s, black people could not enter or leave a white's house by the front door. So strong was this ceremonial rule, researchers observed, that whites would lock the back door, but not the front, when leaving home.[22] Blacks had to address whites by titles: "Boss," "Suh," Mr. or Mrs.; whites would address blacks with first names only. If they did not know blacks by name, whites would use a "generic" first name: Bill, George, or Mary.[23] White people required titles because they had to be treated as representatives of the entire white race, whatever their personal worth; they were symbols as well as individuals. The use of a title also avoided any claim to familiarity, thus protecting the "ideal sphere" of honor around every white person. Whites denied blacks this sphere of honor, privacy, and protected space.[24]

The color line in the South did not separate only the high from the low. It was also the boundary between the pure and the impure, and this, too, was marked in daily life by etiquette. Especially clear illustrations appear in rules followed by many retail stores.[25] Blacks could shop in retail stores—whites did not want to segregate themselves from black money. A black man could try on a hat in the store for fit. A black woman, however, could not. A white clerk might demonstrate it for her, but once a hat sat upon a black woman's head, it could no longer be sold to a white woman. The issue was not that trying on a hat might make the black woman equal. Rather, contact would defile the hat and make it unfit for a white woman to wear. African Americans, that is, were not only "inferior," but also "unclean." An incident observed in Natchez illustrates the same point. A black woman returned a coat she had purchased because it did not fit. Perhaps because the current depression made black customers too valuable to alienate, the store manager accepted the coat back, thereby horrifying two white clerks. " 'This is perfectly terrible; I think it is awful'," said one. " 'We can't put that coat back in stock.' " Another added, " 'I know it. Who wants a nigger coat? . . . Some little white girl will probably come in and buy it and not know it is a nigger coat.' " One of the clerks "hung it up very gingerly and didn't touch it any more than necessary." As the observers noted, "in spite of their widespread uses as nurses and servants, there remains a strong feeling that the color of the Negroes is abhorrent and that contact with them may be contaminating."[26]

The principle involved is the one illuminated in Mary Douglas's classic study, *Purity and Danger*.[27] Douglas argues that ideas of ritual pollution arise as a way to prevent violations of the symbolic order. Dirt . . . is "essentially disorder," or "matter out of place." Social order . . . may be symbolized, and disorder perhaps avoided, by attention to ritual purity and pollution: rules keep order.[28] Hierarchical social orders are often protected with rules involving ritual pollution. The upper group in the social order is conceived to be not merely higher, but also purer; the lower orders are not merely lower, but also unclean. Contact can defile the upper groups with the "dirt" of the lower, but the reverse cannot occur.[29]

The most important of all rules of purity involved sexual contact. As both the progenitors of whiteness and the special repositories of white purity, white women had to be especially protected from defilement through contact, however slight and indirect, whether from a plate, a touch, or a glance, with "unclean" black men and women. The home, as women's "place," especially needed protection, and "protecting" the purity of women enforced simultaneously the boundaries of gender in the white world and the boundaries of race. Sexual contact between black men and white women was an extraordinary threat precisely because it struck so hard at the place where systems of race and gender intersected in the Southern cultural matrix. There is a close similarity here to the thrust, if not the complexities, of the rules governing purity and pollution in Hindu India. There we find extremely elaborate rules governing eating and drinking; there, too, sexual contact between lower caste men and higher caste women was the ultimate defilement of the social order.[30]

A white informant in William Ferris's study of Mississippi folk culture reminisced nostalgically about racial etiquette in his father's era. "My daddy," he said, "liked a niggir as long as he stayed in a niggir's place.... In his days coming up, when they paid them 'tention, the niggir respected the white man. He come to the back door and didn't come to the front door. And he took his hat off when he com in, and if he didn't, you'd ask him 'Niggir, don't you know how to take your hat off your head?' " But when "he got out of a niggir's place [daddy] put him back. And they always said 'yes sir' to him. If he didn't, he would wind up on the ground."[31] The informant's description illustrates well the role of violence in the culture of race. Etiquette maintained boundaries; violence restored them.[32]

While to some extent any violent attacks by whites against blacks served to enforce the color line, the most powerful symbolic acts of racial violence were the lynchings of African Americans by white mobs.... [M]any lynchings of blacks were highly ritualized punishments.[33]

When they involved a large portion of the white community, lynchings displayed white solidarity. To intimidate and warn other blacks, lynchers sometimes paraded their victims, either before or after they were killed, in black areas. Many lynchings took place at the spot in which the alleged crime had taken place. Fire might be used to torture victims, but fire also helped to expiate the harm done to the ritual order, as we can see in those instances in which lynch mobs killed their victims in one place, and burned their bodies in another—at the site of the crime, perhaps, or in a town square. The parts of a lynching victim's body might afterwards be treated as sacred objects, talismans which could bring good luck to the owners.

Blacks in the New South could be lynched for trivial violations of the racial code, but the full ritual display ... generally followed what whites perceived to be the most egregious violations of the boundaries of purity and hierarchy: rape of white women or murder.[34] Southern defenses of lynchings concentrated almost exclusively on the need to punish blacks for sexual violations of white women. As Southern African Americans themselves always knew, however, most lynchings did not involve accusations of rape or attempted rape.[35] Murder was the most common accusation against a lynching victim. For accused murders, highly ritualized lynchings were especially likely when the alleged murder victim was a law officer or woman.[36]

Etiquette and violence were central to the definition and enforcement of the meanings of race because those meanings were, in the words of Michael Omi and Howard Winant, "unstable and 'decentered' " and "constantly being transformed by political struggle."[37] Such long-term developments as the rise of an urban, African American middle class and changes in the status and role of women undermined many of the premises of the South's racial system.

World War I brought new, immediate, and profound challenges to the culture of race in the South. The call for national solidarity in a war fought for "democracy" challenged the idea of a society divided by a color line. The beginnings of massive migration from the South by black workers threatened some (but not all) white economic interests. Perhaps most important of all, some African Americans responded to the opportunities that the war seemed to open by courageously challenging the color line itself. This essay explores, for a single place, some of the consequences of that moment of extraordinary struggle and instability, which in Vicksburg provoked a crisis not only between whites and blacks, but within white society itself.

The city of Vicksburg lies at the southern tip of the Mississippi-Yazoo Delta, the heart of the South's post-Civil War cotton production.[38] In 1917 the city's experience of Civil War and Reconstruction was still vividly remembered. Vicksburg had endured weeks of siege before surrendering on July 4, 1863—five decades later, still a day to mourn rather than celebrate. To the city's whites, Reconstruction was a mythic time of misrule by carpetbaggers and blacks, little more, in their eyes, than a continuation of Yankee occupation. A bloody revolt had ultimately restored southern white rule.[39]

Yet Vicksburg's early-twentieth-century white leaders did not see themselves as nostalgic for the antebellum order, and they had not rejected modern civilization. From Reconstruction onward, the city's white elite had tried to tie Vicksburg by rail and water to national and international markets, and they did not hesitate to seek economic aid for that purpose from the federal government.[40] Vicksburg had ultimately lost out in the competition for the Delta's cotton trade to

St. Louis, Memphis, and New Orleans. After jumping from about 4,000 in 1860 to over 12,000 in 1870, the city's population had only slowly increased to its 1910 level of 20,814. Still, even if Vicksburg remained small and provincial by the standards of Memphis or Atlanta, the city's commercial-civic elite shared with the leaders of those bigger places an "urban ethos." They wanted to be part of a New South, not an old one. They worshiped growth and progress, and believed they could have these without sacrificing order and harmony.[41]

Like their urban counterparts elsewhere in the South, Vicksburg's leaders were conservative and paternalistic in their ideas about race. They accepted unthinkingly both segregation and the elimination of African Americans from the state's political life.[42] Still, they were willing for blacks to have a subordinate part in the march of progress. By the era of the World War, local white newspaper editors, though never challenging the essentials of white racial domination, condemned lynching and found room in their pages to praise black church leaders and black educational efforts.[43]

One of Vicksburg's African American residents in the war years was Dr. John A. Miller. Forty-seven years old in 1918, Miller was born in Virginia, attended the preparatory school at Howard University, and earned degrees from Williams College in 1896 and the University of Michigan's Medical School in 1900. Why he went to Vicksburg is something of a mystery; perhaps simply because it was a city with a growing black population, including a not-insignificant middle class.[44]

John Miller was probably at the turn of the century the best-educated black man in Vicksburg; he may have been the best educated person, period. [However], a 1908 survey of the community gives him barely more than a mention, suggesting that perhaps, even after years of residence, he was considered something of an outsider.[45]

During his nearly twenty years in the city, Miller later wrote, he "never meddled in the white man's affairs and did not dare murmur or complain at the many acts of lawlessness against my race." Except, that is, twice, and the two exceptions tell us a great deal about Miller and white Vicksburg. In 1909 Miller helped to prevent the appointment as a public school teacher of a black woman who was "a public woman for white men." In 1916, Miller unsuccessfully opposed the hiring of a black teacher who "was the proud mistress of a white man." Both times, Miller hired white lawyers to help lobby the school board, and in 1916 he collected an affidavit from "a reputable White Lady" to support his case.[46]

White Vicksburg residents may have seen Miller as a "good negro" who, in trying to punish miscegenation, was accommodating, Booker

95

T. Washington style, to Jim Crow. To Miller and other middle class blacks, however, this action was more protest than accommodation. The authors of a letter about the second case to white lawyer John Brunini explained that they were trying to "overcome the charges of Immorality that are thrown at the race from time to time."[47] Like middle-class blacks elsewhere in the South, they deeply resented white assumptions that all blacks were by nature too sexualized and "immoral" to be able to meet the Victorian standards that whites identified with civilization itself. Their knowledge that white men themselves hypocritically violated those standards with black women only compounded their resentment.[48] Some of Vicksburg's African Americans later told an investigator that discontent over the "immorality of school teachers" whose jobs were "in the hands of white trustees" was a contributing cause of black outmigration from the city.[49] In insisting that whites hire only respectable black teachers, Dr. Miller and other blacks were also insisting that respectability knew no color line.

African Americans like John Miller recognized that American entry into the World War might offer them new opportunities.[50] Mississippi's whites came with alarm to the same realization. Even before the declaration of war, a shortage of industrial labor touched off a massive movement of blacks to northern cities. Some white southerners, fearing the loss of their cheap labor supply, responded with a variety of repressive methods in a vain attempt to stem this tide.[51] For others, however, the Great Migration helped to reinforce the idea that their interests were best served by paternalistic protection of minimal African American rights. If Mississippi wanted to keep its black workforce, one Vicksburg leader wrote, it needed to protect "the hardworking money-making darky" from "injustice by court agencies and robbery by parasites."[52] Lynchings in the state, which had averaged more than fourteen per year from 1900 to 1909 and eight per year from 1910 to 1915, fell to three in 1916 and 1917 combined.[53]

The declaration of war created new concerns for the South's whites. The draft, for example, raised the specter of millions of armed blacks; Mississippi's Senator James K. Vardaman proclaimed that he knew of "no greater menace to the South than this."[54] The sight of black men in official U.S. uniforms bothered many whites, and the idea that black soldiers might meet white women in France as social equals bothered some even more.[55] Each of these complaints—that black soldiers would have access to means of violence, to symbols of public honor, and to social relationships with white women—points to a threat to the symbolic underpinnings of the color line. In response, Vicksburg whites sometimes drove black soldiers off the streets and out of town, and white soldiers in the city beat up black women.[56]

Such anxieties and conflicts were only part of a more complicated story, however. The war called for men and money, including black men and black money. The leading white businessmen, clergy, political leaders, and editors joined to foster and encourage black participation in the war effort. With every draft of African-American soldiers, the city organized an elaborate send-off ceremony. Both white and black speakers praised the civic contributions of newly enrolled black soldiers, who then paraded to the train station with bands blaring.[57] A local judge, in his "patriotic charge" to a grand jury, paid "tribute to the colored soldiers" and "stated that regardless of race prejudice or expressions that when the time came the negro soldiers would cover themselves with glory and would be found giving just as valiant service in the defense of their flag as their white brothers."[58] When Alice Dunbar Nelson visited the city to stimulate war-related volunteerism by African-American women, one white newspaper covering the appearance of this "Prominent Colored Woman" even referred to her as "Mrs." Nelson.[59]

Civic leaders also called upon African Americans to buy war bonds and savings stamps. Vicksburg's War Stamp Savings Committee organized a sales campaign led by George Williamson, cashier of the city's largest bank. The Committee and its many volunteers resorted to highly coercive tactics. Those who refused to pledge the amount determined by an "Allotment Committee" put themselves "in line for a yellow card"—a public display reserved for "pledge slackers."[60]

The campaign climaxed on "War Savings Day," June 28, 1918. In the week leading up to the 28th, local police arrested and fined a British citizen for "acting in a discourteous manner" to members of the Stamp Committee . . . [and charged] a black man, Sam Gaithers, with "interfering with a government loan" for allegedly telling his nephew "that he did not have to buy any of the stamps if he didn't want to."[61] Chairman Williamson took out a full-page newspaper ad warning that if any citizens refused to do their duty, "the Government will see to it that their movements will be watched and their actions will be recorded in Washington."[62]

It was in this charged atmosphere that, sometime in the spring or early summer of 1918, John Hennessey of the War Savings Committee visited Dr. Miller and asked him to subscribe to war bonds. Undoubtedly to John Hennessey's surprise and chagrin, the Miller he called on was not the Washingtonian accommodationist he surely expected, but the man who, with two friends, had just become a charter member of a new chapter of the NAACP.[63] According to his own description, Miller responded to Hennessey's request with complaints about poor treatment of blacks generally, and bad schools and low pay for black teachers in particular. "After discussing these local conditions," Miller continued, "I asked Mr. Hennessee (sic) as a white man now what would you do if your patriotism at home was crushed as the white people of Vicksburg crush the Negroes . . . I added I want you to think over what I have said and come back and I will tell you how many bonds I am going to buy."[64] It would indeed be delightful to have a picture of Hennessey's face at this moment of catastrophic breakdown in the etiquette of race.

As later newspaper reports made clear, even before this meeting with Hennessey, Miller had begun to earn a reputation as a trouble-maker. One paper reported that rumors of Miller's "disloyal" state-ments had been circulating for months.[65] According to another, among the "many disloyal statements" Miller had made in connection with the Liberty Loan and War Savings drives was his claim that "his race got only half a chance in this community anyhow."[66] This report apparently referred to a different incident; when Miller was asked for a contribution of $10 to the Red Cross, he had given only $5, he wrote, because he "had only half [his] rights."[67]

We don't know how Hennessey replied to Miller, but the plain fact was that he and other white citizens of Vicksburg had been put in a dilemma. The war had thrown the color line into confusion, as signi-fied by events as various as parades in the streets and appeals to black patriotism. With the line between black and white no longer so obvi-ously the line between citizen and non-citizen, the white elite had begun to approach some black residents as if they had typical patri-otic feelings and normal patriotic duties.[68] Miller had accepted their unintended invitation to act like a citizen. It was they, and not he, who had first stepped over proper racial boundaries. It is telling that the Stamp Committee did not immediately call out a mob or even visit Miller more discreetly. Instead a member of the Committee called him up and insisted that he buy the extraordinary amount of $1,000 in war bonds—borrowing from a bank to do so, if necessary. Another call came on June 28—War Savings Day—insisting again that Miller sub-scribe to $1,000 in bonds, and threatening to arrest him for sedition if he refused. As Miller later learned from a white friend, the War Sav-ings Committee was trying to trap him "into saying I had advised Negroes not to buy Govt. securities."[69] The Vicksburg elite was going to extraordinary lengths to discredit him, not simply as an uppity black man, but as a disloyal American.

It may have been in part Miller's own position in Vicksburg that made him both a challenger of racial boundaries and a target of those who would reinforce those boundaries. As a professional black man, highly educated in elite Northern institutions, a native Southerner yet perhaps always something of an outsider in Vicksburg, he was himself an embodiment of the impossiblities of clearly defining racial bound-aries. Yet, the events that bracketed the July 23 tar-and-feather attack on Miller demonstrate that the confounding of racial issues with the problem of "loyalty" went well beyond the case of one man. Dave Cook, the first tar-and-feather victim on July 23, was a white man. Those who attacked him claimed that he had said "he would see the United States government in hell" before he would allow any of his sons to be drafted. Clearly, however, a key reason for the attack was that Cook lived openly with a black woman, and that his sons were mulattos.[70] The following night (July 24), the "flying squadron," as the newspapers referred to the leaders of the tar-and-feather episode, appeared at the homes of Ethel Barrett and Ellen Brooks, two poor black women, and poured tar on them. Mob members explained that "neither of the negro women would work, [that they] were living at the expense of the community." The "squadron" promised to clean out Vicksburg until it was "One Hundred Per Cent American"—and un-American types included "all loafers and idlers, whether white or black, male or female." The men planned to "specialize on both white men and negro women who have been living together, with a view of breaking up this practice entirely."[71] By July 1918, not just criticism of war-related policies, but also violation of racial norms in marriage and the refusal of black women to perform menial labor were signs of something less than "100 percent Americanism."

John Miller believed the city's white leadership had provoked the July 23 events and accused Stamp Savings Committee Chairman George Williamson of giving a "direct or indirect" order to attack him. The incident, he declared, could not be blamed simply on the "mob spirit."[72] The response of the white elite, however, suggests a more complex picture and points toward a significant division among whites.

The day after the attack on Cook and Miller, Williamson, Mayor Hayes, and several others published a statement "deeply deplor[ing] the unfortunate incident that took place yesterday afternoon, when a few of our citizens tarred and feathered a WHITE man and a NEGRO, for disloyal acts and utterances." The signers went on to urge "all good citizens, white and black, to avoid every utterance and every act that might lead to a repetition of the outbreak of yesterday," and to assure all "citizens, white and black, that loyalty and proper living will be as highly approved and heartily defended as disloyalty is condemned."[73] Perhaps these gentlemen were simply looking away while other people did their dirty work. But when the two black women were attacked on the night of the 24th—immediately after this statement appeared— elite responses went well beyond denunciation.

One editor branded that second assault "one of the most cowardly that could possibly have been committed," and a reporter suggested that the real motive behind the attack was that one of the women had refused to work for one of the mob's leaders. It soon became clear that

Ethel Barrett was a hard-working laundress and, perhaps most embarrassing for city leaders, both women had husbands serving in the army. The whole incident, one reporter wrote, had "humiliated" the city.[74] A public meeting on July 26 explicitly condemned the attack on the women, and within a week seven men, now labeled "whitecappers," were prosecuted in the city court at the behest of a "citizens committee" and fined for assault.[75]

Of the seven men who had been convicted and fined, five can be identified in local records. Four were partners in the Home Taxi Company in 1918. One of these had been a chauffeur a few years before. Another of the four had been an employee in the maintenance division of the local electric company, and the fifth identifiable participant was a maintenance supervisor in that company. Those identified as "mob leaders," then, consisted of a small group of men who knew each other well. By no means at the bottom of the white occupational hierarchy, they were nonetheless far removed from the world of the business elite in the city, and at least one of them had only recently risen from a relatively menial service occupation. In labeling these attackers "whitecappers," elite leaders thereby identified them with the kind of attacks by white small farmers on rural blacks that had plagued parts of Mississippi earlier in the century. Whitecappers had operated in areas in which whites and blacks competed for good land to rent and often were intent on driving a way African Americans completely. Their activities were anathema to white planters and planter-merchants who depended upon black labor.[76] As against this traditional rural culture of violence, Vicksburg's elite was defending what Joel Williamson has termed the "conservative," paternalistic racism of the South's cultural elites.[77]

Miller's punishment is itself ironic evidence of the contradictions within white racist culture that had been exposed and to some extent created by the war. His was a ritual of shaming, and not, as in lynching, of death. As such, the attack on Miller implied that white Vicksburg had invited him into the circle of honor, as a patriotic American. It was perhaps the shock of recognition that they had done so, as much as Miller's own actions, that confounded Vicksburg's white leaders, for they, as well as he, had bent if not broken the hierarchical boundaries of race. The city's elite had then allowed lesser white men to punish Miller in a way that violated the ideals of "civilization" and democracy for which the World War was supposedly being fought. Only three days after the attack, both Vicksburg newspapers gave front-page coverage to President Woodrow Wilson's denunciation of the lynching of a German immigrant in Illinois, which put "lynchers squarely on the side of Germany."[78] By prosecuting and punishing the crowd leaders for their attacks on the women, Vicksburg's white leaders resolved their dilemma in a way. The court action allowed the city's elite to vindicate the "honor" of Vicksburg without entirely repudiating the punishment of the black physician who had insisted on his own right to honor.[79]

The World War had redrawn the boundaries of inclusiveness, disturbed the color line, and provoked a violent white response in Vicksburg. More than the war itself had created a fear of disorder among whites, however. A white man had violated the color line in marriage. Two poor black women had insisted on some measure of control over their own work. Attacks on them, while occasioned by the war, grew out of anxieties that went beyond the immediate events of the war years. These anxieties, centered on concerns about home and work, and so about gender and class, increased in the aftermath of the war. As a result, a young black man would suffer a terrible death.

To be sure, some of these postwar anxieties grew directly out of the way war had perturbed racial boundaries. Editors and letter writers openly fretted about "the high tension which seemingly exists . . . about the returning negro soldiers," and cautioned readers to ignore "absurd" stories that the "soldiers who went overseas would come back and expect to marry your sisters."[80] Perhaps out of concern about the continuing migration of blacks to the north, local editors also endorsed the "laudable intentions" of a "colored meeting" at the courthouse that condemned lynchings and called for improved wages for black laborers.[81]

More threatening than returning black soldiers, to judge from the attention it received in the newspapers, was the labor strife that erupted in 1919 throughout the United States. Many connected these labor troubles to the success of the Bolsheviks in Russia, who in the popular imagination soon replaced the Huns as a danger to civilization. Newspaper headlines warned how "Bolshevists Would Contaminate World" or were "Threatening Civilization."[82] Strikes in Seattle and Minneapolis, and even crime in New York City, were interpreted as extensions of this worldwide threat: "Seattle Thinks that Bolshevism Grips the City;" "Practical Bolshevism in New York. Unprecedented Reign of Crime and Loot."[83]

Yet the popular media was preoccupied with an apparent upheaval in the proper relations of men and women. This preoccupation seems to have been tied less to the impending ratification of the Nineteenth Amendment to the Constitution, giving women the right to vote, than to threats simultaneously more specific and more pervasive.[84] On the same day that the Vicksburg *Evening Post* reported the "Bolshevik" threat in Seattle, another front page story—based on information received over a "special leased wire"—gave the latest details on the trial of a Mrs. Abbott in Atlanta for the murder of her husband.[85] Throughout the spring of 1919 similar stories dominated the front pages: a murderess in Selma, Alabama; a "shocking murder" in nearby Indianola, in which a "travelling man" was shot down by a white woman while her husband watched; the arrest of a Vicksburg stenographer, charged with poisoning her late husband.[86] When a convention of police chiefs met in New Orleans, "women crooks" shared attention with the "spread of Bolshevism" as leading topics of discussion.[87]

The Bolshevik scare entered into this volatile brew of class and gender anxieties because the Bolsheviks threatened to tear apart the sexual as well as the class order. Newspapers titillated readers with allegations that Lenin presided over "Daily Orgies of Indulgence ... at Bolsheviki Headquarters," and reported that the Bolsheviks were "nationalizing" Russian women and had "declared war on family life." Men were sharing women between them "and consideration for one another's mother or sister is forbidden. All must be treated alike. The most terrible thing is that the women themselves have accepted their 'nationalization' and very little protest is made."[88]

In April, 1919, Rev. Charles Criswell, a "militant pastor," explained to his congregation the connections between sexual scandals and the Bolshevik menace. The world, according to Rev. Criswell, was "on the edge of a volcano," and the twin warnings of the impending explosion were "bolshevism and infidelity." "Making the world safe for democracy is incidental to making every home safe. The world cannot be safe as long as there is an unprotected country in it, any more than any city can be safe if there is an unprotected home in it."[89]

Exactly two days later, the *Evening Post* reported that a "Midnight Visitor"—a black man—had "invaded" two homes, frightened ladies, and "attacked" Mrs. F. A. Arnold.[90] Over the next four weeks, more break-ins by "black prowlers" were reported. Several men were arrested on suspicion, but identifications were uncertain and the "epidemic" did not stop.[91] By May 14 white emotions were at a fever pitch when the *Post*'s headline screamed "Negro Attempts Rape of Young Working Girl." Bloodhounds had tracked the criminal, the paper reported, and authorities had arrested a young black man, Lloyd Clay.[92] The city's sheriff hustled Clay off to jail, hoping for a quick identification by Mattie Hudson, the alleged victim. Then the city could order a quick trial and conviction and hope to avoid a mob scene. The sheriff was no doubt disappointed when Miss Hudson not once, but twice, failed to identify Clay in a lineup.[93]

If Lloyd Clay began to breathe more easily, his relief did not last long. Too many people in Vicksburg were wrought up, and hundreds of whites, convinced of Clay's guilt, gathered before the jail, determined to seize him and administer their own brand of justice. By the evening of the 14th, the crowd had swelled to perhaps 1000, and many of its members were drunk. Shortly before 8:00 p.m. they stormed the jail and seized Clay. Some of the men in the crowd dragged their victim out to the street while others went for Mattie Hudson. What went through the minds of Clay and Hudson as they faced each other that evening can only be imagined. Clay strongly denied his guilt. Though at first "loathe to identify him," Hudson finally told the crowd "that he was the guilty one." In terror, Clay cried out "I'm the man. Give me a pistol and I'll blow my brains out." Such a relatively painless death, however, would not satisfy the mob. They stripped Clay, poured oil over his body, put a rope around him and hung him from a tree at the side of the street. As the rope pulled taut, "the sight of the nude body rising above the crowd increased the excitement." A fire set below his feet lapped at his legs. Without a cry, he "lifted his arms" and "placed his palms together in an attitude of prayer." Finally, many in the crowd began to fire their guns at him, and "even women were seen to shoot revolvers." In the wild firing a white bystander was fatally struck with a bullet. The flesh of Lloyd Clay continued to burn—described in gory detail in local newspapers—after he was dead. Finally the body was cut down and the crowd, in a "hubbub of gloating," rushed in to seize souvenirs.

Defenders of the lynching justified it as whites always had—it was a ritual necessary to restore the racial order. One female "sufferer" claimed that evidence from the bloodhounds and Mattie Hudson "was proof enough to the minds of most people of the identity of the brute. Could our fathers, husbands and brothers take a chance on this man's life?"[94] A white man called the tree on which Clay was hung "a monument to the spirit of manhood of this community who will not tolerate crimes against their women folks."[95]

Yet this lynching, even more than the tar-and-feather attack of the year before, rather than re-establishing order and reinforcing white solidarity, ultimately served to reveal and deepen class cleavages in white Vicksburg. A few days after Clay's murder, a group of the wealthiest and most influential men in the city met publicly to denounce it. In a remarkable inversion of black/white imagery, they resolved that the lynching had "cast an ineffaceable black shadow upon the fair name of our city" and made Vicksburg "the object of abuse and contempt of people in every section of the civilized world." This language was put into a petition which circulated through the city and soon claimed the signatures of nearly ten percent of the adult white male population; the petition called for swift and sure punishment for the lynch mob's leaders.[96]

Vicksburg's white elite repudiated the lynching in part because, in its own disorder, it had failed as ritual. The crowd inflicted "unnecessary" torture, and it caused the death of a white bystander. The "fiendish gloating" of the crowd reminded one local commentator of the "Bolsheviki" themselves, and a reporter called the mob "an amateur organization," implying that it had lacked proper direction from community leaders.[97]

Much worse, many soon realized that Clay was almost certainly innocent. Even the strongest champions of southern bloodhounds could doubt that they had correctly tracked a single scent to a place as public as the railroad station. Mattie Hudson had "been loathe to identify" Clay, and she had made her uncertain identification literally in the face of a howling mob. Clay's brother, furthermore, soon claimed that Lloyd had spent the entire night of the alleged crime with him. Four days after the lynching, the editor of the Vicksburg *Daily Herald* lamented that the "hideous and dehumanizing spectacle" had resulted in the death of an innocent man, "one wholly out of the class of the 'bad negro'."[98]

Finally, in attempting to enforce the boundaries of race, the lynching had ignored the proper boundaries of gender. The mob lynched Clay at the doorstep of a home owned by prominent white women, one of whom was so offended that she asked the city to cut down the tree—the "monument to the spirit of manhood"—where Clay had been hung.[99] Many white women had witnessed the sadistic torture of the nude black man, with its obvious sexual connotations, and several had fired revolvers.

When local commentators deplored the presence of women at the lynching, a Mrs. Emily P. Shaw responded with a remarkable letter to the *Evening Post*. A witness herself to the lynching, she approved of it—a "just mob" had only been "meting out justice." "The day has passed when a woman, 'to be a lady,' must stay behind closed doors. There are times when she should come forth and she is none the less a lady for doing so."[100] Mrs. Shaw in effect denied that white women like herself needed to be protected in their homes. Perhaps her letter raised questions in the minds of some of Vicksburg's white men about the circumstances of Lloyd Clay's alleged assault. The crucial break-in had come in the apartment of a single woman, working and living alone. How could such women, living without the "protection" of a man, ever be kept safe? Indeed, it had been such an unattached woman, working as a stenographer in the city, who had been accused of poisoning her late husband just weeks before.[101] One woman, replying anonymously to Shaw, insisted that "there is an innate feeling in most women that causes them to experience horror at the thought of witnessing such a scene. If I were not sure that this were so with the large majority of women here, I would wish to shake the dust of this city from my feet forever." She vehemently denied that the mob had exhibited a "spirit of chivalry."[102]

These multiple doubts about the lynching led Vicksburg's white elite to repudiate the mob. The language of their condemnation—that the lynching had made Vicksburg "the object of abuse and contempt of people in every section of the civilized world"—suggests a provincial bourgeoisie struggling to identify itself with the standards of a wider world. The "civilized world" was the world of Northern and European civilization, a civilization that a mighty war had just been fought to preserve. Now, as one letter writer put it, Vicksburg had been witness to a "victory for German ideals."[103] As the petition drawn up by the elite circulated through the city in the next few days, Vicksburg's citizens were asked to identify themselves publicly with these values of civilization, and in effect to reject those of a presumably more primitive cultural ideal. The accumulation of names on the petition offers powerful evidence of the ways in which that cultural divide was also a class divide.

The signers included an array of the most prominent business and professional leaders in the city. As far as can be determined, the petition contains the names of white men only. These included the mayor, the heads of every bank, prominent lawyers, the ministers of the major religious denominations, owners of important businesses, the supervisor at the main railroad, and the President of the Board of Trade. Yet the petition contained the names of many men who were not part of that leadership.

The great majority of non-elite signers held clerical and similar white-collar jobs in the city. Most were employed by the elite signers. The signature of W. S. Jones, President of the Merchants National Bank, was closely followed by those of C. E. Downing and Preston Wailes, clerks at the bank. The signatures of W. Conway and T. H. Allein, clerks at Warner and Searles Clothing, followed that of C. L. Warner, the president of the company. The pattern is consistent through more than one hundred such signatures from lower-white-collar workers. By contrast only three identifiable blue-collar workers signed— one carpenter, one electrician and one bicycle repairman. Undoubtedly Vicksburg's white establishment had circulated the petition among themselves, and in each of their businesses had gotten the lower-level employees to sign as well. While it seems reasonable to think that clerical workers might feel intimidated when asked to sign such a petition, the signatures of contractors were not followed by those of carpenters, nor that of the owner of a boiler works by those of boilermakers.[104] The class divide was not simply a matter of income. It was also a matter of culture, as clerks, many of whom were no doubt educated and ambitious to rise in the world of business, chose to identify themselves with the business civilization of Vicksburg's elite.

In the end, the system of race survived these shocks largely intact.

John Miller left for Detroit shortly after the attack on him. The U.S. Department of Justice refused requests by the NAACP to investigate the attack. In Detroit, Miller took up his medical practice again, served on the board of a YMCA branch, and voted with the Republican Party. He died there in 1931.[105] In August, 1918, Alice Dunbar Nelson wrote to her Washington office that since the tar-and-feather incident "the colored brass band will not lead the colored draftees to the station, seeing no cause for making music."[106] The determination of the "flying squadron" to enforce "one hundred per cent Americanism" would be taken up in its own way by the revived Ku Klux Klan of the 1920s.[107]

Despite the efforts of Vicksburg's white elite, Lloyd Clay's killers were never brought to justice. When the Grand Jury met in July, 1919, the presiding Judge compared the mob to the "lawbreaker and agitator" who would bring about "Bolshevism and anarchy and ruin," and charged jury members to "bring Clay's slayers to court." But the Grand Jury was dominated by farmers and planters from the rural areas of Warren County who refused to return an indictment. Frank Andrew, foreman of the jury, Secretary of the Vicksburg Board of Trade, and a signer of the anti-lynching petition the previous spring, resigned in protest, creating "a considerable sensation about the court house and throughout the city," but the resignation had no effect; the judge ordered him not to mention publicly the names of any suspected lynchers.[108] The split in the Grand Jury points out some of the ways the culture of race differed in the rural and urban South, as well as along class lines. The color line would survive until a later generation, following an even bigger war, rose to challenge it anew.

NOTES

1 Vicksburg *Daily Herald* (VDH), 24 July 1918; Vicksburg *Evening Post* (VEP), 24 July 1918. The incident is also documented in Papers of the NAACP (Mf edition: Frederick, MD), August Meier and John H. Bracey, edit. advisors, Part 7, Series A: Anti-Lynching Investigative Files, 1912–1953 (hereafter NAACP), reel 14, frames 1ff, 120–197; and it is discussed and described in Neil McMillan, *Dark Journey: Black Mississippians in the Age of Jim Crow* (Urbana, Ill., 1989), 31, 171, 304–5.

2 VDH, 24 July 1918; VEP, 24 July 1918. . . .

3 Wyatt-Brown, *Southern Honor: Ethics and Behavior in the Old South* (New York, 1982), esp. chaps. 14–16.

4 Cornel West, "Race and Social Theory," in *Keeping Faith: Philosophy and Race in America* (New York, 1993), 268.

5 The argument her is informed by Fredrick Barth, ed., *Ethnic Groups and Boundaries: The Social Organization of Culture Differences* (London, 1969).

6 In the vast theoretical literature on race and racism, useful general studies include Robert Miles, *Racism* (London, 1989); John Rex, *Race Relations in*

Sociological Theory (London, 1983); Pierre van den Berghe, *Race and Racism: A Comparative Perspective* (New York, 1978); Michael Banton, *The Idea of Race* (Boulder, Col., 1978); and Donald Horowitz, *Ethnic Groups in Conflict* (Berkeley, 1985). . . .

7 Oliver Cromwell Cox, *Caste, Class, and Race: A Study in Social Dynamics* (1948, reprint. New York, 1959); quote 393.

8 Barbara J. Fields, "Slavery, Race and Ideology in the United States of America," *New Left Review*, no. 181 (1990), 95–119; Barbara J. Fields, "Race and Ideology in American History," in J. Morgan Kousser and James McPherson, eds., *Region, Race, and Reconstruction: Essays in Honor of C. Vann Woodward* (New York, 1984). . . .

9 . . . . Roediger, *Wages of Whiteness: Race and the Making of the American Working Class* (London, 1991), quote 7.

10 The language of this last sentence in part paraphrases Horowitz, *Ethnic Groups in Conflict*, 105–6.

11 Joel Williamson, *The Crucible of Race: Black-White Relations in the American South Since Emancipation* (New York, 1984); Jacqueline Dowd Hall, *The Revolt Against Chivalry: Jesse Daniel Ames and the Women's Campaign Against Lynching* (New York, 1979), 129–57. An earlier study influenced by Freudian theory is John Dollard, *Caste and Class in a Southern Town* (1937; reprint. Madison, Wisc., 1988), esp. 315–363. . . .

12 Van den Berghe, *Race and Racism*, xx.

13 The argument here is influenced by . . . Clifford Geertz, especially in "Thick Description: Toward an Interpretive Theory of Culture," and "Religion as a Cultural System," in *The Interpretation of Cultures* (New York, 1973), 3–30, 87–125. . . . It should be noted that such "primordial" differences can also be conceptualized as "tribal," "ethnic," or in other ways.

14 . . . . The perspective in the present essay is in the largest sense Weberian, rather than Marxian or Freudian; a plea for such a perspective is made by George C. Fredrickson in "The Historiography of Postemancipation Southern Race Relations," in" *The Arrogance of Race: Historical Perspectives on Slavery, Racism, and Social Inequality* (Middletown, Conn., 1988), 154–160.

15 This is a major theme in Eric Foner, *Reconstruction: America's Unfinished Revolution* (New York, 1988).

16 See Martha Hodes, "The Sexualization of Reconstruction Politics: White Women and Black Men in the South after the Civil War," in John C. Fout and Maura Shaw Tantillo, eds., *American Sexual Politics: Sex, Gender, and Race since the Civil War* (Chicago, 1993), 59–74.

17 On the late 19th century, see Williamson, *Crucible of Race*.

18 I have followed Erving Goffman's definition of etiquette: the "code which governs ceremonial rules and ceremonial expressions" which make up the "conventionalized means of communication by which the individual expresses his character or conveys his appreciation of the other participants"; see "The Nature of Deference and Demeanor," in Goffman, *Interaction Ritual: Essays on Face-to-Face Behavior* (Garden City, NY, 1967), 47–96, quote 54–55; see also Goffman, "On Face Work," in ibid., 5–45. A growing interest in the history of etiquette among U.S. historians was sparked by the translation of Norbert Elias, *The History of Manners. The Civilizing Process*, Vol. I (New York, 1978). . . .

19 The specific event was that "a huge Negro soldier compelled me to take to the gutter, to escape coming in contact with him" and her father had told

her, "My child, you must expect that and many things besides." Georgia Bryan Conrad, "Reminiscences of a Southern Woman," *Southern Workman*, July 1901, 410.

20 For treatments of racial etiquette and examples of common rules, see Bertram Doyle, *The Etiquette of Race Relations in the South* (Chicago, 1937), 142–159, in which Doyle lists rules provided by his black students in the 1930s; Dollard, *Caste and Class*, passim. . . . The phrase "local knowledge" is from Clifford Geertz, *Local Knowledge: Further Essays in Interpretive Anthropology* (New York, 1983).

21 . . . For comparative examples, see John F. Kasson, *Rudeness & Civility: Manners in Nineteenth-Century Urban America* (New York, 1990), 143–146; Greg Dening, *Islands and Beaches: Discourse on a Silent Land. Marquesas 1774–1880* (Honolulu, 1980), 52, 89; Alexandr Nikolaevich Engelgardt, "Letters from the Country, 1872–1887, trans. and ed. by Cathy A. Frierson (New York, 1993), 188–189; . . . Orest Ranum, "Courtesy, Absolutism, and the Rise of the French State, 1630–1660," *Journal of Modern History*, 52 (1980), 426–51. For a general consideration of the symbolic uses of the body, see Mary Douglas, *Natural Symbols: Explorations in Cosmology* (New York, 1982).

22 Allison Davis, Mary Gardner, and Burleigh Gardner, *Deep South: A Social Anthropological Study of Caste and Class* (Chicago, 1941), 22.

23 McMillan cites the case of a white postmaster who defaced the words "Mr." or "Mrs." when these were used on letters addressed to blacks: *Dark Journey*, 24.

24 "Although differing in size in various directions and differing according to the person with whom one entertains relations, this sphere cannot be penetrated, unless the personality value of the individual is thereby destroyed. A sphere of this sort is placed around man by his honor." Georg Simmel . . . quoted in Goffman, "Deference and Demeanor", 62–63.

25 See Doyle, *Etiquette of Race Relations*, p.153.

26 Davis, et al., *Deep South*, 15–16. . . .

27 Mary Douglas, *Purity and Danger: An Analysis of the Concepts of Pollution and Taboo* (London, 1966).

28 Ibid., 2, 35. . . .

29 In the South, many such rules . . . were written into ordinances . . . requiring segregated restaurants, toilets, and drinking fountains. . . .

30 . . . . see, e.g., Gerald Berreman, "Caste in India and the United States," *American Journal of Sociology*, 64 (1960), 120–127; George DeVos and Hiroshi Wagatsuma, *Japan's Invisible Race: Caste in Culture and Personality* (Berkeley, 1966). . . .

31 William Reynolds Ferris, Jr, "Black Folklore from the Mississippi Delta," (Ph.D. diss., University of Pennsylvania, 1969), 289. . . .

32 In the Indian caste system, too, violation of purity rules, especially concerning sexual contact between higher caste women and lower caste men, could bring terrible punishments to the men and women involved. See note 30, above.

33 . . . . [On] the ritualistic aspects of some lynchings [see] W. Fitzhugh Brundage, *Lynching in the New South: Georgia and Virginia, 1880–1930* (Urbana, Ill., 1993), 36–45. . . . See also Williamson, *Crucible of Race*, 183–189; Hall, *Revolt Against Chivalry*, 129–157; Wyatt-Brown, *Southern Honor*, 453–61; Trudier Harris, *Exorcising Blackness: Historical and Literary Lynching and Burning Rituals* (Bloomington, Ind., 1984). . . .

34 According to Brundage, over 85% of Georgia's "mass mobs" [those usually

involving ritualistic elements] were precipitated by charges of rape or attempted rape (48%) or murder (39%). (. . . calculated from Brundage's listing of victims in *Lynching in the New South*, Appendix A. . . . For Brundage's own discussion and accompanying charts, see his chapter 2.) What Brundage calls "terrorist" lynchings, which seldom involved ritual elements, were more likely to have their source in economic conflicts.

35 This was pointed out as early as the early 1890s by Ida Wells. See . . . Mildred I. Thompson, *Ida B. Wells-Barnett: An Exploratory Study of an American Black Woman, 1893–1930* (Brooklyn, 1990), which reprints several of her anti-lynching publications. . . . E. M. Beck and Stuart E. Tolnay have compiled the most complete list of verified lynchings for their book, *A Festival of Violence: An Analysis of Southern Lynchings, 1882–1930* (Urbana, Ill., 1995). I am grateful to Beck and Tolnay for sharing with me their lists for Mississippi and Georgia.

36 . . . . [T]he murders and assaults that most often led to fully ritualized lynchings were attacks on women, or on sheriffs and other officials who symbolized white hierarchy and white control of the community: Brundage, *Lynching in the New South*, 73–80. . . .

37 Omi and Winant, *Racial Formation in the United States From the 1960s to the 1980s* (New York, 1986), x. . . .

38 On the Delta, see especially . . . James C. Cobb, *The Most Southern Place on Earth: The Mississippi Delta and the Roots of Regional Identity* (New York, 1992).

39 William C. Harris, *The Day of the Carpetbagger: Republican Reconstruction in Mississippi* (Baton Rouge, 1979), esp. 634–636, 645–649.

40 They eagerly sought federal help when the Mississippi River threatened to change its course and leave the city's port dry. See Harris, *Day of the Carpetbagger*, 281–284, 547–554; Virginia Colohan Harrell, *Vicksburg and the River* (Jackson, Miss., 1982), 71–73.

41 Blaine A. Brownell, *The Urban Ethos in the South, 1920–1930* (Baton Rouge, 1975).

42 This elimination had been enshrined in the state's constitution in 1890; see McMillan, *Dark Journey*, 38–48.

43 VEP 4 June 1917, 26 July 1918, 17 May 1918; VDH, 5 July 1918. Lynchings had become rare in the immediate vicinity. Vicksburg was in Warren County, which had witnessed, according to the best available counts, 11 lynchings from 1885 to 1994, 3 from 1895 to 1904, and one each in 1907 and 1915. These numbers come from the research of Beck and Tolnay.

44 Sketchy biographical information on Miller is available in *Who's Who in Colored America, 1928–29*, 266, and in Williams College *Reunion Book, 1933*, 21–22. . . .

45 *The Leading Afro-Americans of Vicksburg, Miss. Their Enterprises Churches, Schools Lodges and Societies* (Vicksburg, 1908). On Mississippi's urban middle class, see McMillan, *Dark Journey*, 164–186.

46 Miller to Walter White, Sept. 3, 1918, and Affidavit of Kate D. Hawkins, 11 July 1916, in NAACP Files, reel 14, frames 1, 36. . . .

47 Typescript letter to Brunini titled "Vicksburg, Miss. July 11–16," in the folder "Migration Study. Negro Migrants, Letters From 1916–17," Box 86, Series 6, National Urban League Records, Library of Congress [NUL]. . . .

48 One of the middle-class black informants in John Dollard's classic study of the Delta town of Indianola, Mississippi, "resented the charge of the whites [that all Negroes were immoral] because he knew what they do among

themselves, as well as with Negroes." Dollard pointed out that middle class blacks adopted Victorian sexual standards also as a way of distinguishing themselves from lower-class blacks. Dollard, *Caste and Class*, 424. . . .

49 "Vicksburg," in Folder "Migration Study Mississippi Summary," Box 86, Series 6, NUL. . . .

50 See for example McMillan, *Dark Journey*, 302–304.

51 James R. Grossman, *Land of Hope: Chicago, Black Southerners, and the Great Migration* (Chicago, 1989), Part I.

52 Frank Andrews to Theodore Bilbo, 26 June 1917, typescript copy in folder "Migration Study. Negro Migrants, Letters From 1916–17," Box 86, Series 6, NUL. . . .

53 These numbers are summarized from the database of Beck and Tolnay. . . .

54 Quoted in Jane Lang Scheiber and Harry N. Scheiber, "The Wilson Administration and the Wartime Mobilization of Black Americans, 1917–18," *Labor History*, 10 (1969), 441.

55 After the war Governor Bilbo blamed the reception of Negro soldiers by a "certain class of white women in France" for some of the lynchings that had taken place; see VEP, 2 August 1919.

56 McMillen, *Dark Journey*, 302–307; John A. Miller to Walter White, 3 Sept. 1918, NAACP, reel 14, frames 36ff. . . . In addition, African American women in Vicksburg were not allowed to volunteer for canteen work because white volunteers objected to their wearing the Red Cross uniform: Alice Dunbar Nelson to Hannah Jane Patterson, 23 August 1918, Box 512, Folder 131, Central Office File, Records of the Council of National Defense, Committee on Women's Defense Work, Record Group 61, National Archives and Records Service, Suitland, Md [CWDW].

57 VEP, 17 July 1918.

58 VEP, 8 July 1918. White newspapers also took note of black soldiers serving in France. For other stories about black participation in the war, see VEP, 6 June 1917, 8 April 1918, 22 June 1918, 13 February 1919. . . .

59 VEP, 22 August 1918. Nelson . . . came to Vicksburg as a representative of the Committee on Women's Defense Work of the Council of National Defense. . . . The National Urban League's investigator noted that, since the out-migration of blacks had begun, white men in the town of Greenwood, on the edge of the Delta, "have been seen to tip their hats to colored ladies." "Greenwood," in Folder "Migration Study Mississippi Summary", Series 6, Box 86, NUL. . . .

60 VEP, 26 June 1918. . . .

61 VEP 25 June 1918.

62 VEP 27 June 1918.

63 McMillen, *Dark Journey*, 304. . . . There is no suggestion in the sources that white Vicksburgers knew about the NAACP chapter, but two other African Americans, William P. Harrison, a pharmacist, and D. D. Foote, a dentist, were also members and probably escaped tarring and feathering only because they were out of town on July 23. Harrison, who was later reclassified and drafted by Vicksburg's draft board, told the NAACP that "this fight upon us" came about because "we used both our time and money to fight the wrongs done our people in that section." Harrison to John R. Shillady, 25 September 1918, NAACP, reel 14, f.117.

64 Miller to Walter White, 3 Sept.1918, NAACP, reel 14, frame 36. . . . On the NAACP during the war, see David Levering Lewis, *W.E.B. DuBois: Biography of a Race, 1869–1919* (New York, 1993), 501–580.

65 VDH, 24 July 1918.

66 VEP 24 July 1918.

67 Miller to Walter White, 3 Sept. 1918, NAACP, reel 14, frame 36.

68 David R. Roediger argues that even for white workers in the antebellum North, blacks were seen not only as "noncitizens," but "anticitizens": *Wages of Whiteness*, 57.

69 Miller to John Shillady, 29 Oct. 1918, NAACP, reel 14. . . .

70 VDH, 24 July 1918. Less plausibly, Cook was also accused of saying "there would be no race distinction after the war is won by Germany and the negro and white children will be sent to the same schools." VDH, 25 July 1918. . . .

71 VDH, 25 July 1918.

72 Miller to John Shillady, 8 August 1918, NAACP, reel 14.

73 VEP, 24 July 1918; VDH 25 July 1918. . . . Occupational identifications were made with the Vicksburg City Directory for 1918.

74 VEP, 25 and 26 July 1919; VDH, 27 and 31 July 1919.

75 VEP, 26 and 27 July 1918; VDH, 26, 31 July 1918. The meeting on the 26th was attended by most of the same men who had published the statement condemning the violence against Cook and Miller as well as other leading businessmen and lawyers.

76 William F. Holmes, "Whitecapping: Agrarian Violence in Mississippi, 1902–1906," *Journal of Southern History*, 35 (1969), 165–185; Brundage, *Lynching in the New South*, 19–28. . . .

77 Williamson, *Crucible of Race*, esp. 259–284.

78 VEP, 26 July1918; VDH, 27 July 1918. While Wilson's statement did not touch on race as an issue, it was partly a response to intense pressure brought to bear on Wilson from black leaders in the North and even members of his own administration to condemn racial violence; see Scheiber and Scheiber, "Wilson Administration," 456–457.

79 Almost immediately after that attack on the women, the police chief and mayor claimed that the incident was separate from the earlier attacks on Miller and Cook, but the evidence strongly suggests the same men were instigators in both events. Miller told the NAACP that he had been taken to city hall by, among others, "public auto driver Patterson," almost certainly the same Frank Patterson prosecuted for the attack on the women. . . .

80 VEP 22 March 1919. . . .

81 Ibid., 19 April 1919. See McMillen, *Dark Journey*, 302–307, for a discussion of Mississippi blacks' responses to the war.

82 VEP 5 Feb. 1919; VDH, 26 March 1919.

83 VEP, 7 Feb. 1919; VDH, 8 April 1919.

84 While Mississippi was one of the states that rejected the amendment, the issue generated little newspaper controversy. Many Mississippians, including former Senator James K. Vardaman, nationally known as a staunch champion of white supremacy, supported women's right to vote; see William F. Holmes, *The White Chief: James K. Vardaman* (Baton Rouge, La., 1970).

85 VEP 7 February 1919.

86 VEP, 25 and 26 April 1919.

87 VDH, 15 April 1919. . . .

88 VEP, 28 March 1919, 9 April 1919. The latter story was reprinted from the *London Daily Express*.

89 VEP, 17 April 1919. . . .

90 VEP, 19 April 1919.

91 VEP, 23, 24 April, 7, 8, and 9 May, 1919. . . .

92 VEP, 14 May 1919.

93 Ibid., 15 May 1919. Unless otherwise noted, the detailed description of the events below comes from this source. This day's edition and other documents related to the lynching can be found in NAACP, reel 14, frames 261ff.

94 VEP 16 May 1919. . . .

95 Ibid.

96 Coming at a time when . . . lynching "had little articulate opposition" from editorial writers, religious leaders, or government officials, and when lynchers could expect complete immunity from punishment, such language is doubly remarkable: McMillan, *Dark Journey*, 245–251.

97 See letter from "Prof. J. H. Culkin," and other reports, ibid. . . .

98 VDH 18 May 1919.

99 VEP, 15 May 1919.

100 VEP, 17 May 1919.

101 See note 24, above.

102 VDH, 22 May 1919.

103 Letter from "G.A.S.," VDH, 22 May 1919. . . .

104 Identifications were made in the Vicksburg City Directory for 1918, and for some cases, 1912.

105 *Who's Who in Colored America, 1928–1929*, 266; Williams College *Reunion Book, 1933*, 21–22.

106 Alice Dunbar Nelson to Hannah Jane Patterson, 23 August 1918, Box 512, Folder 131, CWDW. . . .

107 For a treatment of the Southern Ku Klux Klan that emphasizes the importance of gender ideologies . . ., see Nancy MacLean, *Behind the Mask of Chivalry: The Making of the Second Ku Klux Klan* (New York, 1994).

108 VEP, 7 and 12 July 1919. Occupations of Grand Jury members were found in the city directories or the 1910 manuscript U.S. Census of Population.

5

NEW WOMEN

Nancy A. Hewitt

Here, Nancy A. Hewitt examines the "new women" of the 1920s in the southern urban borderland of Tampa, Florida. The mosaic of race and ethnicity in Tampa, a center of cigar manufacturing, was unusual. The labor force in the cigar factories was largely Cuban and Italian. As Hewitt demonstrates, gender, class, and ethnic identity were cross-cutting factors in the shaping of women's public activism in Tampa. By the 1920s, Anglo, Latin, and African-American women had all developed traditions of organization, but the nature and goals of their organizations varied. Working-class Latin women, for example, focused on labor organizing rather than on the (segregated) voluntary associations created by native women, both white and black.

The coming of woman suffrage made a difference in the early 1920s, as women "organized more frequently as women" even as they also "joined mixed-sex associations in greater numbers than ever before." Among women of the same class, "the increasing salience of gender identity to social activism . . . helped bridge differences of nationality among Black (African-American and Afro-Cuban) and white (Latin and Anglo) women." But the "fault lines" in women's activism remained, and in many ways "the expansion of women's efforts and organizations actually highlighted differences among Latin, African-American, and Anglo communities." In the longer run, woman suffrage had less of an impact than either its supporters or its detractors had expected.

* * *

On November 10, 1916, women tobacco stemmers from the Lozano and Sidelo Cigar Company walked out, demanding higher wages. They marched to other factories, calling out the workers, and by nightfall some 1,500 cigar makers had left their benches, and another 8,500 threatened to join them. The spontaneity and militancy of the movement was recognized as the work of women. Celestino Vega, the factory owner, sought "protection" for his male rollers when they were accosted by a "disorderly mob of strikers" who "rushed into the factory deriding and hooting workers ... women, leading the mob, called the men at work 'females' and offered their skirts to those who refused to quit." The actual term used by the women wildcatters was reported in Havana's *La Lucha* as *"afeminadas,"* suggesting that the men were feminine, or even effeminate, rather than that they were women.[1] Though Mayor D. B. McKay was probably unaware of the nuances of the insult, he assured Vega that police would be on hand the next day to secure the premises and protect the male rollers.[2]

Factory owners and city officials were not alone in opposing this strike. The male leaders of the local Cigar Makers' International Union (CMTU) derided the wildcat venture from the beginning and, even though some men joined the strike, accused the women of responding to "blind enthusiasm." The editor of *El Internacional* queried his readers, "May a man now say what he thinks without exposing himself to the dangers of being insulted by his female comrades who offer him their skirts?" The strike was soon settled, though the greatest benefits went to the cigar rollers (mostly men) rather than to the stemmers (all women) who had initiated the action.[3]

If the 1916 walkout had stood alone, it might be considered just a colorful anecdote, but it marked a turning point in women's public and political roles in the Latin community. In [previous strikes in] 1901 and 1910, ... Cuban and Italian women had become politically active—petitioning the governor and the Anglo wives of vigilantes, marching on the mayor's office, attacking strikebreakers, and honoring heroic women through manifestos—but they had justified their actions largely in the language of class solidarity and maternal protection. By 1916 ... women wildcatters chose sexual ridicule over labor solidarity and maternal rhetoric. Although the 1916 walkout failed to achieve its goals, over the next decade, the rising tide of women in the cigar labor force became increasingly critical to union success, and class and ethnic identities became increasingly infused with gender.

Latin women were not alone in their newfound sense of importance to public and political action. In the weeks before the wildcat strike, Anglo women launched a campaign on behalf of a woman school board candidate—Alice Snow—who ran in District 2, which included [the immigrant enclave known as] Ybor City.[4] A year earlier, the Florida legislature had passed the Municipal Reform Act, allowing municipalities to set their own rules on a number of electoral matters.[5] Neighboring cities, including St. Petersburg, instituted municipal suffrage for women; Tampa did not, so women remained dependent on male voters to make their case. Still, they insisted on running a woman candidate and learned a valuable lesson: Alice Snow lost to the Reverend Irwin Walden by only fifteen votes out of nearly four thousand cast, the margin of defeat provided by a set of contested ballots from Ybor City's

Twenty-sixth Precinct.[6] Again, women acting independent of men failed to achieve their goal, but this failure, too, inspired women to demand additional rights based on sex.

The urge to organize around women's issues and concerns also intensified for African American women during this period, as their significance in community efforts expanded. The Tampa School of the Household Arts served as one base for such efforts, but even more important was a new array of women's clubs and women's institutions, including the Willing Workers, the Busy Merry Makers, the Mary Talbert Club, and the Helping Hand Day Nursery. It was in the context of this profusion of single-sex organizing that women joined the effort to regain Black voting rights.

African American women, however, did not follow the lead of their Latin and Anglo counterparts in directly challenging the power and authority of men in their community. Rather, they continued to pursue common agendas in both mixed-sex and single-sex movements throughout the 1910s and 1920s. Now, however, women wielded skills honed in single-sex associations to ensure a critical place for themselves in wider efforts at community advancement. In fall 1920, for instance, they organized with men against a city charter "reform" that would further limit the electoral clout of African American and immigrant neighborhoods. Coming just after the federal woman suffrage amendment was ratified, Black women also used the occasion to launch a voter registration drive, insisting that the new law be implemented in racially inclusive ways.

These bursts of woman-centered activism in the late 1910s and early 1920s made many men take notice and made some, especially Anglo male civic leaders, wary of furthering women's formal political clout. The recognition of women's heightened influence occurred in a period when men were already anxious about female autonomy. On the very day of the wildcat walkout in November 1916, for instance, the *Tampa Morning Tribune* ran an article on women leading public prayers at a national woman suffrage convention, a practice the reporter considered "a rather new departure." That same week, Tampa's Wesleyan Baraca Club was debating the resolution, "That money has a greater influence on men than woman has," indicating that an organization once dedicated to prayer and missionary work had now turned its attention to more secular and gendered concerns. The *Ragged Princess*, showing at one local movie house that week, told the story of a poor orphan girl capturing the heart, and hand in marriage, of a wealthy man through her beauty and charm, while *Fifty-Fifty*, offered at another theater, presented a vampish Norma Talmadge in a tale of marriage, adultery, and intrigue. The *Tribune*, meanwhile, ran a feature story entitled "America a Market for Chinese Slave Women," which provided

Sunday readers with lurid details about prostitution, slavery, and the sale of wives. . . .[7]

Women's actions and the images conveyed in public debates, films, newspaper reports, and advertisements suggested the new opportunities available to women and the anxieties haunting men.[8] Despite the tendency of the national media and many historians to focus solely on the emergence of the "New Woman" in northeastern cities, Tampa residents knew that transformations in gender expectations and experiences also affected Black, Latin, and Anglo women in their hometown.

After 1915, Tampa women pursued public power in increasingly vocal ways and advocated agendas that took sex seriously. Collectively, they demonstrated a new sophistication regarding political action that drew on a range of resources—the Latin heritage of labor militancy, northern models of social housekeeping, the social gospel, racial pride, African American and Latin traditions of self-help and mutual aid, and ideals of the "New Woman." While the passage of the Nineteenth Amendment certainly reinforced this trajectory for some women in Tampa, the dynamics of sexual politics in Latin, African American, and Anglo communities were changing well before its ratification. The issues and timing varied, but in each case, a shift in the balance of public power between women and men occurred before women gained voting rights and proved significant even when the vote failed as an effective vehicle for implementing change.

Many Anglo and African American women eagerly embraced their newly won political rights in 1920. African American women in the South were soon disfranchised, however, which meant that once again they would follow paths traced out by earlier generations of Black women. Latin women, too, worked largely outside electoral politics. But they remained committed to workplace organizing as the most potent weapon in their arsenal, whereas African Americans pursued economic autonomy and community advancement through voluntary associations, church-based organizations, and schools.

Whether or not they wielded the power of the franchise, African American, Latin, and Anglo women each organized more frequently as women and around women's issues in the late 1910s and 1920s. At the same time, they joined mixed-sex associations in greater numbers than ever before, gaining leverage there through the benefits achieved by single-sex organizing. Despite women's increased participation in single-sex and mixed-sex organizations and in campaigns to advance the cause of women and various class, race, and ethnic communities, the fault lines of Tampa activism did not disappear. In some ways, the expansion of women's efforts and organizations actually highlighted differences among Latin, African American, and Anglo communities.*

Whatever Tampa women's attitudes, World War I did not so much transform their activism as accentuate trends already evident. For instance, women's war work provided further justification for the establishment of single-sex associations among Black and Anglo women, quickened the movement of Latin women into the labor force, and fostered women's interest in national and international politics. The crises created by global conflict did not erase the divisions among women activists, however. Instead, the wartime emergency intensified debates over women's proper place in their communities and in the larger society.

For African American women, the war crystallized efforts initiated earlier. In early 1917, graduates of the Tampa School of the Household Arts formed the first Black YWCA in Tampa, under the direction of Blanche Armwood. Its officers, all graduates of the school, dedicated themselves to the "interests of the working girls" and "mutual helpfulness." .... The women who filled the positions of president, vice-president, corresponding and recording secretary, treasurer, and pianist in the new organization—Mrs. Lucy Hall, Mrs. Minnie Lorey, Mrs. Albertha Downing, Mrs. Anna Daniels, Mrs. Hattie Shingles, and Mrs. Bessie Johnson—had not been leaders in earlier organizations; but in January 1917, their names were published in the *Tampa Bulletin*, a local Black paper.[9] The African American YWCA survived for only two years, but it suggested the possibility for an expanded corps of leaders in the community.

Tampa's best-known Black woman activist was Blanche Armwood, who had organized and served as first president of the Colored Women's Clubs of Tampa in 1912. By the end of the decade, she had become a significant player in state, regional, and national organizations. Her very success, however, drew her away from Tampa and local concerns. ... By 1920, she was traveling the country promoting candidates for the Republican party and woman suffrage for the National Association of Colored Women Clubs.[10]

As Armwood's absences from the city lengthened, the leadership of Black women's efforts shifted to teachers and businesswomen still rooted in the community. Mrs. Christina Meacham of the Harlem Academy; Mrs. Emma Mance from the West Tampa School; Mrs. Gertrude Chambers, Mrs. Lila B. Robinson, and Miss Annie House, all hairdressers; and Preston Murray, the wife of a prominent undertaker,

---

* A section on women's activism in Tampa during WWI has been omitted—ed.

were among the most active clubwomen in Tampa during the 1910s and 1920s. They eagerly embraced an African American version of the "New Woman" that emphasized cultural pride and civic activism, even as they remained concerned about the exploitation of southern Black women.[11]

The African American "New Woman," like her white counterpart, was encouraged to adopt new fashions in clothing, hair care, and cosmetics. Black beauticians in the city were especially active in combining innovative styles with racial advancement.[12] Rather than substitute fashion for activism, they used the profits offered by the former to fund the latter. By 1920, Chambers, Robinson, and House—all of whom worked in the same beauty shop—held leadership positions in several Black women's clubs. In the following years, they increased their involvement in these associations, joined in the establishment of the interracial and mixed-sex Urban League, and helped develop the first cooperative efforts with Afro-Cuban women in the city.

Latin women, too, combined work in mixed-sex associations focused on community advancement with activities in single-sex organizations that promoted women's interests. On the political front, Latin women and men raised funds to support the Russian Revolution . . . and the Nicola Sacco and Bartolomeo Vanzetti defense fund. They also joined efforts in some two dozen food and clothing cooperatives founded in the 1910s and held positions of leadership in some. Here, however, they often initiated their own projects. In 1915, Cuban and Italian housewives led the campaign against an ordinance that threatened to increase the price of bread; and in 1917, they sustained a potato, meat, and onion boycott.[13]

Despite cooperative community ventures, it became increasingly difficult for Latin working women to maintain their common ground with men on the factory floor. In March 1917, stemmers pleaded with their skilled male coworkers to join them in "improving the conditions of the stripping department." They conceded that this department was "a proper place for women of our people to earn their living," but they argued women would continue to compete with men for more skilled positions if their conditions and wages did not keep pace with those of the cigar makers. Claiming that "orphan girls, maids who fortunately or unfortunately have no male helper, widows with young children, the victims of divorce, the daughters of large families, the victims of vicious men or of sick or disabled men" constituted the bulk of this work force, the stemmers retreated from their earlier sexual innuendoes and called on Latin men to protect working women. At the same time, they implied that if men refused, competition between the sexes would be the consequence.[14]

Over the next two years, developments in the national industry

further threatened labor solidarity among local Latins. First, the introduction of stemming machines lessened the need for hand workers
and allowed "American girls"—that is native-born women with no
experience—to enter the industry. Second, employers tried to substitute
cans for boxes in cigarpacking, which again allowed unskilled workers,
including women, to replace men in one of the industry's most highly
coveted positions. When packed in boxes, owners demanded that the
top row of cigars be of the same texture, leaf style, and color, which
could be achieved only by highly skilled workers. When packed in
cans, such aesthetic concerns and the skills they required were irrelevant. In 1919, in the midst of a national wave of postwar industrial
strikes, cigar workers in Tampa walked out to protest both stemming
machines and "girl" packers.[15]

What allowed Latin women and men to make common cause despite these structural changes was owners' interest in hiring "American
girls" to pack cigar cans and operate stemming machines. In February
1919, stemmers and cigar makers walked out at [four] factories in West
Tampa after the owners installed stemming machines, which workers
claimed would displace six to eight workers each. The issue, however,
was not only mechanization but also the entrance of native-born white
women as operators. Packers joined the struggle on behalf of their own
issues, demanding that women packers serve the same apprenticeship
as men and be paid the same wages, which would negate employers'
interest in hiring them.[16]

The "American girls" who gained jobs in the cigar industry did not
have a long history of labor activism behind them, but they did not
accept their exclusion without a fight. They immediately sought the
intervention of white civic leaders. A group of twenty-two machine
tenders petitioned Tampa's mayor, D. B. McKay, noting that the "work
is agreeable and we need the wages." "As residents of Tampa and
American citizens," they claimed, "we are entitled to fair play." The
native-born white women hired to operate the stemming machines
shared much with their Latin counterparts; many were also orphaned,
widowed, divorced, or daughters in large families. But the two groups
rarely considered making common cause. Rather, "American girls"
appealed to Anglo civic leaders and national values, while Latin
women struck alongside union men.[17]

Women packers also called on Anglo civic leaders, including the
American Legion and the city council as well as the mayor, but they
turned to white working-class men as well, requesting a separate
affiliation under the auspices of the American Federation of Labor (AFL)
to counterbalance the power of the Latin-dominated Cigar Makers'
International Union (CMIU) packers. The men packers pointed out that
their AFL charter eliminated the need and the possibility for a separate

women's local. The men then struck those factories that allowed women to work without passing through the apprenticeship and the test of packing skills required by their charter. In this case, the factory owners backed down and accepted the terms of the Latin men, releasing the "American girls" they had once hoped would provide them leverage against the unions.[18]

Yet the story of Anglo women versus Latin workers was not quite as simple as it appeared in women's petitions and CMIU protests. The delegation of women packers that sought assistance from the American Legion and the group that petitioned the city council included a more diverse lot than suggested in either the English- or Spanish-language press. Several of the Anglo women had been employed in the cigar industry for some time but in jobs reserved for women. Myrtle Albritton, Rosa Hendrix, and Martha Gouch, for instance, worked as cigar banders before seeking employment as packers. . . . The conflict occurred, then, not because "American girls" sought work in a Latin industry but because they sought work as packers, a "man's" job. Similarly, Latin women protested native-born women working as machine operators not because they were native-born but because mechanization threatened to curtail work for women in general. Many Anglo civic leaders and factory owners, like Latin workers, assumed that native-born women sought these positions because they lacked any tradition of labor militancy. Yet the ethnic identities of several petitioners were more complicated than the term "American girls" suggests. Mary Alonzo, for example, was a native-born white woman, but she married an Italian cigar maker and lived on Garcia Avenue in Ybor City. Similarly, Winona Cabrera married a Cuban cigar maker, Esteban; and the Anglo Cassie Fernández sought work as a packer alongside her husband, Adolphus, who had held that position for several years. Other petitioners, such as Carmen Bussetti, were born in the United States but had been reared in an immigrant family. . . . These "American girls" thus included second-generation immigrants and the Anglo wives of Latin cigar workers.[19]

Despite the complexity of the petitioners' identities, the conflicts of 1919 revealed both the potential for Anglo working women to organize on their own behalf and their capacity to revitalize solidarity between Latin women and men. During the 1919 strike, male union leaders proclaimed the importance of Latin women's support and refused to accept a settlement that would have benefited the most skilled workers, mainly men, but would have left the "clerks, strippers, and banders, [mostly women] to 'paddle their own canoe.'" Forgetting the ridicule they heaped on women wildcatters three years earlier, union leaders now claimed that "labor will ever be subservient . . . so long as they stand divided." Latin men once again embraced their sisters as partners to stave off the entrance of women into men's jobs and the introduction of machinery into cigar factories.[20]

As Latin women and men collaborated to limit Anglo women's entry into the cigar industry, they also campaigned against illicit activities that threatened to turn Ybor City and West Tampa into havens for gambling and prostitution. They attacked both Anglos who invested large sums of money in such activities and Latins who were seduced into supporting them. . . .

Reform-minded Anglo women were equally concerned about the moral condition of Ybor City and West Tampa. After prohibition was finally mandated by the Eighteenth Amendment to the U.S. Constitution in 1918, bootlegging flourished in Tampa. Although there was plenty of evidence that Anglo men were in charge of operations, Ybor City was the primary site of their activities. The WCTU [Women's Christian Temperance Union], now joined by members of the YWCA, the Tampa Civic Association, and other women's organizations, redoubled efforts to clean up the ethnic enclaves and to rescue women and children from the depredations of alcoholic husbands. At least some, however, may have realized that the root problem lay in the profits made by Anglo entrepreneurs, which fueled not only bootlegging in the ethnic enclaves but also political corruption in the city as a whole.

As early as 1912, the *Jacksonville Dixie*—a reform newspaper—had proclaimed, "Tampa is reeking in crime, and gamblers in the open operate in various parts of the city." The king of crime in the city, the report claimed, was Charlie Wall, descendant of [a] prominent pioneer family, . . . and related by marriage to D. B. McKay.[21] In 1916, the *Tribune* had accused McKay, who was the rival editor of the *Tampa Daily Times*, of being the beneficiary of Wall's gambling operations. McKay, married to the daughter of one of the largest cigar manufacturers, was then serving his second term as mayor and running for a third. Gambling and graft were linked to election fraud; and McKay received a large proportion of votes cast in Ybor City, the heart of Wall's machine.

The major form of profiteering in the ethnic enclaves was *bolita*—a numbers game.[22] In Cuba the numbers game functioned under the auspices of the state as the Cuban National Lottery, but in Tampa it flourished as part of a free enterprise system of gambling and graft. Manuel Suárez, a Spaniard, apparently introduced *bolita* to Ybor City in the late 1880s, and thereafter it was closely connected with the saloon trade. By 1900, there were more taverns in Ybor City than in all of the rest of Tampa. *Bolita* games were also being run from grocery stores and coffeehouses and in lavish gambling emporiums, such as El Dorado Club, which also housed prostitutes. The clubs were generally owned and managed by Spaniards and "protected" by Anglo politicians and police. Convinced of the sexual desires and desirability of

Caribbean women and confident that any illicit activities would be ignored, Anglo men haunted these clubs. After the ratification of prohibition, bootlegging joined *bolita* and brothels as a source of enormous profits and payoffs. Anglo sheriffs, county commissioners, mayors, and newspaper editors were linked into the system alongside their Latin collaborators.

Anglo women and Latin labor leaders were no match for the profits generated by gambling, prostitution, and rum-running. Any serious attempt to rein in corruption in Ybor City depended instead on a reconfiguration of local political power. When McKay won the mayoral election for a third time in 1916 based on disputed ballots from Ybor City, his opponents finally had sufficient moral authority to push for charter reform. Their plan, following municipal reform in other American cities, was to replace corrupt ward-based politics with a city commission form of government. Success was still a few years away, but the issue of good government had finally gained center stage.

In the face of these heated debates over political corruption, Anglo women began to question their exclusion from voting and officeholding. Throughout the South, the suffrage cause gained new adherents in the 1910s. In Florida, the first statewide suffrage meeting held in more than two decades opened in Tampa in 1917. Just a year after Alice Snow's defeat in the school board election, the gathering inspired twenty-one local women to organize the Tampa Equal Suffrage League. The war had directed attention to other issues, but members of the league felt certain that women's patriotic activities would reinforce arguments for their enfranchisement. Though claiming to support "equal suffrage," the organization was composed entirely of native-born white women.[23]

At the founding meeting, held in the council chamber at city hall, Snow signed on as a charter member and the organization's first secretary. The other officers . . . were less well known. The president, Ada Price, and vice-presidents, Mabel Bean and Elizabeth Hurn, had not been leaders in local clubs or voluntary organizations. But like Alice Snow, whose son, Fred, worked as a postal clerk, these women had connections to local civic affairs through male relatives. Ada's husband, Ivil O. Price, was active in the Republican party and would run for sheriff on that ticket in 1920; Bean's father had served as postmaster in the 1890s; and Hurn's husband also worked for the post office. The other officers—Sarah Chapman and Jane Davis—had fewer visible ties to political appointments or partisan contests; Chapman was a teacher, and Davis was the wife of a salesman and the mother of a teacher and a stenographer.[24]

. . . . Over the next two years, support for a state woman suffrage bill grew exponentially among Anglo Tampans, partly because those who insisted that voting rights should be regulated only by the states feared passage of a federal suffrage amendment. In March 1919, for instance, the *Tribune* editor declared, "GIVE THEM THE BALLOT," but demanded that it be granted by amending the state constitution, not by ratifying the federal amendment. Women advocates appear to have been less concerned about the *means* of obtaining the vote than about the end. Some supported state legislation granting women the right to vote in primaries (the most important elections in Florida's one-party system); others advocated a state constitutional amendment; and still others favored ratification of the Nineteenth Amendment.[25] Whatever position they took, a growing number of women were now demanding electoral rights.

In spring 1919, a "suffrage conference" was held in conjunction with the annual meeting of the white women's clubs in the city. It attracted representatives from a wide array of local organizations and from state and regional groups whose leaders would have shunned the cause just a few years earlier. The president of the Florida Federation of Women's Clubs and a Virginia leader of the United Daughters of the Confederacy offered rousing pro-suffrage speeches. The UDC spokeswoman advocated primary suffrage as the surest and quickest means of obtaining votes for southern women—which also virtually eliminated the possibility that Black women would benefit from an expanded electorate—and both argued for electoral rights on the basis of women's responsibilities to children, home, and community. A *Tribune* reporter in attendance assured readers that had a straw vote been taken at the conclusion of the meeting, "the women present were unanimously agreed" in favor, as were half the reporters.[26]

On Halloween weekend that year, the Tampa Equal Suffrage League hosted a second suffrage convention, attracting participants from the Tampa Civic Association, the Tampa Woman's Club, and other Anglo voluntary associations as well as attention from Doyle Carlton, a state senator; Dr. Louis Bize, a bank president; William Brorien, the president of the Peninsular Telephone Company; and Fred Turner, the secretary of the YMCA. Speeches by male civic leaders as well as Ada Price, Kate Jackson, and other league officers reflected the now widespread support for female suffrage in the city. The women speakers in particular emphasized the need to educate Florida women for their new responsibilities.[27]

Although racist diatribes against woman suffrage were popular among many southern legislators, Tampa Anglo civic leaders instead emphasized nativist claims for the vote's power to quash immigrant radicalism. Louis Bize declared that the "men of the South must push aside the old idea that the negro women will ever interfere by the voting privilege. It is nothing but a bugaboo." Instead, he claimed, "If there was ever a time when the women should have it [the vote], it is the present when the institutions that our fathers fought for are menaced by this propaganda of bolshevism." Claiming that Bolsheviks have "no religion and no God" and pointing out the links between bolshevism and labor unrest in Tampa, Bize concluded that "if the women had the ballot now, there would be fewer strikes."[28] Once again, the multicultural character of the Cigar City subverted racial orthodoxy, this time in the service of white women's rights.

In the following months, both the Tampa Civic Association and the Tampa Woman's Club sponsored Suffrage Days to keep their members informed on the issue of enfranchisement. Yet the most important weapon Anglo women wielded remained their collective strength as lobbyists. It appears that even as leading clubwomen were drawn to suffrage, leading suffragists were drawn to clubwork. In 1920, both Ada Price and Jane Davis were elected for the first time to offices in the Tampa Civic Association—Price as president—and they carried on their suffrage activities increasingly in the context of larger voluntarist efforts.[29]

Tampa clubwomen also expanded their work within statewide and national organizations, including the Florida Federation of Women's Clubs, the General Federation of Women's Clubs, the WCTU, and the YWCA, all of which now endorsed suffrage. At the October 1917 meeting of the state federation, held in Tampa, president May Mann Jennings, the wife of the former governor and an active suffragist, announced a campaign to double the membership of the organization, urging affiliated clubs to recruit additional members and encouraging them to form new associations. Caroline Hawkins of Tampa was elected vice-president of the state organization and was placed in charge of Americanization and child welfare programs. Kate Jackson was active in raising an endowment fund for the federation and expanding the organization's work on civic development. Local members campaigned for laws regulating child labor, juvenile crime, gambling, prostitution, public health, the environment, and civil service while lobbying for fire escapes at schools, teacher certification guidelines, traveling libraries, women school board appointees, state reformatories for boys and girls, and the abolition of convict leases.[30] All of these efforts would be enhanced if women gained the vote. . . .

In August 1920, when Tennessee became the thirty-sixth state to ratify the Nineteenth Amendment granting woman suffrage, Florida legislators still refused to approve the measure. Nonetheless, Tampa women would soon have the opportunity to test their electoral capacities as a result of the continuing feud over charter reform among local politicians. Supporters of a commission system of municipal government wanted to reduce electoral graft, but their plan would also limit the power of immigrant and African American voters, who, under the existing ward system, could influence the choice of representatives from racially and ethnically homogeneous districts.[31] Charges of corruption in the 1916 mayoral election gave commission supporters their first serious chance at success, but it took until June 1920 for a charter committee to be elected. Just a month later, the committee proposed the replacement of the ward-based city council with a commission, all five members of which would be elected at large. In September, the state's attorney informed Tampa officials that the charter issue could not be resolved through the white Democratic primary but must be introduced to the general electorate, including newly enfranchised women. A binding referendum on the issue was scheduled for October.[32]

Politicians on both sides of the charter issue were suddenly confronted with an unexpected and unfamiliar constituency. A number of Tampa civic leaders voiced anxiety about "what the women voter [will] do with her newly acquired rights and privileges." Some envisioned African Americans flocking to the polls, while others imagined their Anglo counterparts forming "a party run and managed by women only."[33] Local men reassured one another, however, that women *would* "affiliate with one of the two old parties in this country" and that the new type of woman in politics "is not afraid to be charming. She works with, not against, men."[34] To ensure such solidarity, at least among whites, city officials traded in their earlier ambivalence about women's political capacities for paeans to "intelligent" womanhood. The state Democratic party chairman also began urging white women to register in order to counterbalance the feared influx of their African American counterparts. City officials aided the effort by assuring white residents that any Black registrants would be assigned to separate lines at polling places, thereby forestalling fears of racial mingling.

Throughout the fall, accusations that each side was courting Black ballots appeared alongside pleas for white female participation. On September 21, 1920, Wallace Stovall, editor of the *Tribune*, decried the "unexpected and uncouth treatment of the white women of Tampa" by opponents of the proposed city charter. The attack was aimed most directly at the *Tribune's* journalistic rival, the *Tampa Daily Times*, which supported the existing system of electing the council by ward. Stovall granted that the registration of women to vote was newsworthy, but he cried foul when the *Times* "embarrassed" socially prominent and "home-loving" women by making fun of their anxiety at the registration office, ridiculing them as "potential candidates for the office of commission," and, worst of all, printing "the age of those offering to register." Such actions are "certainly indicative," argued Stovall, "that among a certain class the old-time chivalry, deference and honor, reverence and protection, which the Southern gentlemen throw about woman has decayed most lamentably."[35]

In explaining the ill treatment of white women registrants, Stovall pointed to the opposition's deference to potential Black voters. He noted as evidence that "[n]ot one negro woman of Tampa has been embarrassed or humiliated by having cheap fun poked at her" in the *Times*. "Can it be that the opposition knows it can count on Negro women's vote to help defeat the charter . . . adoption of which means a cleaner Tampa, a better governed Tampa, a Tampa such as we have dreamed of?"[36] While concerned primarily with the *Times*'s alleged racial perfidy, the *Tribune* also acknowledged the likelihood that African American women would manage to register and vote. When state officials waived poll taxes for women in 1920 and ruled that the charter referendum had to be decided by the general electorate rather than through the white primary system, they opened the door for Black women's participation, and local officials, caught off guard, had not succeeded in closing it.

Although the *Tribune* suggested that only African American women would oppose the charter, white women were not simply pawns of pro-charter forces. Anglo women leapt into the fray on both sides. Members of the Equal Suffrage League and the Tampa Woman's Club met immediately after ratification to discuss their responsibilities and practically overnight published a pamphlet entitled "An Open Forum on Our Government for Women Voters." They then organized a series of meetings designed to prepare women to cast their first ballots.[37] Ada Price, presiding over one of these gatherings, noted that both Democrats and Republicans now claimed the honor of having produced suffrage for women. "Neither party has us roped and branded," she warned, "and they will never get us gagged."[38] White women thus declared their political independence. . . .

Anglo women were suddenly organizing, attending, and speaking at dozens of political meetings and rallies throughout the city. In early October, Julia Norris, past president of the Florida United Daughters of the Confederacy, spoke "eloquently" on behalf of the proposed charter. But her primary concern, like that of white male civic leaders, was "the heavy registration of Negro women," and she "emphasized the necessity of white women to accept it as their duty to register and vote since equal suffrage is now the policy of the country."[39] And 2,462 white women did register in 1920, constituting 32 percent of all whites on the voter rolls that year.[40]

The concern whites voiced about the potential political power of Black women was not simply a convenient trope for inspiring racial fears and inducing white women to vote. Such fears were certainly at work among charter advocates, but Black women and men were eager to participate for their own reasons. African American registration soared in 1920 when nearly 32 percent of local Blacks signed up to vote, including 1,298 women, who formed over 60 percent of the total Black registrants.[41] African American women claimed the right to vote both to redress men's disfranchisement and to further ongoing efforts at community advancement.[42] They not only registered and voted but also participated in the public debates preceding the referendum. Mrs. Inez Alston, for instance, who had gained community respect and experience in public speaking as a teacher and clubwoman, presided over a series of meetings on charter reform held at Black churches.

Much to the consternation of editor Stovall, several pro-charter advocates, including Julia Norris, Minnie Albury, and Judge Ernest Drumright, agreed to participate in these meetings. The *Tribune* refused to cover the discussion at the Bowman African Methodist Episcopal Church, until its anticharter rival, the *Tampa Daily Times*, pointed out the irony of "Judge Drumright, one of the founders of the White Municipal party and a staunch Democrat, addressing a Negro Republican meeting." Although the *Times* ignored the role of Black women in organizing the event, the *Tribune* noted that it was "earnest negro men and women" who had extended the invitation to Judge Drumright and three white women. Claiming that these "worthwhile negro residents" were seeking "advice and guidance" from the white speakers, Stovall insisted that it was only proper to comply. The danger to the racial status quo lay, he claimed, with the anticharter group, which sought "the support of the motley crowd of black people who were herded to the registration places by the negro policemen" or those registering at the Sunshine Club, a local gambling den that had been recently raided by federal prohibition agents.[43]

Awareness of activism in African American neighborhoods and fear that such efforts would disrupt fragile racial hierarchies help explain why so many Anglos, already in control of elections through the white primary, felt it necessary to further dilute minority voting power through at-large elections. These fears of Black political power ... motivated white civic leaders to enlist the electoral aid of their female counterparts even if they could not entirely control their political opinions.

When the referendum was completed, white women had fulfilled the hopes of charter advocates. On October 20, the *Tribune* headline blared, "Charter Wins by 770, Commission Plan Triumphant Despite a High Vote Cast against in the Town's Black Belt." The story credited the victory to white women. According to the report, they recognized "that it was largely a contest between their votes and those of negroes" and that the new charter would provide "a weapon by means of which they could protect their homes and children." The *Tribune* concluded,

"Tampa women have shown they are able to rock the cradle and the politicians at the same time."[44]

.... Ignoring the anticharter sentiments of some white women and the presence of Black women, the *Tribune* cheered "the advent of women into politics." White women, a reporter claimed, were so eager to participate on election day that they "brought their babies with them in many instances to the polls." Even among Latins and African Americans, the article declared, "the better and more intelligent . . . the higher class, better informed, honest set, . . . helped to win the election by counterbalancing the votes" of the "idle and worthless."[45]

Of course, the *Tribune* reporters could only guess at how any group of city residents had actually voted. They based such speculations on a combination of wishful thinking—wanting to believe that most white women had followed the path to the polls carved out for them by white pro-charter men—and the analysis of precinct totals. The largest number of Black registrants, for instance, lived in . . . areas with the highest anticharter vote margins. . . . The highest pro-charter margins came from precincts . . . where white women had registered in particularly large numbers. . . .[46] Thus, civic leaders had some basis for applauding the "efficiency and intelligence" of white women who cast their first ballots. Hafford Jones, an inspector in the predominantly white Seventeenth Precinct, declared that "the women had voted 99 percent strong in that precinct and that he believed the women of the city deserved great credit for the way they had taken hold of things. He thought that at least one member of the city commission should be a woman."[47]

The reactions to African American voters, especially women, were more vituperative. Amos Norris, husband of the pro-charter advocate Julia Norris and an inspector in the heavily Black Ninth Precinct, claimed that the "worst class of negroes imaginable were present." Norris rejected the ballot of a Black man who purportedly gave the wrong address and several African American women who he thought "were under age." He also swore out a warrant against "Julia Sacio, negress," claiming that she was "paying off" voters at the polling station. Throughout the city, it was reported, "a large number of negroes had been systematically herded into the registration and poll tax offices by a negro policeman, and it is presumed that all of these voted against the charter." In addition, the members of the "old political ring" were accused of "forgetting their color and standing in life sufficiently as to engage in taking negro men and women to the polling places."[48]

Even though Black Tampans had been organizing for political rights, economic justice, and social services for more than a decade, Anglo civic leaders rejected the possibility that African American women and men might justifiably pursue political power on their own terms. Yet the very presence of a Black policeman and hundreds of Black voters reveals their ongoing desire for political power. Unfortunately, even effective organization among local African Americans could be defeated by a combination of racism and political corruption. The advent of woman suffrage did little to change that.

Suffrage actually proved a relatively weak weapon in the activist arsenal of Tampa women from any racial or ethnic group in the 1920s. Most continued to rely on voluntarism rather than voting as the best vehicle for promoting social reform in the city. Anglo women continued to vote, but widespread corruption made voting in local elections practically meaningless for men or women until the 1950s. Moreover, all but a handful of the African American women registered to vote in 1920 were knocked off the rolls by 1924 as white officials imposed racist literacy and poll tax requirements. When they were excluded, so were most of the Black men, who had used woman suffrage as a counterweight against their earlier disfranchisement. Blacks were thus forced, once again, to join Latins, who continued to voice their concerns through community-based organizations rather than electoral politics.

The most severe problems that confronted Latins—declining opportunities in the cigar industry, mechanization, and lack of union recognition—defied electoral solutions. Thus, when Cuban and Italian workers sought change, few viewed the vote as a likely weapon, despite the importance of Ybor City ballot boxes to the careers of Anglo civic leaders. In addition, Florida's poll tax and residency requirements discouraged immigrants from registering. In 1910, fewer than 10 percent of the city's adult Cubans and Spaniards and fewer than 3 percent of adult Italians had even become citizens. By 1930, Tampa ranked at the bottom of American cities with over 100,000 population with respect to the percentage of foreign-born adults who had acquired citizenship and voting privileges; and Latin women were less likely than their male kin to gain the benefits of citizenship, even after the passage of woman suffrage.[49] Woman suffrage, then, like so many other avenues of activism in Tampa, quickly became race-specific.

Latin women, however, made abundantly clear the importance of alternative political strategies and tactics. The industrywide cigar strike of 1910–21 proved the limits of both electoral and economic pressure. Despite growing tensions over changes in the sexual division of labor within the industry, the unity among the nearly 8,700 striking cigar workers was astounding. The union did not even bother to post pickets around the factories: "the committee says they don't need any as they have no fear that strikers will desert the ranks."[50]

Such unity had inspired white reactions from the first days of the strike in July 1920. Just as the charter committee was completing its work, Mayor D. B. McKay, at the behest of Anglo women leaders, offered the Children's Home as a refuge for the children of strikers. The Children's Home, however, which had been gutted by fire in June, had relocated to a refurbished cigar factory; and one of the new vice-presidents of the Children's Home, Mrs. Carolina Vega, was married to the man whose factory had been raided by unruly women four years earlier. He had been among the first to install stemming machines. Moreover, several board members had petitioned the state the previous year for a compulsory education statute that would require stricter enforcement of child labor laws in Ybor City, depriving some families of much needed wages.[51] Recognizing the links between Anglo women reformers and Latin factory owners, the workers rejected the offer, refusing to "leave [their] children to the tender mercy of men [or women] who will try to squeeze the lifeblood out of [us] while living."[52]

Latin families that needed assistance had an array of more palatable alternatives, which had been created by their own collective efforts. The CMIU, as in previous strikes, offered monetary benefits, soup kitchens, and moral support; and the local Labor Temple and mutual aid societies provided places where strikers could meet to exchange not only information but also food, clothing, and other necessities of life. During the 1920 battle over the closed shop, CMIU affiliates also formed the Committee of Public Health to coordinate relief efforts. The committee received donations not only from Latin shopkeepers and community leaders but also from union locals across the country.[53] Individual strikers could seek help as well from the clubs of which they were members. El Centro Asturiano, for instance, offered meeting rooms, medical services, emergency relief, and recreational activities for children throughout the strike. Church-sponsored missions and settlement houses, located in the heart of the Latin enclaves, provided another source of support.[54]

Throughout the summer of 1920, local business and political leaders, who still hoped that woman suffrage would be defeated, expressed far more concern with strikers' solidarity than with woman's rights.[55] Once again, the strategy for disrupting working-class unity involved offering "American girls" opportunities to replace Latin women and men in well-paying factory jobs. On the very day that Tennessee legislators ensured the ratification of the suffrage amendment, a manufacturers' journal, Tobacco Leaf, declared a new day for women, but their focus was economic rather than electoral. Noting that the Tampa strike had already lasted for two months, the Tobacco Leaf assured its readers that "girl packers" from across the country were pouring into the Cigar City and were finding "working conditions superior to their expectations." These young women, "earning twice as much as they have been accustomed" to, were declared the wave of the future by both leading manufacturers and local politicians.[56]

There were signs, however, that the owners' version of events might be more propaganda than reality. The vice-president of the Committee on Public Health was Mrs. Elizabeth Law, who was then head of the tobacco stemmers' union. She was native-born but native-born Black rather than Anglo.[57] A reporter for the *Tampa Citizen*, a labor paper, claimed that in general it was African American not Anglo women who entered stemmers' and packers' ranks during the 1920 strike. Manufacturers' hopes of filling the cigar benches with white women was "swiftly fleeting," declared the *Citizen*, since "American girls cannot be secured as long as they are forced to work at the same benches with negro girls."[58] Given cigar workers' earlier opposition to the hiring of Anglos and the contemporary attacks on Black women voters, Latin women's acceptance of African American coworkers is even more notable. Instead of walking out to protest Law's hiring, the stemmers elected her head of their union. This decision may have been intended more to challenge Anglo civic leaders than to embrace African American rights, or it may have reflected Law's acceptance by Afro-Cuban women, who now dominated the stemming rooms.

Latin cigar workers vied for attention with the charter fight during September and October 1920. When the referendum threatened to overtake union demands in the minds of Anglo residents, Latin women and children regained center stage by leading the "Biggest Labor Parade Ever Seen in Tampa," as one of the newspapers described it. While politicians sought support from local voters, strikers sought assistance from workers nationwide. As the charter battle neared its climax, workers called a mass meeting to reconfirm their commitment to continuing the strike.[59] On October 14, five days before the charter vote, more than twenty-five hundred strikers, "about 50 per cent of them women, crowded the Centro Asturiano Clubhouse to the doors" for a mass meeting called by the Committee of Public Health. . . . One of [the speakers] was Mrs. Cándida Bustamente. . . . Bustamente was active in the Methodist Home Missionary Society in both Ybor City and West Tampa and was preparing to present the local groups' report to the Latin district conference of the Methodist church the following week. Perhaps she was the "old lady" described by an *El Internacional* reporter who "electrified" the audience. Combining traditional paeans to women's familial roles with an anticapitalist jeremiad, she declared, "We, the wives and mothers, must choose to die, together with our children and our husbands, rather than submit to the unparalleled condition of servitude which the manufacturers impose upon us."[60]

Though "no vote was taken," the *Tribune* reported that the participants demonstrated their support for the leaders of the strike and their confidence in achieving victory.[61] Anglo leaders who focused only on the charter fight concluded that "very few Latin women voted, apparently taking little interest in government." Yet most recognized that this group was in fact the most effective among Tampa women in pursuing power by other means.[62]

On November 2, as Tampans in other sections of the city cast ballots in the national presidential election, the union's Committee of Public Health launched a publicity campaign to offset the lurid stories appealing in the local press, which union leaders believed were intended "to stir up mob spirit among the people of Tampa."[63] On November 6, AFL unions around the country participated in a "National Donation Day" in support of Tampa cigar workers. The *Tribune* ignored the effort, focusing instead on the activities of the White Municipal party as it prepared for the election of city commissioners necessitated by the passage of charter reform. The paper was sure, moreover, that the strike would soon be broken, allowing the city to return to normal after months of political and economic turmoil.

The strike, however, lasted another three months, and before it ended, Latin women did turn out to vote. On February 5, 1921, they cast their ballots on a resolution to end the strike.[64] We do not know how women voted, though the resolution passed. We do know that the following fall, women stemmers initiated a general strike. They walked out in protest over "short pay," suggesting that owners had not lived up to their part of the earlier agreement. When the union called a strike vote a few days later, the stemmers proclaimed that they "would stay out on strike regardless of the outcome of the vote."[65] Even within the union, Latin women viewed the ballot as only one instrument for wielding power; another was their control over the first step in the production process.

In the context of labor unrest and the entrance of women into electoral politics, activist identities and alliances were reconfigured. Sex-specific issues and organizations became more central to the activities of Latin, African American, and Anglo women even as women from each group continued to collaborate with men to achieve shared goals. But tensions over women's roles and gender priorities were more evident by 1920, particularly in the contest over charter reform among Anglos and in reaction to changing labor conditions among Latins. Even for African American men, women's prominence in the debates and the vote on charter reform must have caused some consternation.

The heightened focus on gender issues and women's organizations illuminated fault lines within African American, Latin, and Anglo communities, but it also provided the basis for strengthening and creating coalitions among women across these communities. For example, the circle of Latin women participating in Anglo women's voluntary associations widened. The changes were visible in 1921, when Anglo women followed the lead of their African American counterparts and formed a citywide federation, the Tampa League of Women's Clubs. Of course, Black women were excluded from this venture, and no Latin women were elected to a major office. Yet five Latin women served on the twenty-five-member board of directors, representing both older organizations, such as the Friday Morning Musicale and the Children's Home, and newer ones, including the American Association of University Women and the Business and Professional Women. Of course, those Latins who found their way into the offices of Anglo-dominated organizations did not represent the experiences of the masses of first- and second-generation immigrant workers. Mrs. Josefina Diaz, who achieved the loftiest position in Anglo voluntary ranks, served for a year as acting president of the Children's Home. She was married to a cigar factory owner, as was Mrs. Celestino Vega, who joined her on the board of the Tampa League of Women's Clubs. Their younger counterparts were college-educated professional women, mainly teachers, nurses, and the daughters of bankers, insurance agents, and ministers rather than cigar makers.[66]

Although there was some fear that female voluntarism would lose its significance once women gained the right to vote, such was not the case in Tampa.[67] Rather, when charter reform failed to resolve the problems of corruption and cronyism in Tampa politics, well-to-do women expanded their social reform efforts, ensuring that participation in electoral politics would supplement rather than substitute for voluntarism. In this context, Latin women's failure to embrace suffrage in significant numbers had little impact on interethnic cooperation.

African American women were far more committed to suffrage than were their Latin neighbors, but ultimately they were no more effective in using the vote to their advantage. In the context of Black women's disfranchisement, economic strategies reemerged as the lifeblood of racial advancement. It was on this ground that African American and Latin working women built their coalition. Although some Afro-Cuban women had attended classes at the Tampa School of the Household Arts, there was no sense then that they were co-workers with Blanche Armwood and other African American middle-class leaders of the program. Only with Elizabeth Law's election as head of the stemmer's local did Afro-Cuban and African American women forge their first truly collaborative efforts. By the mid-1920s, these connections would be extended by more affluent African American and Afro-Cuban women working on behalf of child care and community improvement.

The increasing salience of gender identity to social activism in the late 1910s and early 1920s helped bridge differences of nationality among Black (African American and Afro-Cuban) and white (Latin and

Anglo) women, at least those of the same class. Formidable barriers to communitywide efforts by women remained, however. Anglo, Black, and Latin activists might declare themselves "New Women," but differences of race and class would continue to obscure commonalities of sex as Tampa activists forged interracial and interethnic coalitions over the following decade.

NOTES

1 *La Lucha*, November 25, 1916. All articles were originally in Spanish, translated by Jane Mangan.
2 On the 1916 incident, see *Tampa Morning Tribune* [*TMT*], November 11, 17, and 25, 1916; and *El Internacional* [*EI*], December 1, 1916.
3 On the male strikers' response and the quote, see *EI*, December 1, 1916. . . . On the outcome of the strike, see *TMT*, November 17 and 25, 1916.
4 Alice Snow is often touted as the first woman in Tampa to run for elected office, but Adele Kossovsky apparently preceded her as a candidate, running in 1910. . . .
5 Randy Gardner and Steven F. Lawson, "At-Large Elections and Black Voting Rights in Tampa/Hillsborough County, 1910–1984," unpublished paper in author's possession, 3.
6 *TMT*, September 19, 1916.
7 Ibid., November 10, 11, and 12, 1916. . . .
8 The "New Woman" has been widely studied by historians, who in recent years have illuminated its working-class manifestations. The work still focuses, however, on northern cities. See, for example, June Sochen, *The New Woman in Greenwich Village, 1910–1920* (New York, 1972); Carroll Smith-Rosenberg, *Disorderly Conduct: Visions of Gender in Victorian America* (New York, 1985), 245–96; Kathy Peiss, *Cheap Amusements: Working Women and Leisure in Turn-of-the-Century New York* (Philadelphia, 1986); Joanne Meyerowitz, *Women Adrift: Independent Wage-Earning Women in Chicago, 1880–1930* (Chicago, 1988); John D'Emilio and Estelle Freedman, *Intimate Matters: A History of Sexuality in America* (New York, 1988), chap. 8; and Nan Enstad, *Ladies of Labor, Girls of Adventure: Working Women, Popular Culture, and Labor Politics at the Turn of the Twentieth Century* (New York, 1999).
9 *Tampa Bulletin*, January 20, 1917, clipping, Miscellaneous file, box 3, Armwood Family Papers, University of South Florida Library [USFL].
10 On Armwood's political career in the late 1910s and early 1920s, see boxes 2–4, Armwood Family Papers,; and Elizabeth Lindsay Davis, *Lifting as They Climb* (Washington, D.C., 1933), 264–65, 287.
11 Annie House married Emma Mance's son in the early 1920s and continued her work as a club leader. . . .
12 Black beauty culture associations were founded nationally in this period with the express purpose of encouraging beauty culturists "to take the full responsibilities as good citizens by participating in civic and community work" as well as promoting their occupation and improving their techniques. . . .; see Tiffany Gill, " 'Never Wanted to Do Anything but Hair': Beauty Salons, Hairdressers, and the Formation of African American Female Entrepreneurship" (paper presented at Rutgers University, Spring 1999), 11 (quote).

13 On communitywide organizing, see Gary R. Mormino and George I. Pozzetta, *The Immigrant World* of *Ybor City: Italians and Their Latin Neighbors in Tampa, 1885–1985* (Urbana, Ill., 1987), 151, 152, 157–59; and *EI*, September 5 and 12 and November 7 and 14, 1919.

14 "The Strippers' Problem," *EI*, March 2, 1917 (original in English). *Tobacco stripper* and *stemmer* were synonymous terms.

15 *TMT*, August 17, 1918, January 16, February 6 and 8, and November 16, 1919; *Tampa Times*, January 7, 1919; *Tobacco Leaf*; March 13, 1919. The events of 1919 were also covered extensively in Havana's *La Lucha*.

16 Ibid.

17 The American stemmers' petition is covered in *TMT*, February 8, 1919, along with the strike of Latin stemmers, which is also covered in *TMT*, February 6, 1919; and *Tobacco Leaf*; March 13, 1919.

18 On women packers, see *TMT*, November 16 and December 5 and 12, 1919.

19 The names of petitioners listed in the *TMT*, December 5, 1919, were linked with information in the Tampa City Directory, 1919, 1920, to determine residence, previous occupation, and husband's or sister's occupation. . . .

20 *EI*, December 1919 (date illegible).

21 Charles E. Jones, "Sodom or Gomorrah-or Both," *Jacksonville Dixie*, June 27, 1912, quoted in Gary Mormino and George Pozzetta, "The Political Economy of Organized Crime, Bolita and Bootlegging in Tampa," n.d. (unpublished paper in author's possession), 417.

22 The discussion of *bolita* and political corruption is based on Mormino and Pozzetta, "The Political Economy of Organized Crime," 416–20.

23 On suffrage campaigns in the South generally, see Marjorie Spruill Wheeler, *New Women of the New South: The Leaders* of *the Woman Suffrage Movement in the Southern States* (New York, 1993); and Elna C. Green, *Southern Strategies: Southern Women and the Suffrage Question* (Chapel Hill, 1997). On the Equal Suffrage League, see Doris Weatherford, *A History of Women in Tampa* (Tampa, 1991), 92–93; and "Florida," in *History of Woman Suffrage* (Washington, D.C., 1922), ed. by Ida Husted Harper, 6: 113–20.

24 On the backgrounds of Equal Suffrage League officers, see Tampa City Directory, 1918; and the *Tampa Daily Times* [*TDT*], October 8, 1920. . . .

25 *TMT*, March 22, 1919, includes an editorial and discussion of a range of women's positions on woman suffrage.

26 See coverage in ibid., March 22 (first quote) and April 1 and 3 (second quote), 1919.

27 Ibid., November 1, 1919.

28 On the activities of the Equal Suffrage League, see ibid., October 28 and 31 and November 1, 1919; Weatherford, *A History of Women in Tampa*, 92–93; Crake, " 'In Unity there Is Strength': The Influence of Women's Clubs in Tampa, 1900–1940" (M.A. Thesis, University of South Florida, 1988), 56–58; and Tampa Civic Association, Minute Book, 1916–23, Hillsborough County Federation of Women's Club Papers, USFL. . . .

29 Tampa Civic Association, Minute Book, 1916–23.

30 Lucy Worthington Blackman, *The Florida Federation of Women's Clubs, 1895–1939* (Jacksonville, Fl., 1939), 30–35; *Florida Times-Union*, October 4, 1917.

31 Although the institution of the white primary minimized African American voting after 1910, white civic leaders continued to voice concern about Black ballots and sought additional ways to ensure African American disfranchisement.

32 On the charter battle, see Gardner and Lawson, "At-Large Elections and

Black Voting Rights in Tampa/Hillsborough County, 1910–1984"; and *TMT* and *TDT*, for July through October 1920, esp. July 24, August 25, and October 2, 6, 14, 20, and 21.

33 *TMT*, August 25, 1920; *TDT*, October 2, 1920. . . .

34 *TDT*, October 2, 1920. . . .

35 Editorial, *TMT*, September 21, 1920.

36 Ibid.

37 Crake, " 'In Unity There Is Strength,' " 67.

38 *TMT*, October 8, 1920. . . .

39 *TDT*, October 6, 1920.

40 For registration figures, see *TMT*, October 18, 1920. For population figures, see U.S. Bureau of the Census, *Abstract of the Fourteenth Census of the United States, 1920* (Washington, D.C., 1923), ii, 4–15, 130–31. . . .

41 Registration and population figures are taken from the sources listed in note 40. The percentages are approximate. . . .

42 . . . see Evelyn Brooks Higginbotham, "In Politics to Stay: Black Women Leaders and Party Politics in the 1920s," in *Women, Politics, and Change*, ed. Louise Tilly and Patricia Gurin (New York, 1990), 199–220.

43 Editorial in the *TMT*, October 11, 1920, quoting the *TDT* article published earlier that week.

44 *TMT*, October 20, 1920.

45 Ibid.

46 For registration totals, see *TDT*, October 18, 1920; on pro-charter and anti-charter vote margins by precinct, see *TDT*, October 21, 1920. . . .

47 *TMT*, October 20, 1920. . . .

48 Norris, quoted in *TMT*, October 20, 1920.

49 For figures on citizenship, see Mormino and Pozzetta, "The Political Economy of Organized Crime," 426, and on corruption more generally, passim. On issues of disfranchisement, see Lawson and Gardner, "At-Large Elections and Black Voting Rights in Tampa/Hillsborough County, 1910–1984."

50 R. S. Sexton to Samuel Gompers, July 31, 1920, reel 36, American Federation of Labor Papers. . . .

51 Even though the union refused the offer, it did donate ten dollars toward the rebuilding fund. . . .

52 Letters column, *Tampa Citizen*, July 20, 1920.

53 The *Cigar Makers' Official Journal* of September 15, 1920 included a list of locals donating to the A.F. of L. Fund in Aid of the Tampa Strikers. . . .

54 On missions, see report on Methodist conference in *TMT*, October 20, 1920.

55 Until August 25, the *Tribune* and the *Times* ran far more articles and editorials on the cigar strike than on woman suffrage or women's emancipation. Between then and October 20, the day of the charter vote, they featured woman suffrage and the charter contest far more prominently. After October 20, they returned to a focus on the strike.

56 *Tobacco Leaf*, August 26 (first quote) and September 23 (second quote), 1920.

57 On Committee of Public Health, see *TMT*, October 15 and November 2, 1920. The editors of *EI* . . . claimed that 30 percent of the city's 8,125 cigar workers were American-born, many of American-born parents, and that the president of the stemmers' union was an American woman. . . . Manufacturers and Anglo civic leaders always used the term *American girls* to mean white women only; union leaders, when they used the term at all, meant native-born women, white or Black.

58 *Tampa Citizen*, August 13, 1920, responding to claims in *Tobacco Leaf* that "American girls," meaning native-born white women, were pouring into Tampa to take jobs as packers that striking Latin men had left vacant.

59 On workers' activities between August and October 1920, see, for example, *TMT*, September 7 and October 15 (quote), 1920. . . .

60 *TMT*, October 15, October 20, 1920; *EI*, October 22, 1920.

61 *TMT*, October 15, 1920. The *TDT*, October 14, 1920, claimed that a vote was taken and that women strikers voted with the majority to continue the strike.

62 *TMT*, October 20, 1920.

63 Letter from Committee of Public Health, ibid., November 2, 1920.

64 Ibid., February 6, 1921 . . .

65 Ibid., November 27, 1921 (quote); *TDT*, November 26, 1921. . . .

66 Tampa League of Women's Clubs, Scrapbook, vol. 1, and Handbook, 1921–22, Tampa League of Women's Clubs Papers, Special Collections, University of South Florida Library; Tampa City Directory, 1922.

67 On the relation of suffrage to women's voluntarism nationally, see Nancy Cott, "Across the Great Divide: Women in Politics before and after 1920," in *Women, Politics, and Change*, ed. Tilly and Gurin, 153–76. . . .

6

DEFIANCE AND DOMINATION

"White Negroes" in the Piney Woods New South

Victoria E. Bynum

This essay is taken from Victoria E. Bynum's fascinating study of Jones County, in southern Mississippi. Settled largely by yeoman farmers and with relatively few slaves, Jones County became a site of serious resistance to the Confederacy during the Civil War. Dozens of Unionists in the county, many of them Confederate deserters, banded together under the leadership of Newton Knight to resist the draft and harass Confederate officials. Stories circulated that this "Knight company" had issued a formal declaration of "secession" from the Confederacy, giving rise to the legend of the "Free State of Jones."

After the war, Newton Knight became a leader in the local Republican Party, and later he left his wife, Serena, to live with Rachel Knight, a former slave. Two of his children from his marriage with Serena married children of Rachel Knight, and, later, Newton Knight himself fathered children with Rachel. The resulting kinship group formed a community of "white Negroes," a "racial island" that stood as a living contradiction to the New South's rigid racial categorizations. From one decade to the next, census takers and courts could judge the same person to be "white," "black," or "mulatto." Jones County's "white Negroes" thus exemplify the way that local history and local circumstances could shape the meanings of "race." As Bynum writes, the "true essence of race was socially rather than biologically determined."

The story of Jones also illustrates the ways that memory helped to shape southern culture and society. In the twentieth century, the memory of the "Free State of Jones," and of Newton Knight in particular, was sharply contested by local residents. Newton's son Thomas wrote a history of the Confederate resisters that was highly favorable to his father, painting him as a kind of Robin Hood—though suppressing information about Newton Knight's interracial social and sexual relationships. Newton's great-niece Ethel Knight wrote a quite different account of Newton Knight's wartime resistance, portraying him as an outlaw and murderer with "a warped and twisted mind" who had forced his children to marry the children of a prostitute. In their different ways, these local accounts of the "Free State of Jones" attempted to force the facts of the past into the mold of the mythological history of the Lost Cause; in doing so they reinforced the edifice of segregation.

* * *

Many Mississippi historians apparently agreed with Josie Frazee Cappleman [state historian for the Mississippi United Daughters of the Confederacy] that the history of the Confederate cause should be written as a "golden romance"—and a golden romance it became.* In the Old South world created by New South writers, wealthy and poor whites, men and women, and blacks and whites all shared a harmony of interests shattered by the invading North. [Studies published by the] Mississippi Historical Society replaced Northern images of a violent, backward South with those of a brave and noble civilization. Beginning in 1898 pro-Confederate rhetoric flooded the pages of the historical society's journal. Authors regularly blamed Northerners and African Americans for the failure of Reconstruction by caricaturing or vilifying Republicans, while praising the motives of the Ku Klux Klan.[1]

Although the stated goal of the historical society was to paint a more truthful picture of the past, its *Publications of the Mississippi Historical Society* proved every bit as slanted as any product of Northern abolitionist presses. . . . Lost Cause historians enshrined Confederate soldiers as heroes and expressed contempt for those who had opposed or deserted the Confederacy. The story of the Free State of Jones moved from the realm of recent history into that of legend, where over time it became distorted by caricatures of ignorant, feuding poor whites, bestial black men, besieged white women, and seductive mulatto women.

Southern white women were both actors and subjects in the revision of Civil War history. In the same *Publications* issue in which Cappleman counseled local and state historians of the Civil War on their mission, Mary V. Duval likewise called on them to replace Northern versions of Southern history with their own. Duval, who authored a history textbook for Mississippi schoolchildren, painted a glowing picture of slavery. She wrote of antebellum white Southerners with "gracious manners" who owned little black "pickaninnies" who "rolled and rollicked from sheer delight in living." The supposedly finer sensibilities of middle-class white women in regard to moral values and domestic life lent authority to their words, while blossoming literary opportunities in the postwar South gave them a new public voice.[2]

---

* Cappleman wrote, "Aye, let us have our history—as it *should* be! Give us the correct version of that unequal struggle. . . . A record that reads more like a golden romance, than a living breathing reality."

North and South, the greater public visibility of genteel white women made the emerging images of freed black men all the more disturbing to middle-class audiences. Alongside Duval's renditions of happy-go-lucky black children emerged those of rapacious black men empowered by corrupt white Republicans. Between 1890 and 1920 white Southern literature—especially newspapers—commonly portrayed interracial sexual relations as the product of sex-crazed black "fiends" ravishing innocent, virginal blondes, rather than as the product of white men raping black women or of blacks and whites participating in consensual sexual relations. It followed that white men such as Newt Knight who had seized power as scalawags during Reconstruction, partly through interracial political coalitions, became traitors to both their government and their race.[3]

As early as 1868 the *Meridian Mercury* provided a lurid description of a black man "skinned alive" in Jones County for having "ravished" a white woman "to the full gratification of his lustful desires." With sarcasm and condescension, the editors noted that during the war, the county had "acquired a wide notoriety for the 'lollty' of its people, many of whom could not be persuaded to be good Confederates." Connecting the unionism of Jones County with new dangers to white women, they commented that "loyalty now means to let the negroes do any sort of devilment without retribution in kind." Such articles helped to spawn a rhetoric of rape fueled by images of vulnerable white women and lustful black men—men who had been freed by the very Union leaders who in 1868 held the reins of power. The message of conservative white editors was clear: only white men, increasingly understood to be devotedly pro-Confederate, could restore honor and order to Southern society.[4]

Following the lead of the *Mercury*, Mississippi newspapers continued to entwine class politics with images of freely roaming black men threatening the purity of white women. In 1895, only one week after the editors of the Clarion-Ledger accused Populists of courting "Negro" support, the paper's headlines screamed that yet another "defenseless white woman" had been "MURDERED BY A NEGRO." The paper warned that if the wheels of justice moved too slowly, "peaceable and law abiding" people would resort to lynching "these negro brutes who murder innocent women and children." Southern white editors seemed to agree that black men, unless controlled by force, threatened to destroy white men's private as well as public lives.[5]

Less than two months later, editors reported that in this case the woman's own husband had hired the black man to shoot her; they did not, however, describe the white man as a "fiend" and a "brute," as they had the black man, only as a "cowardly husband." Nor was the murdered woman any longer "innocent." It now appeared that she had been "very jealous" of her husband, having accused him of "things he never did"; furthermore, her extravagant desires had forced them to live in financial "hot water." A white man's vicious scheme to murder his wife thus became transformed into a tragic story of her domestic failure.[6]

Democrats, dependent on support from plain white men, masked the politics of class behind the rhetoric of race and white womanhood. In 1898 Democrat S. Newton Berryhill, billed as Mississippi's Backwoods Poet, metaphorically portrayed white men who had opposed the Confederate cause as animals who had abandoned their own fair civilization to rape and pillage. Using sexual imagery to bind the interests and history of all pro-Confederate whites regardless of class, he characterized carpetbaggers and scalawags as a "snarling pack" of "jackals black and white" who tear at the South's "lovely form by day, and gnaw her bones by night." Not only did Berryhill delineate clear political and racial lines for all Mississippians, but his imagery also helped to encourage and justify the era's numerous lynchings of black men.[7]

During the South's "lynching era," from 1889 to 1945, nearly 13 percent of the nation's recorded 3,786 lynchings occurred in Mississippi. One of the most vicious mob murders of a black man occurred in 1919 in Ellisville, Jones County. John Hartfield, accused of raping a white woman, was pursued for ten days through three counties before finally being caught and lynched. His public murder was organized by a committee, announced in the newspapers, and attended by a multitude of white people, many of whom carried picnic baskets.[8]

Among those who attended the lynching was fourteen-year-old junior reporter and future novelist James Street. In a collection of essays, *Look Away! A Dixie Notebook*, published in 1936, Street subtly sought to convince readers of the heinous nature of such "justice." Without denying Hartfield's guilt, he juxtaposed the image of the black man's grisly death against that of white folks who simultaneously "ate their picnic on the courthouse lawn, under the Confederate monument." Street gently tugged at the mask of reverence for white female honor by noting the incongruity of the alleged rape victim's appearance on her porch, where she waved to the bloodthirsty crowd. "It seemed to me the woman should have been in seclusion," wrote Street. "I can't say she enjoyed the excitement. Her face looked drawn, but there she was leaning on a bannister and talking with her avengers." He concluded his essay by linking racial hatred to class hatred—and both to reverence for the Confederacy—by noting that Hartfield was hanged from the same sycamore tree used by the Confederacy to hang three of Newt Knight's men during the Civil War.[9]

141

Although Street's voice was one of reason, it did not prevail. Hysterical spectacles of violence, especially lynchings, drove the image of black men as "fiendish brutes" ever deeper into the minds of white people. In 1936, the same year that Street published his account of Hartfield's lynching, B. A. Boutwell offered his own version of the murder to a WPA interviewer. In words dripping with the sentimental treacle of New South rhetoric, Boutwell described the events that led to the pursuit of Hartfield. "Like the cave man of long ages past," he said, "a black fiend had rushed out . . . and seazed one of the most beautiful flowers in the garden of society and dragged her into a nearby woods to satisfy his own beastly desire." Clearly believing that justice was served that day, Boutwell methodically described how the crowd tortured, burned, and mutilated Hartfield's body. Presumably because his seven-page description was so approving and graphic, a WPA official wrote in the margins, "omit this story."[10]

Sixty years after the Ellisville lynching, the power of "black beast" imagery still colored the memories of Jones County's seventy-nine-year-old Hulon Myers, who had attended the incident. Although he disavowed the Klan to an interviewer in 1979, he admitted having been a member of the organization in the 1920s, when the Klan was "all right" because their actions were "the only thing that kept the raping down and all like that." When asked how law officers responded to lynch mobs back then, he replied approvingly that "they just kept hands off most of the time."[11]

So rigidly were the boundaries of race reinscribed by the segregated New South that when Meigs Frost interviewed Newt Knight in 1921, he mentioned neither Rachel Knight [the former slave with whom he lived] nor the mixed-race composition of his homestead. Given that Newt openly lived among his mixed-race kin until his death, it seems likely that Frost, not Newt, censored all mention of Rachel, and it is easy to see why. Frost sought to write a sympathetic story about "Captain Knight" and the Free State of Jones, not an expose about miscegenation. Writing for a white audience during a decade that sanctioned violent enforcement of racial segregation and white domination over blacks, he dared not place a woman of African ancestry at the center of a legendary white uprising. Rachel thus disappeared from sight.[12]

Tom Knight's 1935 biography of Newt made only a veiled mention of Rachel, Georgeanne, and the mixed-race community and totally ignored his father's intimate connections with them. These omissions enabled him to replace painful memories of miscegenation with a glorified interpretation of his father's Civil War exploits. A product of his times, Tom did not merely fear the racist judgments of white society; the shame of being son and brother to members of a mixed-race community strained his relations with his father for most of his adult life.[13]

Ethel Knight, who was almost fifty years younger than Tom, was even more thoroughly immersed in a culture that insisted on purity of race and made the Confederate Lost Cause its dominant symbol. Embarrassed by her great-uncle Newt, she condemned him as a cold-blooded murderer and an outlaw, a man "with a warped and twisted mind, . . . almost wild in his habits." Furthermore, she insisted that Newt had stood ready to murder his own wife and children if they opposed his scheme to force marriages between his and Rachel's children. In an apparent effort to match the "blood and thunder" prose of James Street's *Tap Roots*, Ethel enlivened her stories—at times far-fetched and unsubstantiated—with unknowable details of the Knights' innermost thoughts and feelings.[14]

According to Ethel, Serena [Newt's wife] was essentially Newt's prisoner, appalled by her children's interracial marriages but power-less to thwart her husband's will. Ethel claimed that Serena had attempted to leave Newt during the late 1870s but that he forced her back home by shooting at her from behind briars and bamboo as she attempted to flee. Although Serena's life with Newt may well have been miserable, records verify only that she moved to the home of Molly and Jeffrey sometime before 1900, which hardly suggests that she opposed their marriage.[15]*

Although Ethel was determined to expose Newton as an advocate of miscegenation, she also sought to deny kinship between as many black and white Knights as possible. To this end, she disputed long-standing rumors that Newt had fathered children with both Rachel and Rachel's daughter Georgeanne. To further reduce the number of her black kin, Ethel even claimed that all but one of Molly's children—Otho, the father of Davis—had been fathered by white men rather than by Molly's husband, Jeffrey.[16]

Though she offered not a shred of evidence, Ethel labeled Rachel, Molly, and Georgeanne as whores, prostitutes, and even murderers to serve her own ends. For example, although Molly married Jeffrey while still a teenager and remained his wife until her death, Ethel pro-nounced her a "harlot" who had "launched out upon a career of prosti-tution" even before her marriage. Georgeanne, according to Ethel, was so craven with desire for Newt that she had attempted to murder Serena with an axe and possibly poisoned her own mother just to get to him.[17]

---

* Molly was the daughter of Newt and Serena Knight; Jeffrey was the son of former slave Rachel Knight.

In the segregated South, black women and white women who lived among blacks could be slandered with impunity. Societal stereotypes that posited white women who crossed the color line as sexually promiscuous and black women as naturally lascivious enabled Ethel to portray the mixed-race community as deviant, dangerous, and outside the boundaries of normal, decent society. She obviously had no direct knowledge of any turmoil that rocked the households of Newton, Serena, Rachel, and Georgeanne between 1870 and 1900, yet she filled readers' minds with fantastic and undocumented tales of lust and murder.[18]

Until Ethel published her account, journalists and historians who wrote about the Free State of Jones ignored Newt's interracial relationships, focusing instead on whether or not the county had formally seceded from the Confederacy. In 1886 G. Norton Galloway, a Northerner who billed himself as "historian of the 6th Army Corps," built on earlier newspaper accounts of Civil War Jones County to present deserters as feuding backswoodsmen who created a local "confederacy," wrote their own constitution, and elected "Nathan" Knight, "one of the most illiterate citizens of Jones County," as their president. Galloway claimed that this minirepublic attracted so many dissidents and "miscreants" that the county's population rose from 3,323 to more than 20,000 in little more than a year. He alleged that 10,000 of these people belonged to Knight's "army."[19]

Galloway's highly inaccurate version of the story of Jones County entertained Northerners and ridiculed Southerners with images of "bloody butchery" among men engaged in a fratricidal war, "bloodcurdling in the extreme." Southern whites were portrayed as ignorant and illiterate brutes, no matter on which side of the war they fought. Plainly intending to endorse the civilizing effects of industrialization, Galloway ended by praising Northern capitalists' introduction of lumber mills into Jones County.[20]

Newt Knight, poorly educated but hardly illiterate or ignorant of the world around him, neither fit Galloway's image of him nor celebrated the glories of Northern progress. In an 1887 letter to his brother John in Arkansas, he lamented the fact that missionaries, "skillet-head" doctors, and the lumber industry had penetrated his Piney Woods. Complaining that four steam-powered sawmills regularly interrupted the stillness of Tallahoma Creek, he commented to his brother that "I tell you they are slaien [slaying] them big pines."[21]

Served a steady diet of articles by authors such as Galloway, most middle-class Americans assumed that industrialization would turn back Southern poverty and civilize Southern poor whites. To such readers the Knight Company's Civil War uprising merely demonstrated poor whites' penchant for violence. That image was reinforced in 1891 and 1892 when Albert Bushnell Hart and Samuel Willard drew heavily on Galloway's distorted vision of the Free State of Jones to publish separate articles on the uprising in the *New England Magazine* and the *Nation*.[22]

As the century drew to a close, it was not only Northerners who ridiculed Piney Woods folks. In 1894, as North and South clasped hands across the ruins of war to build an economically "progressive" New South, Dabney H. Maury, the same Confederate general who thirty years earlier had ordered Col. Henry Maury into Jones County, offered a Southern version of the Free State of Jones. In his memoir, *Recollections of a Virginian*, he, too, characterized the deserters as hyper-secessionists, referring to the uprising as an *"imperium in imperio."* Like Galloway, Maury portrayed deserters as degraded poor whites, but from a class-based rather than a Northern perspective. Jones County, which he explained was part of the "vast piney woods that sweep along our seaboard from Carolina to the Sabine," contained the "worst class of our population."[23]

By the close of the nineteenth century, to be Southern was to be white, and to be white was to revere the Lost Cause of the Confederacy. In light of this dictum and Galloway's inaccurate and inflammatory article, two Mississippi historians decided to correct the record in regard to Jones County's Civil War record. In 1898 University of Mississippi professor Alexander L. Bondurant dismissed the legend of Jones County's secession as a pure "fabrication" in an article published by the Mississippi Historical Society. In 1904 Goode Montgomery, a Jones County schoolteacher, attorney, and future mayor of Laurel, expanded on Bondurant's work in the same journal.[24]

Although both Bondurant and Montgomery painted a much more accurate picture of Jones County's "secession," they also displayed passion for more than the mere truth when they assured readers that Jones County was loyal to the Lost Cause. Bondurant hoped to restore the "good name of a county which rendered brave and efficient service to the Confederacy." Montgomery wrote a much more factual, straightforward account than that of Bondurant, admitting that up to 125 Jones County men deserted the Confederate Army and joined the "Newt Knight Company." Still, he emphasized that most men, even those who initially opposed secession, "enlisted early in the war and served until they were mustered out in 1865, as faithful to the Confederacy as any troops in the Southern army."[25]

Raised in Jones County, Montgomery was personally connected to the Free State of Jones through his wife, Nora Herrington, whose maternal grandfather was Prentice Bynum, a member of the Knight band. Montgomery did not mention this connection; instead, he interviewed fifteen Jones County citizens who had lived during the war and who assured him that the Knight band never passed an ordinance of secession from the Confederacy.[26] Two of these interviewees were Jasper J. Collins and William Wesley Sumrall, whom Montgomery described as unrepentant members of the band. In fact, he noted, "no one of Knight's men" with whom he talked "was ashamed to be numbered with that company." Glorification of the Confederate cause seemed not to convince them that they had acted shamefully during the war. They denied the legend that they had seceded from the Confederacy, but their denial was not the product of shame and regret. They denied it simply because it was not true on procedural grounds.[27]

To provide a more civilized image of the Jones County area, Montgomery emphasized that Newt Knight went "wherever his business calls him" and lived "peaceably with his neighbors just like any other farmer." But despite Montgomery's sanguine words, he knew that a sympathetic portrayal of Newt could not include mention that he had crossed the color line. Mississippi lawmakers proscribed biracial education and interracial marriages in 1878 and 1880; the state's 1890 constitutional convention codified the laws and also disfranchised black citizens. By 1904 it was controversial enough for Montgomery merely to mention that opposition to the Confederacy existed among respectable men in Jones County; he dared not present as respectable a man who deserted the Confederate Army and who lived among his black kinfolk.[28]

It is difficult to know how Newt's nineteenth-century friends and associates responded to his disregard for laws that forbade interracial marriages and mandated racial segregation. His 1887 letter to his brother John contained ordinary accounts of activities and deaths among friends and relatives; it certainly did not suggest a man shunned by all white society. Several of his and Serena's children married white partners after the mixed marriages of their siblings had taken place. . . .[29]

Even if kinship ties and shared Civil War experiences forged lifelong loyalties between Newt Knight and some of his associates, he clearly paid a price for ignoring the color line, especially as time passed. In fact, Jasper County's 1900 federal census enumerator went so far as to deprive him of his white identity. A comparison of that year's census with that of 1880 reveals the reconstructed racial identity of many members of the "white Negro" community. In 1880, for example, the census enumerator listed Newton's children Molly and Mat as white and their spouses, Jeffrey and Fannie, as mulatto. Twenty years later the enumerator listed no mulattoes and only one white family in their community: Joseph S. Knight (Sullivan), a son of Newton and Serena, was listed as white presumably because he had married a woman accepted by the community as white. Yet Sullivan's parents and sister Molly were enumerated as black, no doubt because they lived in households that included descendants of Rachel Knight. By contrast, Newton and Serena's son Mat Knight remained "white" because he had separated from Rachel's daughter Fannie, moved out of the community, and married a white cousin. Obviously "race" was no mere matter of biology.[30]

Long before Ethel wrote her book, people whispered that Newt had fathered children by both Rachel and Georgeanne. In fact, many descendants of Rachel Knight's son John Madison "Hinchie" Knight and her daughter Augusta believe that Newt is their direct ancestor. However, while it is certain that Newt and Rachel's children intermarried, the nature of Newt's relationships with Rachel and Georgeanne is speculative. Newt and Serena lived together until at least 1880, and both remained within the family's network of households until their deaths.

Fortunately there are voices far more reliable than Ethel's as to relations within the households of Newt, Serena, Rachel, and Georgeanne. A more believable source on Newt's sexual affairs is ex-slave Martha Wheeler, his contemporary, who pointed out in 1936 that "Rachel was considered [Newt's] woman." After Rachel's death in 1889, said Martha, "her daughter, Georgianne, took her place [with Newt] and separated him from his wife, who went out and lived . . . among her children."[31]

The earliest memories of Georgeanne's oldest daughter, Anna, were of a crowded household plagued by poverty and segregation. "When I was old enough to understand," she wrote, "I discovered myself living in a large family; some of its members were grown men and women, two of whom were married. All lived in the same house, and all except one of the children was older than I."[32] Anna could not attend whites' schools but remembered learning to read and write from playing with white children. Play time was scarce, however, and both girls and boys worked hard, felling trees with axes and chopping cotton all day. She emphasized that "there was no rest for women," for housework awaited their completion of fieldwork. As a child who lived in a household in which people worked "all the time," she felt that she was "always in the way" and that she was "shoved and pushed around."[33]

During the twentieth century, as segregation deepened, most whites shunned the mixed-race community, and some white branches of the Knight family hid their kinship with Newt Knight from their children. Many believed, as did Ben Graves, that "what he did after the war was worse than deserting."[34] Paula Bolan, great-granddaughter of Newt's sister Martha Yawn, did not discover until she was in the eighth grade that she was kin to the county's most famous outlaw. She later learned that her great-grandfather Joseph Richard "Dick" Yawn had once refused to accompany his wife on a visit to her brother Newt's home, even though he had ridden with the Knight Company during the war. Lonnie Knight, a descendant of Newt's brother James (who was also the ancestor of Ethel Knight), was told by his parents, "No, we are not related to that [Newt's] bunch."[35]

Nevertheless, some white friends and relatives continued to admire Newt despite his discredited behavior. During the 1930s, when Tom Knight gathered stories and testimonials for his father's biography, he found several older Jones County folk who still admired Newt's wartime stance. George A. Valentine, whose older brothers had joined the Knight Company, extolled Newt's unionist ideals and described him as a "quiet and peaceable" man. Martha Ellzey Knight, the wife of Newt's younger brother Taylor, told Tom that "she did not know what would have become of the poor little children and women here in Jones County had it not been for Captain Knight and his company [during the war]."[36]

William Pitts, born in 1921 and descended from Newt's brother Albert, remembered that his family seldom spoke of Newt because of the "Negro thing" but nonetheless gave him the "feeling" that the Civil War was so terrible that Newt ought not be judged too harshly. Similarly, DeBoyd Knight and Earle Knight—both descendants of Dickie Knight—and Julius Huff, a descendant of Thomas J. Huff, were all raised with a certain respect for Newt Knight, despite his interracial relationships.[37]

Newt's closest white friend in later years may have been his cousin George "Clean Neck" Knight. Although Clean Neck's father, Jesse Davis Knight, died fighting for the Confederate Army, and although his mother was a Baylis, he and Newt developed a close relationship after the war, perhaps in part because their wives were also kin. . . . Loyal to Newt until the end, Clean Neck died on his one-hundredth birthday in 1952, having lived just long enough to complain that Ethel Knight's book contained "not a shred of truth."[38]

Even had whites wanted to, however, those sympathetic to Newt could do little to change the prevailing norms of society that marked him as deviant. Much more important to the mixed-race community's ability to thrive was Anna Knight [a daughter of Georgeanne], whose conversion to Seventh-Day Adventism first transformed her own life. Anna discovered Adventism around 1890 during the church's intense campaign to evangelize the South under the leadership of the charismatic prophetess Ellen G. White. . . . Adventism give Anna the tools with which to educate and reform the habits of her kinfolk.[39]

Under the auspices of the Seventh-Day Adventists, Anna not only taught the "three Rs" and Adventist theology in her Sunday school, but she also convinced her relatives to accept Adventist reforms in their diet, dress, and social behavior. Although she lived outside the

Knight community most of her adult life, she influenced the community's development more profoundly than did Newt Knight himself. To gain the skills and authority to redirect the course of the community, however, she had to first leave Mississippi, which she did under the sponsorship of the church.[40]

Shortly after joining the Adventist Church, Anna moved to Chattanooga at the invitation of church elder L. Dyo Chambers and his wife, who then provided for her education. In 1895 Anna moved to Battle Creek, Michigan, where she trained as a missionary nurse at the church's American Medical Missionary College. After graduating from its nursing program, she fulfilled the college's required self-supporting medical missionary work by establishing a school for her Mississippi kinfolk.[41]

Anna escaped Mississippi at a critical point in the life of a young African American woman in the 1890s South. To make so sudden a move (she was barely sixteen years old), she had first to reject her mother's and grandmother's lives as models for her own. Like them, she never married, but unlike them, she never had children. As a devoutly pious woman writing a church-sponsored autobiography, she did not openly discuss sexual matters but hinted at sexual tensions when she described how a raging thunderstorm once halted a dance party that she had attended against her better judgment. Convinced that the storm was God's warning, she wrote, "From that time on I never took part in any more card parties or dances. Jesus saved me from all such things."[42]

The storm occurred around 1889, the year of Rachel Knight's death. Just as Anna was reaching womanhood, her forty-nine-year-old grandmother died. . . . Two years after Rachel's death, in 1891, Anna's mother, Georgeanne, gave birth to Grace, a child fathered by either Newt or another white man.[43] The life that lay before Anna must have been made chillingly clear by the lives of her mother and grandmother. Although she eventually returned to live in the South, she escaped rural Mississippi and gained protection against sexual exploitation and poverty within the nurturing environment of Seventh-Day Adventism.[44] As Ethel Knight's book makes abundantly clear, many whites refused to consider Rachel and Georgeanne, both unmarried black women with light-skinned children, as anything other than prostitutes or concubines of white men. When Anna returned to Jones County, around 1898, white men there were confronted by a dignified, educated missionary rather than a pretty and vulnerable woman whose "black blood" made her sexual fair game. And just in case anyone questioned the seriousness of her purpose, she packed a revolver "and sometimes a double-barreled shotgun" when she taught Sunday school.[45]

Anna was also attracted to Adventism because of the church's racial tolerance, reflective of its origins among the antebellum Millerites, who were abolitionists. Adventists challenged both gender and racial barriers in their evangelical missions, particularly in the postbellum South but, like other institutions, were eventually forced to segregate their facilities. Anna remembered that when she joined, however, "white and colored worshiped together." As the church's black membership grew, so, too, did fierce opposition to race-mixing, often from within the church itself. According to Anna, after she enrolled in the Adventist Graysville Academy in Tennessee, several students' parents protested her admission. Her sponsors then withdrew her and arranged for her to receive private tutoring.[46]

In 1898, two years before the Jasper County census enumerator designated all members within the mixed community as "black," Anna opened a private school in Soso for the Knight children under the sponsorship of the Seventh-Day Adventist Church. According to her, white neighbors burned this first school to the ground around 1902. She then traveled to India as a missionary for the church, leaving the Knight community without a school for over five years. At the urging of her relatives, she returned to Mississippi around 1908 and directed the rebuilding of the school in nearby Gitano in Jones County.

Because of the demands of Anna's work as a teacher and missionary, she educated her sister Grace, who eventually replaced her as teacher of the school. For most of her life Anna lived and worked at Oakwood College, which the Adventist Church founded for African Americans in 1896 in Huntsville, Alabama. Many mixed-race Knights received their grade school education from Grace and then left the area to attend high school at Oakwood College. These two schools became their most important resources for battling against total debasement under increasingly strict racial segregation.[47]

Although Anna and Grace became two of the community's most important figures, the presence of such an imposing white male as Newt Knight enabled the community to survive and grow Although he exercised his sexual prerogative as a white male by boldly crossing the color line, he deviated from the usual pattern of interracial relations by sanctioning his children's marriages and by openly living among Rachel, Georgeanne, and his mixed-race descendants. It would appear that his lifelong reputation as one who lived as he chose—a right he had successfully defended with arms during the war—discouraged many direct challenges to his shocking postwar behavior. As Maddie Bush emphasized in 1912, Newton still "toats [sic] his old gun."[48]

Newt's presence may have protected Rachel's oldest son, Jeffrey, from prosecution or mob violence when Jeffrey married Newt's daughter Molly. This marriage might easily have inflamed whites' fantasies about black males' lust for white women, but the fact that Jeffrey looked "almost" white may have enabled some to ignore his marriage. Most did not challenge it because Newt either had "given" his daughter to him or, as Ethel Knight would have it, forced his own daughter to marry a black man. To most whites it seemed not so much that Jeffrey had challenged white males' exclusive access to white women, but that he reaped the benefits of a white father's misuse of patriarchal authority. Indeed, racist whites did not expect a black man to refuse the "gift" of a white woman. Like Ethel, they considered Molly tainted and incapable of respectability.[49]

But Newt Knight, particularly as an old man, could not prevent all the dangers inherent in a society in which blacks were controlled through violence as well as segregation. In late November 1920, less than two years before Newt's own death, Stewart Knight, Rachel's son (and perhaps Newt's) was murdered. Sharp Welborn, a white man who reportedly lived near him, was convicted of manslaughter. Stewart, light-skinned and well dressed, may have aroused resentment for his lifestyle among his white neighbors. Although Welborn's apparent motive was robbery, some of Stewart's relatives believe that an incident involving a white woman precipitated the attack.[50]

The heightened role of the Ku Klux Klan in the Jones County area raises the question of whether Stewart's murder was racially motivated. Not only was John Hartfield lynched in Ellisville in 1919 but so, too, was an unidentified black man lynched in Estabutchie, Jones County, during the same year. Only two years after Stewart's murder, a large parade of robed Klansmen marched in the streets of Hattiesburg [in neighboring Forrest County]. That same year, on October 23, 1922, twenty-five klansmen warned "Mr. Letow," a black man who owned a restaurant in Hattiesburg, to move his business from the white to the black section of town.[51]

The Klan hit closer to home around that time when it intruded on two Baptist churches, one in Laurel, Jones County, and the other in nearby Moselle, Covington County. On October 20 the *Laurel Daily Leader* reported that the First Baptist Church of Laurel had received a visit from Klansmen clothed in "full regalia" who left behind a "well-filled purse" and a warning that the Klan was sworn to protect the "purity of womanhood" and "100 percent Americanism." The very next day the Klan visited the Moselle Baptist Church in Covington County. The *Daily Leader* reported that the Reverend C. F. Austin dutifully seated the men near the pulpit and "delivered a dramatic eulogy on the historical record of the Klan from the days after war strife until the present day." An approving Klan once again left money and a letter outlining its guiding principles for the accommodating minister.[52]

In this dangerous and circumscribed world, members of the Knight community made difficult personal choices. Many married their light-skinned cousins to assure that their children would be equally light-skinned. In the process they created enclaves of people who were neither "white" nor "black," with complex and doubled lines of descent from both Rachel and Newt Knight. Florence Blaylock, a great-granddaughter of Rachel Knight, remembered the importance of skin shade and hair texture within the racial system in which she grew up. The realization that many mixed-race Knights did not consider themselves "black" was driven home to her as a child when she heard a light-skinned, pretty cousin insist that "if a black man ever tried to talk to me, I would slap his face!" Florence's own racial identity was complicated, however, by her light-skinned father's marriage to brown-skinned Eddress Booth rather than to one of his light-skinned cousins. The children of Oree and Eddress Knight inherited varying shades of skin and hair texture, which meant that some could ignore segregation ordinances, while others had no choice but to obey them.[53]

In 1939 black sociologist E. Franklin Frazier characterized communities such as the Knights' as "racial islands."[54] As Mississippi's racial climate worsened, however, many of the lightest-skinned Knights left their protective enclave to seek acceptance elsewhere as whites. Newt and Serena's son Mat separated from Fannie and in 1895 married a white cousin (under Mississippi's antimiscegenation laws, no divorce was necessary). Several of Mat and Fannie's children moved to Texas before 1920 and successfully blended into white society. Their descendants were told only that their grandmother (Fannie Knight) was a "full-blooded Cherokee Indian." Similarly, several grandchildren of Jeffrey and Molly Knight moved to Arkansas after 1920, where they explained their olive skin to their children and neighbors by transforming Serena Knight, their white grandmother, into an Indian, while ignoring Rachel, their mulatto grandmother. According to their version of the family's history, Newt Knight had met Serena in Oklahoma, where she arrived via the Cherokee Trail of Tears.[55]

Despite these Knights' erasure of their African ancestry, to say that they passed for white is to accept a social construction of race that lacks a logical scientific basis. Given many of the Knights' physical appearances, it is more accurate to say that Mississippi forced them to pass for black. As retired black Kentucky politician Mae Street Kidd commented in 1997 about her own white appearance, "It's so very obvious that I'm so much whiter than I am black that I have to pretend to be black." Like Kidd, the Knights knew from direct experience that the true essence of race was socially rather than biologically determined, as demonstrated by their ability to be white in one region of the country and black in another.[56]

Certainly, the Knights could not remain in the Jones County area and expect to be accepted as white. In a 1914 court dispute over the estate of the deceased Mat Knight, Fannie Knight, by then married to Dock Howze, was interrogated by attorney Goode Montgomery as to her and Dock's true racial identities. Despite Fannie's description of herself as "Choctaw and French" and of Dock as "Choctaw and Irish," Montgomery insisted that they were "Negroes," to which Fannie replied, "Well, you will have to do your own judging." When Montgomery next asked her if she was "living with niggers," Fannie conceded, "Yes sir, I stay on that side." To be "on that side" in the segregated South was, of course, evidence of Fannie's blackness, no matter how light her skin. This reality led the daughters of Fannie's sister Georgeanne—Anna, Grace, and Lessie Knight—along various paths of racial identification. Grace remained in the community, never married, and lived as a black woman despite her white appearance. Lessie married a white man and moved to Texas, where she lived as a white woman, though she frequently returned home on visits. Anna never married, lived outside Mississippi for most of her life, yet identified herself as a "colored" woman.[57]

By 1923, the Knight community's first generation had passed away On February 16, 1922, less than a year after his interview with Meigs Frost, Newt Knight died. The editors of the Ellisville Progress wrote a remarkably sympathetic obituary, taking pains to explain why he had deserted the Confederate Army. Newt and "his followers," they wrote, "held that after the twenty negro law was passed ... they had no interest in the fortunes of the confederacy." The editors acknowledged that "there was a great deal of truth" in their convictions but lamented that Newt had "ruined his life and future by marrying a negro woman."[58]

Six months later Georgeanne died, followed by Serena in 1923. These deaths inevitably changed the community. Some white neighbors remember Klan harassment of Knights during the 1930s, including one instance in which a white man was beaten "because he had dated a Knight girl." Many Knights moved away during this period, but those who remained in the Jones County area looked ever more to Anna and Grace Knight and to the Adventist Church for protection against the worst effects of racial prejudice and segregation.[59]....

The "white Negro" community existed in defiance of every tenet of the New South creed. Twentieth-century racism, reshaped between 1890 and 1920 by the architects of segregation, reinforced many Americans' desperate determination to deny any and all African ancestry. Perhaps with even greater urgency, many continued to explain olive skin as the legacy of distant Indian, Spanish, Portuguese, and even Carthaginian—but never African—forebears.[60] White people's denial of black ancestry was certainly not surprising in a white supremacist society that claimed by the turn of the twentieth century that one drop of "African" blood overpowered all other blood in determining one's racial identity. If most planter- and yeoman-class Southern whites denied knowledge of their darker-skinned kinfolk during the nineteenth century, few Southern whites of the segregated twentieth-century South would admit even to socializing with blacks.

The belief by many that "one drop" of African blood made one black culminated in 1948 with the miscegenation trial of Davis Knight, a grandson of Molly and Jeff.* That trial, however, was about much more than simply one man's racial identity. As the nation inched closer to a confrontation over segregation, many white Southerners feared what lay ahead. In opposing Davis Knight's claim to whiteness when he married across the color line, they once more took their stand, this time with the Lost Cause of segregation.[61]

A casualty of Davis Knight's battle over racial identity was Tom Knight's romanticized portrayal of the Knight Company as a band of heroic white yeoman farmers who acted in defense of liberty and the safety of women and children. Largely because of Davis's trial, Ethel Knight successfully replaced Tom's version of the Free State of Jones with her own, a tale that featured a demented white man, a manipulative green-eyed mulatto woman, and one hundred or more men who were persuaded to join a misbegotten plot to overthrow what she believed was the noblest government on earth—the Confederacy.

NOTES

1 Josie Frazee Cappleman, "Importance of the Local History of the Civil War," *Publications of the Mississippi Historical Society* [*PMHS*] 3 (1900): 111. . . . For Lost Cause versions of the Civil War and Reconstruction in *PMHS*, see esp. J. S. McNeilly, "The Enforcement Act of 1871 and the Ku Klux Klan in Mississippi," 9 (1906): 171; W. H. Hardy, "Recollections of Reconstruction in East and Southeast Mississippi," 4 (1901), 105–32 and 7 (1903), 199–215; and S. S. Calhoon, "The Causes and Events that Led to the Calling of the Constitutional Convention of 1890," 2 (1902), 105–9.

2 Cappleman, "Importance of the Local History of the Civil War"; Mary V. Duval, "The Making of a State," *PMHS* 3 (1900): 157, 161–65. Cappleman and Duval demonstrated the important role played by women in creating the Myth of the Lost Cause. See LeeAnn Whites, *The Civil War As a Crisis in Gender: Augusta, Georgia, 1860–1890* (Athens, Ga., 1995), 160–98, and

---

* When David Knight, a great-grandson of Newt Knight, married a white woman after World War II, the Jones County prosecutor brought him to trial for violating Mississippi's anti-miscegenation law. The trial turned on whether he was in fact "white" or "black." A determination at the trial that he was "black" was overturned by an appeals court.

Rebecca Montgomery, "Lost Cause Mythology in New South Reform: Gender, Class, Race, and the Politics of Patriotic Citizenship in Georgia, 1890–1925," in *Dealing with the Powers that Be: Negotiating Boundaries of Southern Womanhood*, ed. Janet L. Coryell, Thomas H. Appleton, Jr., Anastatia Sims, and Sandra Gioia Treadway (Columbia, Mo., 2000). On Mississippi, see Karen L. Cox, "Women, the Lost Cause, and the New South: The United Daughters of the Confederacy and the Transmission of Confederate Culture, 1894–1919" (Ph.D. diss., University of Southern Mississippi, 1997). On the Southern movement to "correct" the historical record in favor of Lost Cause values, see Fred A. Bailey, "The Textbooks of the 'Lost Cause': Censorship and the Creation of Southern State Histories," *Georgia Historical Quarterly*, 75 (fall 1991): 507–33.

3 Neil R. McMillen, *Dark Journey: Black Mississippians in the Age of Jim Crow* (Urbana, Ill., 1989), 245; Jacquelyn Dowd Hall, " 'The Mind that Burns in Each Body': Women, Rape, and Racial Violence," in *Powers of Desire: The Politics of Sexuality*, ed. Ann Snitow, Christine Stansell, and Sharon Thompson (New York: Monthly Review Press, 1983), 328–49; William Pierce Randel, *The Ku Klux Klan: A Century of Infamy* (Philadelphia: Chilton, 1965), 82. . . . On other interracial Southern communities of the postbellum South, see esp. Mark R. Schultz. "Interracial Kinship Ties and the Emergence of a Rural Black Middle Class: Hancock County, Georgia, 1865–1920," in *Georgia in Black and White: Explorations in the Race Relations of a Southern State, 1865–1950*, ed. John C. Inscoe (Athens, Ga., 1994), 141–72; Adele Logan Alexander, *Ambiguous Lives: Free Women of Color in Rural Georgia, 1789–1879* (Fayetteville, Ark., 1991); Kent Anderson Leslie, *Woman of Color; Daughter of Privilege, 1849–1893* (Athens, Ga., 1995). . . .

4 Article from the *Meridian Mercury*, reprinted in the Ralls County (Mo.) *Record*, Apr. 30, 1868.

5 *Jackson Clarion-Ledger*, Oct. 17, 1895.

6 Ibid., Dec. 12, 1895.

7 Lipscomb, "Mississippi's 'Backwoods Poet,' " *PMHS* 1(June 1898), 11. . . .

8 McMillen, *Dark Journey*, 229, 244–45.

9 James Street, *Look Away! A Dixie Notebook* (New York, 1936). I have found no evidence to suggest that Street's statement about the sycamore tree was true.

10 Interview with B. A. Boutwell, unpublished WPA records, Jones County, RG 60, vol. 316, Mississippi Department of Archives and History. Boutwell . . . gave the date of the lynching as 1917 but was surely describing the June 26, 1919, lynching of John Hartfield. . . .

11 Interview with Hulon Myers by Orley Caudill, Mississippi Oral History Program, vol. 349, 1979, University of Southern Mississippi [USM], 33–37. On the history of the 1920s Ku Klux Klan, see esp. Nancy MacLean, *Behind the Mask of Chivalry: The Making of the Second Ku Klux Klan* (New York, 1994).

12 *New Orleans Item*, Mar. 20, 1921.

13 Thomas J. Knight, *The Life and Activities of Captain Newton Knight and His Company and the "Free State of Jones"* (1935; rev. ed, Laurel, Miss., 1946), 96–97. . . .

14 Ethel Knight, *Echo of the Black Horn*, 293, 300, 31 5. The phrase "blood and thunder" is from Thomas L. McHaney, "James Street: Making History Live," in *Mississippi's Piney Woods: A Human Perspective*, ed. Noel Polk (Jackson, Miss., 1986), 125. . . .

15 Knight, *Echo of the Black Horn*, 264–70; US. Bureau of the Census, Federal Manuscript Census, 1900, Jasper County, Miss.

16 Knight, *Echo of the Black Horn*, 315.

17 Ibid., 264–65, 278–79 (quoted passage), 300, 303, 309, 311–12.

18 Paula Giddings, *When and Where I Enter: The Impact of Black Women on Race and Sex in America* (New York, 1984), 86–87; Martha Hodes, *White Women, Black Men: Illicit Sex in the Nineteenth-Century South* (New Haven, 1997), 131–32, 162–63.

19 G. Norton Galloway, "A Confederacy within a Confederacy," *Magazine of American History*, Oct. 1886, 387–90; *Natchez Courier*, July 12, 1864; *New Orleans Times-Picayune*, July 17, 1864.

20 Galloway, "Confederacy within A Confederacy," 387–90. On Northern ridicule of Southern whites as illiterate, feuding, and backward, see Altina L. Waller. *Feud: Hatfields, McCoys, and Social Change in Appalachia, 1860–1900* (Chapel Hill, 1988), 195, 206–34.

21 Newton Knight to John Knight, Apr. 3, 1887, reprinted in Winnie Knight Thomas, Earle W. Knight, Lavada Knight Dykes, and Martha Kaye Dykes Lowery, *The Family of John "Jackie" Knight and Keziah Davis Knight, 1773–1985* (Magee, Miss., 1985), 351–53.

22 Albert Bushnell Hart, "Why the South was Defeated in the Civil War," *New England Magazine*, n.s., 4 (Dec. 1891): 95–120; Dr. Samuel Willard, "A Myth of the Confederacy," *Nation*, Mar. 24, 1892, 227. . . .

23 General Dabriey Herndon Maury, *Recollections of a Virginian in the Mexican, Indian, and Civil Wars* (New York, 1894), 200–3, 246–47.

24 Alexander I. Boudurant, "Did Jones County Secede?" *PMHS* 1 (1898): 103–6; Goode Montgomery, "Alleged Secession of Jones County," *PMHS* 8 (1904): 13–22.

25 Bondurant, "Did Jones County Secede?" 106; Montgomery, "Alleged Secession of Jones County," 21.

26 Bondurant interviewed three former Mississippi governors, John M. Stone, Robert Lowry (the Confederate colonel who led a major raid on Knight's band during the war), and Anselm J. McLaurin, and a Jones County chancery clerk, E. B. Clark. See Boudurant, "Did Jones County Secede?" 103–6, and Montgomery, "Alleged Secession of Jones County," 13–22. . . .

27 Montgomery, "Alleged Secession of Jones County," 18–19; *New Orleans Item*, Mar. 20, 1921.

28 Montgomery, "Alleged Secession of Jones County," 17–19. On increased legal and extralegal persecution of interracial marriages beginning in the 1880s, see Hodes, *White Women, Black Men*, 176–97; Glenda Elizabeth Gilmore, *Gender and Jim Crow: Women and the Politics of White Supremacy in North Carolina, 1896–1920* (Chapel Hill, 1996), 71; and W. Fitzhugh Brundage, *Lynching in the New South: Georgia and Virginia, 1880–1930* (Urbana, 1993), 58–62.

29 Mary E. Welborn and Sarah E. Welborn, daughters of Aaron Terrell Welborn, married Tom Knight and Joseph Sullivan Knight, respectively, in 1878 and 1880. Ulysses Grant Welhorn, son of Caroline Welborn, married Susan Knight in 1888.

30 U.S. Bureau of the Census, Federal Manuscript Censuses, 1880, 1900, Jasper County, Miss. According to the U.S. Dept. of Commerce, *Twenty Censuses: Population and Housing Questions, 1790–1980* (Orting, Wash, 1979), 22, 33, census enumerators for 1880 were instructed to designate people of African ancestry as either "black," or "mulatto," according to their physical appearance. In 1900, just four years after the U.S. Supreme Court sanctioned racial

segregation in *Plessy v. Ferguson* (1896), they were instructed to designate people of any degree of African ancestry as simply "black."

31 George P. Rawick, ed., *The American Slave: A Composite Autobiography*, supplement, ser. I, vol. 10, Mississippi Narratives, pt. 5 (Westport, Conn., 1972), 2268. Georgeanne's four children were John Howard, born 1872; Anna (Rachel Ann), born 1874; Grace, born 1891; and Lessie, born 1894. [A summary of the genealogical evidence has been omitted—ed.]

32 U.S. Bureau of the Census, Federal Manuscript Census, 1880, Jasper County, Miss. Consistent with Anna Knight's memory, the 1880 census enumerator listed Rachel's household separately from Newt and Serena's. . . . The census enumerator's listing of the Knight households is a tangle of confusion, however. Several Knights are double-listed. . . .

33 U.S. Bureau of the Census, Federal Agricultural Census, 1880, Jasper County, Miss.; Anna Knight, *Mississippi Girl: An Autobiography* (Nashville, 1952), 12–13, 18, 27.

34 B. D. Graves, Hebron Community Meeting, June 17, 1926, Lauren Rogers Museum of Art, Laurel Mississippi.

35 Paula Bolan, e-mail message to author, Apr. 19, 2000, and Lonnie Knight, e-mail messages to author, Jan. 28, 29, 2000, ML-USM.

36 Thomas J. Knight, *Life and Activities of Captain Newton Knight*, 17, 37 (second quoted phrase), and 87 (first quoted phrase), 96–97. Tom Knight provided an obtuse, confused discussion of Rachel and Georgeanne's efforts to send mixed-race Knights to a newly built schoolhouse around 1870, referring to them only as "Negro women." George Valentine was the younger brother of Richard H. Valentine, who appeared on Newton Knight's company "muster list" during the Civil War. Martha Ellzey married Taylor Knight, Newton's brother, in 1871. . . .

37 William Pitts, telephone conversation with author, Feb. 16, 2000; DeBoyd Knight, conversation with author, Aug. 9, 1993; Earle Knight, conversations with author, June 28–30, 1994; and Julius Huff, conversation with author, Aug. 8, 199 3, McCain Library and Archives, USM [ML-USM]. When I asked William Pitts what he thought of Ethel Knight's book, he pronounced it unfair to Newt and mostly "fiction.". . . .

38 According to Ethel Knight, George "Clean Neck" Knight (who earned his nickname because he wore his collar so high that hair did not grow on his neck) was one of only two whites who attended Newt's funeral: see *Echo of the Black Horn*, 326–27. . . .

39 On Ellen G. White, see esp. Ronald L. Numbers, *Prophetess of Health: Ellen G. White and the Origins of Seventh-Day Adventist Health Reform*, rev. and enl. ed. (Knoxville, 1992). Works that illuminate religious movements in which women promoted racial uplift include Nell Irvin Painter, *Sojourner Truth: A Life, a Symbol* (New York: Norton, 1996); Gilmore, *Gender and Jim Crow*; Evelyn Brooks Higginhotham, *Righteous Discontent: The Women's Movement in the Black Baptist Church, 1880–1920* (Cambridge, Mass., 1993); Mary E. Frederickson, "Each One Is Dependent on the Other: Southern Churchwomen. Racial Reform, and the Process of Transformation, 1880–1940," in *Visible Women: New Essays on American Activism*, ed. Nancy A. Hewitt and Suzanne Lebsock (Urbana, Ill., 1993), 296–324; Cynthia Neverdon-Morton, *Afro-America Women of the South and the Advancement of the Race, 1895–1925* (Knoxville, 1989); and Jacqueline Anne Rouse, *Lugenia Burns Hope: Black Southern Reformer* (Athens, Ga., 1989).

40 Numbers, *Prophetess of Health*, 93–101. Seventh Day Adventists strongly

supported the Temperance Movement; for this reason, claimed Anna, moonshiners regularly harassed her. See Anna Knight, *Mississippi Girl*, 83–84.

41 The American Medical Missionary College was sponsored by the Seventh-Day Adventist Battle Creek Sanitarium from 1895 until 1910. . . .

42 Anna Knight, *Mississippi Girl*, 26–27. . . .

43 Annette Knight, interview with author, Soso, Miss., July 22, 1996, ML-USM. As Darlene Clark Hine has written, "The combined influence of rape (or the threat of rape), domestic violence, and a desire to escape economic oppression born of racism and sexism" motivated many young black women during this era to flee the South. See Darlene Clark Hine, "Rape and the Inner Lives of Southern Black Women: Thoughts on the Culture of Dissemblance," in *Southern Women: Histories and Identities*, ed. Virginia Benhard, Betty Brandon, Elizabeth Fox-Genovese, and Theda Purdue, eds. (Columbia, Mo., 1992), 177–89.

44 Knight, *Echo of the Black Horn*, 265, 309. . . .

45 Anna Knight, *Mississippi Girl*, 84.

46 . . . Anna Knight, *Mississippi Girl*, 20–29, 48–49 . . .; On Anna Knight's encounter of racial prejudice, see ibid., 20–32, 41–47, 71–75. . . .

47 Ibid., 14–15, 75–92, 159–70.

48 Quoted from Address of M. P. Bush, Feb. 17, 1912, Rogers Museum.

49 Knight, *Echo of the Black Horn*, 296–300. On societal condemnation of white women who crossed the color line, see Martha Hodes, "The Sexualization of Reconstruction Politics: White Women and Black Men in the South after the Civil War," *Journal of the History of Sexuality* 3 (Jan. 1993), 402–17, and Laura F. Edwards, "Sexual Violence, Gender, Reconstruction, and the Extension of Patriarchy in Granville County, North Carolina," *North Carolina Historical Review*, 63 (July 1991), 237–60.

50 *Laurel Leader Call*, Dec. 9, 1920; Annette Knight, taped interview with Florence Blaylock, Soso, Miss., June 29, 1996, and Yvonne Bevins and Anita Williams, taped interview with Florence Blaylock, July 4, 1996 (tapes in possession of Florence Blaylock, Soso, Miss.). . . .

51 "The Lynching Century: African Americans Who Died in Racial Violence in the United States: Names of the Dead, Dates of Death, Places of Death, 1865–1965" (www.geocities.com/Colosseum/Base/8507/NLPlaces2.htm); *Laurel Daily Leader*, Oct. 23, 1922.

52 *Laurel Daily Leader*, Oct. 20, 21, 1922. In 1979 Hulon Myers recalled how the Klan "would go in and march around and they would hand the preacher a letter, maybe it would have a hundred dollars in it" (interview with Hulon Myers, 33).

53 Florence Blaylock, telephone conversation with author, Mar. 5, 2000, ML-USM.

54 E. Franklin Frazier, *The Negro Family in the United States* (Chicago, 1939), 215–45.

55 Melba Riddle, e-mail message to author, Nov. 3, 1999; Rhonda Benoit, e-mail message to author, Jan. 14, 2000; Frances Jackson, e-mail message to author, Apr. 30, 2000, all at ML-USM.

56 Wade Hall, *Passing for Black: The Life and Careers of Mae Street Kidd* (Lexington, Ky., 1998), 176–77.

57 Anna Knight, *Mississippi Girl*, 14–15; Annette Knight, conversation with author, Soso, Miss., July 22, 1996, and Florence Blaylock, Dorothy Marsh, and Olga Watts, conversation with author, Soso, Miss., July 22, 1996, ML-USM;

Deposition of Fannie House (Howze), in *Martha Ann Musgrove et al. v. J. R. McPherson et al.*, Jan. 27, 1914, case no. 675, Chancery Court of Jones County, Laurel, Miss., copy in Kenneth Welch Genealogy Files. . . .

58 *Ellisville Progressive*, Mar. 16, 1922.

59 Memories of the Klan's harassment of whites were described by Frances Gandy-Walsh, e-mail message to author, June 28, 2000, ML-USM. Dates of deaths are from individual tombstones. . . .

60 John Shelton Reed, "Mixing in the Mountains," *Southern Cultures* 3, no. 4 (spring 1998), 29.

61 On developing notions of race and "whiteness," see esp. Leon Litwack, *Trouble in Mind: Black Southerners in the Age of Jim Crow* (New York, 1998); Grace Elizabeth Hale, *Making Whiteness: The Culture of Segregation in the South, 1890–1940* (New York, 1998); and David R. Roediger, *The Wages of Whiteness: Race and the Making of the American Working Class* (New York, 1991).

7

PILGRIMAGE TO THE PAST

Public history, women, and the racial order

Jack E. Davis

Here, Jack E. Davis analyzes the "Natchez Pilgrimage," an annual event focused on tours of the antebellum mansions in this Mississippi city. The Pilgrimage began during the Great Depression as a way to bring tourists into the town. It was, Davis writes, "the consummate history lesson," when "Natchez became a fantasy world in which the past seemed to co-exist with the present."

That fantasy world showed the Old South as whites wanted it to have been—a superior culture in which happy slaves served dominant but kindly masters and mistresses. Blacks in Natchez had roles in the Pilgrimage only as subordinates, not as "decision makers in the production of history." And, while the Pilgrimage was created and organized by Natchez women and in some ways valorized their place in history, it also advanced "traditional patriarchal attitudes," displaying women only in "traditional roles."

Like other authors in this volume, Davis argues for the importance of culture in the formation of New South history. The Pilgrimage, he writes, was an expression of "white cultural identity," and illustrates his argument that "at bottom, segregation was a function of white perceptions about blacks and black culture."

* * *

"Natchez Pickaninnies," reads the caption of the circa-1930s black and white photograph found in a local history monograph. In it four black children, with arms wrapped around their knees, are huddled together on the side of a downed tree. Their clothes are worn and tattered and bear the look of hand-me-downs. All four are bare-footed and obviously poor. The faces of three share the same dispassionate expressions. The fourth, the biggest boy, wears a floppy hat smartly cocked back on his crown, and he reveals a faint grin. Presumably, they were not accustomed to being in the focal point of a camera lens. It is also safe to assume that they were unaware that the camera would make them part of the local historical record, one that today is recognizably incomplete and misinformed.[1]

The photograph comes from a small book titled *Natchez of Long Ago and the Pilgrimage*, by Katherine Grafton Miller. In itself, the photograph is not degrading. But within the context of Miller's 1938 book, it assumes a specific social meaning and purpose. The Natchez pickaninnies are alone among the book's fifty-three other photographs ennobling whites and antebellum traditions: hoopskirted belles, aristocratic men, magnolia-shaded mansions, and black mammies and footmen tending to all. Miller's account of historic Natchez and "the golden days of the Old South" offered to white readers an inflated conception of their heritage and culture. The compliant servants and the barefooted pickaninnies render the book's only images of black life. Their unflattering contrast to the white material elegance carries a subtextual message that undoubtedly reinforced the assumption of difference between two cultures.[2]

Miller likely was not interested in subtextual messages. She wrote her book as a tribute to the Natchez Pilgrimage, a weeklong spring event in which private antebellum homes were opened to the public for an admission price. Miller was a founder and the exalted empress of the Pilgrimage, which began in the early 1930s and ultimately evolved into a community mnemonic more powerful than the Lost Cause creed, history textbooks, or any other local ritual or ceremony. It was the consummate history lesson—animated, inspiring, and righteous. During Pilgrimage week, Natchez became a fantasy world in which the past seemed to co-exist with the present. One could hardly know Natchez without knowing the Pilgrimage. The latter was the undergirding of a burgeoning local tourist industry, an industry that quickly grew to rival farming and manufacturing and eventually to surpass both.

Along with Miller, fellow members of the all-female Natchez Garden Club created the Pilgrimage and oversaw its operations. They elevated their spring event to a commanding status in the community by selling nostalgia to locals and tourists; it was an elixir in great demand. In a sense, the garden club women privatized public history. Yet their efforts went beyond profitmaking. In the tradition of their nineteenth-century foremothers, they served as the trustees of the local historical memory, and with their Pilgrimage, they raised the historical consciousness of Natchezians. Indeed, public history in Natchez is noteworthy for the expanded moral force it gave women. They were the trusted keepers of white culture and the vessels of its regeneration. They "sanctified history," said a longtime Natchez resident. "They've made it holy; they've made a religion out of it."[3]

Theirs was a civil religion given to value consensus rather than spiritual truth-seeking. It tolerated and nurtured only pleasant images of and messages about white heritage. Pilgrimage festivities dwelled on themes of innocence, simplicity, family, and virtue, and they brought to life a vision of the Old South that was deeply embedded in the regional imagination. David Donald, a native Mississippian, describes that vision as one of "magnolia-shaded plantations, where young gallants rode to foxes, cheered on by damsels in hoops and crinolines, and where happy pickaninnies divided their time between eating watermelons and serving mint juleps to the Old Massa." If that South, as Donald contends, "never existed outside of fiction," then by way of historical depiction, fiction flourished in Natchez. History's chief fabricators, the garden club women resurrected with their Pilgrimage a dream world of the past that shaped beliefs and perceptions in modern-day Natchez.[4]

In the qualities of spirit, Natchez and the Pilgrimage were one. The city, in fact, appropriated as its own the motto garden club members adopted in the 1930s for their annual Pilgrimage. "Natchez, 'Where the Old South Still Lives' " summed up concisely the image both wanted to convey to the world and did so with extraordinary success. As one observer of the Pilgrimage remarked in 1935, there is a "sense of timeless quality about this romantic little town." More than four decades later, the Pilgrimage moved a *Boston Herald* writer to describe Natchez as a page out of *Gone with the Wind*. "[D]uring Pilgrimage," the author noted, "it is possible to believe that there is still a land of cotton, where old times are truly not forgotten."[5]

The Pilgrimage indeed assured that the past would be not forgotten and thus sustained history's role as a social determinant. Like the photograph of pickaninnies that provided a visual reference from which whites could contrast their imagined cultural elevation, the Pilgrimage animated an age of unquestioned white virtuousness. It was an age when the racial order allowed white southerners to march civilization to a pinnacle of greatness never reached before or after. This was the Pilgrimage myth. It was also the cultural reality that defined whites' social standing, as well as that of blacks, in southern life. The Pilgrimage myth was not created to justify racial traditions or to placate white guilt over the treatment of blacks. The former did not carry the latter, but the Pilgrimage did create a context that heightened the sense of whiteness and of a racial other. The spring event was a product of pre-existing myths, a producer of new ones, and a disseminator of both.*

---

* A section on the origins and early years of the Pilgrimage, from 1932 to 1944, has been omitted—ed.

.... Within a decade of its inception, the Pilgrimage had grown into a major tourist event of the Southeast. Miller and the Pilgrimage organizers were credited with developing a tourist trade at a time when travel agents described Mississippi as underdeveloped and wanting for interesting places. Each year, the hostesses of the Natchez homes were "receiving" an increasing number of visitors, and in 1977 a fall Pilgrimage was added. By the 1980s, a half million tourists were flocking to Natchez annually to see living history, and each year homeowners earned several thousand dollars for opening their private lives to visitors. "You didn't have a half a dozen houses fit to come see," said former mayor Troy B. Watkins of the early years. With the Pilgrimage, the garden club women made "a success out of nothing. And it was nothing."[6]

Natchez always had its history and tradition though. Miller and the others turned both into a livelihood, and Natchez seemed to have regained the prominence it formerly commanded in the antebellum South. In later years, the 1930s in Natchez were remembered not only for their economic hard times, but for a "Renaissance" in commercial and cultural life initiated by the founding of the Pilgrimage. The garden clubs were, by Watkins's account, "probably more responsible for bringing Natchez out of the doldrums back in the 30s. That was a bunch of determined women at the time."[7]

The evidence of a local revival was in the restored physical elegance of the mansions. Most of the homes on tour were of early to mid-nineteenth-century vintage. One of Natchez's great contributions to that period was its grand domestic architecture. The inclusion of Federal and Greek revival forms gave Natchez an architectural grandeur that compared to its celebrated citizenry. The local nabobs engaged local master builders, many originally from the East, who duplicated a national trend of integrating classical forms, common in public architecture, into domestic design. Many of the skilled workers in wood and plaster, as well as the landscape gardeners, were both locals and European immigrants. Slaves lent their own carpentry and bricklaying skills and, of course, their muscle. Clay and timber were the principal building materials and were available locally. Decorative work came from abroad: iron from Spain and Belgium and stained glass from the latter. The nabobs furnished their mansions with French and English pieces and Italian paintings. Elevated locations enhanced the stately appearance of the houses, removed residents and guests from mosquito-infested bottomlands, and provided the master with a perch from which he could watch over his labor. The mansion was his most prominent expression of success and social rank. He built it on the idea of familial permanence and social continuity, bequeathed it as a home place and symbol of status to be possessed by his children and grandchildren. Like a surname it was part of his legacy.[8]

One of the mansions that contributed to Natchez's larger legacy and that represented local architecture "at its best" evolved in part from the efforts of a woman, Jane Surget White. Eldest daughter of Pierre Surget, she gave her hand to John Hampton White, a shrewd and consequently wealthy land speculator previously from North Carolina; it was a strategic union for both White and the Surgets. Sometime around 1816 they commissioned the construction of a new mansion, which she named Arlington. Her husband died in 1819 during a yellow-fever epidemic. Yet evidence indicates that she had been the original force behind Arlington's planning and construction. The Whites hired an architect-contractor, who was probably from Philadelphia, and they apparently allowed him to study existing local design before beginning his own Natchez project. What he created reflected a "Southern Colonial" form that would become commonplace in Natchez.[9]

The result was a sturdy, two-story brick structure of Georgian precision. Inside were seventeen-and-a-half-foot ceilings, eight rooms, including a music room and library, and a rear gallery. Handcarved rosewood furniture complemented cornices of like design above the windows and interior doors. Up and downstairs front entrances, with fanlighted transoms and glass side panels, led in from a large portico, fronted by four Tuscan columns supporting a frieze-trimmed pediment. The white-pillared facade, which later came to epitomize the southern mansion in the popular imagination, had not reached most other parts of the South at the time of Arlington's construction. White did not live long enough to realize her own role in helping to establish a trend in southern architecture. Legend has it that she hosted a ball to celebrate the opening of her new home, was overcome by the festivities, and died in her sleep that night. Whatever the circumstances of her death, she foreshadowed an architectural matriarchy that characterized twentieth-century Natchez. Her family descendants would help build the Pilgrimage and would display their own homes.[10]

In those later years, the great houses such as Arlington were tangible reminders of the South's unique past. On speaking tours promoting the Pilgrimage, Miller said Natchez's "houses show history-making events and epochs." In the minds of white southerners, such homes conjured up the style of life of a "vanished culture" that prevailed when graciousness and an easy pace defined the norm, when the South commanded a certain sense of order, permanence, and leadership.[11]

Even after the Civil War assailed the South's sense of itself, the surviving mansions stood as the ultimate vestiges of security and restoration. Perhaps the best known example of this symbolism is the place of Tara in *Gone with the Wind*. In the climax of Margaret Mitchell's romance, after Sherman's fiery procession sweeps through Atlanta, Scarlett retreats to the family plantation in the North Georgia countryside. Her life and livelihood have been ravaged by the war. But there the family home, Tara, still stands, cast in immortality. Its very survival of the war is portentous. It is the nourishment of Scarlett's being, easing her despair and granting her hope and a future. Without such great houses as Tara in their stories, southern writers of the early tradition could not have conveyed the desired sense of place and ordered civilization, not to mention romance, to their readers.[12]

Before Mitchell's *Gone with the Wind*, Mississippi's Stark Young recognized the singular importance of the stately residence as a device to establish the setting of an Old South novel of popular appeal. He chose Natchez as the setting of *So Red the Rose* in part because he saw its antebellum mansions as "the richest things of their kind in America." They were rich in visual splendor, family and regional heritage, and symbolism. . . . In actuality, columned mansions of Natchez's collection and plantation houses of Tara's cinematic magnificence did not dominate the architectural landscape of the Old South; they represented the exception—and Natchez's exceptionalism.[13]

Mitchell herself understood this historic fact. She fought vigorously with Hollywood filmmakers to keep columns off Tara. Writing a close friend, she said she wanted to keep it consistent with "the healthy, hearty, country and somewhat crude civilization" of North Georgia, the book's setting for Tara. She had found the domestic scenery in the film adaptation of *So Red the Rose* overly spectacular and artificial. One reviewer referred to the 1935 movie as "history-in-hoopskirts." That Hollywood and the movie-going public confused the Natchez houses on the screen with an architectural standard of the Old South truly grieved her. She did not "know whether to laugh or to throw up" at the thought that the producers of *Gone with the Wind* might try to duplicate the showy grandeur of Natchez.[14]

But Mitchell was waging a losing battle against a powerful cultural myth. Fellow southerners of her and Young's day and race saw white-columned mansions as a lost norm and attached a meaning to them that went beyond mere shelter, taste, and even wealth; they were manifest proof of the ascendancy of southern white civilization over all other civilized societies. One society that offered an acceptable comparison to the grand Old South was that of the Athenian Greeks, whose architectural style provided a source of inspiration for the latter-day civilization.[15]

The women of the Pilgrimage believed that the great homes continued to bestow the same meaning of prestige and social position as they did for the original occupants. To the garden clubs, Natchez's architectural contribution to the nineteenth century also belonged to the twentieth. This was the legacy of Jane Surget White and the others, or at least that was how the Pilgrimage women perceived it, and they undertook the responsibility of perpetuating it. They looked upon that responsibility as a cultural mission defined by history. As the organizers of the Pilgrimage, they were also prophets of white cultural integrity. History played an integral role in their collective stewardship.

The mansions of Natchez provided the visual props to the mythic story of their idealized culture. When Mississippi newspaperman and writer Hodding Carter visited the Spring Pilgrimage in the early 1940s, he observed that each mansion "has its unending story of hope and change and lost greatness and despair." Another observer attributed Natchez's far-reaching attraction to not only its "hallowed atmosphere" of "august abodes" but also to the Pilgrimage's success at preserving "the spirit of the Old South." He called Natchez's tourists "culture-seekers" and described the old river city as a last remnant of "the cream of American culture."[16]

The more pleasant scenes of that Old South civilization were brought to life every spring in the Confederate Pageant, a stage production that became part of the Pilgrimage in the early years. . . . Visitors were treated to "beauteous" southern belles in hoopskirts, pantaloons, and ball gowns, and stalwart young beaux in frock coats, military dress, and fox-hunting jodhpurs. All graced a series of animated tableaux that composed the pageant. Locals from every generation performed in skits and dances celebrating antebellum culture. With the musical score dominated by songs of Stephen Foster (a southern favorite who was actually a Yankee), the whole effect gave profound life to moonlight-on-magnolia romanticism.[17]

The pageant was a myth-building reenactment of an "enchanted way of life," to which whites held an intransigent faith, even though it never truly existed. The tableaux avoided the tender subjects of southern defeat and intolerance and instead followed a patriotic thematic line—from the "Unfurling of Old Glory" to the wedding of Jefferson Davis and Natchez's Varina Howell to past time soirees and a Confederate farewell ball. The pageant pointedly associated Natchez with "great" men of history, however indirect the connections with those men, including Jefferson Davis, John James Audubon, and the infamous but honorable Aaron Burr. "[A]ll these are Natchez," proclaimed the 1992 pageant program guide, as were "Romance, grandeur, chivalry, wealth," and "Adventure, action, boldness, strength."[18]

The cultural heroes and the self-congratulatory images were parts of the social relationship that twentieth-century white southerners forged with the past. That relationship gave meaning to life, while it substituted for the larger and elusive American relationship with economic prosperity, educational prominence, military success, and national respect. One might interpret the ceremonious exaltation of the mythic past as the collective yearning to inhabit it, to turn back the calendar far enough to escape the feeling of loss, which was heightened by conditions breeding runaway social change: the Great Depression, World War II, and later the cold war and the civil rights movement. "We, as a new generation in a changing South," noted the program for the 1940 pageant, "take pride in preserving that which seems best in our glorious heritage."[19]

Along with the grandeur, one outstanding feature of the pageant was the presence of children. Participation in the pageant was a family tradition, with two or three generations taking the stage together year after year. No less than Little League or the Girl Scouts, the pageant was part of the upbringing of children of garden club members. For example, one six-year-old girl whose family regularly devoted itself to Pilgrimage activities was described in 1984 as being "like any other little girl," except that she had a large bedroom with twelve-foot ceilings, a closet with hoopskirts and pantalets hanging among her blue jeans, and a dresser covered with countless Pilgrimage party invitations. Children were groomed at an early age for a succession of parts in the pageant, often starting as a young maypole dancer and working up to a member of the royal court.[20]

Every pageant had two royal courts—each representing a garden club. Presiding over the courts were a king and queen. It was not unusual to find in some families a mother who had passed along her queen's tiara and scepter to her daughter, or a boy who had followed in his older brother's footsteps as king. Candidates for royal couple were required to be students and were judged on citizenship, academic achievements, and, of course, family and background. Once the couples were chosen and announced, an anticipated moment in some circles, the local newspaper played up the qualifications of the selectees. As was tradition, the respective royal couples were honored at a private "Royal Ball" of pageant participants. They were then introduced to the public at the Confederate Pageant, where family and friends sat conspicuously in the "Royal Box" along with the garden club presidents. The women wore hoopskirts and the men equivalent formal attire. In the closing tableau, the royal families and guests stood in glorification of the not-forgotten South to honor the king and queen, cueing the rest of the audience to rise as the music of "Dixie" filled the auditorium.[21]

From the pageant and Pilgrimage came a palatable history of order, innocence, and leisure. As one garden club member put it, the Pilgrimage organizers were "trying to make something pleasant and happy. They are not trying to show anything that was unattractive." . . . . In the Pilgrimage version of antebellum Natchez, society was a natural bias born out of family loyalty and regional and racial pride. That version was codified into law in 1940 when the garden clubs persuaded city aldermen to institute an ordinance mandating the licensing of all tour guides. Applicants were required to pass an exam, developed by the two clubs, in local history, horticulture, architecture, and "cultural facts." Violators of the ordinance could be fined up to fifty dollars and jailed up to ten days.[22]

Historical truth that subverted vaunted images of bravery, honor, and solidarity had no place in Pilgrimage lore. By means of omission and hyperbole, the historical message of the spring ritual insulated the dominant culture from scurrilous realities and extolled ideal group values and virtues. Tourists did learn about the rowdy river life at Natchez-under-the-Hill, but the local trustees of history humorously sloughed it off as a bawdy other world worthy only for its contrast to the culture on top of the hill. Not completely taken in by the pomp and ceremony of the Pilgrimage, Hodding Carter understood that the stories of the Natchez elite were festooned in myth, like moss on the oak trees that shaded them. "It is pleasant and easier," he wrote, "to fit old Natchez to a pattern of brave gentility shrouded in candlelight, and of quiet breeding that is the presently dismissed handmaiden of wealth, and of community integrity as unassailable as the classic proportions of a Corinthian pillar." Carter knew that tourists encountered a portraiture of Natchez life in the Old South that was incomplete.[23]

One of the Pilgrimage's more egregious omissions was an explanation of how Natchez's extraordinary collection of mansions escaped Yankee pyromania during the "War between the States." What the Pilgrimage did not tell tourists is that Natchez had the distinction of surrendering on two separate occasions to Union forces. Following the forty-four-day struggle required to seize Vicksburg, Natchez submitted to Union occupation without a fight. Natchezians welcomed their enemy, according to historian Ronald Davis, with "waving handkerchiefs and unfurled American flags." They then turned their mansions into "perfect hotel[s]" for high-ranking officers. More than a century after embers cooled in Vicksburg, residents there would remember Natchez's wartime hospitality as a traitorous deed.[24]

What the Pilgrimage did promote was the idea of a surviving aristocracy. However one wishes to define aristocracy, in Natchez the word was associated with wealth, intelligence, family, and continuity. One early sentimental historian said of old Natchez that men of only the best breeding populated the region, talented men "of education and high social standing." These were the words of "Major" Steve Power, whose work Miller consulted when forming her own vision of Natchez past. The myth of local exceptionalism was so enduring that Natchez society impressed even H. L. Mencken, whose haughty standards not even the Anglo Saxons themselves could meet. He called the old Natchez elite "one of the best the Western Hemisphere has seen" and thus propagated the myth himself. Long after the deaths of its originators, the myth betrayed itself in a 1992 Pilgrimage program guide that described old Natchez as "an early magnet for men with a lust for life. . . . A bustling river town full of passion, power, and paradise."[25]

The elite of Natchez were not without wealth, of course. Even before the founding of the Pilgrimage, locals habitually boasted that antebellum Natchez was unsurpassed in terms of personal fortune. That claim contained, to quote one recent historian, "elements of mythmaking that would take on new dimensions with the introduction of the 'Natchez Pilgrimage.' " Antebellum Natchez had been indeed a cosmopolitan city, and concentrated within the district was an impressive number of family fortunes. This was the era that the Pilgrimage resurrected, when Natchez could lay claim to a portion of estates valued over $100,000 that was greater than that held by America's wealthy in Newport, Rhode Island, and in the Eighteenth Ward of New York City. Yet the so-called local nabobery was a group constantly in flux, with shallow, mostly early nineteenth-century roots. If there were those who inherited wealth—and thus social status—and those who brought their wealth when they came to Natchez, there were also the nouveau riche, those who rose to social prominence by way of successful business ventures. Such traits might ordinarily be considered commendable, but the Pilgrimage preferred the inherited qualities of bloodline over those acquired by way of common ambition.[26]

In sensing something extraordinary about their history and community, Pilgrimage folks showed an almost messianic fervor in their resolve to share Natchez with the rest of the world. "It is 'noblesse oblige,' " noted a local history, "on the part of the members of the Garden Club, who work and give that their good purposes may be served." Beyond the Pilgrimage's economic benefits was the self-gratification that Natchez's reborn greatness would not go unrecognized in other corners of the globe. If Yankees could not respect the modern South, their enthusiasm for the Pilgrimage revealed an enduring appreciation for what the South had once been. Natchez is a "modern miracle," noted a writer in *Better Homes and Gardens*. Those who have made it so "deserve a nation's thanks," for one "will come away with a feeling of awe, and a prayer for the perpetuation of such haunting sweetness." A 1935 *New York Times* article complimented Natchez as a "romantic little town . . . tinged with a nostalgia for days and manners that are gone; with regret that this culture went down in ruin."[27]

Even the image of Katherine Miller in the founding of the Pilgrimage was tinged with mythic nostalgia. Considered the personification of Natchez itself, Miller in organizing the first Pilgrimage was acclaimed as a brave woman who singlehandedly overcame mountainous obstacles of public pessimism and complacency to restore Natchez to its former glory. One Natchez historian, Harnett T. Kane, described Miller as having "the pent-up energy of a buzz-bomb ... a combination of Miss Nelly of N'Orleans and Tallulah Bankhead, with a slight dash of P. T. Barnum." With Natchez caught in the economic grip of the depression and teetering at the brink of financial ruin, Miller made the momentous decision to sell, by another observer's account, "the last thing that we have left to sell of our Past: the Past itself." With Miller at the helm, the opening day of the first official Pilgrimage in 1932 was depicted as an epochal event, a cataclysm in the course of Natchez's future that occurred with the redemption of its history. The garden club women invested time, sweat, money, and new gray hairs in preparing for the opening day, with no assurance of success. Failure would mean shame. "Suddenly it happened," wrote Kane, reconstructing the first day into a great climax. "From all directions, by car, bus, and train, people were pouring in."[28]

The romantic genesis also included stories of families and their ancestral mansions being delivered from the insuperable depths of ruin. Many of the families indeed had suffered depression-wrought hardships, and their houses consequently fell into disrepair. Pilgrimage profits afforded the restoration of Natchez's antebellum architecture and the continued tenancy of the old families. Yet in Pilgrimage lore, a commiserating eyebrow was raised to those whites who had fallen from luxury to live in reduced circumstances. The Grecian columns and white porticoes had become a mere facade behind which families survived without the usual platoon of servants and with, instead, plenty of bare cupboard space and tax bills. The image that was projected smacked of a modern-day Lost Cause comparable to the suffering of ancestors who forfeited their slaves and fortunes during the Civil War. It was another chapter of pathos in the South's beleaguered history, one that ignored the perpetual economic instability of blacks and many whites. In his sentimental rendition of the elite's misfortunes, Kane wrote that the downtrodden elite "had only the house, a place they could not afford to heat in the winter, in which they must live through the summer without ice." They were "too poor to paint, too proud to whitewash," he wrote in hackneyed description of the South's evanescent fortunes. "Granddaughters of mansion builders walked a mile or so into town from the big house to save a nickel."[29]

The myth of genteel poverty and the founding of the Pilgrimage was so profound that in 1950 it became the material of a modern romance novel. In *The Natchez Woman*, Alice Graham (a descendent of an old Natchez family) forges fiction with real-life themes, such as love, divorce, death, tragedy, ruin, and the Pilgrimage founding. All add up to a soppy melodrama. Graham depicts the Pilgrimage founding as a fateful turn of events that spared many elite from economic privation and public embarrassment. The book's protagonist is Jane Elliston, the archetypical garden club woman. Jane finds her ancestral home slipping from her financial grasp, and transforming, Graham writes, "like a coagulation of leaves in the swamp, disintegrating, giving out an unhealthy atmosphere." Jane grows increasingly disillusioned with the burdens of an elite life. "I had to fight the house," she says, "just as I had to fight the land. Rule it, not let it rule me." She and her husband cannot seem to turn a profit from their five plantations, so they subject themselves to accepting tourism as a necessary means of living. Her husband, Alec, moans about their shifting existence. "I feel harried," he says. "We have to skimp and save and almost starve ourselves here at home to put on a show, then we work ourselves to rags over the plantations." Jane complains, too, but she sees a "certain brilliance" in the Pilgrimage that offers a way out of her family's economic plight. "I don't want to live in a measly way," she says. "I want to live in a grand way, and to do that we have to have money."[30]

The theme Graham explores here is one of survival, which in Pilgrimage lore was an attribute attached to beleaguered mansion owners. During the Great Depression, poverty among the elite took on an elevated class distinction of sorts. Dire straits were associated with virtuosity for the old families who withstood the test of character by weathering the destabilizing atmosphere of the national economic crisis. Not all made it; many lost their homes. But those who did lose, as the tale went, were victims of incontrovertible conditions. They had, after all, come from good stock, where estimable values and upstanding character had been part of their upbringing. Their impoverishment was, as Pilgrimage folk saw it, the consequence of circumstance, or in the worst case, individual failure—but not culture.[31]

The Natchez elite failed to rationalize poverty among nonelite poor, black and white, in the same fashion. The cause of one group's poverty was different from the other's, as whites saw it, and was related to the cultures of the respective races and an individual's relationship with his or her culture. The southernized version of history communicated and legitimized the ideas of a culture of poverty (essentially black) and a culture of prosperity (essentially white), while the Pilgrimage did its part by celebrating whiteness and keeping history in the mind's eye. When whites glimpsed at history through the animation of the Pilgrimage, they saw a society and omnipotent culture that heralded traditional values of work, family, and education, those values believed to be central to the progress of civilization. "You have some values that are not based on money alone," said Grace MacNeil, scion of the Surget family. Whites saw themselves as the progenitors of fundamental American values and the lone human embodiment of those values."[32]

Probably the most crucial source in the South for taught values was the family, a central theme in the Pilgrimage. As one observer of Mississippi culture put it, "Families carry on the rich and vital culture which nourishes the spirit of their kin, molding, reshaping, and renewing them . . . in generation after generation." Family was an individual's strongest link with the past, and out of the repository of history came one's heritage and ultimately one's identity. Family represented continuity over change, tradition over innovation, and security over disruption; and the integrity of family assured the continuing stability of culture and society. Mississippi had a relatively small population (2.5 million in 1980), and all but one city (Jackson) had populations of fewer than 50,000. Family and kinship ties that laced this small-town state formed the cohesive fabric of Mississippi society. The Pilgrimage indeed paid elegant tribute, as one Confederate Pageant narrator put it, to "continuity of family and homeland across the generations."[33]

By no coincidence, family and social relationships have traditionally been favorite themes of some of Mississippi's fiction writers. Among those writers is novelist Ellen Douglas (pen name for Josephine Haxton), a native of Natchez and a descendent of its antebellum homes. Many of her stories are set in the imaginary town of Homochitto, a place that holds fast to social traditions. When writing about the fictitious community, she is often describing the manners and culture of her birthplace. She does just that in her first book, A Family's Affair, published in 1962. . . . "At its best," one reviewer noted, A Family's Affair "projects the sights, sounds, and rhythms of true Mississippi life." Fleshing out the central themes in Douglas's fiction reveals much about the actual in Natchez.[34]

In A Family's Affair, the varied lives of Douglas's characters come together in a saga about family life. She carries her story from the early twentieth century through three generations of the Andersons and McGoverns, a clan of cousin intermarriages and of Scotch ancestry. At its core, the book is both a testament to and a study of the value and meaning of family: an individual's need of a support structure, despite that person's own inner strengths; the complex patterns of kinship relationships and choosing an acceptable mate; and the utility of and emphasis on family loyalty.[35]

The women of Douglas's novel are the heart and soul of family life. They do not simply belong to their respective family; their own strengths are its foundation of stability. The book's story revolves primarily around the life of Kate Anderson, beginning with her acceptance of widowhood and forfeiture of remarriage to plan instead the futures of her three daughters. After her husband's death, Kate tried to keep the family plantation going. But "flood had compounded debt," forcing Kate to move her daughters and son to her mother's house in town. Although their financial stability is in question, their social status is not. They are among the impoverished elite. In Homochitto, as in Natchez, "poverty was more than respectable . . . and by its inverse standards the Andersons were the last word in aristocracy." A firmly determined woman, Kate Anderson knows that if she raises her three daughters within the dictates of their social class, they can still marry well.[36]

Family perpetuity and continuity serves as an important subtheme in Douglas's narrative. The Anderson and McGovern women cast their vision toward the future, which counterbalances that of the more present-minded men. In choosing a husband, one of Kate's daughters, Charlotte, plays her role well. She looks for the traits that would ensure a stable future for the family they would have together. She cares less about a prospect's "good looks or money" than about "strength and honor, and intelligence." As a result of prudent deliberation, Charlotte would marry "late, at twenty-five, for it took her a long time to find a man who met her standards . . . and her family's."[37]

For her part, Kate is pleased with Charlotte's choice, for already "he had made his reputation for stability" and "had everything she wanted in a son-in-law." Charlotte pursued and won the heart of Ralph McGovern, whose attributes Charlotte locates in her mother-in-law to be, Julia. In herself, Julia "demanded honor—virtue, good faith, loyalty and courage, and in everyone else she assumed it." After marriage and motherhood, Charlotte accepts her culturally determined task to indoctrinate in her own children the cultural values exemplified in her mother-in-law, including the "inflexibility of character" that Ralph and his brothers inherited from their parents. As Charlotte had learned, and as she teaches her children, their actions must remain above reproach or risk bringing shame on the family.[38]

Douglas's story of family life closes with the funeral of Kate Anderson. In the end the family members come "together because of her life, not her death," Douglas writes. "They all knew this, and knew that the others knew it, as clearly as if they had said it to each other." Even after Kate's death at eighty-five, the family takes her spirit as their moral compass and bond. In memory, her ideals, those of her society and culture, will be given continuity.[39]

Although prim and pure, yet anything but naive, Douglas's women are not helpless creatures of fragility and idleness. They indeed defy the mythic formulation of the southern lady. It is safe to assume that Kate Anderson and her fictional cohorts were conjured from Douglas's mental synthesis of historical and contemporary images. Yet their portrayal as the central, virtually unimpeachable executioners of moral authority and governesses of family honor and virtue does not reflect the errant fantasy of a fiction writer. These very character compositions affirm the value of *A Family's Affair* to the task of demystifying the garden club women of Natchez and their role as community historians. In their domestic responsibilities, social graces, as well as assertive posture, women of the Natchez elite were the real-life equivalent of Douglas's fictional characters.

More than sixty years earlier, Natchez historian Steve Power described a similar unreproachable woman of Natchez. He wrote that women were "trained in all that constitutes nobility of soul and sentiment, intelligence and purity, and their influence dominated the whole." Such paramount virtues also carried women through the crisis of war and destruction, according to Power and other local historians. "Reared in luxury from the cradle, every fine instinct carefully trained . . . too sad to weep, too proud to complain, they stooped with dignity and took up the broken thread of life and like their divine prototype 'went about doing good.' " Prophetically, he continued: "This was the work of those greathearted women who lived in those Natchez homes after the war."[40]

Indeed, Power's complimentary prose places his work perhaps closer to the description of a pulp novel than of a serious history. But whether derived from historical truth or contemporary projection, or both, the image he invoked reveals a persistent pattern of female assertion when placed next to the fictional Kate Anderson and the factual Katherine Miller. The female descendants of "those great-hearted women who lived in those Natchez homes" founded the Pilgrimage on their own initiative for the sake of their houses, their families, and their history, and they revitalized an idyll that would have comforted Power. Their initiative was consistent with gender conventions of the day, or at least with a contemporary view of proper womanhood. Mississippian David Cohn wrote in a 1940 *Atlantic Monthly* article, "Natchez Was a Lady," that "Many a war-broken Southern family owed its resuscitation to the valor of its women, and this is largely true of the recent rise of Natchez."[41]

White women of Natchez found within the Pilgrimage a unique public repository for preserving history, heritage, and the culture. Southern society expected white women to be unblemished paragons of moral rectitude, and by example and nurturance they gave assurances to the perpetuation of the dominant culture's values. As late as 1947, the Natchez Garden Club reminded its members that they "shalt be an example in thy home." The Pilgrimage facilitated their labor. It was a veritable instructional aid that gave viable proof to the veracity of their lessons. It animated a way of life—the best of civilization—that whites could equate with their values and principles.[42]

It also enhanced the public life of women, even as it reinforced the social hierarchy. With the Pilgrimage, white women enlarged their circle of influence outside the family, developed and applied organizing and business skills, and in some instances expanded their political activities, especially on issues dealing with tourism or the community's appearance. To the standard texts that purged women from the historical record, the public history over which white women had control offered a correction that noted their involvement in celebrated historical events and activities, casting them as anything but passive objects. . . . One of the common qualities that the Pilgrimage shared with American pageants was the advancement of traditional patriarchal attitudes toward women, despite the enriching contributions to their contemporary lives. Whether at home teaching children the values of the culture or fostering the established social order through public history, white women were perpetuating their own second-class status. Repudiating what felt like the natural order of humanity and the sexes was rare. The southern white woman instead expected her pedestal, and she reached suppliantly for the supporting hand of her man as she took her place upon it.[43]

Just as public history fixed women in traditional roles, it fixed blacks in their prescribed social function and place. Unlike women, blacks were not decision makers in the production of history. They had little, if any, voice in public history, and there were no sympathetic whites advancing an objective perspective of black contributions. Quaint figures trimming the romantic image of the Old South, blacks were presented as abiding slaves engaged in the seemingly inconsequential activities of the wet nurse and the cotton picker. Presumably, their masters single-handedly turned fortunes out of the land and built mansions with their fortunes, apart from the "inconsequential" labor of the enslaved.

Consistent with their designated place in southern society, blacks played only menial parts in the Pilgrimage, both behind the scenes and in the public eye. They manned the crews needed for cooking, cleaning, and preparation for a countless number of all-white private and public parties and to serve the month-long stream of visitors. One early source describing and promoting the Pilgrimage mentioned: "Perhaps a grizzled, bent, old ex-slave stands to bow you in, or a strapping, courteous young negro will direct the parking of your car and reply if you question him . . . that his people have been here since 'befo' de' War' in the service of the same family. . . . [Or] a little colored boy stoops and wipes your shoes lest you have the embarrassment of taking unnoticed souvenirs of park and garden."[44]

Blacks also played conspicuous roles in the animated scenes of the Pilgrimage. Guests were treated to landscapes of belles and beaux flanked by heavyset black "mammies," who wore traditional checked-gingham dresses with large aprons, colorful bandanas wrapped around their heads, and performed the servile duties of slave days. In one of the more popular tableaux, happy blacks, each with a canvas sack slung over a shoulder, stood behind a row of cotton bolls and entertained the audience with slave songs. The painted backdrop captured the world of the enslaved: a field high in cotton, a slave shack, and an outdoor privy. Completing the stereotype were two black children placed in the foreground eating watermelon.

Another favorite of locals and guests was a "chorus of 100 voices" performed at a local black church. The musical performances were variously called "Heaven Bound," "Straight and Narrow Path," and "The Evolution of the Negro Spiritual." Whichever name, the theme was always the same: the slave's journey was a continual ascent, beginning with heathenish Africa and concluding with the Promised Land. But it was God's inscrutable will, as in any biblical story, that there should be suffering along the way. For the African, it came with the cruel slave traders, who were implicitly northern and ruthlessly greedy. Redemption came with sale to the kindly white southerner, proof of the journey's upward direction. Southern civilization brought Christian conversion and earthly grace; it was the final stop and preparation for entering the gates of heaven.[45]

White minds turned the ethereal performances into an earthly validation of the righteousness of their system. In her scrapbook on the Pilgrimage, Miller pasted a Natchez Democrat clipping that described "Heaven Bound" as altogether "creditable," and as giving "an insight into the simple faith and possibilities of the colored race." A 1952 article in the journal of the Natchez Garden Club, Over the Garden Wall, revealed a self-deluding notion of the past when it noted, "A cherished testimonial to masters and slaves is the fact that the spirituals though born in slavery contain no note of bitterness. They voice the cardinal virtues of patience, forbearance, love, faith, and hope."[46]

To white ears, the crooning of a mournful spiritual was one of the few contributions of black culture to southern civilization. From slavery to the era of television, black performers had always pleased the senses and sensibilities of whites, in part because they exhibited the unthreatening, childlike qualities that whites considered the finest attributes of blacks. The joyous singing in the Pilgrimage was a reassurance to whites that the "old timey darkey" was still around or reemerging in the contemporary black character. The Natchez Democrat's editor wrote in 1934: "Nature has endowed members of the negro race with the great gift of music ... and their melodies have brought happiness to millions." From the white perspective, the spiritual singer was little different from the "old time mammies." Both existed for the purpose of improving the quality of life of whites, and both fulfilled the wistful vision of the faithful servant. When ninety-six-year-old Aunt Alice, who had served six generations of families at Melrose, died in 1936, her obituary in the *Democrat* was almost nostalgic. It described her as "another of those typical old negro mammies of 'befo de war' ... a trusted and valued *part* of the household" (emphasis added). Only typical old Negroes were honored with an obituary in Natchez's white newspaper.[47]

For blacks, the Pilgrimage was a conflicting experience with confounding consequences. While it subjected them to roles that strengthened racial stereotypes, it offered the opportunity to bring a few tourist dollars into the black community. In 1956, for instance, blacks who were part of the Confederate Pageant cast earned forty-five to fifty-four dollars for eighteen performances. The addition of the spirituals in 1933 in fact began as a black idea, sold to the garden club as a fund-raiser for a library for the black schools. Dolores George (pseudonym), who came from an established black family, participated in "Heaven Bound" from the time she was a young girl until she left for college in the 1940s. She earned a little money for her performance, while the church kept a portion for expenses. During the Pilgrimage, her brother made extra money by chauffeuring visitors around Natchez. A neighbor, Laura Davis, was engaged to make costumes for the Pilgrimage.[48]

But this kind of economic exploitation of the Pilgrimage came with social costs. During the 1941 Pilgrimage, a teacher from the all-black Natchez College complained that the singers in the cotton-picking tableaux were dressed "in costumes which were demeaning to the race." Apparently, some of the singers agreed. How and if the matter was resolved is unclear, but protestations of this nature were rare before the civil rights struggle of the 1960s. Until then, blacks continued to play the roles of affable servants. Similar to blacks who internalized the white image of blackness, those who participated in the Pilgrimage reinforced white reality by sending a false message, certainly unintentionally, to whites about the universal acceptance of the racial order.[49]

Voicing antipathy for the Pilgrimage publicly would have questioned the white sense of goodness. Whites believed that in allowing blacks to participate in the Pilgrimage and to share in white heritage they were doing a service to the black community. Writer and garden club member Ethel Fleming articulated this idea in a WPA project. According to her, "It was indeed fortunate for the negroes of Natchez and vicinity that the highest type of white people settled here. That culture and refinement of the Masters and Mistresses is still reflected in the lives of the descendants of their slaves as well as in the descendants of the free negroes who lived here." Natchezian Steve Power pronounced a similar historical gospel decades before when he asked whether the transformation of the "untutored savage" to the "trusted servant" was a "miracle wrought by magic." He found the answer in the "benign influences" of the "Southern matron" who undertook "the task of civilizing, training and protecting those who were dependent on her."[50]

White women, women of the Pilgrimage, committed themselves to the norm of racial superiority expressed in Power's words. Commonplace to that norm was the notion that there was nothing degrading about a system that allowed the best to rise above those, white and black, who were in need of oversight. Southern white women were certain of the goodness of the southern way of life, just as they raised their sons and daughters to believe in the righteousness of their class and race—sons and daughters who often grew up to be elitists themselves. Like their male counterparts, women feared the downfall of civilization in the absence of an enforced racial hierarchy. Southern civilization's very integrity reflected that of heir own. If male authorities imposed this line of thinking upon them, women did not protest it. Instead, a persistent ideology of race and class bonded the two sexes.[51]

Favored by both men and women, segregation was the most salient expression of biracial society. No exception, Natchez had the usual physical duplication in public conveyances: restrooms, waiting rooms, water fountains, schools, movie theater seating, hospital wings, recreational areas, cemeteries, and neighborhoods—and even a separate "All Negro Fair," which featured livestock, crafts, and produce. The practice of segregation actually was somewhat less rigid than the ideal. But it was the idea of segregation that counted most. The locally owned retail shops, for instance, waited on customers in turn rather than by race, and white nurses cared for black patients at the municipal hospital. The county-operated poorhouse gave refuge to destitute elderly of both races before it closed its doors in the 1940s.[52]

At the other extreme were also outright exclusions. Until the 1960s, blacks could not use the municipal parks, and their only entry to white-owned restaurants that served blacks was through the back kitchen door. The most sacred forbiddance, of course, was black male sexual intimacy with white females. That restriction accommodated the white male privilege that, according to one school of thought, most completely defined the system of racial supremacy: access to women of both races.

Sexual boundaries were only one aspect of a larger, more complex problem. At bottom, segregation was a function of white perceptions about blacks and black culture. Searching for the reason for segregation, Robert Penn Warren in 1954 addressed the question to an anonymous Mississippi planter, "the very figure of Wade Hampton or Kirby Smith" (who could easily have been from Adams County). The planter articulated that reason in an unqualified single-word reply: "Character." To whites, blacks were culturally distinct, not only with respect to folk ways, but also in terms of their group code of conduct and behavior. The majority of blacks were regarded as emotionally and intellectually undeveloped, therefore lacking individual initiative and responsibilities. Whites located the origins of these presumed racial perversions in what they saw as a flawed value system and a deficient set of group norms. While holding up the historical figures of George Washington Carver and Booker T. Washington as cultural aberrations, the editor of the *Natchez Democrat* wrote, "the mass of the negroes show no inclination to self-advancement and achievements." The subordinate position of blacks was ascribed not to white self-interests nor to an oppressive social structure, but to an inherent inferiority of blacks themselves. Immutable conditions of culture, as whites saw it, were the chief impediment to black economic and social advancement. In its alleged state of arrested development and moral deficiency, black culture predetermined the plight of blacks as the South's lower caste and as the dominant among the poor.[53]

Based on these assumptions, segregation was necessary to retain racial and cultural integrity. Unchecked social interaction—even in circumstances not conducive to interracial sexual relationships—was tantamount to cultural commingling, and risked debasing white culture. Instead of blacks absorbing the traits of the "superior" white culture, the reverse might happen: whites would abandon the better attributes of their own culture for a diminished set of norms and values (as white poor had allegedly done). As one white Natchezian put it, blacks "have a carefree approach to so-called moral values, cultural standards, that whites would love to pick up." However imperfectly, institutional safeguards such as segregation were intended to stay the human impulse to moral depravity. At the same time, whites fancied themselves as stewards of humanity, morally and socially obliged to lift blacks from their cultural abyss. After all it had been whites, especially women, according to a local family biographer, who had exercised "that subtle, potent charm ... which transformed the very nature of the colored race from the savage imported from the wilds of Africa to the faithful, well-trained servant."[54]

Women were indeed inseparable from the practice of racial separation. At the core of the ideology of segregation were opposing cultural images of the fair flower of white womanhood and the aggressive black buck of an oversexed race. No greater "unconscious tribute was paid to Southern women by the severest critics of the social order," wrote Steve Power, when Reconstruction regimes deemed former slaves "worthy to stand side by side with the Caucasian."[55]

Psychosexual fears and socioeconomic competition can only partially explain the religious-like intensity behind the protected female and the lynched rapist. The link between white womanhood and culture better explains the motivation, not wholly chivalrous, driving that intensity and why women themselves were inclined to contribute to it. As was the case in the life and legacy of Kate Anderson, southern civilization was eternal in the white woman. Her unsullied body and soul were integral to not only the moral and spiritual integrity of the culture but also to its regeneration. She was the giver of life, and from her womb, the race and culture were reproduced. The system of segregation aided in securing her against her black pursuer and from what his behavior represented, the defilement of womanhood and the debasement of culture. Whites linked the preservation of the white southern way of life to that of feminine purity; without one or the other, the collapse of civilization was certain.[56]

A 1954 court case involving a Natchez women suggests just how deeply rooted in the culture was the fealty to protected white womanhood. One Mary Dunigan, who was white, brought a suit of libel against the *Natchez Times* for inadvertently identifying her in a news article as black. Dunigan's attorney argued that the error had caused her significant public humiliation. The case followed the conventional route of appeal to the Supreme Court of Mississippi, where the justices sided with the plaintiff. "Under Mississippi law," the decision read in part, "to assert in print that a white woman is a Negro is libelous per se." The court apparently did not appreciate that a label that was considered demeaning to a white woman might also bring grief to those called Negro. For a brief moment in her life, Dunigan had been made into an "Artificial Nigger," to borrow a short-story title from Flannery O'Connor. She became the creation of the white mind, an inverted perception of fact. In both instances—libeled woman and "Negro"— the image attached was incomplete without a near opposite and artificially exalting image about whiteness.[57]

Nothing raised the historical concept of cultural dissimilarities to a higher level of public consciousness than did the Pilgrimage. It was a public-sanctioned affair for white self-indulgence. Its very existence depended on the collective notion of white cultural superiority and on identifying the white race positively within the context of favorable and unfavorable images. At the same time, the Pilgrimage spotlighted stereotyped images of blacks and sustained the perception of cultural deficiencies by retreating the tone and tempo of the slave South.

In a sense, Natchezians, like other southerners, were prisoners of their history. It was a prison of which white women had been the architects and the builders and from whose walls neither male nor female cared to escape. History provided the cognitive basis for a two-tiered social order divided by race. Dismantling the caste system—changing attitudes and perceptions—would require not only rewriting history but overturning it, if not escaping it.

Until that day came, judgment day, whites embraced public history as a civil religion. The message of the Pilgrimage was delivered and received like the gospel of an evangelical minister: thrust into the open hearts of a willing flock. The worshiping of the past in Natchez was not so much a calculated defense of a system—and the beliefs and behavior behind it—as it was a search for and expression of cultural identity. Among those who carried the past in their minds with the passionate devotion that an evangelical carries the Bible, to quote Friedrich Nietzsche, "their cultivation of history [did] not serve pure knowledge but life." Ironically, life in Natchez was, David Cohn noted, lived "with the dead." To the living, the message of the Pilgrimage was clear—that white culture was endowed with the best of qualities from which all groups in southern society had benefited.[58]

NOTES

1 Katherine Grafton Miller, *Natchez of Long Ago and the Pilgrimage* (Natchez, 1938), 37.
2 Ibid., 5.
3 Interview with Marty Nathanson, by author, March 26, 1993.
4 David Donald quoted in Charles Sallis, "Images of Mississippi," in *A Sense of Place: Mississippi*, edited by Peggy W. Prenshaw and Jesse O. McKee (Jackson, Miss., 1979), 69.
5 *New York Times* [*NYT*], March 17, 1935; "A Page from *Gone with the Wind*," *Boston Herald American*, March 25, 1979; Elmer T. Peterson, "The Old South Lives Again!" *Better Homes and Gardens*, February 1938, 34–50; *Natchez Democrat* [*ND*], March 4, 1972. . . .
6 Troy B. Watkins interview; J. Oliver Emmerich, "Collapse and Recovery," in *A History of Mississippi*, ed. by R. A. McLemore (Hattiesburg, 1973), 106.
7 Troy B. Watkins interview; *Report of Self Evaluation; ND*, March 13, 1962, November 12, 1970; *Jackson Clarion-Ledger*, March 26, 1978; *Washington Post*, April 3, 1977; "Great Comeback," *Over the Garden Wall*, September 1955, 6.
8 Many of the scholarly studies of Natchez architecture are terribly flawed. . . . The most accurate study on Natchez architecture is Ronald Miller and Mary M. Miller, *The Great Houses of Natchez* (Jackson: University Press of Mississippi, 1986); and Ronald Miller and Mary M. Miller, *Natchez National Historical Park, Historic Resource Study* (Natchez, 1977).
9 J. Frazier Smith, *White Pillars: Early Life and Architecture of the Lower Mississippi Valley Country* (New York, 1941), 117 ("at"). Constructed in 1812, Auburn was actually the first home of this design in Natchez. See Miller and Miller, *Natchez National Historical Park*, 30–31.

10 Miller and Miller, *Natchez National Historical Park*, 115–17; Harnett T. Kane, *Natchez on the Mississippi* (New York, 1947), 166–69; Grace MacNeil interview; Nola Nance Oliver, *Natchez: Symbol of the Old South* (New York, 1940), 10–13.

11 *Birmingham News*, clipping, n.d., Miller Scrapbooks ("houses"); Oliver, *Natchez*, dust jacket ("vanished"); F. Gavin Davenport, *The Myth of Southern History: The Historical Consciousness in Twentieth-Century Southern Literature* (Nashville, 1970), 34 n.

12 Margaret Mitchell, *Gone with the Wind* (Garden City, N. Y., 1954), 266–67, 277, 287–88. . . .

13 Stark Young to Claribel Drake, February 2, 1935, Stark Young Letters, Mississippi Department of Archives and History [MDAH];. . . . *Stark Young, a Life in the Arts: Letters, 1900–1962*, ed. by John Pilkington (Baton Rouge, 1975), 119 (quote); Stark Young to Julia Young Robertson, March 18, 1935, ibid., 585, 617n.

14 Steven H. Scheuer, editor, *Movies on TV, 1988–1989* (New York, 1987), 729; Darden Asbury Pyron, *Southern Daughter: The Life of Margaret Mitchell* (New York, 1991), 370–72.

15 For a discussion of Greek Revival architecture of the Old South, see Smith, *White Pillars*.

16 Hodding Carter, *Lower Mississippi* (New York, 1942), 234, 251; Thomas Craven, "Culture of Natchez," newspaper clipping, n.d., in scrapbook. Accretion. box 1. NGCR ("culture-seekers").

17 Elmer Peterson, "The Old South Lives Again!" *Better Homes and Gardens*, Feb. 1938, 34; Executive board minutes, March 26, April 23, 1936; "The Confederate Pageant," *Over the Garden Wall*, March 1955, 6–9; "Seventh Annual Pilgrimage Tour Guide," 1938; and "Natchez Pilgrimage Guide," 1947, all in Natchez Garden Club Records [NGCR].

18 "A Mansion," *Over the Garden Wall*, March 1955, 11; "The Confederate Pageant, 1992," Confederate Pageant program guide, in author's possession.

19 "Confederate Ball: 9th Annual Pageant of the Original Natchez Garden Club, March 24–April 7, 1940," box 3, Garden Clubs of Misssissippi Records [GCMR]; Miller. "Natchez Is a Fairy Story"; Ruth Audley Beltzhoover interview. Some whites regarded the Old South luminaries as religious saints and martyrs. See Charles Reagan Wilson, *Baptized in Blood: The Religion of the Lost Cause, 1865–1920* (Athens, 1980), 25.

20 Carolyn Vance Smith, *Secrets of Natchez: From a Journalist's Notebook* (Natchez, 1984), 9–17.

21 Interview with Anabel Young Maxie, by Graham Hicks, August 25, 1981, MDAH; Interview with Mary Jane Beltzhoover, by author, March 27, 1993; Virginia Beltzhoover Morrison, Katherine Blankenstein, and Rebecca Benoist interviews; *ND*, April 2, 1969; Attendance at the Confederate Pageant, by author, March 27, 1992.

22 Anonymous interview ("trying"); Natchez Board of Aldermen [NBA] minutes, September 10, 1940; *Code of the City of Natchez, Mississippi, 1954*, Chapter 24, "Tourist Guides" ("cultural"); Mayor W. J. Byrne to Mrs. W. A. Sullivan, October 8, 1940, and Mrs. W. A. Sullivan to Honorable W. J. Byrne, October 23, 1940, Correspondence, box 3, NGCR. The city ordinance still exists, and Pilgrimage Tours administers the exam.

23 Carter, *Lower Mississippi*, 234, 251.

24 Ronald L. F. Davis, *Good and Faithful Labor: From Slavery to Sharecropping in the Natchez District, 1860–1890* (Westport, Conn., 1982), 59–62 ("waving");

Mrs. Harry C. Ogden to Mrs. Hanun Gardner, September 9, 1938, box 3, Henrietta Henry Papers, MDAH ("perfect"); Miller and Miller, *Natchez National Historical Park*, 111; Ronald L. F. Davis, *The Black Experience in Natchez* (Eastern National Park and Monument Association, 1994), 133; James M. McPherson, *Battle Cry of Freedom: The Civil War Era* (New York, 1989), 626–38; Kane, *Natchez*, 274–75; Nola Nance Oliver, *Natchez: Symbol of the Old South* (New York, 1940), 92.

25 Newspaper clipping, n.d., Miller Scrapbooks ("of"); Miller, *Natchez Long Ago*, passim; Mencken quoted in David L. Cohn, "Natchez Was a Lady," *Atlantic Monthly*, January 1940, 14. . . .;"The Confederate Pageant, 1992" ("an").

26 Morton Rothstein, "The Changing Social Networks and Investment Behavior of a Slaveholding Elite in the Ante-Bellum South: Some Natchez 'Nabobs,' 1800–1860," in *Entrepreneurs in Cultural Context*, edited by Sidney M. Greenfield, Arnold Strickon, and Robert Aubrey (Albuquerque, 1979), 67–68 (quote); William Scarborough, "Lords or Capitalists? The Natchez Nabobs in Comparative Perspective," *Journal of Mississippi History*, 75 (Sept. 1988), 239–67; D. Clayton James, *Antebellum Natchez* (Baton Rouge, 1968), 136–61.

27 Georgia Willson Newell and Charles Cromartie Compton, *Natchez and the Pilgrimage* (Southern Publishers, 1935), 5, 39 ("It"); Peterson, "The Old South Lives Again!" 34–50 ("modern"); *New York Times*, March 17, 1945.

28 Kane, *Natchez*, 337–41. See also Newell and Compton, *Natchez and the Pilgrimage*. Cohn, "Natchez Was a Lady," 15 ("the last").

29 Michael Wayne, *The Reshaping of Plantation Society: The Natchez District, 1860–1880* (Urbana, Ill., 1990), 71–109; Kane, *Natchez*, 335. . . .

30 Alice Walworth Graham, *The Natchez Woman* (Garden City, N.Y., 1950), 218–20.

31 See Editorial, *Over the Garden Wall*, 2.

32 *Jackson Daily News*, December 14, 1985.

33 Joanne V. Hawks, "A Historical Assessment," in *Rituals: The Importance of Family in the Development of Mississippi Society*, edited by Joanne V. Hawks and Mary Emma Graham (Jackson, Miss., 1986), 3–5; Mary Emma Graham, "Family as a Literary Theme," in ibid., 6–8; "What Shall Children Do with their Parents?" *Over the Garden Wall*, February 1949, 13, 19; Willie Morris, "A Sense of Place and the Americanization of Mississippi," in *A Sense of Place*, ed. Prenshaw and McKee, 3–13; Walker Percy, "Mississippi: The Fallen Paradise," *Harper's*, April 1965, 166–71; Sam Jones, narrator, 1994 Confederate Pageant, Natchez, Mississippi.

34 *New York Times Book Review*, July 8, 1962, 18 (quotes); Anthony Walton, *Mississippi: An American Journey* (New York, 1997), 25–28.

35 Ellen Douglas, *A Family's Affair* (Boston, 1961), 40–41.

36 Ibid., 33. . . .

37 Ibid., 33, 37, 40–41.

38 Ibid., 36–37, 433.

39 Ibid.

40 Steve Power, *The Memento: Old and New Natchez* (Louisville, Ky., 1897), 8, 13, 14.

41 Cohn, "Natchez Was a Lady," 15.

42 "Ten Commandments of the Modern Wife," *Over the Garden Wall*, October 1947, 5 (quote). . . . For a commentary about domesticity in southern society, see Anne Firor Scott, *The Southern Lady: From Pedestal to Politics, 1830–1930*

(Chicago, 1970); Catherine Clinton, *The Plantation Mistress: Woman's World in the Old South* (New York, 1982). Clinton offers the most insightful and, consequently, valuable examination of the thesis of southern women as keepers of culture.

43 Blair, *Torchbearers*, 120–30.

44 Newell and Compton, *Natchez and the Pilgrimage*, 23 (quote); *Memphis Commercial-Appeal [MC-A]*, February 23, 1941. Interview with Marion Kelly Ferry, by Graham Hicks, November 17, 1981. Interview with Clarence C. Eyrich Sr. and Clarence C. Eyrich Jr., by Elliot Trimble, August 12, 1981; and Interview with Mr. and Mrs. Joseph F. Dixon, by Graham Hicks, n.d., all in MDAH.

45 *MC-A*, February 23, 1941; "Natchez Pilgrimage Week." Natchez Pilgrimage brochure, 1933, box 7, folder 68, James Allen and Family Papers, MDAH: *ND*, March 15, 26, 1933; February 25. 1987; Allison Davis. "The Negro Church and Associations in the Lower South," June 1940, Carnegie-Myrdal Study, The Negro in America, Schomberg Collection Negro History, reel 5, 42–43, 68.

46 *ND*, clipping, n.d., Miller Scrapbooks ("creditable"); Mary P. McVeigh, "Negro Spirituals," *Over the Garden Wall*, April 1952, 20 ("A cherished").

47 *ND*, December 1, 1934 ("Nature"), May 6, 1936 ("Another"); Interview with Elliot Trimble, by author, September 17, 1993.

48 Interview with Dolores George [pseud.], by author, July 17, 1996; Interview with Charlotte Mackel Harrison, by author, December 22, 1996; Interview with, Mary Toles, by author, May 2, 1998; Library of Congress Copyright Certificate, April 23, 1936, issued to Julia Walker Harrison for "Heaven-bound Pilgrims," copy in author's possession; Natchez Pilgrimage brochures, 1965 and 1966, Natchez Pilgrimage Papers. Seventh Annual Pilgrimage Tour Guide, 1938, and Natchez Pilgrimage Guide, 1947, in Publicity and Promotions file; Executive board minutes, November 15, 1933, box 1; and Check Stubs file, box 11, all in NGCR.

49 Natchez Pilgrimage Historical file, box 7, NGCR ("Possible Evidence").

50 Ethel L. Fleming, "Achievements and Social Conditions of Negroes," Adams County Education, Negro Organizations file, WPA Projects Files, RG 60, box 217, MDAH; Power, *The Memento*, 13.

51 See Jacquelyn Dowd Hall, *Revolt against Chivalry: Jessie Daniel Ames and the Women's Campaign against Lynching* (New York, 1979); Donald L. Grant, *The Anti-Lynching Movement: 1883–1932* (San Francisco, 1975). . . .

52 Interview with Ruth Dumas, by author, August 19, 1992; Marty Nathanson interview; *Jackson Clarion-Ledger*, July 3, 1979; Davis et al., *Deep South*, 38–39, 457–58; "Democracy in Mississippi," *Crisis* 34 (November 1927): 296; "Deep in Dixie: Race Progress," *U.S. News and World Report*, February 26, 1954, 53–4; U.S. Commission on Civil Rights, *Hearings before the United States Commission on Civil Rights*, Administration of Justice, February 16–20, 1965 (Washington, D.C., 1965), 2: 69.

53 *ND*, August 6, 1948; Robert Penn Warren, "Segregation," in *The Robert Penn Warren Reader* (New York, 1987), 245–46. . . .

54 Elliot Trimble interview ("have"); Allison Davis, Burleigh Gardner, and Mary R. Gardner, *Deep South: A Social Anthropological Study of Caste and Class* (Chicago, 1941), 19–20; John Dollard, *Caste and Class in a Southern Town* (Madison, Wisc., 1988), 88; Elizabeth Dunbar Murray, *My Mother Used to Say: A Natchez Belle of the Sixties* (Boston, 1959), 188–89. . . .

55 Power, *The Memento*, 14.

56 On these various points, see Dollard, *Caste and Class in a Southern Town*, 134–72; Joel Kovel, *White Racism: A Psychohistory* (New York, 1970); Clinton, *Plantation Mistress*. . . .

57 *Natchez Publishing Company v. Dunigan*, No. 39135, Supreme Court of Mississippi, May 24, 1954, found in *Southern Reporter*, 2d ser. (Saint Paul, West Publishing, 1954), 72: 681–87.

58 Friedrich Nietzsche, *The Use and Abuse of History* (Indianapolis, 1957), 10; Cohn, "Natchez Was a Lady," 14.

8

LE REVEIL DE LA LOUISIANE
Memory and Acadian identity, 1920–1960

W. Fitzhugh Brundage

W. Fitzhugh Brundage's essay on the Acadian "revival" beginning in the 1920s illustrates the ways in which public memory could be manufactured to create a "usable past." The Acadians (or "Cajuns") originated from a migration to southwestern Louisiana of French-speaking people expelled from Nova Scotia by the British in 1755. Motivated in part by the same commercial impulses as the Natchez women discussed in the essay by Jack E. Davis in this volume, a small number of Louisiana activists molded a highly romanticized vision of the Acadian past. In a process similar to the one that scholars have traced for Appalachian regions of the South, these men and women promoted a mythic view of an unchanging Acadian culture. The view owed much to Henry Wadsworth Longfellow's popular epic poem, "Evangeline." In effect, Brundage argues, Acadians were placed "outside the flow of southern history" with its messy realities of slavery, war, and racial conflict.

* * *

The recent Cajun "revival" in Louisiana is a striking example of the revitalization and reassertion of ethnic identity in the modern South. The music, food, and folkways of the descendants of the French settlers of southwestern Louisiana have become so familiar as to be clichés. Fast-food restaurants sell Cajun-spiced hamburgers, television advertisers use Cajun music to evoke an atmosphere of *bon temps*, and architects crowd subdivisions with faux-Acadian homes. Meanwhile, public authorities have promoted the preservation of the French language in Louisiana, designated Acadiana as a distinct cultural region, and even officially denounced derogatory slang references to Cajuns.

The campaign to preserve and promote Cajun culture during the past three decades has attracted considerable interest. For some observers, the recent Cajun revival demonstrates the possibilities for mobilized communities to slow the erosion of their inherited culture. For other observers, the modest accomplishments of the revival underscore the corrosive and relentless absorption of distinctive communities into modern and mass consumer culture. In a real sense, both assessments are valid. An understanding of the origins of the Cajun revival underscores the ability of a small number of cultural activists to promote consciously and to mold systematically regional culture. It also reveals that the revival of Acadian or Cajun culture, from its inception, has been woven inexorably together with its commercialization.

The contemporary renaissance of all things Cajun may be traced to the activities of a small but prominent group of Acadian enthusiasts active during the quarter century after 1920. The stated goal of the Acadian revival was to make both Acadians and Americans mindful of the Acadian heritage in Louisiana. For all of their professed reverence for traditional culture and their wish to forestall the cultural effects of "progress," the revivalists themselves were powerful instigators of cultural change. By looking upon the residents of southwestern Louisiana as a vulnerable culture whose traditions were tenuous and would persist only through insistent reeducation by cultural enthusiasts sensitive to traditional culture, the Acadian revivalists advocated deliberate cultural intervention. Because of their status and power, they were able to institutionalize their ideas about Acadian identity. They defined what Acadian culture was and adapted decidedly modern means—pageants, films, radio, festivals, and publications —to promote appreciation of it.

In the process, the Acadian revivalists crafted representations of the Cajun past that became tropes—ubiquitous depictions so widely known that their meaning required little if any explanation. Over time their notions took root within Acadians' conceptions of themselves and their culture and precluded considerations of the contemporary realities of Acadia, to say nothing of the dynamics of change in the region. This rendering of Acadian history has had far-reaching consequences for the perceptions of Cajuns. The Acadian "movement" institutionalized a Cajun ethnic consciousness that stressed the "otherness" of white non-Cajun southerners. Cajuns, the revivalists told themselves and others, were not really of the South; the peasantlike Acadians had no place in the familiar narrative of southern history as told by other white southerners. The historical twists and turns of the region's past—slavery, sectionalism, and the traumas of the New South—happened to other people elsewhere. In a real sense, the revivalists placed the Acadian saga outside the flow of southern and, indeed, American history.

The central theme in the Acadian revival of the twentieth century has been the presumption that the Acadians are a people united by a tragic history. Louisiana Acadians trace their origins to peasant settlers who migrated from France to the west coast of "Acadie" or Nova Scotia, beginning in 1604. There they lived in scattered settlements, tended subsistence crops, and raised cattle. Neither their geographic isolation nor their wary attitude toward colonial officials could protect them from the recurring contests between the English, French, and Indians over the surrounding region. After France ceded Nova Scotia to Great Britain in 1713, the British distrusted the loyalty of the French-speaking and Catholic Acadians. During the subsequent half century, British officials endeavored to coerce the Acadians into renouncing their professed neutrality. Finally, at the onset of the Seven Years' War in 1755, British authorities ordered the expulsion of the Acadians.[1]

During the ensuing exile—the so-called *grand dérangement*—about eight thousand Acadians were scattered from Massachusetts to Georgia. Deprived of everything except their movable possessions, the Acadians lost their lands to Anglo-American settlers whom the British trusted. The American colonies received the exiles with open hostility; they, after all, were displaced French at a time of war between the Anglo-Americans and the French. Any realistic hopes of returning to Acadia ended with British victory in 1763. Consequently, Acadians eager to escape their de facto prisoner-of-war status in the British colonies began to migrate to the French colony of Louisiana. Even after Spain acquired Louisiana, the colony continued to welcome the Acadian diaspora from across the Atlantic rim for the remainder of the eighteenth century.[2]

The Louisiana Acadians, like their predecessors in Nova Scotia, sought out isolated regions suited to their agricultural and stock-raising traditions. Their communities clustered along the Mississippi River west of New Orleans, along Bayou Lafourche, and especially around Bayou Teche, the center of "la Nouvelle Acadie." But, as though mocked by fate, the Acadians soon faced growing numbers of Anglo-American and West Indian Creole settlers who, along with their slaves, flooded into southern Louisiana following the Louisiana Purchase in 1803. Acadians responded in various ways to the new settlers. Some, like the Mouton family of Lafayette, clawed their way into the planter elite otherwise dominated by Anglo-Americans and Creoles. Other Acadians occupied a middle ground as small semicommercial farmers and cattlemen. A third group retreated to the fringes of settlement and eked out an existence as subsistence ranchers, trappers, and fishermen.

The Civil War and the subsequent economic transformations of the New South exacerbated these divisions among the Acadians. While the Acadian elites embraced the Confederacy, other Acadians displayed much less fervor, especially after frequent raids by both Union and Confederate troops stripped the region of much of its wealth. At war's end, the Acadian elite united with their Anglo and Creole counterparts in a ferocious vigilante campaign to restore their traditional political and economic control over the region. They joined in welcoming the arrival of railroads, modern rice cultivation, and oil production. These innovations eroded the cultural cohesiveness that a shared language, religion, and traditions once had provided the Acadian exiles.[3]

For all of the changes that overtook the Acadians of Louisiana during the nineteenth century, they nevertheless acquired a reputation as tradition-bound peasants. In the eyes of urbane Louisiana Creoles, who took pride in their continued cultural ties with France, the Acadians lacked cosmopolitan refinement. Likewise, Anglo observers ridiculed the rustic Acadians for their purported lack of ambition and resulting poverty. In addition, their alleged hedonism, manifested in dancing, feasting, gambling, and drinking, grated on the sensibilities of many Protestant Anglos.[4]

These negative depictions of Acadians were offset partially by competing, romantic renderings, especially Henry Wadsworth Longfellow's exceptionally popular poem *Evangeline*, published in 1847. Longfellow recounted the exile of the Acadians from their idyllic homeland by tracing the ill-fated romance of two Acadians, Evangeline and Gabriel. Separated on their wedding day by the grand dérangement, Evangeline and Gabriel endured the hardships of the Acadian dispersal. Longfellow's resilient heroine subsequently tracked her Gabriel to Louisiana, where he had fled. To her dismay, she discovered that he had departed shortly before her arrival. After years of fruitless searching for him, Evangeline eventually devoted herself to nursing at a Philadelphia hospital. There, at the close of Longfellow's poem of pathetic and unfulfilled romance, she found her fiancé on his deathbed.

However much Longfellow's poetic epic deviated from the recorded history of the Acadians, it nevertheless created a powerful and enduring depiction of Acadian culture that reached audiences around the world. The poem revived awareness of the eighteenth-century deportation of the Acadians, and the figure of Evangeline came to personify Acadian tenacity and devotion to tradition and Catholicism. Not surprisingly, those Acadians in Canada and Louisiana who were anxious to refute pejorative stereotypes of Acadians adopted Longfellow's Evangeline as their Joan of Arc.[5]

Louisiana Acadians embraced Longfellow's mythical account of the Acadian diaspora, but they revised it to accentuate the purported historical authenticity of Evangeline and her life in Louisiana. If Longfellow's poem depicted the steadfast courage of the Acadian exiles, it simultaneously contributed to the idea that they "had abandoned the fatherland and mortgaged their heritage for a new life in an

exotic, semi-tropical land."[6] Moreover, Longfellow's Evangeline had
lingered only briefly in Louisiana. Intent on claiming the mythical
Evangeline for southwestern Louisiana, Felix Voorhies, a St. Martinville
judge of Acadian descent, proclaimed in the 1890s that she had been,
in fact, an actual person, Emmeline Labiche. On the basis of the purported recollections of his grandmother, published in newspapers
and eventually collected in *Acadian Reminiscences*, Voorhies maintained
that Labiche had tracked Louis Arceneaux, the Gabriel of Longfellow's
poem, to St. Martinville, Louisiana, only to discover that he had married. The real-life heroine, then, had died of grief and, Voorhies reported,
was buried in the quaint town.

The impact of Voorhies's account was considerable. It "authenticated the now nationally famous Evangeline myth and planted it
firmly in the bayou country," explains Carl Brasseaux.[7] In addition,
Voorhies's sentimental vision of traditional Acadian folkways and
his admonition to Louisiana Acadians to both remember the grand
dérangement and "always be proud to be the sons of martyrs and
of men of principle" anticipated the subsequent Acadian revival.[8]
Together, Longfellow's poem and Voorhies's quaint "reminiscences"
promoted and authenticated the notion of a distinctive Louisiana
Acadian heritage and culture.

That members of the white elite in southwestern Louisiana enthusiastically embraced Voorhies's account of Evangeline in part reflected
their perception of the waning of Acadian traditions. Members of the
regional elite, like their counterparts elsewhere in the country, evinced
worry about the threat that rapid economic and social change posed to
inherited values.[9] These concerns appear to have been especially acute
among elite Acadians—merchants, planters, lawyers, and public officials—who moved back and forth between Acadian communities and
the larger Anglo world of Louisiana. Almost certainly their exposure
to and assimilation into "American" life made them keenly aware of
both the distance that separated them from their ancestors and the
condescension of both Creoles and Anglos toward their heritage.
Acadian elites, like elites elsewhere, equated culture with ancestry. By
resurrecting Acadian heritage and culture they sought to validate their
personal and community identity. Thus, their interest in celebrating
their heritage did not imply hidebound opposition to modernity or
progress. To the contrary, for genteel Acadians, who were clustered
in the towns of the region, especially Lafayette, the "Hub City" of
Acadian Louisiana, the promotion of Acadian heritage went hand in
hand with local boosterism.

That interest in Acadian culture was respectable and "progressive,"
rather than merely whimsical, was evident in the attention devoted to

it by the voluntary associations and clubs of the region. These voluntary associations offered forums in which self-conscious Acadians and their non-Acadian allies could promote commerce and civic pride while also expressing their deliberate idealization of Acadian heritage. The prominence of such associations as outlets for organized contemplation of the local past is hardly surprising. Elsewhere in the nation, clubs, especially women's organizations, assumed the leadership of campaigns to promote an understanding of history and its relationship to the present. In keeping with this pattern, women's clubs in Lafayette conducted several yearlong, systematic surveys of Louisiana history, with special emphasis on the Acadian experience.[10] Similarly, in 1914 the Lafayette Forum, an elite civic club, listened to Judge Julian Mouton, a member of the distinguished Acadian family, describe the history of "pathos, courage, and loyalty" of "the peaceful peasants" who had settled the region.[11]

These genteel civic boosters and antiquarians recognized the need to extend the reach of their nostalgia to the larger Acadian population, whose attitudes were essential to the perpetuation of Acadian culture. Public festivals seemed well suited to this task. As early as 1914 members of the Lafayette Forum established the Acadian Pageant Company, which, by means of a " 'presentation of history through history, allegory, poetry and the stage,' proposed to demonstrate that nowhere in America was there a 'more picturesque, romantic, or distinctive history' than in the 'land of Evangeline.' Their planned pageant, to be staged by a cast of hundreds of the 'lineal descendants of the Acadians,' would portray a history 'of thrift and peaceful contentment' in Nova Scotia and subsequent British 'TYRANNY' and forced exile."[12] Like pageant enthusiasts elsewhere during the early twentieth century, the Lafayette planners intended their celebration to be an avowedly didactic spectacle that would yoke the educational innovations of the Progressive Era to the dramatic arts, thereby both promoting community unity and enabling residents to teach themselves and others about their heritage.

Nearly a decade passed before pageant boosters fulfilled their ambition to create a communal spectacle that retold the Acadian past. The centennial celebration of Lafayette Parish in 1923 provided an ideal pretext for their historical production. Intent on applying the latest techniques to the staging of the huge show, centennial organizers enlisted a professional pageant artist to supervise it.[13] On 6 April 1923 between 4,000 and 6,000 spectators (at a time when the population of the town was about 10,000) watched the cast of approximately 2,000, including students from Lafayette's public schools and many of the town's voluntary associations, perform the three-and-a-half hour-long Attakapas Trail Pageant.[14] Initial plans for the pageant, perhaps reflecting the earlier pageant plans, had focused almost exclusively on the romantic tragedy of Evangeline as a personification of Acadian perseverance and valor. The nineteenth-century history of the Acadians and their role in the Civil War apparently merited little attention. One pageant planner had suggested to the pageant supervisor, "HOW much of the Civil War you want to emphasize, *you* know. I would recommend very little."[15] The performed pageant, however, did incorporate a tableau devoted to the Civil War and even the emblem of nineteenth-century modernity, the railroad. Even so, the Acadian theme remained conspicuous; the third act depicted "the simple village life of the Acadians" and their quaint domestic traditions and old "Village dances." Moreover, to help spectators transcend the chasm of time and to make tangible the connection between the Acadians and their past, one of the performers wore a dress that her grandmother had made a century and a half earlier after arriving in Louisiana from Nova Scotia.[16]

The Lafayette pageant displayed both the nostalgia and the boosterism that would characterize the subsequent Acadian revival. But it remained a single event that could not long sustain a collective identity. In keeping with the tenor of the times, Acadian boosters began to take tentative steps toward forming organizations to promote their cultural identity. This impulse drew on many sources of inspiration, including the Catholic Church. Some of the French Canadian priests who served the region introduced Acadians to the linguistic and cultural nationalism then developing among French Canadians. As early as 1924, for example, a Canadian priest toured the area recruiting members for an international society of Acadians. Although he failed to attract a substantial following in the region, he did increase local awareness of the quickening international campaign for Acadian unity.[17]

Tourism provided another, albeit decidedly secular and commercial inspiration for the organized promotion of Acadian identity. The Louisiana landscape immortalized by Longfellow had attracted sightseers throughout the late nineteenth century, but the inconveniences of rail travel had limited their numbers. Automobiles now enabled affluent northern refugees from winter to flock to the region's colorful attractions. At a time of growing enthusiasm for vacation travel within the United States, residents of southwestern Louisiana embraced tourism as a way simultaneously to promote their heritage and to pad their wallets. Local boosters, no less than in other areas of the South, looked with envy at Florida's booming tourist-driven development.[18]

Growing awareness of the needs and interests of tourists led to demands for the beautification and promotion of local sites, such as the so-called Evangeline Oak in St. Martinville where the "real" Evangeline allegedly glimpsed her beloved Gabriel.[19] Business leaders in the region implored their neighbors to seize the commercial opportunities that the tourists represented. C. T. Bienvenu, editor of the *St. Martinville Weekly Messenger*, for example, urged, "With the increased number of tourists now coming to us . . . I feel that the time has arrived for St. Martinville to organize and maintain a wide awake and active organization" to respond to the interest in "the sturdy, lovable and valiant Acadian pioneers who settled here nearly two hundred years ago."[20]

No one better appreciated the potential significance of the Acadian past as a draw for tourists than Susan Evangeline Walker Anding. Although she could not claim Acadian ancestry, she nevertheless nurtured a strong attachment to all things Acadian that she traced to her lifelong exposure to Acadian culture and a sentimental bond with her fictional namesake, Longfellow's Evangeline. The epitome of the industrious clubwoman of the era, she earned a regional reputation as an irrepressible promoter of civic organizations and good roads. In 1925 she proposed establishing a permanent national monument to Evangeline and the Acadians in St. Martinville. Not coincidentally, the monument would be located on the Pershing, the Evangeline, and the Spanish Trail national highways (stretching from California to Florida and from Texas to Canada), which she also promoted.[21]

Susan Anding hitched the apparatus of civic organizing and applied the techniques of advertising to the cause of Acadian cultural identity. Employing her uncanny promotional skills, she coaxed newspaper editors, public officials, and members of the Acadian, Anglo, and Creole elites of southwestern Louisiana to join her Longfellow-Evangeline National Monument Association. As early as 1925 she exploited the latest technology when she broadcast her monument plans to radio listeners across the Deep South. Borrowing an idea from the campaign to fund a monument to the Confederacy at Stone Mountain, Georgia, she appealed to school children in Louisiana to contribute their pennies to the construction fund for the Evangeline Park. She also organized booths at state and local fairs that raised money for the planned monument.[22]

The most successful of her publicity ploys was her use of "charming costumes of the period when Evangeline lived" to arouse interest in and evoke the romance of the Acadian past. She first experimented with representing a lifelike Evangeline in 1926, when she exhibited a mannequin clothed in an Evangeline costume at the Philadelphia Sesquicentennial Exposition. So popular was the exhibit and so well suited to the commercial aesthetic of the era that it subsequently was moved to the window of a New York City department store. In 1928, in what a local newspaper saluted as "a progressive stunt," she chaperoned a group of real-life "Evangeline girls" to the Republican and Democratic National Conventions. Wherever the "Evangeline girls" went, their quaint garb of "prim white hats, tight black bodices, loving blue satin dresses, and wooden shoes" attracted attention.[23] From their quaint convention booths, draped with Spanish moss and outfitted with an old Acadian spinning wheel, the latter-day Evangelines distributed tourist literature and retold the history of "Evangeline Country."[24] The following year Mrs. Anding escorted another group of appropriately clad "girls" to President Herbert Hoover's inauguration.[25]

The success of Evangeline as a motif for Acadian identity was hardly happenstance. Longfellow's Evangeline, of course, was an established literary icon. But the impulse to personify Evangeline bespoke the publicity-crazed tenor of the era. Susan Anding's genius was to adapt the parlor game of tableaux vivant to serve the ends of a modern publicity campaign. By swaddling the "Evangeline girls" in (purportedly) historically accurate attire, she catered to the contemporary nostalgia for the authenticity and charm of yesteryear. If Acadian "girls" induced nostalgia, their "tight bodices" and perky demeanor simultaneously radiated a sex appeal attuned to the modern taste for beauty queens. In addition, there were powerful reasons why the icon of the Acadian revival would be feminine. Like other images of women in contemporary advertising, the idealized Acadian "girls" remained static in time, seemingly sheltering traditions from the forward rush of progress. The combination of their old-fashioned attire and props of domesticity, such as spinning wheels, conjured timeless values of family, community, and heritage that encouraged Acadians and others to acknowledge those traditions even as they withered. Moreover, no mythical male Acadian figure could have evoked romance the way the "Evangeline girls" did. Men powerless to protect their dependents, such as the Acadian patriarchs who were expelled from Nova Scotia, could not easily be turned into heroic figures. But a romantic heroine like Evangeline, who was buffeted by historical forces she could not have been expected to control, actually proved her womanly virtue through her victimization during the Acadian expulsion. Thus, she, far better than any male figure, could become an allegory for Acadians in general.[26]

Susan Anding's campaign was remarkable for the publicity it garnered and for its propagation of many of the tropes of the Acadian revival. But it was less successful at raising funds for the Evangeline Park. She secured a modest contribution of state funds and land, but the park's subsequent slow development prompted her critics to complain in 1929 that she had not conducted the drive "in a business-manner fashion."[27] In 1930 her poor health provided a genteel pretext for easing her out of power and for turning the campaign over to a newly established Longfellow-Evangeline Park Commission.[28] Soon thereafter her ambition for a park commemorating Evangeline came to pass. By the late 1930s park managers boasted that the park housed "more relics and antiques of real Acadian articles [than can] be found anywhere [else]."[29] In addition, they made the convenient (and mistaken) discovery that an old house on the park grounds was the reputed home of Louis Arceneaux, the purported inspiration for Longfellow's Gabriel. The restored home provided a setting of "incomparable and picturesque fascination" in which lecturers and exhibits helped visitors "to understand the pride with which natives keep alive and relive the exploits of their ancestors."[30]

The opening of the Longfellow-Evangeline Park and the resulting tourist interest in it and nearby St. Martinville permanently inscribed the narrative promoted by the nascent Acadian revival onto the landscape. Anding's campaign wed the relentless boosterism of the era with the emerging interest in promoting Acadian self-esteem. She prodded Acadians and non-Acadian sympathizers to organize and present their collective history in new ways and to new audiences. When she invited communities to establish chapters of the Evangeline Park Association, she also encouraged them to imagine themselves as united by their shared Acadian heritage. Thus, when the Chambers of Commerce in the five counties surrounding the proposed Evangeline monument issued public announcements claiming the title of the "Acadian heartland" in 1927, they made manifest the "imagined community" that Anding had helped to inspire.[31]

If Susan Anding helped to fuse a sense of place with the Acadian identity, Dudley LeBlanc, an Acadian raconteur of uncommon ability, strengthened the link between the Acadian identity and the distant past. Unlike Anding, LeBlanc was a descendant of Acadian exiles and had lived in the French-speaking world until he entered Southwestern Louisiana Institute (now the University of Southwestern Louisiana) in Lafayette. After graduating he became rich by peddling everything from patent medicines and tobacco products to burial insurance. His years as a traveling salesman trained him in the use of flamboyant advertising and promotion to appeal to the tastes and traditions of "the people."[32]

When LeBlanc's boundless ambition led him into public life, he applied his well-honed skills of salesmanship to politics. From his first campaign in 1923 until the end of his long political career in the 1960s, he touted his Acadian identity. In 1926, for instance, while representing St. Landry Parish in the state legislature, LeBlanc enthusiastically supported the proposed Evangeline Park by securing $10,000 of state funds for it. He subsequently reminded voters of his concern for Acadian heritage by recruiting members of the Longfellow-Evangeline Association to endorse him at campaign appearances. He also shamelessly employed the symbols of Acadian heritage in his campaigns. In 1926, for example, he delivered a stump speech beneath the branches of the Evangeline Oak in St. Martinville.[33] He sprinkled his speeches with the Acadian patois (when he did not deliver them entirely in French) and incorporated Acadian music and food into his electioneering.[34]

LeBlanc's interest in his ethnic heritage fueled his enthusiasm for forging ties between Acadians in Louisiana and in Canada. Almost certainly his friendship with Father Fidele Chiasson, a French-Canadian priest in Mamou, Louisiana, with a long-standing interest in French Canadian nationalism, was a catalyst for this project.[35] In addition, LeBlanc's knowledge that his ancestors had been prominent Acadian exiles in the eighteenth century inspired his activism. In 1928 he led a delegation of four Acadians and Father Chiasson to a convention of North American Acadians held in Massachusetts.[36] Addressing the six thousand gathered delegates, LeBlanc described the Louisiana brethren as the "most romantic and tragically unfortunate of all the [Acadian] exiles." So well received was his speech that the Democratic National Committee recruited him to campaign in the French-speaking communities of New England on behalf of Democratic candidates. Beyond deepening his appreciation of the uniqueness of Louisiana Acadians, the experience inspired LeBlanc to promote the cultural union of French communities in North America.[37]

LeBlanc's widening ties with the North American Acadian community brought him into contact with F. G. J. Comeaux of Halifax, Nova Scotia, an ardent Acadian activist. In February 1930 Comeaux visited Lafayette and encouraged LeBlanc to organize a "pilgrimage" of Louisiana Acadians to the 175th anniversary commemoration of the Acadian expulsion from Nova Scotia.[38] LeBlanc eagerly embraced the cause and organized mass meetings that drew French-speaking audiences from across southwestern Louisiana.[39] He also founded the Association of Louisiana Acadians, whose membership was limited to descendants of the Acadian exiles. Borrowing from Susan Anding's publicity techniques, he and his association invited each Acadian community to appoint an Acadian "girl" as its representative at the Canadian celebrations.[40]

On 11 August 1930 thirty-eight Louisianans, including twenty-five "Evangeline girls," began a two-week pilgrimage to Canada. The color-fully costumed Acadians attracted widespread publicity. A news service filmed the spectacle that the "girls" presented throughout the trip; national newspapers reported their visit with President Hoover at the White House; banners on the sides of their Pullman cars announced them as "Acadians of the Evangeline Country" and boomed LeBlanc's gubernatorial candidacy (which, not coincidentally, he announced just before the pilgrimage); and radio and public speeches by the "picturesque" Acadians reached audiences across the Northeast and Canada.[41]

Beyond garnering national publicity, the trip intensified the identification of the "pilgrims" with their Acadian heritage. LeBlanc gushed that "the reuniting of this long separated people was most touching. . . . There were many things to be recalled . . . and many common customs and characteristics to be noted."[42] One of the returning "Evangeline girls" raved that the trip "helped to cement us closer to the land from whence we came to the north." To be in Nova Scotia, she continued, "brought back to me the stories of our earlier exile often heard from the older people. . . . I never felt that I was anywhere else but at home."[43]

LeBlanc and his Canadian partners longed to perpetuate this revived sense of shared identity among Acadians. In the following April, LeBlanc organized a visit by 138 French Canadians to Louisiana. Throughout their five-day tour of the major Acadian communities, the Canadians were barraged with images of Evangeline. During visits to all of the shrines associated with the lovelorn Acadian exile, young men dressed as Gabriel and the "Evangeline girls" who had toured Canada the previous year (and other costumed women) greeted the Canadian tourists. The shared faith and language of the Acadians also figured prominently in the celebrations. One measure of the importance attached to Catholicism as a core element of Acadian identity was the 28 Canadian clerics, including a bishop, who joined the pilgrimage. At churches important in the early history of the Louisiana Acadians, the Canadians and their hosts preformed Mass.[44] And at a time of declining French proficiency in Louisiana, the Canadian visitors and their Louisiana chaperones pointedly delivered most of their public speeches in French. LeBlanc scheduled a regionwide French language contest to coincide with the visit.[45] With the Canadian visitors watching during the unveiling of a monument commemorating Evangeline in St. Martinville, he awarded medals to young Acadian essayists who had recounted "the peaceful life in Acadia before the exile; the cruelties and sufferings of the Acadians when they were exiled; how they settled in Louisiana; [and] their present modes and customs."[46]

The transnational Acadian exchanges continued in subsequent years. In 1936 LeBlanc led another pilgrimage to Canada. He again organized a group of "Evangeline girls" to represent Acadian communities along the gulf coast from Beaumont, Texas, to Pensacola, Florida.[47] As in the past, the pilgrims attracted national publicity. In addition to visiting the hallowed home of the Acadians in Nova Scotia during the two-week, five-thousand-mile tour, the Louisianans stopped for a visit with President Franklin D. Roosevelt, were feted in Baltimore by the governor of Maryland, attended a Mass in their honor at St. Peter's

Cathedral in New York City, visited with the celebrated Dionne Quintuplets in Canada, and attended the Texas Centennial. Ten years later, after an interruption caused by World War II, LeBlanc escorted twenty Canadian "Acadian girls" on a grueling tour of southwestern Louisiana. Promoted as part of a "patriotic movement organized to create good will between the Acadians of Louisiana and the Acadians of Canada," the tour highlighted Acadian folk dances and music. The women delivered more than thirty concerts in Acadian communities from the Texas border to Baton Rouge.[48]

The various tours prompted an outpouring of expressions of pride in Acadian identity and heritage. In 1931 the *Opelousas Clarion-News*, for example, saluted the Canadian visitors by affirming that "We are of French descent here. . . . We are proud of our heritages, proud of our accomplishments. . . . These Northern Acadians are part of our French blood and they are related to us by close bonds of sympathy. . . . We trust that the visit of the Acadians . . . will rededicate this romantic bond [between our two sections]."[49] . . .

Beyond promoting Acadian awareness by organizing ongoing contacts between Louisiana Acadians and their "cousins to the north," LeBlanc's signal contribution to the Acadian revival was to codify a historical narrative of Acadian victimhood. In 1927 he published *The True Story of the Acadians*, which he subsequently revised and republished in 1932 and again in 1967. The hardships of exile, of course, had figured prominently in both Longfellow's *Evangeline* and Voorhies's *Acadian Reminiscences*. But neither Longfellow's epic poem nor Voorhies's family lore claimed the precision or credibility of formal historical scholarship. Recognizing the power that the scholarly trappings gave to historical narratives, LeBlanc employed the tools of scholarship, which previously had been used to stigmatize Acadian heritage and folkways, to bolster Acadian pride.

LeBlanc intended his book to be a manifesto of Acadian historical consciousness. He complained that previous accounts of the Acadian experience had "distorted the facts in order to shield the British government from the responsibility of having committed the crime." He, in contrast, insisted on the credibility of his account: "Every controversial statement in this work is supported by authorities with appropriate citations" and "these statements cannot be successfully contradicted." He conceded that his narrative of the Acadian "persecutions" did not rest on new research. Instead, it was a pastiche of lengthy quotations from published histories and primary sources interspersed with breathless celebrations of Acadian heritage. LeBlanc recounted the tragedy of the "simple," "moral," "temperate," "happy," "peaceful," "chaste," and "noble" Acadians who fell victim to a perfidious and cruel British campaign to condemn "a noble race into utter oblivion." Whereas the survival of the Acadians in the decades immediately following their expulsion from Nova Scotia was "a miracle," their subsequent century and a half in Louisiana held little interest for him. He denied any rupture between tradition and modernity and ignored the effects of change. He was satisfied to vouch for the integrity of Acadian culture by pointing to Acadians' continuing fealty to Catholicism. And LeBlanc, like enthusiasts for Appalachian culture who boasted of the purported Elizabethan authenticity of mountain dialects, touted the French spoken by the Louisiana Acadians as "actually classical." "If you are an Acadian," LeBlanc triumphantly concluded, "you have just cause to be proud of your ancestors. . . . No other race of people in the world ever could claim what you can justly and proudly boast for yours."[50]

The significance of LeBlanc's ethnic boosterism should not be exaggerated. In principle, his Association of Louisiana Acadians represented the institutionalization of the Acadian revival. But, in reality, the organization was little more than a vehicle for LeBlanc's caprices. It endured in a state of suspended animation until temporarily revived during his pilgrimages. He displayed little interest in either sustained or comprehensive cultural preservation. Instead, his compulsive hucksterism was always conspicuous in his celebrations of Acadian identity; without fail, LeBlanc's promotion of all things Acadian coincided with either his latest business enterprise or his candidacy for public office.[51] He also revealed condescending attitudes toward the very culture that his association purportedly preserved.[52] Nevertheless, his hagiography of the Louisiana Acadians and promotion of Acadian pride were conspicuous contributions to the nascent Acadian revival. His charismatic personality, shrewd entrepreneurship, and prestige among his fellow Acadians enabled him to extend the reach of the Acadian revival far beyond the private parlors and Chamber of Commerce meeting rooms where it had its origins. His periodic pilgrimages became ritualized expressions of historical memory that explicitly asserted historical continuity. Beyond reminding participants about the past, the elaborate transnational festivities represented the past so that participants became, if only temporarily and symbolically, contemporaries with mythical events. We should not underestimate the power of these performances to diffuse and establish the enduring cultural authority of the Acadian revival.[53]

Without the contributions of Louise Olivier, an Acadian activist, a skeptic might dismiss the Acadian revival as little more than LeBlanc's ethnic chest-thumping and Susan Anding's publicity stunts. Most early promoters of Acadian heritage, including LeBlanc, displayed little concern for preserving traditional folkways. Aside from the mythical attire sported by women dressed as Evangeline and the retelling of some Acadian stories, the marrow of Acadian culture— handicrafts, music, and folkways—had been virtually ignored by previous Acadian boosters. Olivier, in contrast, waged a long campaign to revive "authentic" Acadian folkways. She was, by no means, unique in her deep affection for the French language and Acadian culture. But, unlike other enthusiasts, she was a professional cultural activist who brought specialized training and endless stamina to the campaign to preserve Acadian culture.

Olivier, like LeBlanc, had a deep personal attachment to the Acadian community she pledged to serve. Born in the Acadian village of Grand Coteau and educated at Catholic convents there and in New Orleans, she earned degrees in music and French. After teaching French in public schools and at the Louisiana State University (LSU), she received an appointment in 1938 as the field representative of an LSU-sponsored program to promote the French language throughout Louisiana. The position called upon her expertise in both music and French while also encouraging her interest in Acadian folk culture.

Her teaching experience made Olivier keenly aware of what she perceived to be the erosion of traditional Acadian culture. "Personally," she explained in 1943, "I feel we are outstanding people saturated with relics of a passing culture!"[54] "Unfortunately," she lamented, "within the last fifty years there has been such a rapid change in the new generations of the descendants of the Acadians brought by modern progress—The customs and even the language of the Acadians are fast disappearing."[55] Traditional Acadians needed to be reinforced in their presumed struggle to hold onto their culture in the face of "progress." Because of her standing as an expert on Acadian folkways, Olivier exerted considerable influence over the value attached to various expressions of Acadian culture. Her self-appointed task was to moderate the destructive impact of modernity by reeducating Acadians to value their traditional culture. She, for instance, advocated purging vulgar modern influences from Acadian music and helped organize a national folk festival to honor the musical traditions she valued. Old Acadian songs were good; newer music was not. Instead of judging new songs or musical styles as evidence of the continued creativity of Acadian culture, she saw them as woeful degeneration. She cautioned an organizer of the National Folk Festival in 1953 that any Acadian bands selected to perform at the festival "would have to be polished, weeded out, advised and directed. They are gradually losing their identity, acquiring cow-boy traits. In other words, they are no longer 'Cajun bands' but 'cow-jun bands.'"[56] Her taste and principles similarly led her to value such essentially archaic artifacts as braided palmetto fans and woven baby bonnets above other forms of Acadian handicrafts.

Her early efforts included pioneering one of the first sustained and widespread campaigns to preserve French in Louisiana. Building on LeBlanc's precedent of broadcasting weekly French-language radio programs, Olivier launched an ongoing series of live French broadcasts.[57] She attracted large audiences for these broadcasts as well as to participate in local French programs. Over time, she expanded these "Assemblées" by recruiting public school administrators, teachers, and community activists in Louisiana's French-speaking parishes to help stage festivities that focused on local traditions. In addition, she organized French clubs to perpetuate the use of the language after the conclusion of the "Assemblées."[58]

Her more enduring contribution to the revival was her promotion of Acadian handicrafts during the 1940s and 1950s. Wartime exigencies, especially gasoline rationing, sharply curtailed her ability to travel and promote French throughout the state. Consequently, she redirected her energies to an ambitious campaign to "preserve as a culture the traditional crafts of our Acadian ancestors," "to furnish an outlet for the self-expression of our women of Acadian ancestry and to develop initiative and independence among them," and "to find a market for the handicraft objects produced."[59] She drew inspiration for her plans from the tradition of handicraft promotion that extended from the earliest London Settlement houses of the late nineteenth century to the Appalachian handicraft revival movement of the teens and twenties.[60]

Beginning in 1942, Olivier enlisted traditional weavers, quilters, sunbonnet makers, and palmetto braiders to produce items for traveling displays of Acadian crafts that were exhibited at public libraries, club meetings, and fairs. Convinced of the value of establishing "THIS MOVEMENT AS AN INDUSTRY," she installed permanent exhibits, including craft demonstrations by Acadian women dressed in Evangeline attire, at the Longfellow-Evangeline State Park and other state facilities.[61] She coaxed organizers of local festivals, such as the Crowley Rice Festival and the Abbeville Dairy Festival, to incorporate the preservation of "the French language, customs, etc." into their annual celebrations.[62] Through these measures, Olivier had earned by the 1950s national recognition for her campaign to promote and preserve Acadian crafts and folkways.

Yet Olivier was not entirely successful in imposing her sensibilities or zeal for "authentic" Acadian culture on the Acadian revival. She, like Anding and LeBlanc before her, employed Evangeline outfits to arouse public interest in her campaign. She comforted herself that although the women she recruited to staff the craft displays wore clothes intended to evoke romance, they at least, unlike previous "Evangeline girls," were actual artisans. Although she was largely responsible for the incorporation of Acadian culture in the fairs and festivals that proliferated during the 1940s and 1950s, she nevertheless resented the superficial respect accorded it.[63] Her frustration with frivolous evocations of Acadian heritage mounted during the Louisiana bicentennial celebrations of the Acadian expulsion in 1955, when she complained that "all that seems to count consist of noise and glitter. I am so tired of hearing *a pretty girl on a shiny float* and police escorts and brass bands, etc. that I could scream."[64]

The significance of Olivier's labors cannot be measured solely by the actual sales of the Acadian crafts that she promoted. Such sales were never large; in 1956 the total value of woven shirts, napkins, bedspreads, and braided palmetto fans sold totaled less than $10,000.[65] A better gauge was her success at attracting wide publicity for Acadian crafts and encouraging merchants to develop their own sources of these crafts.[66] Her project encouraged thirty-some Acadian craftswomen to revive and perpetuate trades that otherwise had little marketable value. Most important, her signal contribution to the Acadian revival was to institutionalize systematic cultural intervention in southern Louisiana and to introduce there the techniques of cultural preservation that had been applied in various other "folk" communities in the United States and Europe. By doing so, she established a precedent for continuing state funded support for the promotion of the French language and Acadian folkways.

The target of Louise Olivier's sternest criticisms—the Acadian bicentennial celebrations of 1955—was nevertheless the most spectacular expression of the Acadian revival or what Olivier called "Le Reveil de la Louisiane." The yearlong festivities represented the naturalization of the region's Acadian heritage. They incorporated virtually all of the themes and techniques that had been employed to represent Acadian heritage during the past two decades. Beginning in 1954, the Acadian Bicentennial Commission (ABC), funded with $100,000 from the state, developed extensive plans to commemorate the expulsion of the Acadians. Directed by Thomas J. Arceneaux, a professor and administrator at the University of Southwestern Louisiana who flaunted his direct descent from Louis Arceneaux (the alleged real-life Gabriel of the *Evangeline* tale), the ABC planned a complex, yearlong celebration of Acadian heritage.

The bicentennial opened on 1 January 1955, when Acadian singers and dancers performed at the nationally televised halftime ceremonies of the Sugar Bowl championship football game. Two weeks later residents of Lafayette welcomed a delegation of Canadian Acadians to the annual Camellia Pageant. The Canadians then undertook a "goodwill tour" of southwestern Louisiana. In February the Acadian bicentennial provided the theme for the Lafayette Mardi Gras celebrations.

In April, a "pilgrimage to the Mother Church of Acadians" in St. Martinville incorporated the selection of an official "Evangeline" to promote the bicentennial, a nationally publicized reenactment of the first Acadian wedding in Louisiana, and a Mass celebrating the perpetuation of the Acadians' faith. During the summer, the commission's Evangeline toured Louisiana, made radio and television appearances, and performed at Bastille Day festivities near New Orleans. In August, Arceneaux led a two-week Louisiana Acadian pilgrimage to Canada that included radio and television appearances and concert performances. During the fall the Abbeville Dairy Festival, the New Iberia Sugar Festival, and the Ville Platte Cotton Festival incorporated bicentennial themes into their festivities. The culmination of the year's program was the Acadian Bicentennial Climax Celebration held in St. Martinville. During the four-day event, the Acadian folk festival championed by Louise Olivier and directed by Sarah Gertrude Knott, the founder and director of the National Folk Festival, staged performances by Pete Seeger and other musicians of the music of Acadiana and Louisiana. The festivities closed with a pageant, featuring a cast of hundreds, depicting the tragic life of Evangeline.[67]

The influence of the Bicentennial Commission extended beyond fairgrounds and public spectacles. Throughout 1955, the ABC encouraged voluntary associations to participate in the celebrations and to study Acadian culture and history. Intent on incorporating Acadian history and culture into school activities, the commission, along with the Louisiana State Department of Education, published and circulated a booklet entitled *Our Acadian Culture—Let's Keep It!* The aim of the booklet was clear—"to instill a desire in our people to perpetuate our Acadian heritage." Teachers were encouraged to organize activities such as listening to French language newscasts, visiting places "rich in Acadian folklore" like the Evangeline State Park and St. Martinville, and corresponding with French children in Canada and elsewhere. More than a brief primer of Acadian history, folk songs, and cuisine, the booklet represented an important step in incorporating the narrative of Acadian exile and the contemporary defense of Acadian cultural traditions into public education.[68]

The commission also explicitly integrated commercial aims into the bicentennial celebrations. Indeed, the original plans and most of the funding for the ABC came from the Louisiana Department of Commerce and Industry. The priorities of the department were threefold: "to provide Louisiana with a suitable vehicle which will (1) attract new tourist money into the state, (2) display the state's Acadian heritage in the most favorable light and (3) establish Louisiana, for years to come, as a prime tourist vacation spot."[69] Advertising for the bicentennial was linked with the department's burgeoning tourist promotion program as well as with the "Holiday in Dixie" campaign, a private effort to promote tourism in Louisiana. This shameless boosterism and commercialism that so offended Louise Olivier may have been unprecedented in scale or intensity, but it was only the continuation of a tradition that Susan Anding, Dudley LeBlanc, and Olivier herself had contributed to. Strung out over the course of a year, the centennial celebrations fused the spectacle of recurrent invocations of Evangeline and the trauma of the expulsion with tireless appeals to preserve authentic Acadian culture and to promote tourism.

The unfolding of the Acadian revival in Louisiana during the first half of the twentieth century mirrors the evolution of historical memory elsewhere in the South (and the United States). The Acadian boosters, no less than the white "Anglo Saxon" elites of the late-nineteenth-century South, were eager to create a usable past. But they had in mind uses for their past quite distinct from those of earlier historical activists. As early as the 1930s, the tourist brochures, advertisements, and souvenirs that invoked the Acadian and southern past had, in a real sense, commodified it. The locally sponsored pageant in Lafayette presaged the future; it retained some of the solemn ritual that had been conspicuous in previous historical representations, but it also incorporated robust doses of local boosterism and spectacle intended to promote and entertain at least as much as to edify. This mix of boosterism and revelry, which found its fullest expression in the Acadian bicentennial celebration, was an essential element of the emerging tourist industry in Louisiana and the South in general. Since the 1920s the promotion of Acadian culture and consumerism have been inextricably linked. Because Anding, LeBlanc, and their ilk reduced the complexity of Acadian history to a romantic essence, it was ideally suited to adaptation to tourism. They remembered only those events closely linked to the romantic episodes in Acadian history: St. Martinville was a suitably romantic shrine of Acadian memory, Evangeline was an ideal tragic heroine, and Acadian folk traditions were appropriately quaint. Local and state authorities not only have encouraged this romanticization, they also have aided tourists in their pursuit of the romantic by literally mapping history onto the landscape. State agencies in Louisiana and across the South funded parks and historic sites and cluttered the highways and byways with markers that alerted motorists to picturesque historical events and personalities. State tourist bureaus likewise provided curious travelers with brochures that cataloged the historical sites that merited attention; in Louisiana, for instance, the state tourist bureau developed a distinctive promotional campaign for "Acadiana." In these various ways, the marketing methods of the last century have come to be incorporated into the transmission of Acadian historical memory.

The Acadian revival also is a conspicuous example of the increasing role of the state in the promotion of historical memory and revived folkways in the South. Although the voluntary organizations that initiated the revival remain active, their role in the promulgation of memory increasingly has been over-shadowed by the state. The extension of state authority into matters past was gradual, beginning with small steps. From a modest beginning when the Louisiana legislature contributed $10,000 to the Evangeline park campaign in 1928, the state's involvement in the Acadian revival has mushroomed to include tourist promotion, state parks, and festivals. (In 1999, for example, the State Department of Culture, Recreation, and Tourism hosted the World Acadian Congress.)[70] Perhaps the most visible demonstration of state commitment is the state-funded Council for the Development of French in Louisiana (CODOFIL). Founded in 1968 by Lafayette-based cultural activists, CODOFIL has aggressively promoted bilingualism and awareness of Cajun (and French) culture in public education.[71] Finally, state largess has undergirded the emergence of the academic study of Acadians, especially at the University of Southwestern Louisiana, the home of the Ragin' Cajuns.

Elsewhere in the South, state promotion of historical awareness followed a similar trajectory, beginning modestly with the establishment of state archives and museums, subsequently expanding to include elaborate historical pageants and festivals, and more recently swelling to embrace countless historical sites and annual festivals. Eventually, all southern states created bureaucracies to study, plan, and market their pasts as tourist attractions. State and local governments now maintain or contribute public funds to operate literally hundreds and hundreds of historic sites. Thus, historical memory has become part of public policy in Louisiana and in the South. Now that the principal responsibility for representations of the past has been assumed by public institutions, debates about memorializing the past necessarily are both public and political.

The legacy of the Acadian revival between 1925 and 1955 is inescapable in contemporary Louisiana. The Cajun identity has attained an influence and a stature far beyond the ambitions of the earliest boosters. A century ago Acadians were obscure if exotic figures overshadowed in the national consciousness by the romantic Creoles of Louisiana. Since then, the success of the Acadian quest for power and social cohesion in the polyglot culture of Louisiana has been so great that much ink now is devoted to informing Louisianans and outsiders alike that the French culture of the state includes white and black Creole as well as Cajun traditions. Indeed, some blacks in southwestern Louisiana openly resent the now-conventional narrative of the region's history that focuses on the Acadians and marginalizes the African American experience. Bemoaning the "cultural piracy" that has appropriated African American traditions as "Cajun," blacks claiming descent from French and Spanish colonists have founded an Un-Cajun Committee and C.R.E.O.L.E., Inc. The group's president, Melvin Caesar, explains: "I'm not against what they (Cajuns) have done. They have marketed their culture very well, and we should learn from them and progress from their success."[72] That these voices of protest, however ineffective, are vented at all testifies to the suffocating achievements of Acadian revivalists.

Yet, despite the apparent success of the marketing of Acadian tradition, Acadian/Cajun identity has acquired the appearance of what sociologist Herbert Gans calls "symbolic ethnicity" or what columnist Maureen Dowd labels "designer ethnicity." Cajun dances, festivals, and exhibits may be commonplace, but these nostalgic leisure activities, some observers contend, comprise the only important and distinctive contemporary expressions of Cajun identity.[73] Otherwise, Acadian/ Cajun symbolic references are free-floating and nearly ubiquitous signifiers that have been reduced to mere commercial slogans that adorn every conceivable type of business in Acadiana. Still unresolved more than a half century after the beginning of the Acadian revival is the complex and unstable relationship between the marketplace and Acadian "traditions." Thus, the irony that was evident in the Acadian revival at its origins persists. For all of the distinctive local color of the Acadian "Revival," it nevertheless displayed such quintessentially modern American traits as longing for folk tradition, discomfort with "progress," and zeal to commercialize culture and adapt it to contemporary tastes.

NOTES

1 Carl A. Brasseaux, *The Founding of New Acadia: The Beginnings of Acadian Life in Louisiana* (Baton Rouge, 1987); Naomi E. S. Griffith, *The Acadian Deportation: Deliberate Perfidy or Cruel Necessity?* (Toronto, 1969). . . .

2 Brasseaux, *Founding of New Acadia.*

3 Carl A. Brasseaux, *From Acadian to Cajun: Transformation of a People, 1803–1877* (Jackson, Miss., 1992); James H. Dormon, *The People Called Cajuns: An Introduction to an Ethnohistory* (Lafayette, La., 1983), 63–69; Lawrence E. Estaville, Jr., "Changeless Cajuns: Nineteenth-Century Reality or Myth?" *Louisiana History* 28 (Spring 1987), 117–40. . . .

4 Dormon, *People Called Cajuns*, 33–43, 55–63.

5 . . . see Carl A. Brasseaux, *In Search of Evangeline: Birth and Evolution of the Evangeline Myth* (Thibodaux, La., 1988), 9–14, passim. . . .

6 Brasseaux, *In Search of Evangeline*, 44–45.

7 Ibid., 19.

8 Felix Voorhies, *Acadian Reminiscences: The Story of Evangeline* (1907; reprint, Lafayette, La., 1977), 106.

9 Michael Kammen, *Mystic Chords of Memory: The Transformation of Tradition in American Culture* (New York, 1991), esp. pt. 2; James M. Lindgren, *Preserving the Old Dominion: Historic Preservation and Virginia Provincialism* (Charlottesville, Va., 1993).

10 In 1927, 1928, 1929, and 1954, club members would again undertake lengthy studies of Louisiana and Acadian history. See Anuual Programs, Women's Club of Lafayette Papers, box 1, Edith Garland DuPre Library, University of Southwestern Louisiana (hereafter USL).

11 Jerome Mouton, "History of Lafayette," Paul DeBaillon Collection, . . . USL.

12 E. L. Stephens Papers, box 6, folder 49, Hill Memorial Library, Louisiana State University, Baton Rouge (hereafter LSU). . . .

13 David Glassberg, *American Historical Pageantry: The Uses of Tradition in the Early Twentieth Century* (Chapel Hill, 1990).

14 *Lafayette Advertiser*, 6 March–7 April 1923.

15 Undated, unsigned draft of "Pageant of Attakapas Country," in Attakapas County Pageant Manuscript, MS 16, USL.

16 *The Attakapas Trail: A History of Lafayette Parish with Complete Pageant Score and Prologues* (Lafayette, La., 1923).

17 *St. Martinville Weekly Messenger* [*SMWM*], 23 February–22 March 1924.

18 *Opelousas Progress*, 7 November 1925.

19 See, e.g., *SMWM*, 25 February 1925.

20 *SMWM*, 8 May 1926.

21 Glenn R. Conrad, "Susan Evangeline Walker Anding," *Dictionary of Louisiana Biography* (Lafayette, La., 1988), 14.

22 Susan Anding's campaign may be followed in the *St. Martinville Weekly Gazette* from 1925 to 1931. For a summary of her efforts, see Brasseaux, *In Search of Evangeline*, 36–39.

23 *Opelousas Clarion-Progress*, 14 March 1929. . . .

24 *SMWM*, 7 July 1928; *New Iberia Weekly Iberian*, 12 July 1928.

25 *SMWM*, 23 June 1928; *New Iberia Weekly Iberian*, 28 June 1928; *New Iberia Enterprise*, 30 June 1928; *Opelousas Clarion-Progress*, 7–14 March 1929.

26 Jackson Lears, "Packaging the Folk: Tradition and Amnesia in American Advertising, 1880–1940," in Jane S. Becker and Barbara Franco, eds., *Folk Roots, New Roots: Folklore in American Life* (Lexington, Mass., 1988).

27 *SMWM*, 13 July 1929. . . .

28 *SMWM*, 13 July, 3, 17 August 1929, 8 February 1930; *Opelousas Clarion-News*, 23 January 1930.

29 Brasseaux, *In Search of Evangeline*, 46.

30 *Second Biennial Report of the State Parks Commission of Louisiana, 1936–1937* (New Orleans, 1937), 65; *Fourth Biennial Report of the State Parks Commission of Louisiana, 1940–1941* (New Orleans, 1941), 28 . . .

31 *SMWM*, 22 January 1927.

32 Floyd Martin Clay, *Coozan Dudley LeBlanc: From Huey Long to Hadacol* (Gretna, La., 1973), chap. 1.

33 *St. Martinville Weekly Messenger*, 4 September 1926.

34 During his campaign for the position of public service commissioner he delivered, by one count, eighty-two speeches in French, *SMWM*, 10 September 1926; *Abbeville Meridional* [*AM*], 27 October 1928.

35 LeBlanc acknowledged "the great part he played in bringing me to an appreciation of my Acadian heritage." Dudley LeBlanc, *The True Story of the Acadians* (n.p., 1932), i.

36 *Lafayette Tribune*, 31 August 1928; *SMWM*, 8 September 1928; *AM*, 8 September 1928.
37 *AM*, 27 October 1928.
38 *AM*, 1 March 1930.
39 *SMWM*, 15 March 1930.
40 *AM*, 28 June, 19 July 1930; *New Iberia Enterprise*, 12–19 July 1930; *New Iberia Weekly Iberian*, 17 July 1930; *SMWM*, 26 July 1920.
41 *LDA*, 13, 25 August 1930; *Opelousas Clarion-News*, 14, 21 August 1930; *AM*, 16 August 1930; *New Iberia Enterprise*, 16 August 1930; *SMWM*, 16 August 1930; *New Iberia Weekly Iberian*, 4 September 1930.
42 LeBlauc, *True Story of the Acadians*, 90.
43 *Opelousas Clarion-News*, 4 September 1930. . . .
44 *New Iberia Weekly Iberian*, 16 April 1931; *New Iberia Enterprise*, 18 April 1931.
45 The previous year, during the Louisiana pilgrimage to Canada, the French consul in Montreal had given LeBlanc medals to be awarded to Louisiana high school students who wrote the best essays in French on "The Exile of the Acadians." *AM*, 6 September 1930; *New Iberia Weekly Iberian*, 11 September 1930.
46 *SMWM*, 4 April 1931.
47 *New Iberia Enterprise*, 19 June 1936.
48 *LDA*, 9–22 October 1946; *Opelousas Clarion-News*, 10, 24 October 1946; *New Iberia Enterprise*, 10 October 1946; *SMWM*, 11–25 October 1946; *Abbeville Progress*, 12 October 1946; *New Orleans Times-Picayune*, 12 October 1946; *Crowley Weekly Acadian*, 17 October 1946; *Opelousas Daily World*, 18, 20 (quotation) October 1946; *AM*, 19 October 1946.
49 *Opelousas Clarion-News*, 16 April 1931.
50 Dudley J. LeBlanc, *The Acadian Miracle* (Lafayette, La., 1966), viii, 46, 81, 367.
51 The announcements for the 1936 pilgrimage, for instance, proclaimed: "Remember that this tour is intended to advertise the natural resources of Louisiana. It is planned to call the attention of the industrial leaders of the East and of the North to the wonderful resources of Louisiana, to its favorable climatic conditions and to its wonderful labor conditions." *LDA*, 10 August 1936. . . .
52 For all of his proclaimed attachment to Acadian culture and language, LeBlanc nevertheless announced that he hoped that the 1946 tour of the "Acadian girls" would prod rural Acadians in Louisiana to adapt to progress, including to learn English. . . . *New Orleans Times-Picayune*, 12 October 1946.
53 The tradition of Acadian "pilgrimages" persists. In August 1999 thousands of Acadians from Canada and the United States gathered in "Acadiana" to take part in the second Congres Mondial Acadien. *New York Times*, 16 August 1999.
54 Louise Olivier to H. B. Wright, 23 April 1943, Acadian Handicrafts Project Records (hereafter AHPR), box 1, LSU.
55 Olivier to Henry D. Larcade Jr., 11 August 1949, AHPR, box 5, LSU.
56 Olivier to Clay Shaw, 23 March 1953, AHPR, box 4, LSU.
57 Elizabeth Mae Roberts, "French Radio Broadcasting in Louisiana, 1935–1958" (M.A. thesis, Louisiana State University, 1959), 88–89.
58 Olivier boasted that "through the medium of the Assemblée, the younger generation became acquainted with and learned something of its French heritage [and . . .] all generations had an opportunity to meet on an equal footing and make practical use of their common language." "Resume of

Louisiana State University French Project Activities, 1938–1944," undated [1944?], AHPR, box 1, LSU.

59 Ibid.

60 On the handicraft movement that influenced Olivier, see Jane S. Becker, *Selling Tradition: Appalachia and the Construction of an American Folk, 1930–1940* (Chapel Hill, 1998), and David E. Whisnant, *All That Is Native and Fine: The Politics of Culture in an American Region* (Chapel Hill, 1983).

61 Olivier to "Grace," 18 March 1944, AHPR, box 1, LSU.

62 See various festival announcements, AHPR, box I, 3, LSU.

63 The festivals "bore me," she fumed. "They are getting to be more and more like street fairs. . . ." Olivier to Sarah [Gertrude Knott], undated [1956?], AHPR, correspondence 1955–56, box 7, LSU.

64 Olivier's complaints about the crass commercialism of the bicentennial celebrations hinted at her recognition that her own project also commercialized Acadian culture. Olivier to "Keed," 15 March 1955, AHPR, box 5, LSU.

65 "Sales Records in 1956–1957" [1957?], AHPR, box 2, LSU.

66 See, e.g., "Ways of the Bayou Country," *Recreation* 40 (July 1946), 207–8, 220; *Craftsman* 11 (December 1946), 332–43; *Travel* (January 1947), 21–23; and Marjorie Arbow, "It Pays to Play with Your Family," *Farm and Ranch* 84 (October 1954), 47.

67 The best source for information on the bicentennial celebration is the Acadian Bicentennial Commission Collection (hereafter ABCC), USL.

68 *Our Acadian Heritage—Let's Keep It!* (n.p.: Louisiana State Department of Education . . . , 1954)

69 Edwin L. Reed, Director, Advertising and Promotion, Louisiana Department of Commerce and Industry, 30 June 1954, ABCC, box 3, USL.

70 *New Orleans Times-Picayune*, 30 May, 24 August 1997, 14 January 1998.

71 On CODOFIL, see Robert Lewis, "L'Acadie Retrouvée: The Remaking of Cajun Identity in Southwestern Louisiana, 1968–1994," in Richard H. King and Helen Taylor, eds., *Dixie Debates: Perspectives on Southern Cultures* (New York, 1996), 67–84.

72 *New Orleans Times-Picayune*, 11 August 1997.

73 Herbert J. Gans, "Ethnic Invention and Acculturation: A Bumpy-Line Approach," *Journal of American Ethnic History* 12 (Fall 1992), 44–45 (Gans and Dowd). On contemporary Cajun culture, see Marjorie R. Esman, "Festivals, Change, and Unity: The Celebration of Ethnic Identity among Louisiana Cajuns," *Anthropological Quarterly* 55 (October 1982), 199–210; "Tourism as Ethnic Preservation: The Cajuns of Louisiana": *Annals of Tourism Research* 11 (1984), 451–67; and *Henderson, Louisiana: Cultural Adaptation in a Cajun Community* (New York, 1985), esp. chaps. 10–11.

9

SOUTHERN SEEDS OF CHANGE, 1931–1938

Patricia Sullivan

As noted in the Introduction to this volume, historians now identify the New Deal as a period of significant change in the South. Here, Patricia Sullivan traces the careers of three exemplary activists in this era: Charles Houston, an African American whose experiences as a soldier in World War I propelled him into a legal career as the foremost civil rights lawyer in the United States; Lucy Randolph Mason, a descendant of a famous Virginia founding father who became a key organizer of the new union federation, the Congress of Industrial Organizations; and Palmer Webb, also a Virginian, who attended the University of Virginia in 1931 and was active in a number of radical causes. These three, along with others who had become dissenters against the South's racial and class order, were among the founders of the Southern Conference on Human Welfare, an alliance of reformers and radicals who together represented a potentially formidable challenge to white supremacy. They also illustrate three of sources of change in the South in the 1930s: renewed activism from African American-organizations and individuals; the radicalization of many young white southerners by the experience of the Great Depression; and the dramatic expansion of union organizing drives under the favorable auspices of Franklin Roosevelt's New Deal.

* * *

"At the heart of the dark labyrinth of America's complex problems is the crisis in the South," wrote University of Virginia student Palmer Weber in 1938. Weber commended Franklin Roosevelt's successful effort to focus national attention on the region with the widely noted *Report on the Economic Conditions of the South.* Southerners themselves had finally become conscious "of the inherited shackles of tenancy, disease and illiteracy." Such general social problems, he noted, had become "accepted subjects of discussion," and this was a significant development. "But," Weber continued, "the black thread in the crisis ridden pattern of [the region's] social culture has not yet been examined. Neither Mr. Roosevelt nor the Southern New Dealers have publicly considered the social significance of the Southern Negro."[1]

... [T]he Roosevelt administration carefully avoided any suggestion that it aimed to upset the racial status quo in the South. But Roosevelt's attempt to purge southern obstructionists in the 1938 primary elections and bring the South into line with the national Democratic Party implicitly challenged the political foundation of white supremacy.* Roosevelt's ill-fated intervention supported the political aspirations of disfranchised groups who had mobilized in response to the depression and the New Deal. It resulted in the founding of the Southern Conference for Human Welfare (SCHW), a biracial coalition dedicated to ending voter restrictions in the South and completing the liberal realignment of the Democratic Party.

By 1938 a loose political network had developed around the labor movement, local branches of the National Association for the Advancement of Colored People (NAACP), voter leagues, Communist Party initiatives, and New Deal programs. During the 1930s a small number of individuals from widely different backgrounds gave form and direction to the democratic activism that developed outside of the insular structure of southern politics. Palmer Weber, Charles Houston, and Lucy Randolph Mason serve as useful examples of the range of leadership that emerged. Palmer Weber, a native of Smithfield, Virginia, was a radical student organizer at the University of Virginia before joining southern New Dealers in Washington in 1940 and the SCHW'S legislative fight to abolish the poll tax. Charles Hamilton Houston, a brilliant legal mind and strategist, traveled tens of thousands of miles throughout the South, building the NAACP'S southern-based campaign to equalize education and secure voting rights. Lucy Randolph Mason, whose Virginia lineage stretched back to George Mason, a signer of the Declaration of Independence, became the leading public representative of the Congress of Industrial Organizations (CIO) in the South and worked as a union publicist and voting-rights proponent.

The political development of Palmer Weber during the depression years suggests the eclectic nature of the evolving democratic movement. A student of Karl Marx and Thomas Jefferson, Weber participated in the Communist Party during the 1930s as well as the student movement, labor-organizing activities, and the NAACP's pioneering challenge to racial discrimination in public education. Weber was a self-described

---

* Franklin D. Roosevelt had campaigned against conservative Democrats running in the 1938 off-year elections—ed.

free radical, confined by neither orthodoxy nor organizations. Like many others of his generation, he was convinced that the depression had exposed the bankruptcy of capitalism as an economic and political system and had opened the way for a complete reconstruction. Marxist analysis informed Weber's understanding of the causes of the depression and his belief that class consciousness and struggle were essential vehicles both for securing economic justice and for realizing the democratic process "in its full and rich sense." Jeffersonian ideals and the U.S. Constitution provided the political and legal basis for acting. Socialism, as Weber understood it, complemented Jefferson's vision of a dynamic democratic society, which held that nothing was unchangeable or inalienable except the natural rights of man. "The original impulse in socialism," Weber observed, "was how do you arrange social institutions so that social injustice is eliminated. . . . It's not an end in itself. The end . . . is the development of mankind."[2]

When Weber arrived at the University of Virginia in the fall of 1931, he was well-grounded in the social values and philosophical framework that shaped his political development. The small tidewater community of Smithfield, Virginia, where Weber had spent his first twelve years, was nurturing and secure, "a marvelous place to grow up," he later recalled. Across the James River from Jamestown, Smithfield was steeped in the traditions of the Old Dominion. It was a graceful river town that wore the prosperity of an earlier age. Weber, who lived with his mother, brother, and maternal grandparents, described his family as "poor, honest white people." They "went by water": Grandfather William Pittman, known locally as Captain Billy, was an oysterman. All members of the family were expected to work and contribute to the welfare of the household. One of Weber's earliest memories was of his grandfather "putting a one and a half pound hatchet in my hand . . . because I had to learn to make kindling wood . . . my brother and I had the responsibility to keep the wood boxes full." The centrality of work also encouraged an enterprising spirit driven by the "opportunity to make a nickel." As a young boy, Weber took advantage of everything within his reach to earn spending money: he collected scrap iron, shined shoes, sold newspapers, picked cotton, helped on the oyster boats, and after receiving a bicycle for Christmas, became a delivery boy for the dry goods store and the post office.

Weber's social activism was rooted in the church, which was central to community life in Smithfield. Every Sunday his family attended the Baptist Church for morning and evening services; each year he won a medal for perfect Sunday school attendance. The primary lesson that informed Weber's social values was the idea of stewardship: the idea "that your life is not your own, that your life is in effect a trust— you are a trustee of a life that has been given to you by something greater than yourself." There was something larger than personal well-being, something "that demanded your attention and allegiance." He embraced a fundamental belief in the brotherhood of all mankind, the basis for his later response to the issue of racial discrimination. As a child, he grew up in a segregated world. But he recalled: "Racism never took hold of me. I never absorbed it in the way some southerners did." He attributed this to his family's basic decency and lack of racial hostility, as well as his Christian values.

Diagnosed with glandular tuberculosis at the age of twelve, Palmer left the insular world of Smithfield and traveled 150 miles to the Blue Ridge Sanitarium, which sits in the shadow of Thomas Jefferson's Monticello. His five years at the sanitarium provided a formative educational and intellectual experience. In his eagerness to make himself useful and earn money to enlarge his stamp collection, Weber took on a number of jobs that brought him into daily contact with the patients in the adult ward of the sanitarium. Here was, he remembered, "a whole collection of people in the midst of dying and getting well, all of whom were concerned with the state of the human soul, the state of economics and politics. "It was "a magic mountain type of experience where you had a continual dialogue going on." A Greek immigrant and a railroad worker from Richmond engaged the young Weber in his first discussion of socialism, based on the debate between Harold Laski and Sumner Schlecter in *Current History*. Francis Franklin, a recent graduate of the University of Richmond and a student of Samuel Chiles Mitchell, introduced Weber to the Buddhist sutras and Mohandas Gandhi's *Young India*. He also read Gandhi's correspondence with Leo Tolstoy on nonviolent civil disobedience. Plato's *Dialogues*, the *Communist Manifesto*, and current issues of *Foreign Affairs* were shared by others and discussed. And Weber, who became superintendent of the sanitarium's Sunday school, pursued a thorough study of the Old and New Testaments. When he enrolled in the University of Virginia at the age of seventeen, Weber was a committed student of philosophy. "I wanted to understand the answers to the meaning of life, why people did this, why they did that, what things they held of value. I wanted to study ethics. I wanted to study politics."

While the state of Virginia was slipping deeper into the depression in the fall of 1931, the University of Virginia maintained its reputation as one of the country dub colleges of America, a place where students took great pains to dress well and master the etiquette of play. Palmer Weber did not have the time, the resources, or the inclination for either. A $100 gift from Dr. William Brown, the superintendent of the sanitarium, plus $100 from his mother and a $100 scholarship covered Weber's first year of study. He "worked like a sledgehammer" to stay at the head of his class, a goal that was necessary to maintain scholarship assistance. And he succeeded. Virginius Dabney, historian of the University of Virginia, described Weber as probably the most brilliant student at the university during the 1930s. He completed his bachelor's degree in three years, graduating Phi Beta Kappa, and continued for a Ph.D. in philosophy. During his time in Charlottesville, only his deepening involvement in political activity would compete with his rigorous academic schedule. Often, politics took precedence over academics.[3]

"You could describe me as a Gandhi socialist, Christian socialist, a Marxist socialist, any kind of variation where it was a questioning of authority or where an effort was made to bring justice," Weber recalled. Justice was central, very much as in Plato's *Republic*. Weber compared Plato's famous statement "giving each man what is his own" to Marx's "from each according to his ability, to each according to his need." There was one guiding question, according to Weber: "How do you carry out justice? What is your responsibility . . . as a citizen to see that the body politic embodies justice?" Thus, the study of philosophy, of social institutions, of economic history, was essential but not sufficient. Paraphrasing Marx, Weber explained, "The philosophers have interpreted the world in various ways; the point, however, is to change it." Weber "did anything that was within reach . . . that represented in practice trying to bring some justice into [the] local community, in race relations, in student discussion, whatever."[4]

Palmer Weber was the primary catalyst of a small but vocal student movement, which interacted with a national student movement that grew up around campus unrest during the early years of the depression. The Virginia movement had its origins in a Marxist study group of roughly twenty-five students, organized by Weber in 1932 as a spin-off of a reading group directed by Rev. William Kyle Smith, secretary of the local Young Men's Christian Association (YMCA). Later in 1932, Francis Franklin enrolled in the graduate program of philosophy at the University of Virginia. Through his connections with the state Communist Party headquarters in Richmond, he, Weber, and three or four other students joined the party, an affiliation that was openly acknowledged.

As a Marxist organization in the South, the Communist Party had a special appeal as an action-oriented organization, as demonstrated by its efforts in behalf of the unemployed and disfranchised workers and its bold defense of nine young black men in the widely publicized Scottsboro trials. Moreover, by 1932, students were stretching beyond the narrow sectarianism that dominated national party policy. The Communist-led National Student League (NSL), founded in 1931, provided an organizational framework for student protest and linked it to scattered movements on the labor, civil rights, and civil liberties fronts.

In addition to marking a departure from the tradition of campus radicalism, the NSL broke from the orthodoxy of the Third Party period that ruled the students' adult counterparts in the Communist Party. . . .

In December 1931, a small group of students from various New York City colleges, some members of the Young Communist League and some sympathetic to the Communist approach, responded to the new mood of political interest and urgency by establishing the National Student League. The NSL, which proposed to mobilize students for political action, marked a major breakthrough for the American student Left. The NSL built an autonomous movement, responsive to the concerns of students. It also provided a vehicle for realizing and acting on the connections between the economic troubles facing America's youth and the deeper social crisis generated by the depression.[5]

In implementing its founding pledge to build a mass movement among the nation's college students, the NSL pioneered Popular Front techniques and strategies in direct contradiction to the militant sectarianism of official Communist Party policy. The NSL endured occasional criticism from the Communist Party leadership, but the party hierarchy evidenced no interest in controlling "the seemingly unimportant world of student organizing." NSL founders included Joseph Starobin, Max Gordon, Joseph Clark, and Robert F. "Rob" Hall. They represented a new generation of radical activists, and their ideas about socialism and politics would help shape the course of the party during its heyday. The students were adherents of the American Communist Party's militant anticapitalism and looked to the Soviet Union as "the world's only worker-run, depression proof country." Organizing, however, took precedence over orthodoxy. Rob Hall's membership in the party represented a direct outgrowth of the economic and political concerns that had led this native Alabamian to Columbia University in 1929 to study agricultural economics under Rex Tugwell. Hall recalled that he "grew into" the party. "This was what you believed. These were the people you worked with." Citing Marx's prediction that the peaceful development of socialism could be realized in England and the United States, Hall looked toward political organization and action as prelude to the democratic realization of a socialist state in America.[6]

The NSL-led expedition to aid striking miners in Harlan County, Kentucky, in March 1932 signified the political baptism of the student movement. Socialists and unaffiliated students, as well as Communist Party members, were among two busloads of students carrying relief to the miners. Hall, the group's organizer, emphasized the nonconfrontational nature of the trip; students were advised to forgo proletarian fashion, such as leather jackets, for dresses and suits and to avoid revolutionary rhetoric. The purpose of the trip was to investigate conditions in the coalfields and provide humanitarian assistance. However, the hostile reception awaiting the students in Kentucky ensured that the students would draw national attention to the desperate conditions of the striking miners and on the routine civil liberties violations encountered by unionization efforts and prolabor supporters. Stopped at gunpoint on the highway and hauled into court, the students were harassed by the local prosecutor as "Russian-born Jewish Communists" and then carried to the state line and forced to leave. The delegation continued on to Washington to appeal for federal protection of the constitutional rights of the striking miners. Hall's testimony before a subcommittee of the U.S. Senate Committee on Manufactures aided liberal senators in their battle for a congressional investigation of the coal strike.[7]

. . . . Political action joined to Marxist analysis initiated a process of questioning and radicalization that shaped a new student culture in the 1930s. . . . Student organizers mobilized youth around campus-based problems such as cuts in student assistance, fraternity control of student government, the establishment of book cooperatives, free speech for political dissidents, and antiwar protest and linked student activism to the broader social movements of the depression decade. In the process, this activism supported and created opportunities for interracial associations and political action.

The student movement at the University of Virginia carved out multiple areas of activism. With the exception of the strike for peace in 1935, however, student protest at Virginia never engaged more than several dozen young men. Yet these students spearheaded a successful challenge to fraternity control of student government, organized a cooperative bookstore, and mobilized one thousand students and faculty members as part of the nationwide student strike for peace in April 1935. Working through the Liberal Discussion Group and a local chapter of the NSL, they succeeded in publicizing social and racial issues that had never been raised on white college campuses in the South. They sponsored a series of interracial lectures; speakers included Ronald Ely, president of the student union at Virginia Union University, a black college in Richmond, and leading Communist Party figures such as J. B. Matthews and Earl Browder. When the university refused to let Richard B. Moore, a black Communist, speak on campus grounds, Palmer Weber asked, "What manner of small-minded men have inherited Mr. Jefferson's University?" His column blasted the university administration for violating "the ancient and revered traditions of free speech and free thought . . . in the futile endeavor to support social mores," mores that could "no longer be justified." The controversy won attention in the northeastern press; it was the last time such a restriction was imposed.[8]

Weber's politics and organizing skills were tested by the peculiarities of southern politics and race relations and were forged in the changing contours of national politics. He served as a student representative on the Virginia State Committee of the Communist Party, was the first president of the Virginia chapter of the NSL, and joined the national board of the NSL in 1935. When Earl Browder visited Charlottesville in 1936 to discuss the upcoming presidential election, Weber told Browder that he was ready to engage in full-time organizing work either for the party or with a labor union. Browder advised Weber to stay at the university and complete his Ph.D.; the party needed competent people.

On 1 May 1934, in the first of a series of columns he published intermittently over the next four years in *College Topics*, the student paper at Virginia, the twenty-year-old Weber, writing as a strident Marxist, appealed to his readers: "The future of youth lies in the rising tides of the industrial prolerariat, may we grasp their hands in unity and struggle with them this May day." But as he acted on this challenge, participating in local efforts to organize the unemployed and workers at a local textile plant, Weber's political understanding increasingly reflected the social and economic realities of Virginia and the South in general. Commenting on his organizing efforts among the unemployed of Charlottesville, Weber recalled: "There was no community leadership. . . . It was just as though you had people released from slavery." If there were two hundred jobs in the textile mill, there were three thousand people waiting to be hired for any available opening. There was one brief, unsuccessful strike at the Ix textile mill on the outskirts of Charlottesville, where Weber and several others were arrested for distributing leaflets. Desperate conditions and police repression of union activity seemed to defy the most resourceful organizers.[9]

Race became a dominant factor in Weber's analysis of the South's economic and political structure and a defining element in his development as an activist and organizer. More than any other issue, lynching exposed the routine lawlessness and antidemocratic ideology that permeated southern society in the guise of white supremacy and states' rights. In a series of columns urging the passage of federal antilynching legislation, Weber argued: "Let it be repeated that those people who keep hollering about States Rights and the American form of government are the very people who violate the American constitution. They are the people who have limited the franchise in the South to the point where not one third of the Southern people vote. They are the people who never mention the decades long violation of the thirteenth, fourteenth and fifteenth amendments to the constitution. Rather, keeping their foot firmly in the Negro's face, violating his every human and legal right, they spend their effort hollering about States' Rights."[10]

Supported by a series of studies published in the early 1930s, Weber debunked the charge that lynch victims had been accused of rape; only 16 percent in the previous fifty years had been so accused. "Negroes have been lynched in the South," Weber explained, "for asking [for] a

217

written receipt for a bill paid, or a written contract for tenancy, or for slapping a white man, or for talking back, or a hundred other reasons that reflect the struggles of the Negro people to obtain a better living for themselves." Lynching was "outright terror used in the South to keep Negro tenants and workers in an inferior economic position . . . to beat down their protests . . . to [deny] them simple civil liberties." Such brutal, state-sanctioned suppression of citizenship rights was a national problem, Weber argued, and required federal action.[11]

Weber's racial concerns complemented an emerging movement among southern black activists to challenge the legal and political foundation of white supremacy. Acting decisively on its commitment to fight racial discrimination, the NSL provided a forum for black and white students, one that went beyond the formal interracial "get-togethers" that had characterized groups like the Commission on Interracial Cooperation (CIC), the Young Women's Christian Association (YWCA), and other tentative engagements. Contrasting the NSL'S 1933 "Student Conference on Negro Student Problems" with these efforts, a Howard student observed, "The sugary spirit was absent; instead there was a common resolve to go back to the South and, for that matter, many areas of the North and tackle shoulder to shoulder the problems of discrimination." The NSL brought black and white southern colleges into the national student movement and linked the small handful of student activists on southern campuses around common programs of action. James Jackson, a Virginia Union University delegate to the NSL conference, recalled that the NSL provided "the foundation and the basis" for organizing students at black colleges, where conservative administrations often exceeded white colleges in their repression of student protest.

In the summer of 1935, students from several colleges in Virginia, including William and Mary and the University of Virginia, met at Virginia Union University in Richmond. The group drafted a model bill calling for increased expenditures on education, equal allocation of state funds among black and white students, and an end to segregation.[12] At the end of the conference, an interracial delegation of students went to the State House to present the bill. James Jackson recalled:

> Palmer was mister finger-in-your-chest, an aggressive type. With him in the lead we all marched from the conference to the state capitol in Richmond, under the arrogant glare of Stonewall Jackson, sneering down on us. Palmer just opened the door to the State Assembly and said, "Gentlemen, we have business," and we all marched up to the front. He said "Mr. Speaker, here is Mr. Jackson. He has a proposal to present to this house." And so with no further ado, I read the draft of this

bill to abolish segregation. Towards the end of my reading—I didn't get to the last chapter—the Speaker banged the gavel on his desk. He said this session is over, and we'll give you boys ten seconds to get out.[13]

Virginia, like all other southern states, did not provide access to graduate education or professional schools for black students. In the fall of 1935, Alice Jackson, the sister of James Jackson, applied for admission to the graduate school at the University of Virginia. Jackson's application was part of the NAACP's initial legal challenge to racial discrimination in public education, a challenge that would culminate with the *Brown v. Board of Education* ruling two decades later. The University of Virginia chapter of the NSL supported Jackson's application and invited a representative of the NAACP to address an NSL-sponsored student forum on the case. Despite efforts to inform student opinion, Jackson's application garnered little support among the university's student body. Weber estimated that a scant 5 percent favored Jackson's admission to the graduate school.

The university refused Jackson's application on the grounds that "the education of white and colored persons in the same school" was "contrary to the long established and fixed policy of the Commonwealth of Virginia." Student supporters of Jackson's admission protested the university's action with a statement that won notice in the *New York Times*. "We ask whether a long established policy is never to be changed; we ask whether in the present time of general political reaction and antagonism against racial minorities it is not necessary to assert the right of equal opportunity for all people regardless of color or creed. In short, we criticize the Board's stand because it simply implies the desirability of continuing education inequality. We are confident that every liberal, radical and Christian thinker will concur with us in this protest." The state of Virginia met the challenge posed by Jackson's application by hastily establishing an out-of-state scholarship program for black students seeking graduate and professional education.[14]

Palmer Weber's political interests and activities extended beyond the student movement into Charlottesville's black community. Most black people in Charlottesville were dependent on the University of Virginia for their livelihood, and few were willing to engage in overt protest activity. But Weber found allies in the black community who were open to the possibilities of collective action. He collaborated with Randolph White, a black technician at the University of Virginia hospital, in a successful effort to organize hospital workers to secure an eight-hour day and increased wages and to get black patients "out of the basement," the location of the segregated ward. Weber met frequently with White and his associates to plan strategies and to lobby state officials to improve conditions at the hospital. White and Weber often traveled to Staunton, Virginia, to aid organizing efforts among black workers at Mary Baldwin College. Attempting to explain Weber's enlightened racial views and political activism, White observed: "Palmer was a po' boy. He had a rough time. He was in the same boat." And, White recalled, they shared a mutual understanding of the importance of organizing. The established economic and political powers "didn't care nothin' about the individual." White added: "Whether you're white or black, they'll just cut you down, like mowin' hay. But when people band together, you can do a whole lot."[15]

By the end of 1938, Weber had drifted beyond the orbit of the Communist Party; he found it, as an organization, to be increasingly irrelevant to the political changes that were happening in the South. The Democratic Party had become the most promising arena for realizing a biracial political coalition capable of securing social and economic change in the South. With the large-scale crossover of black voters to the party of Roosevelt in the 1936 election, northern Democrats were speaking more boldly for equal rights. In an article titled "The Negro Vote in the South, "Weber reported on a less noted but equally significant development in the South, where there was a growing movement among black southerners to vote in the all-white Democratic primary. Racial unity was, he explained, something to be achieved, for it existed only "in part in scattered organizations and localities." Its full realization, he predicted, depended on the growth of black and white unity "in labor organizations, among tenant farmers, and in the Democratic primary."[16]

Charles Hamilton Houston also navigated the possibilities created by the economic dislocation and shifting political alliances of the depression years. As chief legal counsel for the NAACP, he was uniquely able to recognize openings in the South's caste-bound society. Starting in 1934, Houston began traveling extensively in the South, observing and documenting conditions in black communities, becoming familiar with local leadership and organizations, and encouraging the renewed political interest and activism evident in the early 1930s. Although Houston's personal experiences were very different from Palmer Weber's, both acted on a common set of beliefs about the central role of race and region in the economic and political contests that were reshaping the nation. "The work of the next decade," Houston wrote NAACP Executive Secretary Walter White in 1934, "will have to be concentrated in the South."[17]

Charles Houston was slightly older than the New Deal generation of black activists. He was born in Washington, D.C., in 1895 and . . . was part of Washington's black middle class. The grandson of runaway slaves, Houston inherited a strong sense of racial pride and benefited from William and Katherine Houston's commitment to provide their only son with the best education possible. From Dunbar High School, he went on to Amherst College, where, during his first year, he was the only person of African descent at the college. "The alienation born of racism," wrote biographer Genna Rae McNeil, became a "catalyst for Charles's . . . personal self-reliance."[18] He graduated Phi Beta Kappa in 1915 and delivered a commencement address on the life of Paul Laurence Dunbar, despite protests from faculty members unfamiliar with the subject.

Formal education was interrupted by service in World War I, an experience that fundamentally shaped Houston's personal expectations and goals. The daily indignities heaped on black soldiers in the segregated armed forces were compounded by his experience as a judge-advocate, during which he witnessed the blatant disregard of fairness and justice when black soldiers were the subjects of prosecution. Houston wrote, "I made up my mind that I would never get caught again without knowing something about my rights; that if luck was with me, and I got through this war, I would study law and use my time fighting for men who could not strike back." In the fall of 1919, Houston enrolled in Harvard Law School and became the first person of his race elected to the editorial board of the *Harvard Law Review*. During his second year, he organized a student luncheon at Harvard for Marcus Garvey, who, Houston later explained, "made a permanent contribution in teaching the simple dignity of being black." After obtaining an LL.B. and a doctorate in law from Harvard, he received a Harvard-sponsored scholarship to support a year of study in comparative law at the University of Madrid. Spain afforded Houston an experience of racial egalitarianism that "colored [his] entire life on the race question."[19]

With the normal channels of political participation closed to black Americans, Charles Houston envisioned a unique and critical role for black lawyers. As early as 1922, Houston proposed that there must be a black lawyer in every community, preferably trained at black institutions by black teachers. Applying the innovative theory of social jurisprudence advanced at Harvard by Roscoe Pound, Felix Frankfurter, and others, Houston explained that through the creative exploration and application of the Constitution, the black lawyer could achieve reforms that were unattainable through traditional political channels. Houston applied his vision as a member of the Howard University Law School faculty (1924–35), where he was appointed vice-dean in 1929. He transformed the school from a nonaccredited night school into a full-time, accredited program and created a laboratory for the development of civil rights law. The rigorous course he implemented reflected his conception of social engineering and the responsibilities of black leadership. The black lawyer, Houston maintained, should "be trained as a social engineer and group interpreter." He added, "Due to the Negro's social and political condition . . . the Negro lawyer must be prepared to anticipate, guide and interpret his group's advancement." Houston educated a generation of black civil rights lawyers, many from the South, who would implement the NAACP's protracted assault on the legal foundation of white supremacy.[20]

By enhancing the power of the federal government, the economic crisis of the depression and the advent of the New Deal reinforced Houston's emphasis on national citizenship. He was alert to the vastly expanded range of possibilities for political education and action, possibilities created by the social dislocation and government experimentation of the 1930s. Houston investigated the racial application of New Deal programs and publicized cases of discrimination, lobbied the Roosevelt administration for fair treatment, testified before Congress on the racial implications of a wide array of legislation, and played a leading role in the fight for antilynching legislation. The development of racially progressive political views among white liberals won Houston's attention. Speaking to groups like the Virginia Commission on Interracial Cooperation and the YWCA, he cautioned them not to act "out of any sentimental interest in the Negro." It was in the self-interest of white liberals to confront the race problem, which, he warned, could "yet be the decisive factor in the success or failure of the New Deal." Their goal, Houston advised, should be to "free white America from the senseless phobias and contemptuous arrogance towards all peoples of the non-nordic stock." He acknowledged the magnitude of the task but suggested that they strive to make their "own generation open its eyes" and realize when it was "cutting off its nose to spite its face." He noted, "The South is doing [this] when it squeezes Negro wages and as a consequence cuts down his consuming power in the community." And he urged them to "save young America from the blight of race prejudice."[21]

Houston publicized promising legal developments that might offer new tools for advancing the movement. Judge James A. Lowell's ruling in the case of George Crawford was one example. In 1933 the Boston judge refused to extradite Crawford, a black man accused of murder, to Virginia on the grounds that the state excluded blacks from serving on juries in that state. Houston anticipated the "opening up of a new underground railroad for Negroes in the South" if Lowell's ruling was upheld. The principle, Houston explained, was simply that Virginia, which was making the request for extradition, could not "invoke the United States Constitution on the one hand for the purpose of obtaining extradition and on the other hand kick the United States Constitution by denying the Negroes the right to serve on juries." Further attention was drawn to the matter when Virginia Congressman Howard W. Smith introduced a bill calling for Judge Lowell's impeachment. George Crawford was finally returned to Virginia and tried for murder. He was represented by an all-black defense team led by Charles Houston for the NAACP.[22]

The early years of the New Deal coincided with Houston's deepening involvement in the NAACP. As the association's legal counsel and trusted adviser to Executive Secretary Walter White, Houston played a critical role in the NAACP's development during these years. By the early 1930s, the NAACP was in the process of completing a major transition, at least at the national level, away from the predominantly white-led organization founded in 1909 and toward an expanding role for black leadership and a greater reliance on black membership. But the New York-based organization continued to maintain a narrow legal focus, tended to rely on prominent white constitutional lawyers for its major cases, and remained remote from the lives and experiences of the majority of black Americans, especially those living in the South. The brief flurry of branch activity in the South after World War I failed to reach much beyond the professional classes and receded by the late 1920s. The NAACP meeting in Oklahoma in 1934 marked the first time a national convention had been held in the South since the Atlanta meeting of 1921. Speaking to the national convention in 1933 and 1934, Houston joined a chorus of voices in urging a major revision of association policy and priorities to meet the crisis of the depression. "Take the Association home to the people in 1934," he implored the Oklahoma gathering.[23]

A case in the 1930s exposed the inadequacy of the NAACP's approach to the South. When news of the arrest of nine young black men charged with raping two white women near Scottsboro, Alabama, reached New York in the spring of 1931, Walter White had no local contacts to call on for a direct report. The nearest NAACP branch, in Chattanooga, had collapsed in 1930. White followed the case in the press, which relied primarily on southern newspapers, and the NAACP remained aloof. Meanwhile, when Charles Dirba, assistant secretary of the International Labor Defense (ILD) and a member of the Communist Party's Central Committee, read about the arrest, he telegraphed Lowell Wakefield, a party organizer in Birmingham, whom he urged to conduct a careful investigation of the case. Wakefield and Douglas McKenzie, a black organizer for the League of Struggle for Negro Rights, attended the trials in Scottsboro. Dependent on a weak and ineffectual team of defense lawyers, the young men were quickly tried and sentenced to death, amid a mob atmosphere. The ILD immediately acted to secure representation for the appeal of the case and publicized the "legal lynching" of the Scottsboro defendants. The ILD won the acclaim of much of the black press and its readership, which chided the NAACP's belated efforts to wrest control of the case from a group that had acted boldly and decisively.[24]

The unfolding of the Scottsboro case, recalled Robert Weaver, was comparable to the dramatic impact of Bull Connor turning the hoses and dogs on young black protesters in Birmingham some thirty years later. "It was a great shock to a large number of people, and made many people face up to a situation which they would have not faced up to before." The ILD'S fight on behalf of the defendants would not be confined to the courtroom, though it did win a major case before the U.S. Supreme Court with *Powell v. Alabama* (1932), which extended the rights of criminal defendants. Through mass demonstrations, the ILD brought the case and the larger racial and economic reality it represented before the nation and won international attention. By contrast, the cautious, legalistic approach of the NAACP, which sought to secure a measure of justice by appealing to the goodwill of white southern moderates, fell flat. In 1934, Charles Houston predicted that the Scottsboro case would one day be acknowledged as a "milestone" in American history.[25]

The Scottsboro case challenged the NAACP to broaden the focus of its campaign against lynching. As Houston viewed it, "relief from physical terrorism" was at the basis of all black progress. He agreed that it was the essential prerequisite to all other struggles for equal rights and "necessary in order to get people to go into court." Though Houston campaigned for federal antilynching legislation, he questioned the tendency of the NAACP to focus on the passage of the bill as the sole cure for lynching in the South. Observing that local elected officials permitted lynchings, Houston argued, "You give nine million Negroes the ballot and they will settle the question of lynching." Scottsboro, he explained, was a judicial lynching with the same social effect "as though a mob had taken them and strung them on a telephone pole." Houston predicted that the "extra-judicial" mob lynchings would turn into "judicial and official lynchings unless the drive of the liberal forces" was "carried way beyond a federal anti-lynching law to complete justice in the courts and to true universal suffrage."[26]

Throughout the 1930s, Charles Houston referred to the Scottsboro case as a pivotal event in the development of black protest. The ILD'S "uncompromising resistance to southern prejudice," he explained, "set a new standard for agitation for equality." As a symbol of "the whole position of oppression of the Negro people in America," the Scottsboro case "fused all the elements of the Negro people into a common resistance more than any other issue within a generation." Whereas most black people had tended to "stay away" from black people in trouble— "with the idea of not letting trouble spread to themselves"—they joined in the fight for the "Scottsboro Boys" because they "were made to feel that even without the ordinary weapons of democracy . . . [they] still had the force . . . with which they themselves could bring to bear pressures and affect the result of the trial and arbitrations." Furthermore, he explained, "The Communists have made it impossible for any aspirant to Negro leadership to advocate less than full economic, political and social equality and expect to retain the respect and confidence of the group."[27]

For Houston, ideological disputes about Communist Party assumptions and goals were of little consequence. What mattered were the patterns of interaction that developed between Communist Party organizers and black people in Alabama. Unlike traditional civil rights and interracial groups, which maintained a paternalistic approach to the "masses," Communists worked among the sharecroppers and unemployed, "offering them full and complete brotherhood, without regard to race, creed or previous condition of servitude." Consequently, they were "the first to fire the masses with a sense of their raw, potential power, and the first to openly preach the doctrine of mass resistance and mass struggle: Unite and Fight!" Through their organizing efforts, Communists turned the attention of blacks to the issue of class and emphasized its relation to racial oppression.[28]

Although Houston concentrated his organizing efforts within the black community, he viewed this as part of a broader effort to build class-based alliances among southern blacks and whites. "The white and black miners in the Birmingham district have presented the ultimate solution," he observed in 1934, "by forming together in one common union to fight shoulder to shoulder for their common interest." That same year, Houston told the annual convention of the NAACP that permanent black progress against injustice and discrimination in the South would depend on whether or not blacks could form an alliance with poor whites, because the separation of the two races was impeding the progress of both. "Together they can win against the forces which are seeking to exploit them and keep them down. Separately they will lose and the other fellow will continue to win."[29]

Houston never doubted that the NAACP had a unique role to play as potentially the most effective black organization in the country, but the role would require a major reorganization and reorientation of the association's program. By the time Houston assumed responsibility for the NAACP's legal campaign against racial discrimination in education in 1934, he was prepared to mediate between the national office and its potential southern constituency. Houston was an astute student of the region and its people, having traveled through the South extensively, always on multipurpose trips. A month-long trip late in 1934 was typical. He visited eleven towns in Georgia, the Carolinas, and Virginia, several of them more than once. He spoke at thirteen black colleges, recruited applicants for Howard University Law School, consulted with black lawyers in each state, spoke in churches, attended the district conference of the African Methodist Episcopal (AME) Zion Church in Rock Hill, South Carolina, and met with teachers groups, NAACP branches, and the North Carolina statewide conference of the Tobacco Workers Union. On the same trip, he investigated school facilities, rural conditions, and the administration of federal relief and jobs and, with the assistance of Edward Lovett, began to document his findings with photographs and films. All the while, he deliberately cultivated support for the NAACP's program and sought out individuals "of force, vision . . . [and] keenness" who had the capacity to "be effective on the race issue in the South."[30]

Houston's efforts to expand the base of NAACP activity in the South were equaled by his steady drive to place the southern situation at the center of national NAACP deliberations. He pressed for a reorganization of the association's structure so that the southern membership could participate in defining the national program. In supporting the nomination of Roscoe Dunjee, editor of the *Oklahoma Black Dispatch*, to the NAACP national board, Houston advised White: "Dunjee is a man of the people, and knows the Southwest situation." Certainly, he added, White needed someone on the board who could vocalize "the aspirations of that section."[31]

A critique of the proposed program for the NAACP annual conference in 1935 contrasts Houston's vision with the conventional leadership that dominated the national office. Houston wrote Assistant Secretary Roy Wilkins that the program emphasis on appealing to white southern goodwill and on pursuing "nationally known names" was irrelevant to the economic and political crisis facing the great majority of black Americans. Commenting on the preview of White's speech on the antilynching fight, Houston said: "Walter can tell all he wants about the change in white southern sentiment. We don't want to waste an evening listening to it. [He] should tie up lynching with all the evils we suffer from; show how it perpetuates political disfranchisement, what that means; how it keeps down labor organizing, etc.; how it keeps down protest against intolerable relief conditions, etc., etc."[32]

Houston compared the proposed program for the annual convention with the Conference on the Economic Status of the Negro, organized by John P. Davis and Ralph Bunche and sponsored by the Joint Committee on National Recovery and the Social Science Division of Howard University earlier that year. "The presence of workers gave this conference an impact of reality wholly different from the usual gabfest conference," Houston advised Wilkins. The NAACP, he insisted, must concentrate on the vital problems of unemployment and relief.

He volunteered to bring some relief workers up from the South, and he suggested that his films on relief in Alabama, education facilities in South Carolina, and NAACP-organized picketing be shown. Houston wanted workers, sharecroppers, and victims of relief discrimination to participate in the various panels. "They may not make grammatical speeches," he told Wilkins, "but their very presence is more eloquent than all the prepared speeches you could present." And it would indicate that the association was "getting away from being paternalistic and becoming fraternalistic with the masses of Negroes."[33]

Under Houston's direction, the NAACP's legal campaign against racial discrimination in education stimulated the revival and expansion of NAACP branch activity. Beginning with a protracted challenge to the most blatant inequities in public education, namely the denial of graduate and professional educational opportunities to black students and the racial basis of teachers' salaries, Houston and his associates crafted a strategy that steadily eroded the legal foundations of segregation. Houston's insistence on working with all-black counsel had particular resonance in southern courtrooms. Here, often for the first time, black people witnessed one of their race functioning in a context of total equality, calling white state officials to account in full public view. Such trial scenes were reenacted in pool halls and barbershops. By 1938, Houston noted, hopefully, that the fight for graduate and professional education was "generating spontaneously out of the group itself"; every case had "been fought by Negro lawyers who practically donated their services."[34]

Houston's efforts in the South, an associate recalled, were fueled by his confidence in the capacity "within the black community and the Negro race to bring about change." The legal campaign was a slow and deliberate process, which sought to establish roots in local communities. In endless rounds of meetings with small and large groups throughout the South, Houston and Thurgood Marshall, his protégé and former student, explained the mechanics of the legal fight, its political significance, and its relationship to broader community concerns. They routinely encouraged people to pay their poll tax, persist in the effort to register and vote, and organize political clubs, explaining that legal victories must be backed up by organized pressure and support. Often they found people fearful of initiating litigation or political action and, in some cases, apathetic about the need for struggle. "This means we have to . . . slow down," Houston would say, "until we have developed a sustaining mass interest behind the programs . . . The social and public factors must be developed at least along with and if possible before the actual litigation commences."[35]

Yet subtle signs of change abounded. Houston reported on organized attempts by black citizens in South Carolina, Alabama, and Texas to gain admission to the all-white Democratic primary elections in 1934. Voting clubs increasingly appeared in black communities throughout the region. Based on extensive fieldwork during the later 1930s, Ralph Bunche reported that in a number of southern cities, blacks elected "bronze" mayors in mock election campaigns that followed a regular campaign with posters and meetings. Bunche and his team of investigators also found a growing movement among black southerners at least to attempt to register and vote in the face of legal restrictions and potential reprisals. Bunche noted, "Despite the hardships frequently imposed by registrars . . . increasing numbers of Negroes in the South are demonstrating an amazing amount of patience, perseverance and determination . . . and keep returning after rejections until they get their names on the registration books." In 1937 Arthur Shores, the only practicing black attorney in the state of Alabama, filed suit against the Board of Registrar in Bessemer, Alabama, on behalf of eight schoolteachers who had been disqualified by the board. The board reversed itself and issued registration certificates, beginning the long struggle to break down discriminatory registration procedures in Alabama.[36]

Bunche and others documented direct links between New Deal initiatives and growing black political participation. Peter Epps, a Works Progress Administration (WPA) worker in Columbia, South Carolina, was typical. When asked whether blacks on a local farm ever talked politics, Epps replied: "They's talked more politics since Mistuh Roosevelt been in than ever befo'. I been here twenty years, but since WPA, the Negro sho' has started talkin' 'bout politics." A 1938 WPA directive served as an inadvertent spur to black political participation. In an effort to defuse conservative charges that the agency fraudulently sought to influence the votes of its beneficiaries, WPA administrator Elizabeth Wickenden prepared a notice to accompany every WPA check and to advise the recipients that they were free to vote for whomever they pleased. Wickenden was inundated with reports of black southerners showing up at the courthouse with a notice from the WPA endorsing their right to vote.[37]

The 1936 election gave form to the sea change in political attitudes and aspirations that had been shaped, in large part, by the rhetoric and initiatives of the early New Deal. Roosevelt's embrace of class-based politics absorbed much of the energy generated by nascent independent movements on the Left. The campaign also marked the political debut of the new industrial unions of the CIO. Working through the Labor NonPartisan League (LNPL), CIO unions organized local get-out-the-vote campaigns in nearly every state, among white and black workers, with no pretense to being "nonpartisan." The LNPL was unabashedly a part of the Roosevelt reelection machinery and was key to the president's historic landslide at the polls. Commenting on "the tremendous proportions of the victory based on labor, farmer, and lower middle class voters," Palmer Weber pointed to the parallels in American history, most recently the capture of the Democratic Party by the Populists in 1896. "This grand American tradition of an alliance," he observed, had sharpened class antagonisms in the past and, he predicted, would do so once again. And, because the election had been fought and won on the basis of class politics, Roosevelt would not be able to contain the consequences."[38]

The election also marked the culmination of a three-year effort on the part of the Roosevelt administration to fully engage the tentative allegiance of black voters, who had been steadily drifting away from the party of Lincoln. The battle for the northern black vote emerged as a major feature of the 1936 campaign. For the first time, the black vote was a part of the political reporting in the national press, and both parties pursued an aggressive advertising campaign in the black press. Although the Roosevelt administration failed to endorse any racially sensitive policies, such as antilynching legislation, it presided over a national convention that, for the first time, opened its doors to the equal participation of black reporters and the handful of black delegates in attendance, drawing a howl of protest from Senator E. D. Smith and the South Carolina delegation. Mary McLeod Bethune and other members of the "Black Cabinet" took part in a sophisticated campaign aimed at black voters; the campaign included an extravagant, multicity celebration of the seventy-third anniversary of the Emancipation Proclamation. These appeals only reinforced the bonds woven by New Deal relief and jobs, ensuring Roosevelt's sweep of the black vote. "The amazing switch of this great group of voters," wrote political analyst Frank R. Kent, "is the real political sensation of the time."[39]

The successful wooing of the northern black vote dominated the rhetoric of southern conservatives as they swelled the ranks of the anti-New Deal coalition. "Acceptance of the Negro on terms of political equality," stormed Senator Smith, had "humiliated the South."[40] But the black vote was still tightly confined by law and custom in the South. It was the new labor movement, working in tandem with the Roosevelt administration and congressional supporters, that immediately threatened to penetrate the "Solid South" and undermine the economic and racial status quo. During 1937 and 1938, the CIO sponsored its first southern organizing drive, providing critical reinforcement to efforts that had taken root among industrial workers and sharecroppers earlier in the decade and generating a reaction that further exposed the police repression, violence, and political disfranchisement that pervaded southern society.*

The CIO tapped into the generation of southerners who had emerged from the student movement, the YWCA and YMCA, and earlier labor-organizing efforts. Of the 112 organizers initially employed by the CIO to work in the South, most were southern-born and many were women. James Jackson, the former student organizer for the NSL and founding member of the Southern Negro Youth Congress (SNYC) in 1937, worked as an organizer for the CIO among black tobacco workers in Richmond, where more than five thousand workers signed up and seven union contracts were secured. The CIO provided an infusion for Highlander Folk School in Tennessee, which had struggled since 1931, with little success, to nurture trade union leadership among industrial workers and farmers. In 1937, Highlander became the CIO'S primary vehicle for training southern organizers. In Birmingham, Alabama, the CIO's Steel Workers Organizing Committee (SWOC) launched a drive in the summer of 1936, invigorating the Popular Front movement that had grown up around earlier Communist-led efforts among the unemployed, sharecroppers, and industrial workers. Under the CIO umbrella, these diverse and widely scattered movements created a southern network and a spur to more effective political action and organizing.[41]

The popular image of union activists as northern troublemakers with foreign ideas met its most effective challenge in the person of Lucy Randolph Mason, the CIO's primary publicist in the South. She was a Virginian of prominent lineage, the great-great-granddaughter of George Mason, a signer of the Declaration of Independence and author of the Virginia Bill of Rights. "People could place her," a contemporary recalled. A slight woman with white hair, she was the quintessential southern lady. "When Miss Lucy entered a union meeting, the men instinctively got to their feet."[42]

Lucy Randolph Mason was born in 1882. Her family lived in West Virginia and Georgia before finally settling in Richmond in 1891, where Mason's father, an Episcopal minister, served as rector of Grace Church. From her parents, Mason imbibed religious values informed by the Social Gospel, with its commitment to community service and social reform. Her political development was further shaped by her exposure to factory life in Richmond at the turn of the century; she was particularly sensitive to the plight of working-class women. Mason endorsed

---

* A section on the background of the founding of the Congress (originally, Committee) of Industrial Organizations in 1935 and its early successes in organizing major industries has been omitted—ed.

the union movement and the expansion of suffrage as essential to the advancement of social justice, and she devoted her efforts to both. She was a leading force in the woman's suffrage movement in Richmond and in 1914 became the first industrial secretary of the YWCA in the South. Mason served as general secretary of the Richmond YWCA during the 1920s and honed her skills as a lobbyist and publicist for legislation regulating working conditions for women and children. A wide-ranging community activist, Mason did not avoid the implications of racial discrimination; she publicly acknowledged that it inhibited any real progress toward economic and social justice. In 1929 she was the only white reformer to oppose a Richmond City Council measure requiring residential segregation.[43]

In September 1932, Mason became general secretary of the National Consumer's League (NCL), which provided a national focus for her efforts to secure protective labor legislation in the South. Almost immediately, the New Deal sparked the revival of the flagging, forty-year-old feminist organization and created possibilities for reaching beyond the state-based focus of the NCL'S program. In April 1933, Mason wrote that she felt "a curious lift and thrill, as if some great adventure were just around the corner." Mason was part of the network of women in the wave of new talent that populated New Deal Washington and that helped shape legislation and policy. She represented the NCL at the National Recovery Administration (NRA) hearings on wage and hour codes, where she joined the opposition to the racial wage differential, and she consulted with New Deal legislative strategist Ben Cohen and others on the drafting of minimum-wage legislation. Her lobbying efforts in Washington brought her into contact with labor leaders such as Sidney Hillman and David Dubinsky and with Eleanor Roosevelt, who became a friend and confidante. Played out against the futile efforts to secure state legislation regulating working conditions in the South, her experience also convinced her of the necessity of federal initiatives and support to secure fundamental reform. By the time Mason joined the CIO in July 1937, it was clear to her that the future of New Deal reforms would depend largely on what happened in the South. A strong labor movement, she believed, was essential to translating Roosevelt's regional support into a politically effective constituency.[44]

Mason worked primarily with the Textile Workers Organizing Committee (TWOC); the effort to organize the South's major industry was at the core of the CIO'S drive. Her confidence that the labor movement could advance economic and political reform in the South was quickly tested by the unbridled power of local authorities to defy federal law and basic constitutional protections. "When I came South I had no idea of the frequent attacks on people peacefully pursuing legitimate purposes," she reported to President Roosevelt in August 1937. "I am appalled at the disregard of the most common civil rights and dangers to bodily harm to which organizers are often exposed." As the CIO'S bold offensive rallied progressive forces in the South, it also helped to galvanize powerful anti-New Deal and antilabor forces in the South and in Congress. Mason wrote to Eleanor Roosevelt that organizing efforts met a solid bloc of resistance from "civil authorities, the press and all other agencies," while company spies infiltrated the ranks of the union movement and while the Ku Klux Klan and other vigilante groups terrorized and assaulted union members and labor organizers. Nineteen southern organizers were murdered between 1936 and 1939. By the end of 1937, early signs of progress had dissipated.[45]

During a textile strike in Tupelo, Mississippi, late in the spring of 1938, Mason met with Joseph Gelders, who suggested a southwide conference on civil rights to organize an effective opposition to the wave of terror and repression. Gelders—a Birmingham native, a former University of Alabama professor, and the southern representative of the National Committee for the Defense of Political Prisoners—had been the subject of widely publicized hearings early in 1937 before the La Follette Committee on antilabor violence in the South. Because of his activities on behalf of Jack Barton, he had been beaten and left for dead by guards employed by the Tennessee Coal and Iron Company. Barton, a longtime member of the International Union of Mine, Mill, and Smelter Workers in Bessemer, Alabama, had joined the Communist Party in 1933 and had been arrested under an antisedition law. After being denied legal representation and a jury trial, Barton was fined and sentenced to hard labor; court officials refused to accept bail from the ILD. Gelders was abducted during his investigation of the case. Though publicly known, his attackers were never brought to trial. In an examination of the circumstances surrounding Barton's arrest and trial and Gelders's beating, the La Follette hearings exposed how industry and local government conspired to suppress labor organizing and political activity in the South.[46]

Gelders's discussion with Mason coincided with the preparation of the *Report on the Economic Conditions of the South*. Mason arranged for Gelders to meet with Eleanor Roosevelt to discuss his plan, and this was followed by a meeting between Gelders and the president at Hyde Park in June 1938, on the eve of the summer primary elections. Both Eleanor Roosevelt and the president endorsed Gelders's idea but advised that the scope of the conference be broadened to address the entire range of problems confronting the South, as put forward in the report. And the president specifically urged that the conference act on the issue of voting rights, beginning with an expansion of the campaign to abolish the poll tax.[47]

Immediately following his session with the president, Gelders

convened a small group in Birmingham to plan for a regional conference late in the fall. One of the first people Gelders contacted was H. C.
Nixon, chairman of the Southern Policy Committee (SPC), who played
a major role in organizing the conference. The Birmingham committee
also included Rob Hall, a founder of the NSL, who had returned to his
native Alabama in 1934 and was district organizer for the Communist
Party. Birmingham Congressman Luther Patrick, Judge Louise Charl-
ton, a member of the Alabama Democratic Committee, and William
Mitch, director of the Alabama CIO, also aided in organizing and local
arrangements. They coordinated their plans with the president's advisory committee on southern economic problems. Late in July, Gelders
and Judge Charleton met with Lucy Randolph Mason and Clark
Foreman in Atlanta, where Foreman was managing Lawrence Camp's
challenge to Senator Walter George in the Democratic primary. The conference aimed to provide southerners with a collective way to address
the *Report on the Economic Conditions of the South*.[48]

While conference planners built on the pioneering work of Howard
Odum's cadre of social scientists at Chapel Hill and the deliberations
of the SPC, they acknowledged the limitations of both approaches.
Lucy Mason expressed the sentiment best: "The South cannot be saved
by middle class liberals alone—they must make common cause with
labor, the dispossessed on the land and the Negro. . . . Some may find
it too shocking to have the other three so articulate about their needs.
But this is the basis for progress in democracy, economic justice and
social values in the South." Organizers drew from the networks that
had grown up around the New Deal, labor organizing efforts, and
local reform movements, and they succeeded in bringing together what
was arguably the most diverse meeting of southerners to occur up to
that time.[49]

Business executives, labor organizers, WPA workers, state and federal
government officials, members of Congress, sharecroppers, newspaper
editors, and college professors and students were among the twelve
hundred people who gathered at Birmingham Municipal Auditorium
over Thanksgiving weekend in 1938. Roughly 20 percent of the delegates were black, and they sat and mixed freely with the white participants. Arthur Raper remembered it as "one of the most exaggerated
expressions of change in the South . . . here was a revival, a bush-
shaking, something that just jumped up." For Virginia Durr, "[It was] a
wonderful sort of love feast because it was the first time that all of these
various elements from the South had gotten together. And we were not
segregated." In a more sober, but still hopeful assessment, black poet
Sterling Brown said that the conference was a sign that the South was
"on the move." He added, "The hind wheel may be off and the axle
dragging, but the old cart is hovering along."[50]

For three days the participants met in small groups to discuss sections of the NEC report; Eleanor Roosevelt, Supreme Court Justice Hugo Black, and University of North Carolina President Frank Graham addressed the plenary sessions. The conference adopted a number of proposals, which called for state and federal action to redress the economic imbalances that had stifled the development of the region's people and its resources. The conference endorsed federal antilynching legislation and equal salaries for black and white teachers. John P. Davis, Clark Foreman, and Mary McLeod Bethune were among those elected as officers of a permanent organization, further indicating a new departure for southern reform. In establishing itself as a permanent organization, the SCHW embarked on the challenging if vaguely defined task of creating and organizing a political movement capable of advancing its resolves. Whereas the matters of strategy and organization were left for future deliberation, the group was unexpectedly compelled to confront the issue of racial custom, something that white southern liberals instinctively avoided.[51]

Conference leaders had not intended to make an issue out of segregation; nonsegregated meetings had been held before in the municipal auditorium. But halfway through the second day the Birmingham police, led by Eugene "Bull" Connor, informed conference organizers that a municipal ordinance requiring segregation in the auditorium would be enforced. Under threats of arrest, and with limited options available, participants decided to comply with the ordinance so that the meeting might continue. Whites sat on one side of the auditorium, blacks on the other. Further attention was drawn to the matter when Eleanor Roosevelt, arriving late for the afternoon session, sat among the black participants. A policeman immediately informed her that she would have to move. Roosevelt did not move to the white side. She took her chair and put it on top of the line set down to divide the two sides. "That was a glorious moment," recalled Rob Hall. Later that evening, when questioned about the incident, Roosevelt avoided outright condemnation of legalized segregation. "I do not believe that is a question for me to answer," she said. "In the section of the country where I come from it is a procedure that is not followed. But I would not presume to tell the people of Alabama what they should do." Her explanation hardly dulled the symbolic import of Roosevelt's action. The *Afro-American* observed, "If the [white] people of the South do not grasp this gesture, we must. Sometimes actions speak louder than words."[52]

Bull Connor's intrusion placed the issue of segregation squarely before the new organization. After several hours of discussion and debate, conference organizers voted that the SCHW would never again hold a segregated meeting. Although this resolution hardly justified the claims of critics that the SCHW was a "racial equality" organization, the group's response marked an important departure from the customary caution of white southern liberals who shrank from any overt challenge to racial segregation. Several prominent politicians in attendance, including John Bankhead, Lister Hill, and Luther Patrick, avoided further association with the group. The episode, and its consequences, made it easier for the SCHW to move beyond traditional white southern liberalism and work with the movement that was developing around the NAACP's legal campaign to end voting restrictions and racial discrimination in the South.[53]

The end of 1938 found the New Deal in retreat on Capitol Hill, with southern conservative Democrats leading the charge. That same year, the Supreme Court, now dominated by Roosevelt appointees, ruled that Lloyd L. Gaines be admitted to the University of Missouri Law School, giving the NAACP its first major legal victory in the campaign for equal education. Pauli Murray, whose application to the University of North Carolina had been rejected solely on racial grounds, observed that *Gaines* was the "first major breach in the solid wall of segregated education since Plessy." It was "the beginning of the end."[54] Black southerners, in increasing numbers, continued to petition state Democratic parties for admission to the primary elections; the NAACP would soon prepare to take another challenge to the Supreme Court in its twenty-year legal battle against the all-white primary. In 1939, the SCHW launched a movement to abolish the poll tax. Its lobbying campaign for federal anti-poll-tax legislation made the right to vote a national issue.

Although the legislative phase of the New Deal may have ended by 1938, its political consequences for the South, for African Americans, and for the Democratic Party were just beginning to be realized. Palmer Weber and Charles Houston were among those who maintained that the fate of New Deal reform would depend largely on what happened in the South. "The economic wage slavery and social suppression cursing the South today stood between the progressive forces of the New Deal and the recovery and reform they sought," observed Houston. Weber concurred. Perhaps, he wrote hopefully in November 1938, "as the tides of liberalism run deeper, the value of racial cooperation will come to be understood–even in the far South."[55]

NOTES

1 Palmer Weber, "The Negro Vote in the South," *Virginia Spectator*, Nov. 1938, 6. [The *Report on Economic Conditions in the South* was issued by the National Economic Council of the Roosevelt Administration in July 1938.]

2 Unless otherwise noted, sources for the discussion of Palmer Weber's early life and later reflections include Weber interviews with author, 9 September 1978, 17 November 1980, 24 February 1984.

3 Virginius Dabney, *Mr. Jefferson's University: A History* (Charlottesville, Va., 1950), 152.

4 Palmer Weber, "The Five Together: Locke, Rousseau, Smith, Jefferson, Paine," unpub. manuscript in author's possession.

5 Ibid., 71–93.

6 Ibid.; Rob Hall interview with author; Ellen W. Schrecker, *No Ivory Tower: McCarthyism and the Universities* (New York, 1986), 28, 65.

7 Robert Cohen, "Revolt of the Depression Generation: America's First Mass Student Protest Movement," (Ph.D. diss., University of California, Berkeley, 1987), 93–122.

8 *College Topics*, 18, 22 May 1934, 26 November 1935; Robert Cohen, "Revolt of the Depression Generation," 385.

9 *College Topics*, 1 May 1934; Weber interview with author, 24 February 1984.

10 *College Topics*, 28 October 1938.

11 Ibid., 27 November 1937.

12 Cohen, "Revolt of the Depression Generation," 494–98; Johnetta Richards, "The Southern Negro Youth Congress: A History" (Ph.D. diss., University of Cincinnati, 1987), 17; Sarah Alice Mayfield, "Southern White Students and Race Relations" (address before the 24th Annual Conference of the NAACP, 30 June 1933), NAACP, microfilm, reel 9; George Streator, "Negro College Radicals," *Crisis* 41 (1934), 47; Preston Valien, "I Attended the NSL Conference," *Crisis* 41 (1934), 67–8; Monroe Sweetland, "Negro Students Superior," *Crisis* 41 (1934), 68; Langston Hughes, "Cowards from College," *Crisis* 41 (1934), 226–28.

13 James Jackson, panel presentation on the Southern Negro Youth Congress, Harvard University, 12 July 1995.

14 *College Topics*, 21 September, 10 October, 22 October, 24 October 1935. . . . Weber interview with author, 9 September 1978.

15 White interview with author; Randolph White, "F. Palmer Weber: A Giant," *Charlottesville Albemarle Tribune*, 28 August 1986.

16 Weber, "The Negro Vote in the South," 25.

17 Charles Houston to Walter White, 1 November 1934, NAACP, microfilm, reel 16. (Unless otherwise noted, references to Houston's correspondence and speeches are from NAACP, microfilm, reel 16.)

18 Genna Rae McNeil, *Groundwork: Charles Hamilton and the Struggle for Civil Rights* (Philadelphia, 1983), 32.

19 Ibid., 42; Charles Houston, "An Approach to Better Race Relations" (address to 13th national YWCA Convention, 5 November 1934). Records file collection, YWCA of USA, New York, microfilm, reel 32.

20 McNeil, *Groundwork*, 52, 71, 84–85.

21 Houston, "Approach to Better Race Relations."

22 "Address by Charles H. Houston before the Twenty-fourth Annual Conference of the [NAACP], 2 July 1933," 6, NAACP, microfilm, reel 9; McNeil, *Groundwork*, 88–101. George Crawford was found guilty by an all-white jury and sentenced to life in prison.

23 August Meier and Elliot Rudwick, "The Rise of the Black Secretariat in the NAACP, 1909–1935," in Meier and Rudwick, ed., *Along the Color Line: Explorations in the Black Experience*, (Urbana, Ill., 1986), 94–127; Meier and Rudwick, "Attorneys Black and White: A Case Study of Race Relations within the NAACP," ibid., 128–73; "Memo from Mr. White . . . 11 November 1933," NAACP, microfilm, reel 16; Charles Houston to Walter White, 21 May 1935.

24 Dan T. Carter, *Scottsboro: A Tragedy of the American South* (Baton Rouge, 1969), chs. 1–2.
25 Weaver interview with author, 16 April 1992; Houston, "Approach to Better Race Relations."
26 Charles Houston to Executive Staff, "Memorandum re: Further Steps in Anti-Lynching Campaign, 2 March 1938," and Charles H. Houston, speech delivered to ILD National Conference, Washington, D.C., 8 July 1939; Robert L. Zangrando, *The NAACP Crusade against Lynching, 1909–1950* (Philadelphia, 1980) 140.
27 McNeil, *Groundwork*, 121.
28 Houston, "An Approach to Better Race Relations."
29 Ibid.; "Negro Should Unite with 'Poor Whites'-Houston," press release, NAACP Annual Convention, July 1934, NAACP, microfilm, reel 9; Roy Wilkins, "NAACP Meets in Oklahoma," *Crisis* 41 (1934): 229.
30 Charles Houston to Walter White, 2 November 1934, 4 November 1934, and Charles H. Houston to Edward P. Lovett, 14 November, 10 December 1934.
31 Houston to Walter White, 5 November 1934.
32 Houston to Roy Wilkins, 22 May 1935.
33 Ibid.
34 Carter interview with author; Charles Houston, "A Challenge to Negro College Youth," *Crisis* 45 (1938), 14–15; Meier and Rudwick, "Attorneys Black and White," 153; Houston to Walter White, 21 May 1935.
35 Weaver interview with author, 16 April 1992; McNeil, *Groundwork*, 135; Franklin interview with author.
36 Houston, "Approach to Better Race Relations"; Ralph Bunche, *The Political Status of the Negro in the Age of FDR*, ed. by Dewey W. Grantham (Chicago, 1973), 72, 87–88, chs. 12–15; Linda Dempsey Cochran, "Arthur Davis Shores: Advocate for Freedom" (M.A. Thesis, Georgia Southern College, 1977), 26–27; Shores interview with author.
37 Bunche, *Political Status of the Negro*, 429.
38 Palmer Weber, *College Topics*, 11 November 1936, 29 January 1937; Steven Fraser, *Labor Will Rule: Sidney Hillman and the Rise of American Labor* (New York, 1991), 356–72; Nancy J. Weiss, *Farewell to the Party of Lincoln: Black Politics in the Age of FDR* (Princeton, N.J., 1983), 203.
39 Weiss, *Farewell to the Party of Lincoln*, 189–208; Frank R. Kent, "The Great Game of Politics," *Baltimore Sun*, 12 November 1936, 1.
40 Smith quoted by Weiss, *Farewell to the Party of Lincoln*, 186.
41 Fraser, *Labor Will Rule*, 378–88; Richards, "Southern Negro Youth Congress," 42–3; John M. Glenn, *Highlander: No Ordinary School, 1932–1962* (Lexington, Ky., 1988), 44–46; Robin D. G. Kelley, *Hammer and Hoe: Alabama Communists during the Great Depression* (Chapel Hill, 1990), 142–51.
42 Durr interview with author, 25 June 1992.
43 John Salmond, *Miss Lucy of the CIO: The Life and Times of Lucy Randolph Mason, 1882–1959* (Athens, Ga., 1988), 1–49.
44 Ibid., 50–74.
45 Ibid., 79; Lucy Randolph Mason to Eleanor Roosevelt [ER], 1 February 1938, ER Papers, Hyde Park, N.Y.; Fraser, *Labor Will Rule*, 397–99.
46 Thomas Krueger, *And Promises to Keep: The Southern Conference for Human Welfare, 1938–1948* (Nashville, 1967), 3–6, 16; Jerold S. Auerbach, *Labor and Liberty: The La Follette Committee and the New Deal* (Indianapolis, 1966), 94–97. . . .
47 Krueger, *And Promises to Keep*, 16; Rob Hall interview with author; Joseph

Gelders telegram to Franklin Roosevelt, 10 July 1940, FDR Papers, Hyde Park, N.Y., PPF 5664; H. C. Nixon to Brooks Hays, 27 July 1938, National Policy Committee Papers, Library of Congress, [NPC], box 3.

48 H. C. Nixon to Brooks Hays, 27 July 1938, NPC Papers, box 3; Lucy Randolph Mason to ER, 28 July 1938, ER Papers; Rob Hall interview with author.

49 H. C. Nixon to Brooks Hays, 27 July 1938; H. C. Nixon to Francis P. Miller, 16 September 1938; H. C. Nixon to Francis P. Miller, 19 October 1938; all in NPC Papers, box 3. Sarah Newman Shouse, *Hillbilly Realist: Herman Clarence Nixon of Possum Trot* (University, Al., 1986), 110.

50 Raper interview with author; Durr and Dombrowski interview with author; *New South*, January 1939, 6–7.

51 *New South*, January 1939, 6–7.

52 Rob Hall interview with author; Roosevelt, *This I Remember*, 173–74; *Richmond Times Dispatch*, 23 November 1938; Pauli Murray, *Song In a Weary Throat* (New York, 1987), 113.

53 George Tindall, *The Emergence of the New South, 1913–1945* (Baton Rouge, 1967), 637; Krueger, *And Promises to Keep*, 38–39.

54 Murray, *Song In a Weary Throat*, 115.

55 Charles Houston, Speech to ILD Conference, 8 July 1939; Weber, "The Negro Vote in the South," 6.

10

"YOU MUST REMEMBER THIS"

Autobiography as social critique

Jacquelyn Dowd Hall

The essays by Jack E. Davis and W. Fitzhugh Brundage in this volume show how memory in the guise of "history"—whether the product of scholarly research or of popular and commercial impulses—could serve to undergird the New South's racial order. Jacquelyn Dowd Hall's essay on the life of Katherine Du Pre Lumpkin, the daughter of a Confederate veteran, shows that memory and history could also serve as a liberating force.

Lumpkin's childhood was suffused with traditional images and stories of the Lost Cause, but, as an adult, Lumpkin began to carefully reexamine the "ghosts" from her own past. By connecting her remembered past to new research on southern history, she was able to uncover a "countermemory" of the southern past that, in turn, informed and fueled her own reformist impulses. Thus Lumpkin, no less than conservative white supremacists, made use of history "as a technique of power and the search for a past that provides a sense of agency and a lever for critique."

Hall also argues that Lumpkin's path of self-discovery can serve as an example to historians, who might well "consider the ways in which their own autobiographies have helped to shape their understandings of the past, and how these considerations may also help to reshape the way historians write history." She calls on historians to leaven their scholarship with "poetics"— the "realm of memory, creativity, and imagination." Historians, she writes, should not assume an "Olympian stance" toward their subjects, but acknowledge that "history is entangled with memory and that implicates us in the history we write."

* * *

Critics often lament a decline in historical literacy and worry about how little Americans know about the past. And yet, in the United States and throughout the world, historical memory has become both a cultural obsession and a powerful political weapon. The people of

239

South Africa, to take just one example, have staked their hopes for reconciliation on the conviction that memories of atrocities must not be erased; the victims' testimony must be heard and acknowledged, and the perpetrators must admit what they have done. At the same time, in Rwanda, in the former Yugoslavia, in Ireland, and elsewhere around the globe, narratives of supposedly ancient grievances and hostilities can justify brutality, knitting people together in "imagined communities" that can exclude and kill, with no sense of guilt.[1]

Such narratives, like all memories, depend upon forgetting. To function at all, we must forget most of the scenes and sensations that constitute the vast rush of "experience" or overlay them with what Sigmund Freud called "screen memories," memories that protect us from fear, anxiety, and pain. Turning memories into stories—whether humble life stories or pretentious master narratives—is also a potent form of forgetting. For every narrative depends on the suppression and repression of contrary, disruptive memories—other people's memories of the same events, as well as the unacceptable ghosts of our own pasts.[2]

We are what we remember, and as memories are reconfigured, identities are redefined. Indeed, we are never outside memory, for we cannot experience the present except in the light of the past ("all beginnings," writes Paul Connerton, "contain an element of recollection"), and remembering, in turn, is an action in the present. The pressure of events puts a chain of associations in motion; these ongoing reconstructions help secure the identities that enable us to navigate, legitimate, or resist the present order of things. And yet when we speak and write *as historians*, we tend to position ourselves above and beyond memory, which we devalue as self-serving and inexact.[3]

Memory, according to Pierre Nora, is organic and continuous, "affective and magical." It "only accommodates those facts that suit it; it nourishes recollections that may be out of focus or telescopic, global or detached, particular or symbolic. . . . [It] takes root in the concrete, in spaces, gestures, images, and objects." History, in contrast, is an "intellectual and secular production." It "calls for analysis and criticism." It "belongs to everyone and to no one, whence its claim to universal authority." Suspicious of "myth" and "legend" as well as of the vagaries of personal memory, historians take it upon themselves to piece together a plausible narrative from scattered, surviving shards. In that sense, as Nora argues, historians can represent a past that seems disconnected from living memory. And yet, for better and for worse, history can also serve as a stay against forgetfulness, perpetuating memories that secure a murderous sense of group identity or that totalitarian regimes try murderously to stamp out. Even when memory and history clash, they are still intertwined.[4]

Indeed, history commonly receives its guiding impetus from memory. Try as we may to break free from the overarching narratives of our time, they persist in the underlying structures of the stories we tell. To challenge those narratives, we often turn to countermemories—memories that resist the biases, exclusions, and generalizations embedded in official versions of the past. History is animated by memory in other, more ineffable ways as well. We bring to our writing the unfinished business of our own lives and times; moreover, the experience of traveling so long in the country of research *becomes* our past, for our stories grow from a process of remembering and forgetting our encounters with the relics, fragments, whispers of an always already-recollected time. In all these ways, we live both the history we have learned through reading and research and the history we have experienced and inherited, passed down through the groups with which we identify, sedimented in the body, and created through talk.[5]

This essay springs from my own engagement with the interplay between history and memory in the American South. It is about the politics of history—by which I mean both the use of history as a technique of power and the search for a past that provides a sense of agency and a lever for critique. It is also about the importance of leavening politics with poetics. Politics demand that we choose a side, take a stand. Poetics demand that we hold seemingly contradictory beliefs at the same time, that we embrace multiple levels of meaning, that we think metaphorically (glimpsing "connections on the basis of a deep logic that underlies any use of words"), that we acknowledge the ways in which beauty and tragedy, good and evil are entwined. The politics of history usually entail an Olympian stance toward our subjects, who cannot talk back, who are dead and gone. Poetics require a different stance, one that acknowledges how history is entangled with memory and that implicates us in the history we write.[6]

The book from which this essay is drawn revolves around politics and poetics, memory and history in the lives of three remarkable sisters: Katharine Du Pre Lumpkin (1897–1988), author of *The Making of a Southerner* (1946), a classic coming-of-age autobiography; Grace Lumpkin (1891–1980), a proletarian novelist, best known for *To Make My Bread* (1932), a novel about the famous Gastonia, North Carolina, strike of 1929; and Elizabeth Lumpkin Glenn (1881–1963), the eldest, a celebrated orator for the Lost Cause at the dawn of the twentieth century. Here I will tell two interwoven stories. First, the story of the South's Lost Cause, the rerembering of the past that the Lumpkin sisters absorbed. The Lost Cause, I will argue, relied on two kinds of repression—the burying of traumatic or unacceptable experiences in the unconscious and the silencing of dissident voices and competing social memories. But it also carried with it possibilities for revision, footholds for contestation, contingency, and change.[7]

My second story turns on Katharine Lumpkin's rewriting of southern history in the 1940s, a rewriting that lay at the heart of her autobiographical project. . . . The main characters are William Lumpkin, the father who made of the Lost Cause not just a story told but a cult enacted, Elizabeth, the true believer, and Katharine, the scholar, the heuristic value of whose work I want to explore. I end with a meditation on history and memory, remembering and forgetting, politics and poetics in historical writing today.

My structure is recursive; like memory, it does not move in a straight line. For example, I rehearse the story of the Lost Cause from a succession of points of view: mine, as a historian of the South; Katharine's, as an autobiographer; and then mine again, as I reflect on the possibilities that Katharine's project suggests. And I am concerned less with unraveling the complexities of biography . . . than with exploring the phenomena that travel under the sign of "memory and history." First, personal memories (the chains of association that seem to come unbidden to the mind, rely on concrete images, and split and telescope time); second, social memories (the shared, informal, contested stories that simultaneously describe and act on our social world); third, history (the accounts we reconstruct from the documentary traces of an absent past); and, finally, political imagination (the hope for a different future that inspires and is inspired by the study of the past).[8]

Katharine Du Pre Lumpkin was the seventh and youngest child in a family that produced some of Georgia's most prominent planters, lawyers, and politicians. Her father, William Wallace Lumpkin (1849–1910), came from a relatively modest branch of the Lumpkin clan. But the distinction hardly mattered. For long after the children of slave owners had abandoned the plantations and thrown in their lot with the New South's railroads, towns, and textile mills, lineage mattered more so than we can easily imagine, so much so that when William Lumpkin died, his obituary ended with a litany of famous "relatives and predecessors" while omitting the names of his children entirely. So much so that even Katharine would always fear bringing "disgrace on the family name."[9]

The South seceded from the Union when William Lumpkin was twelve years old. A few months after his fifteenth birthday, with Gen. William Tecumseh Sherman poised to take Atlanta, he joined the army, spending the final months of the war as a private in Fighting Joe Wheeler's ragtag cavalry, harassing Sherman's troops as they abandoned their supply line north and cut a gash of destruction from Atlanta to the sea. William's parents had named him William *Pittman*

Lumpkin. By the time he returned from war, he was calling himself William *Wallace* Lumpkin after the thirteenth-century Scottish patriot, known to late-twentieth-century movie goers as "Braveheart," who died fighting against English rule. Straggling homeward after the surrender at Appomattox, he cast himself as a romantic hero and stored up tales of the "mad carnival of destruction" perpetrated by Sherman's troops. Studying history, Katharine would come to see Sherman's march as her father never could—as a military maneuver that quickly ended a terrible, costly conflict, the bloodiest conflagration the country had ever known. But as a child she had only her father's stories, which could still fill him with cold fury and, beneath that, a smoldering memory of impotence and disgrace.[10]

Slavery, as William Lumpkin remembered it, was a domestic idyll, peopled by African Americans who willingly catered to his needs and whims, images from a child's dream of unstinting availability and unconditional love. We are all fugitives from childhood, "never completely escaped," and the desires and anxieties of his generation were marked forever by the intimate relations between slaveholder and slave. They were also marked by war and emancipation, which shattered William's childhood Eden. Reconstruction, he believed, dealt it a final blow.[11]

When her father spoke of the "dark days of Reconstruction," Katharine remembered,

> it was as though his words were wrung from him, for he obviously hated the memories. Yet it seems that he felt he must tell the story, lest we have no concrete images such as haunted him. "Lest we forget," he would say to us. . . . We were told how our world . . . was ruled by . . . rank outsiders who had come in, so it was said, to feast like harpies upon a prostrate country, to agitate and use for personal aggrandizement the hapless black man, to dare to rule in place of the South's own foremost leaders. And to be ruled by Negroes! Ruled by black men! . . . The slave ruling over the master!

William himself "was spat upon, and his Mother insulted to his face." Summoned to membership in the Ku Klux Klan, he helped smash Reconstruction and restore white Democratic rule.[12]

Still, as Katharine put it, "the South might be 'restored,' but not the old life for Father." He married well, choosing Annette Caroline Morris (1856–1925), a beautiful, accomplished girl from a middle Georgia planter family like his own. But by the time Katharine was born, William had been reduced to working for the railroad, an obscure lieutenant in the army of salesmen, dispatchers, and ticket sellers that sped the South's new transportation system along its ever-multiplying tracks. Transferred to Columbia, South Carolina, at the turn of the century, the Lumpkins found themselves expelled from the magic circle where their name carried weight. In exile, William's identity came to rest on two props: first on his family, where he was, Katharine said, "head and dominant figure, leader, exemplar, final authority," and then on the movement to commemorate the South's Lost Cause. In practice, the two were inseparable. William's role in the movement gave him stature in his children's eyes; their participation, in turn, demonstrated his success as a father. The pageantry of the Lost Cause and the social relations of the family reinforced one another. Each cultivated race, class, and regional loyalties where they could grow most virulently: in the hearts of vulnerable and idealistic children.[13]

The celebration of the Lost Cause began almost as soon as the Confederacy surrendered, led by the Ladies Memorial Associations that took up the work of public mourning in a society blighted by fratricidal war. The movement reached its apogee, however, not in the postwar backwash of bitterness, uncertainty, and raw, dazed, inconsolable grief, but during Katharine's turn-of-the-century childhood, when it was shaped by quite different needs and circumstances. Inchoate and often contradictory at first, the narrative of the Lost Cause now gained a new cogency and persuasiveness.[14]

Despite the demise of Reconstruction, African Americans across the South had continued to vote and even to hold political office. At the same time, the capitalist reorganization of agriculture fanned the resentments of poor farmers and up-country whites, sparking an interracial Populist movement, the most powerful threat to white solidarity and elite rule that the South—and, arguably, the country—had ever seen. "Here," Katharine wrote, "were white Southerners pitted not against outsiders, but battling among themselves. . . . Conservative men would not, if they could prevent it, let overtake them this threat to the white South's solid front."[15]

It was, many feared (or pretended to fear), "Reconstruction all over again." And across the South, Democratic politicians, many of whom were too young to have fought in the Civil War, blamed their ineffectual, nostalgic fathers—aging soldiers such as William Lumpkin—for what had come to pass. Rallying their forces against "Negro domination," they made white women the centerpiece of violent disfranchisement campaigns. Manufacturing rape scares, they whipped up support by charging that black men's access to politics, however limited, had aroused their desire for that other perquisite of white manhood: access to white women. Campaign parades featured floats bearing girls dressed in white with banners crying, "Protect Us," fluttering above their heads. African American men, politicians everywhere thundered, "must never be strong enough to threaten white women"; and white women, they implied through rhetoric and action, "must never be strong enough to protect themselves." Through propaganda, terror, and manipulation, New South leaders succeeded in doing what the men of William Lumpkin's generation had never quite had the stomach or the freedom from national scrutiny to do. They drove blacks out of politics altogether, locked a system of legal segregation into place, and destroyed even the memory and thus the possibility of an interracial opposition.[16]

Emerging victorious from the white supremacy campaigns, white leaders turned with fresh self-confidence, energy, and conviction to commemorating the region's past. Disfranchisement, segregation, and the battle for memory went hand in hand. Spearheaded by voluntary associations such as the United Confederate Veterans (UCV) and the United Daughters of the Confederacy (UDC), supported by small-town elites, buttressed by the South's first generation of professional historians, and amplified by new technologies of mass communication and entertainment, this effort created a landscape of memory that still surrounds us today. Dotted with what Nora has famously called *lieux de mémoire*—sites for anchoring memories even as they threatened to slip away—that terrain sentimentalized slavery; reconfigured the Civil War as a noble lost cause fought, not to preserve slavery, but to uphold the constitutional principle of states' rights; lauded the courage and sacrifice of soldiers on both sides of the battle; and portrayed Reconstruction as a tragedy that justified disfranchisement and segregation.[17]

It goes without saying that neither the trauma of slavery for African Americans nor their heroic, heartbreaking freedom struggle found a place in that story. But the Lost Cause narrative also suppressed the memories of many white southerners. Memories of how, under slavery, power bred cruelty. Memories of the bloody, unbearable realities of war. Written out too were the competing memories and identities that set white southerners one against another, pitting the planters against the up-country, Unionists against Confederates, Populists and mill workers against the corporations, home-front women against war-besotted, broken men.[18]

Brought to life on the screen in *The Birth of a Nation*, the Lost Cause narrative made its way, with amazing speed, not just into southern public memory but also into American popular culture. Indeed, the Lost Cause offered "ironic evidence that the South marched in step with the rest of the country." For as migrants from eastern Europe transformed northern cities, industrialization sparked violent class conflict, and the United States emerged onto the world stage as a leading imperial power, embattled native aristocrats everywhere commissioned sculptures of American heroes and revived colonial and classical architectural themes, projecting an image of a unified Anglo-Saxon social order onto the face of an increasingly polyglot nation.[19]

In the South, white women stood at the center of this battle for public memory, just as they had served as centerpieces of the white supremacy campaigns. And together those intertwined movements both widened women's horizons and "ensured that they did not venture too far." Turn-of-the-century rape scares hedged white women about with a lingering and debilitating fear: fear of the black rapist but also fear of what would happen if they broke the bargain of ladyhood, which linked the right to protection with the obligation to obey. The rhetoric of the Lost Cause, by contrast, pictured Confederate women as courageous, self-reliant, and strong. The UDC, the South's largest and most powerful women's organization, shared with its predecessors, the Ladies Memorial Associations, a commitment to bolstering vanquished and disheartened veterans and keeping the memory of the dead alive. But it was also committed to immortalizing the heroism of Confederate women, whose valor, its leaders believed, had been every bit as important as men's. It is telling, and typical, that when Katharine's mother published her reminiscences, she evoked a long procession of soldier's funerals but closed with a paean to the home front: "Truly, those were days not only to try men's souls, but to put to the test all that was greatest in the souls of the women!"[20]

UDC leaders were determined to assert women's cultural authority over virtually every representation of the region's past. This they did by lobbying for state archives and museums, national historic sites, and historic highways; compiling genealogies; interviewing former soldiers; writing history textbooks; and erecting monuments, which now moved triumphantly from cemeteries into town centers. More than half a century before women's history and public history emerged as fields of inquiry and action, the UDC, with other women's associations, strove to etch women's accomplishments into the historical record and to take history to the people, from the nursery and the fireside to the schoolhouse and the public square.[21]

Both Katharine's mother, Annette, and her older sister Elizabeth joined the UDC soon after its founding in 1894. Elizabeth quickly became a sensation on the veterans' reunion circuit. Speaking throughout South Carolina, Georgia, and Virginia, she "electrified Confederate assemblies as has no other human being," or so the newspapers claimed. She was, reported one observer, "transcendingly superior to any man or woman I have ever seen in any role on any stage." At the close of her speech, "strong old men" supposedly "threw their arms around each other and wept."[22] .... [A]t their South-wide reunion in Louisville, Kentucky, in 1904, the veterans named Elizabeth the "Daughter of the United Confederate Veteran."[23]

It is easy to see . . . Elizabeth Lumpkin as [a] spectacle and object of speculation, [a body] onto which men could project fantasies of eternal vigor, sometimes even a body that could be literally embraced. Elizabeth assured the elderly soldiers that, "old and gray and wrinkled" though they might be, they could still enjoy the love of a young girl, if only vicariously. "I love you," she proclaimed, "you grand old men, who guarded with your lives the virgin whiteness of our South." We daughters can only envy the "honor our lovely mothers gloried in . . . . *they* could love and marry Confederate soldiers! . . . . We can [only work for them] with tireless fingers . . . run with tireless feet." At a reunion in Georgia, a phalanx of guards was required to protect her "from the ardor of the enthusiastic and admiring veterans." When fifteen-year-old Grace began to take Elizabeth's place as a veterans' reunion speaker, her youth seemed to provoke the crowd even more. Told at a 1906 reunion that a woman was going to speak, the veterans sighed in resignation. A speech by a woman "in any assemblage where men are present," the newspaper admitted, "is generally regarded with a half sinister indulgence." "But there came a surprise. It was not a woman at all, but a . . . child-woman. She appeared under the influence of an occult power, and as she spoke the soldiers stood upon their feet and cheered wildly." Then they rushed the stage, grabbed her hands and kissed her—congratulating her father, who stood at her side.[24]

The kisses of the father and the father's friends: a textbook example of the seduction of the daughter in the Freudian family romance. These "child-women," like the "protect me" girls in the white supremacy floats, told their fathers' stories and followed their mothers' fate. Like the sexualized racism that made rape and rumors of rape the folk pornography of the Bible belt, the Lost Cause thus surrounded women's bodies with a strange brew of lust and etherealization. Walter Hines Page, an expatriate who became one of the New South's sharpest critics, saw other similarities as well. Just as the architects of the white supremacy campaigns had recruited women to help them split interracial alliances and drive black men out of public life, so the "wonderful military relics" of the Lost Cause duped women into helping them cling to their waning power.[25]

True enough. But, like the Lost Cause itself, the presence of women orators signaled, not just the comforting persistence of tradition, but the unsettling swirl of change. The newspapers portrayed Elizabeth's flights of oratory as spontaneous outpourings of emotion. In reality, they were the polished products of education and practice. She had studied oratory at Brenau College-Conservatory, a tiny women's college in north Georgia. From 1903 to 1905, at the height of her speaking career, she headed the department of reading and expression at Winthrop Normal and Industrial College, a school founded at the behest of South Carolina's militant farmers to train white women for teaching and other occupations.[26]

Like Athena, sprung from the head of Zeus, Elizabeth was a classic father's daughter; she memorialized the veterans and promoted the Lost Cause until the day she died. But she also threw herself into a wide range of women's civic associations, admonishing the "brainy, helpful women in the South" to uplift the "helpless, hopeless people in the Southern mills," promoting public libraries, and chairing the Red Cross during World War I ("helping humanity" at the expense of her health and her family, or so her mother feared). After her husband's early death, Elizabeth managed the hospital he had founded in Asheville, North Carolina, ran an inn, and became the first woman in a long line of planter-lawyers to win admittance to the bar.[27]

In the years before World War I, women like Elizabeth Lumpkin Glenn thus summoned the Confederate dead for a new purpose: to sway public opinion in favor of social reforms. By idealizing the Old South as a society based not on New South materialism but on *noblesse oblige*, they sought to promote a more expansive sense of community responsibility. By documenting a heritage of women's strength and achievement, they hoped to inspire contemporaries to action and to silence critics of women's expanding public role.[28]

UDC leaders, like organized southern women generally, saw education as the region's best hope for progress and reform. Dedicating themselves to the generational transmission of memory, they pursued a vigorous censorship campaign, using their influence with local school boards to ensure that "pernicious histories" were banned and "true histories" adopted. By the turn of the century, the historical commissions of the UCV and the UDC could announce what they saw as a "historical awakening": new state history textbooks sympathetic to the Confederacy, many of them written by women, had infiltrated the schoolrooms of Katharine's youth. . . .[29]

After World War I, the influence of the UDC waned, along with that of organized women generally. This was due in part to the rise of a younger generation of women, including Katharine, who began to search out new patterns in the tangled threads of memory and history and to weave new futures from what they found. But the erosion of women's authority was also a measure of their success in prodding southern state legislatures to assume responsibility for archives, museums, and other representations of the past.

Along with this expansion of state responsibility came the professionalization of historical writing. Indeed, by the 1920s, a cohort of professional male historians trained in a new archive-based, seminar-driven "scientific" history was revolutionizing the study of the American past. Among the most influential of the new professionals were two prolific southerners: William A. Dunning of Columbia University, whose disciples churned out monograph after monograph documenting the "criminal outrages of Reconstruction," and Dunning's brilliant student Ulrich B. Phillips, whose adumbration of the plantation as a paternalistic "school of civilization" made him the country's preeminent historian of slavery. These university-based historians, drawing a sharp line between themselves and the amateurs, purged the Lost Cause narrative of its rancor and exaggeration, its fierce attachments to place and kin. In so doing, they transformed it into a story that the whole (white) nation could accept. Women found themselves identified with imprecise, dilettantish, nostalgic "memory"; the new professional history belonged to men. The authority of history, in turn, relied on the prestige of science and the deployment of an impersonal voice, an innovation as critical to historical writing as the discovery of perspective was to painting. Organized women had taken the lead in creating the South's landscape of memory. But it was the new history, cleansed of its association with "scribbling women," that stamped the Lost Cause narrative with the authority of scientific truth.[30]

Two decades later, on the cusp of World War II, Katharine Du Pre Lumpkin turned to autobiography as social critique. *The Making of a Southerner* is about an escape from childhood. It could not have been written if Katharine had not sprung herself free from the past.[31] It is also marked by a "doubled subjectivity": The *I* of autobiography is both the narrator and the protagonist, the recollecting self and the recollected self, the teller and the told. Once Katharine was the book's protagonist, an impressionable, vulnerable girl who had, as she put it, "learned both behavior and belief at a time when those around us were peculiarly disturbed." Now, in the 1940s, as she writes, she has become the narrator, a woman who has completely altered her outlook, "rejecting as untenable on any ground whatsoever . . . the Southern system of white supremacy and all its works." Yet she takes pains to stress, not her uniqueness or the success of her flight, but her commonality with her readers. She is both an outsider and everywoman. Like us, she is steeped in memory, yet capable of freedom. Speaking in the first person, she seeks, not just to critique the past, but to perform her own movement from past to present. Her writing embodies a promise: Change can occur—has already occurred—from within.[32]

The Making of a Southerner pivots on a chapter entitled "A Child Inherits a Lost Cause." The book begins by retelling Katharine's father's, and even her grandfather's, stories: The action takes place before she is born. When her protagonist does appear, almost halfway through the book, Katharine presents her as *tabula rasa*. Although "saturated with words and phrases," she remains a virtually disembodied watching, listening child. That child gains a voice and a body when she is baptized in the sentiments of the Lost Cause at a veterans' reunion in 1903.[33]

Katharine tracks that event, and her family's starring role in it, not just through the byways of memory but also in the material traces of the past, discovering as she does so tensions, contradictions, and hypocrisies that she could never have perceived at the time. (She can see in the newspapers, for example, how veterans' reunions became "good business" as power shifted from old soldiers like her father to their chamber of commerce sons.) But her goal is not to use the historian's privileged view of the past to secure her own and her readers' sense of progress and superiority. What she wants is harder and less conventional: She goes "back to the contemporary documents," seeking to "relearn from the sources," both to provoke and to resituate memory by combining the adult's ironic backward glance with the remembered sensations of how that long-ago pageant registered in the mind and body of a wondering, six-year-old child.[34]

Her account is a bricolage into which she builds her own memories, family stories, and contemporary newspaper accounts. The crowd, she writes, surges forward, cheering the parade and punctuating the speeches with "clapping, stamping, . . . singing." Men doff their hats; women flutter their handkerchiefs; schoolchildren spread the streets with a carpet of flowers. Katharine too sings and claps and stamps her feet until her spine "could not stand any more tingles." Then comes the crescendo, the moment, as Katharine put it, that "a child would never forget": The parade ends and twenty-one-year-old Elizabeth steps forward to address the gathering on opening night. Then, as if that were not enough, William Lumpkin stars in the tableau that crowns the final day. "Lights were extinguished. We waited while the curtain descended and rose again. Gleaming through the darkness was a bright camp fire with a kettle hanging from a tripod. Around the fire one could see men in bedraggled uniforms. One soldier lounged up to the fire—'Quaint reminder of long ago as he stood in the half light, pipe in mouth, pants tucked into his socks, coatless and collarless,' He began to tell a tale of war . . . 'lights gradually brightened . . . the speaker was recognized . . . Col. W. W. Lumpkin, a soldier of the Confederacy again.' " (William, of course, was only a private. Like many a southern gentleman, he acquired the sobriquet of "colonel" in the after echo of war.)[35]

"Their mother teaches them their prayers; I teach them to love the Lost Cause," William always said. Indeed, in the Lumpkin household the Lost Cause became a mode of education and an emblem of intimacy and family love. Confederate reunions offered the most impressive stage for the Lumpkins' pedagogical efforts. But they were not sufficient. William and Annette also seized the most quotidian moments of family life to forward their children's moral and political education.[36]

"To be sure," Katharine wrote, "much was handed on to us incidentally," conveyed in the rituals, ceremonies, and pleasures of family life, sifting into consciousness "as softly . . . as snow floats down on a still winter night . . . but it was not my father's way to leave our lessons to chance. Nor yet indeed my mother's." Annette Lumpkin had been educated in the classics by a beloved Irish tutor and had taught school briefly after the Civil War. Both parents solicited their children toward reading and writing. In the Lumpkin household, books signaled affection; they were also a gateway to the world. Each afternoon, under their mother's tutelage, the children spent an hour reading aloud: the usual suspects—the novels of Thomas Nelson Page, the poetry of Alfred, Lord Tennyson, and the life of Robert E. Lee, but also the works of Charles Dickens and all the great nineteenth-century realists, with their heroes caught up in history's narrative sweep.[37]

Every week ended with a family ritual called the "Saturday Night Debating Club." . . . . "And what a game! . . . And how the plaster walls of our parlor rang with tales of the South's sufferings, exhortations to uphold her honor, recitals of her humanitarian slave regime, denunciation of those who dared to doubt the black man's inferiority, and, ever and always, persuasive logic for her position of 'States Rights.' " At school, Katharine used that training to triumph in lopsided debates on the question "Are Negroes Equal to White People?" More than thirty years later, she could remember her own fervor and the burst of applause when she finished her peroration: "and the Bible says that they shall be hewers of wood and drawers of water forever!" She also remembered how she and her friends banded together in a children's Ku Klux Klan. With costumes made from worn-out sheets, cut to pattern by their mothers, they met in secrecy to plan "punitive expeditions against mythical recalcitrant Negroes." Transmitting memory through movement, ritual, and play, sedimenting in their bodies the gestures of racial dominance, they performed the ideologies that adults' narratives conveyed. "It was," Katharine remembered, "truly a serious game, and in a sense we were serious children bent on our ideals."[38]

As soon as Katharine was old enough to contribute to the project of commemoration directly, her father took her by trolley to recite at a veterans' camp on the outskirts of town. But instead of the glamour she expected, she found a sad collection of lost and bewildered men. Unlike Elizabeth, who basked in her moment on the stage, Katharine gave only a perfunctory performance. "After the first time I went as a duty," she remembered, "but it held no lure for me." The grateful veterans gave her a portrait of herself, an enlarged photograph tinted and set in an ornate gilt frame. She, however, recoiled at the sight of her garish double. That eerily touched-up image was not who she wanted to be. Even her parents were embarrassed, and they never hung the picture on the wall.[39]

The self that Katharine's mother mirrored back to her was a different story. Annette's learning was a "proud family possession, more particularly among her daughters. "Perhaps," Katharine reflected, "we took peculiar pleasure in it, feeling our own prestige advanced, who were but females in a world of male superiority." All three loved to tell the story of how Annette's tutor encouraged her to read the New Testament in Greek when she was eight years old and then, when she was ten, put her to work on John Locke's *Essay Concerning Human Understanding*. And all three remembered Annette as the one, in Grace's words, who "made me wish to write."[40]

"The situation," Katharine said, "was anomalous." Certainly, William and Annette believed in hierarchy, deference, and difference, in men's authority and women's "secondary and supplementary" role. Women were to "sit silent when men were speaking; not to pit our opinions against the more knowing males." Women were "creature[s] of intuition" who needed "the firm, solid frame of a male protector and guide." Yet even as they absorbed such precepts, the Lumpkin sisters were learning contrary lessons—from their mother especially but also, however inadvertently, from their father. Chief among them was the belief that "those who have brains are meant to use them," girls and boys alike.[41]

The Lost Cause, mixed as it was with the pleasures of reading and the provocations of debate, endowed Katharine with a sense of mission: the preservation of the past in the present, the burden of southern history, in all its *gravitas* and entangling self-deceptions. To her, growing up in the wake of Populism and the white supremacy campaigns, there was no doubt that the Lost Cause, whatever else it might mean, symbolized the struggle to reconstitute white supremacy on new grounds, to reinstate, under new conditions, the proper "relation of superior white to inferior Negro. . . . No lesson of our history was taught us earlier, and none with greater urgency than the either–or terms in which this was couched: 'Either white supremacy or black domination.' " Soldiers might perish, slavery might end, mansions might crumble, but as long as whites retained their dominance over blacks, Katharine's whole world taught her, the South's cause "had not been lost."[42]

Those lessons might have forestalled curiosity, trapping Katharine, as they trapped her parents, in the coils of a racism secured by an iconic, nostalgic understanding of the past. Instead, she acquired a love of history from which a devotion to critical inquiry could grow. What saved her, she believed, was not her own will, intelligence, and pluck, but the contradictions and contingencies to which she was exposed. "Here was a South," she reflected, "that had made us what we were in my childhood; to all appearances, it was a highly fixed, stable environment, frozen in its ways. But this same South could and did refashion some of its children. Some of us, although molded in the image of a bygone day . . . yet found the South itself so dynamic, so replete with clashing incongruities, that these could start us down the road toward change." For Katharine, those "incongruities" began in childhood, in the anomalies of her upbringing in a household where girls were expected both to excel and to defer; in the experience of exile, which gave her an outsider's ability to see things that she otherwise might not have seen; in the turn-of-the-century anxieties that the Lost Cause myth could not erase; in her position as the youngest child, the one who was different, who looked on from the sidelines, thrilled by the spectacle of the Lost Cause but not quite taken in.[43]

Looking back on her childhood from the vantage point of the 1940s, Katharine stressed two moments of rupture on which that child's refashioning turned. The first was, as she put it, "traumatic for me": an innocent sun-dappled morning, the sound of screams, a glimpse of her father beating the family's black cook. In her writings, biographical as well as autobiographical, racial violence lay at the heart of southern families. She opened her 1974 biography of the feminist-abolitionist Angelina Grimké with Grimké's memories of the cries of slaves, the sight of a boy her own age so crippled from a whipping that he could barely walk, and the wild rages of her beloved brother, so extreme that she feared he would beat a slave to death. These scenes from Angelina's childhood provided a source of "disturbing knowledge" upon which she, like her biographer, would later act. When I met Katharine in the 1970s (just as her study of Grimké was going to press), the memory of violence in her own family, refracted now through her long engagement with Angelina Grimké, had, if anything, gained in psychic charge. She spoke of the beating in a whisper, explicitly comparing herself to Grimké, who had also cringed at the sight of "someone helpless, in the throes of those who rule." For both women, remembering was a conscious political act.[44]

The second point of rupture, which supplemented Katharine's consciousness of racism with a perception of grinding class inequity, was what she called "A Sojourn in the Sand Hills": the family's move to a hardscrabble farm, where she found herself for the first time in intimate contact with black and white rural poor. By the time she left for college in 1912, Katharine claimed, "I was by no means entirely at home with my old heritage. Enough had gone on in the time-and-place limits of my short lifetime to disturb this seeming rapport. It could have come to nothing, of course—a passing flurry of doubts, and then forgetfulness. Perhaps it would have come to very little if I had chanced to be a student in less dynamic years."[45]

Following Elizabeth to Brenau College, Katharine encountered the action-oriented, optimistic message of the Social Gospel as it was spread through the region by the traveling secretaries of the Young Women's Christian Association (YWCA). It was these "far-sighted professional women," Katharine remembered, who "propelled . . . me . . . into this whole fascinating outside world." Hungry to "unravel the mysteries of why men behaved as they did and perhaps what could make them behave differently," she made her way to New York in the wake of World War I, tracing a path well worn by aspiring southern women at the time. . . .

Hired as a YWCA student secretary, [Katherine] plunged into the post-World War I peace movement, with its increasingly radical linkages to social reform. At the same time, she helped lead the YWCA's pioneering effort to build an interracial student movement in the Jim Crow South. Traveling with her black YWCA colleagues through a region that now seemed both familiar and strange, she saw the privileges and deprivations that had always surrounded her, hidden in plain sight. She also glimpsed the possibility of solidarities that transcended the claims of memory and kin. Eventually Katharine left the South again, first to complete a doctorate in sociology at the University of Wisconsin and then, on the cusp of the Great Depression, to take a one-year job at Mount Holyoke College. There she met a radical economist named Dorothy Wolff Douglas. By the time the year ended, they had moved to nearby Northampton, Massachusetts, and committed themselves to a partnership that would last for almost thirty years.[46]

From the Social Gospel, with its dream of creating the kingdom of God on earth, Katharine had taken a sense of agency, a conviction that she could resist her world's "mores" and intervene in its institutions. Sociology—the science of society—had extended that lesson: It gave her a secular angle of vision from which to question the common sense of her place and time. It also offered her the independence of a professional career devoted, not to the prescriptions of womanhood, but to the seemingly genderless life of the mind. There was, however, a price to pay. Fleeing her father's stories, seeking a career in teaching and research, she found herself still speaking in a patriarchal tongue. The objectivist, scientist assumptions of her discipline screened out moral urgency, muted political passion, and discouraged her regional and race concerns. Her early writings (focused on delinquency and the working-class family and generally couched in bloodless prose) bore the marks of exercises undertaken less from passion than from expediency: an outsider's attempt to get past the gatekeepers and win acceptance in a highly exclusive club.[47]

By the late 1930s, however, Katharine had begun to see herself, not as a potential insider in the academy, but as a permanent outsider—with all the penalties and advantages her welter of regional, sexual, and professional marginalities entailed. Entering the job market just as the stock market crashed, she could not find a teaching job; over the next two decades, professionalization and discrimination pushed women and radicals to the margins of the academy and stamped both sociology and history as masculine domains. In response, and with Dorothy's backing, she helped found alternative institutions: first a Council of Industrial Studies at Smith College, whose work foreshadowed the new labor history of the 1970s, then an independent Institute of Labor Studies that tracked labor relations during World War II. The depression, in the meanwhile, inspired a new left-wing political movement, which Katharine and Dorothy wholeheartedly embraced. That movement helped to realign the South in the American imagination—as "the Nation's No. 1 economic problem." Southernness, for Katharine, acquired a more positive meaning. It became a location from which to speak with authority about the burning issues of the day. Seizing that place and that moment, she began to write less cautiously and more politically. As the thirties gave way to the war years, she "came out" as a southerner, first in a book called *The South in Progress* and then in *Making of a Southerner*, the autobiography that became her most enduring work.[48]

The Making of a Southerner, although concerned with the long arm of the past, took as its point of departure "the fact of change." That point, to Katharine, was critical, for she believed that white supremacy was alive and well, not just in the South, but throughout the country and the world. She also believed that the South in the 1940s stood at a crossroads similar to the one it confronted in the 1890s. Her parents' generation and their successors had opted for reaction and repression, fastening upon the South a system of class and race domination that her generation now had a chance to undo. The New Deal, the rise of the Congress of Industrial Organizations, the impact of the war—all, it seemed, were propelling southerners into a freer postwar world. It was to those citizens in transition that *The Making of a Southerner* was addressed. By describing her upbringing as a white southern woman, Katharine sought to persuade them to identify with her. Then, by taking them step by step through her own transformation (as she remembered, researched, and represented it), she hoped "to deepen and clarify [the] process of aroused thinking" in which they were already engaged.[49]

She used the tools of history to read new meanings into childhood memories and to question the stories on which she was raised. She took her cues from a small group of radical scholars—including W. E. B. Du Bois and C. Vann Woodward—whose work on black history and Populism was beginning, by the 1940s, to challenge the authority of Phillips and Dunning, the towering figures who had helped give the Lost Cause narrative the ring of scientific truth. Through them, she discovered a new regional past—that of the "white millions whose forebears had never owned slaves" and the "Negro millions whose people had been held in slavery." But, unlike the revisionists, she placed a woman, herself, at the center of southern history. Categorically rejecting the racism and censorship that underlay the "historical awakening" of her youth, she nonetheless returned, albeit perhaps unconsciously, to the project initiated by her mother's and sister's generations: the project of etching women into the historical record and using that history to change the world. She chose as her heroes brave black politicians and white Populists (all men, to be sure), but also the black and white women reformers who, in the 1920s, had helped her see the world anew. Her history, like that of her predecessors, was driven by an urgent sense of mission, not by a quasi-scientific search for objective truth. And, like theirs, her narrative had a utopian dimension: It aimed, not just to describe the world as it was, but to bring into being "what has never been."[50]

The Making of a Southerner resonates with Katharine's foremothers' efforts in another way as well. It is—to borrow Studs Terkel's phrase—a "memory book" in which she layers her own memories into other traces of the past: her parents' stories, her older sisters' writings and memories, historical documents and newspaper accounts, the histories and sociologies she read. Throughout, she deploys history against memory, but she also gives memory its due, by showing not only how it can cripple the present, but also how it is always in process, always emerging in the present, and therefore always open to emancipatory uses. Her stance combines the critical perspective of the modern scholar with the forbearance of the autobiographer who keeps faith with other times, other selves.[51]

The new histories that began in the 1970s—social history, labor history, African American history, women's history—have been wildly successful in transforming the theater of the past. They have created entirely new scenes and filled them with actors who played no role in the Lost Cause narrative that Katharine learned. And yet, for all the innovations and advances, the conventions of historical *writing* have hardly changed at all. In that regard, even feminist scholars have tried to use the masters' tools to dismantle the master's house. Katharine Du Pre Lumpkin struggled mightily in her time to acquire and deploy those tools—to use the weapons of social science and revisionist history to demystify the memories and histories that she absorbed as a child. But as long as she remained entirely within those disciplinary frameworks, she could not speak with political effect. In the 1940s, she cast aside those conventions and that impersonal voice. Daring to speak in the first person, she tried to create a new kind of writing, a new way of interweaving memory and history, poetics and politics, without blurring the distinctions between the two.[52]

The 1990s has seen a striking and unprecedented turn to first-person writing, especially among feminist literary scholars. Historians have met this phenomenon—and the "return of the author" more generally—with a mixture of hostility, anxiety, and relief. For Katharine, the *I* of autobiography was an embodied, remembering, reading, and writing self, a self participating with others in the reconstruction of social memory. She asked not, "Who am I?" but, like so many black and white southern writers before her, "Who are we and how can we use both memory and history to reinvent our regional identities?" That approach is the antithesis of "narcissism," the charge that is sometimes leveled at the turn to autobiography today. As such, it may prove particularly useful to historians, who care so much for the social and depend so much on the warrant of facts.[53]

Katharine's rewriting of the Lost Cause, together with my rewriting of her project, may also suggest directions for the study of memory even as they show just how urgent and difficult that study can be. There is no doubt that the Lost Cause dominated the social memory of the "white South" and, indeed, of much of "white America." Hegemonic, in this case, is not too strong a word. Here, if anywhere, was an understanding of the past that evoked intense emotion, provoked action, and worked evil in the world. But the Lost Cause was not a replication of an old original, a banner mechanically transferred from one generation to another. It was a retelling in a new context in which white southerners used history as a resource to fashion new selves and a new society from the materials of the old. William Lumpkin's stories, for example, were bent to the political moment even as they drew on living memory and on unfinished mourning for a childhood cut short. Those twice-told tales could still evoke powerful emotions in the postwar generation, but as they traveled they became ever more malleable. Appropriated by a younger generation of businessmen and politicians, they served to promote national reconciliation, to forward modernization, and to wrap a mantle of Old South legitimacy around a New South elite. Yet even this party of remembrance, effective as it was, could not know in advance, nor control, what would happen when its stories were retold. Even at its height, moreover, the Lost Cause could not stamp out counter-memories. The ex-slaves created their own sites of memory. Black historians fought persistently to make sure that such memories survived. And even the planter class produced sons and daughters like Katharine Du Pre Lumpkin, who, thinking first through their families and then through the ever-widening circles in which they were involved, struggled to rewrite, re-remember, and spring free from—while also honoring—their vexed and painful yet precious pasts.[54]

To comprehend such a contested, multileveled process, we need both poetics and politics, imagination and critique. We cannot, for example, see William Lumpkin's longings simply as utilitarian covers for political ends. Nor can we see history—whether written by the self-styled scientific scholars of the turn of the century or by our own late-twentieth-century selves—simply as the enemy of memory. As we abandon such reductions and dualities, ever more challenging questions will emerge. How, in practice, is memory transferred from one generation to another, impressed in the body, and sustained by every-day performance of self? What is—or should be—the relation between individual memory, social memory, and history, between how people in general make sense of their personal and collective pasts and how historians practice their craft?[55] And, most important perhaps, how can we explain why some pasts triumph, motivating actions, shaping societies, maintaining their emotional charge, while others flicker into burnt-out meteors, spinning hollow shells?

Katharine Du Pre Lumpkin fashioned autobiography into history and, at the same time, used her professional knowledge of the past to re-remember her childhood, resituating her memories in a new perspective derived both from research and from the left-wing politics of her time. She made history a weapon for dismantling social memory, but she also used memory (and autobiography) to breathe life into history. Her aim was to speak to readers beyond the academy in a believable and compelling voice and to demonstrate, through her own example, that even the most lethal and tenacious social memories have their fault lines, contradictions, and emancipatory uses.

We too could benefit from at once questioning and *using* the differences between memory, autobiography, and history. "Historical sense and poetic sense should not, in the end, be contradictory," wrote Robert Penn Warren, "for if poetry is the little myth we make, history is the big myth we live, and in our living constantly remake." Too often in our living, unspoken hierarchies prevail: historical sense overrules poetic sense; modes of explanation that highlight structure (or discourse) eclipse agency; written texts trump oral sources; master narratives override local knowledge.[56] If, as some critics suggest, we have lost our audience, perhaps it is because we have invested too much energy in maintaining—or reversing—these hierarchies and too little in Katharine's project: writing that emphasizes not our expertise but our common condition, writing that troubles the boundaries between poetics and politics, memory and history, witnessing and writing, acting and research.

NOTES

1 Michael S. Roth, *The Ironist's Cage: Memory, Trauma, and the Construction of History* (New York, 1995), 11–12. Benedict Anderson argues that the modern nation-state depends on the oscillation between remembering the stories that secure national identity and burying beneath the surface of consciousness the injustices that secure the nation's imagined borders. Benedict Anderson, *Imagined Communities: Reflections on the Origin and Spread of Nationalism* (London, 1991), 187–206. For the suggestion that the fragmentation of postmodernism has produced an obsession with memory and a veritable memory industry, see Andreas Huyssen, *Twilight Memories: Marking Time in a Culture of Amnesia* (New York, 1995); and David Lowenthal, *Possessed by the Past: The Heritage Crusade and the Spoils of History* (New York, 1996).

2 Roth, *Ironist's Cage*, 9–17, 201–11; Marita Sturken, *Tangled Memories: The Vietnam War, the AIDS Epidemic, and the Politics of Remembering* (Berkeley, 1997), 1–12; and Sigmund Freud, "Screen Memories" (1899), in *The Standard Edition of the Complete Psychological Works of Sigmund Freud*, trans. and ed. James Strachey (24 vols., London, 1953–1974), 111, 301–22. Popular understandings of Sigmund Freud tend to visualize memory as a reservoir of imprinted experiences waiting to emerge. But as Marita Sturken points out, Freud offered compelling images of the constructedness, as well as the endurance, of memory. Sturken, *Tangled Memories*, 3–4. . . . See Maurice Halbwachs, *The Collective Memory*, trans. Francis J. Ditter Jr. and Vida Yazdi Ditter (New York, 1980). For a critique of Halbwach's conflation of individual and collective memory, see James Fentress and Chris Wickham, *Social Memory: New Perspectives on the Past* (Cambridge, Mass., 1992), ix–xii, 1–8. For an example of how oral history provides access to the process by which memories are created in dialogue with others, see Samuel Schrager, "What Is Social in Oral History?," *International Journal of Oral History*, 4 (June 1983), 76–98.

3 Paul Connerton, *How Societies Remember* (New York, 1989), 1–40, esp. 6; David Thelen, "Memory and American History," *Journal of American History*, 75 (March 1989), 1117–29. On the notion that "life consists of retellings," that we experience the present only by taking account of the past, see Edward M. Bruner, "Experience and Its Expressions," in *The Anthropology of Experience*, ed. Victor W. Turner and Edward M. Bruner (Urbana, 1986), 3–30, esp. 12. . . .

4 See Pierre Nora, "Between Memory and History: *Les Lieux de Mémoire*," *Representations*, 26 (Spring 1989), 7–25, esp. 8–9. Nora mourns the postmodern erosion of organic memory and deprecates the critical-rational operations of history, yet he still believes that the historian, "half priest, half soldier," has a responsibility for preserving the "worked over" memories that now constitute our only link with the past. For the ambiguities in Nora's position, see Steven Englund, "The Ghost of Nation Past," *Journal of Modern History*, 64 (June 1992), 299–320. . . . For the intertwining of memory

and history, see Raphael Samuel, *Theatres of Memory*, vol. I: *Past and Present Contemporary Culture* (New York, 1994).

5 William Cronon, "A Place for Stories: Nature, History, and Narrative," *Journal of American History*, 78 (March 1992), 1347–76; Davis and Starn, "Introduction"; Susan A. Crane, "Writing the Individual back into Collective Memory," *American Historical Review*, 102 (Dec. 1997), 1381–85; Shannon Jackson, "Performance at Hull-House: Museum, Microfiche, and Historiography," in *Exceptional Spaces: Essays in Performance and History*, ed. Della Pollock (Chapel Hill, 1998), 261–93. For "body memory," see Connerton, *How Societies Remember*; 25–36, 72–104. . . .

6 Thomas McLaughlin, "Figurative Language," in *Critical Terms for Literary Study*, ed. Frank Lentricchia and Thomas McLaughlin (Chicago, 1990), 80. . . . In literary theory, poetics usually refers to the study of the conventions that inform given texts, but I am using the term more generally to evoke the realm of memory, creativity, and imagination.

7 My study of the Lumpkin sisters is tentatively entitled *Writing Memory: Katharine Du Pre Lumpkin and the Refashioning of Southern Identity*. Katharine Du Pre Lumpkin, *The Making of a Southerner* (New York, 1946); Grace Lumpkin, *To Make My Bread* (1932; Urbana, 1995). . . .

8 I am arguing for fluidity between these phenomena rather than for rigid distinctions. For example, when personal memories are organized into narratives that contrast the "there and then" with the "here and now," they can be seen as informal histories, with their own modes of evidence and analysis. For my understanding of what I call "social memory" (but that others call collective, cultural, or public memory), I am drawing on the works cited above and on Patrick H. Hutton, *History as an Art of Memory* (Hanover, 1993); Daniel Gordon, review of *History as an Art of Memory* by Patrick H. Hutton, *History and Theory*, 34 (no. 4, 1995), 340–54; and Sarah Maza, "Stories in History: Cultural Narratives in Recent Works in European History," *American Historical Review*, 101 (Dec. l996), 1493–1515. . . . I have been influenced by involvement with oral history, whose practitioners cannot avoid grappling with issues of memory.

9 Lumpkin, *Making of a Southerner*; 10–11, 99–108; *Columbia State*, March 14, 1910, 1; Katharine Du Pre Lumpkin, *The Emancipation of Angelina Grimké* (Chapel Hill, 1974), 10.

10 Lumpkin, *Making of a Southerner*, 49, 72–73. For the name change, see Bryan A. Lumpkin, "Lumpkin," [Dec. 1936], typescript genealogy, Katharine Du Pre Lumpkin Papers (Southern Historical Collection, University of North Carolina, Chapel Hill) [SHC] [and various manuscript census records]. On the "mad carnival," see George C. Rable, *Civil Wars: Women and the Crisis of Southern Nationalism* (Urbana, 1989), 172.

11 Jennifer Fleischner, *Mastering Slavery: Memory, Family, and Identity in Women's Slave Narratives* (New York, l996), 1.

12 Lumpkin, *Making of a Southerner*; 86–99, esp. 86–87, 139; Elizabeth Lumpkin Glenn to K. Dear (Katharine Lumpkin), n.d., Lumpkin Papers.

13 Lumpkin, *Making of a Southerner*; 99, 121; Katharine Du Pre Lumpkin, "Lecture to Prof. Harlow's Class," Spring 1947, 8, Lumpkin Papers; Grace Lumpkin, *The Wedding* (New York, 1939) 18–19; Grace Lumpkin, "A Miserable Offender," *Virginia Quarterly Review*, 11 (April 1935), 281–88. For the notion of a magic circle of belonging, see Hollinger F. Barnard, ed., *Outside the Magic Circle: The Autobiography of Virginia Foster Durr* (University, Ala., 1985).

14 On the Lost Cause, see Rollin Osterweis, *The Myth of the Lost Cause, 1865–*

1900 (Hamden, 1973); Gaines M. Foster, *Ghosts of the Confederacy: Defeat, the Lost Cause, and the Emergence of the New South, 1865 to 1913* (New York, 1987); Charles Reagan Wilson, *Baptized in Blood The Religion of the Lost Cause, 1865–1920* (Athens, Ga., 1980); Fred Arthur Bailey, "The Textbooks of the 'Lost Cause': Censorship and the Creation of Southern State Histories," *Georgia Historical Quarterly*, 75 (Fall 1991) 507–33; and Catherine W. Bisher, "Landmarks of Power: Building a Southern Past, 1885–1915," *Southern Cultures* (Inaugural Issue 1993), 5–45. On the role of women and gender in the construction of the Lost Cause and the South's early-twentieth-century historical awakening, see, more generally . . . Karen Lynne Cox, "Women, the Lost Cause, and the New South: The United Daughters of the Confederacy and the Transmission of Confederate Culture, 1894–1919" (Ph.D. diss., University of Southern Mississippi, 1997); Drew Gilpin Faust, *Mothers of Invention: Women of the Slaveholding South in the American Civil War* (Chapel Hill, 1996); Grace Elizabeth Hale, *Making Whiteness: The Culture of Segregation in the South, 1890–1940* (New York, 1998); . . . . LeeAnn Whites, *The Civil War as a Crisis in Gender: Augusta, Ga., 1860–1890* (Athens, Ga., 1995); and Cheryl Thurber, "The Development of the Mammy Image and Mythology," in *Southern Women: Histories and Identities*, ed. Virginia Bernhard et al. (Columbia, Mo., 1992), 87–108.

15 Lumpkin, *Making of a Southerner*; 127–30, esp. 128–29.

16 I am drawing here on Anastasia Sims, *The Power of Femininity in the New South: Women's Organizations and Politics in North Carolina, 1880–1930* (Columbia, S. C., 1997), 33–40, esp. 33, 34, 38, 39; Glenda Elizabeth Gilmore, *Gender and Jim Crow: Women and the Politics of White Supremacy in North Carolina, 1896–1920* (Chapel Hill, 1996), 61–118; C. Vann Woodward, *Origins of the New South, 1877–1913* (Baton Rouge, 1951), 235–63, 321–49; James L. Leloudis, *Schooling the New South: Pedagogy, Self, and Society in North Carolina, 1880–1920* (Chapel Hill, 1996), 133–41; and J. Morgan Kousser, *The Shaping of Southern Politics: Suffrage Restriction and the Establishment of the One-Party South, 1880–1910* (New Haven, 1974). . . .

17 Bisher, "Landmarks of Power"; Nora, "Between Memory and History."

18 For the trauma of war, see Eric T. Dean Jr., *Shook over Hell: Post-Traumatic Stress, Vietnam, and the Civil War* (Cambridge, Mass., 1997). . . . Some historians have suggested that the Lost Cause helped reintegrate veterans into southern society. But it can as well be seen as a collective "screen memory" that overlay less acceptable memories, memories that required tremendous energy to "forget." . . . .

19 Edward L. Ayers, *The Promise of the New South: Life after Reconstruction* (New York, 1992), 334; Bisher, "Landmarks of Power," 7.

20 Sims, *Power of Femininity in the New South, 40*; Jacquelyn Dowd Hall, *Revolt against Chivalry: Jessie Daniel Ames and the Women's Campaign against Lynching* (New York, 1993), 149–57; Jacquelyn Dowd Hall, " 'The Mind that Burns in Each Body': Women, Rape, and Racial Violence," in *Powers of Desire: The Politics of Sexuality*, ed. Ann Snitow, Christine Stansell, and Sharon Thompson (New York, 1983), 328–49; Elizabeth Waring McMaster, *The Girls of the Sixties* (Columbia, S.C., 1937), 105. . . .

21 Brundage, "White Women and the Politics of Historical Memory in the New South"; Sims, *Power of Femininity in the New South*, 128–54; Cox, "Women, the Lost Cause, and the New South."

22 *Columbia State*, Aug. 20, 1905, 3. . . .

23 Foster, *Ghosts of the Confederacy*, 97, 136–37; photocopy of letter fragment

from Elizabeth Lumpkin Glenn, n.d. (in Jacquelyn Hall's possession); *Columbia State*, Aug. 20, 1905, 3.

24 *Confederate Veteran*, 12 (Feb. 1904), 69, 70; ibid., 13 (July 1905), 298; *Columbia State*, Sept. 25, 1904, 11; newsclip, Nov. 13, 1906, 8, 10 (in Hall's possession): *Columbia State*, Nov. 14, 1906, 1; Foster, *Ghosts of the Confederacy*, 136. . . .

25 Hall, *Revolt against Chivalry*, 150; Sims, *Power of Femininity in the New South*, 135; Walter Hines Page, *The Southerner, a Novel: Being the Autobiography of Nicholas Worth* (New York, 1909), 160.

26 On Elizabeth's career, see Annual Departmental Reports, 1903–1905, box 2 (Winthrop College Archives, Rock Hill, S.C.); Katharine Du Pre Lumpkin to My Dear Sister (Elizabeth Lumpkin), Jan. 3, 1904, Lumpkin Papers; and *Columbia State*, Sept. 25, 1904, 11.

27 Elizabeth Lumpkin Glenn, "Bitterroot," [1950] (in Dr. and Mrs. William Glenn's possession); Annette Lumpkin to Sister, Feb. 19, 1924 (in Joe Lumpkin's possession); *Confederate Veteran*, 14 (Nov. 1906), 494–96, esp. 495, 496; newsclip, *Asheville Citizen*, Feb. 15, 1963 (in Hall's possession).

28 See Sims, *Power of Femininity*, 135–37; and Montgomery, "Lost Cause Mythology in New South Reform."

29 Wilson, *Baptized in Blood:* 149; Lumpkin, *Making of a Southerner*; 126–27; Bailey, "Textbooks of the 'Lost Cause' "; Fred Arthur Bailey, "Free Speech and the 'Lost Cause' in Texas: A Study of Social Control in the New South," *Southwestern Historical Quarterly*, 97 (Jan. 1994), 453–77. . . .

30 On the professionalization of southern history and the marginalization of women, see W. Fitzhugh Brundage, [*The Southern Past: A Clash of Race and Memory* (Cambridge, Mass., 2005)].

31 See Jennifer Fleischner's brilliant study of such "escapes from childhood" in slave autobiographies: Fleischner, *Mastering Slavery*, 1.

32 Sidonie Smith, *A Poetics of Women's Autobiography: Marginality and the Fictions of Self-Representation* (Bloomington, 1987), 17; Lumpkin, *Making of a Southerner*, 128; Katharine Du Pre Lumpkin, "Lecture to a General Audience," 1947, 2, Lumpkin Papers. On the utopian and performative aspects of feminist criticism, which aims at "seizing authority from men at the same time that it seeks to redefine traditional models . . . of authority, power, and hierarchy," see Tania Modleski, *Feminism without Women: Culture and Criticism in a "Postfeminist" Age* (New York, 1991), 41–58, esp. 48, 53. On the dialogue between authors and readers, see Norine Voss, " 'Saying the Unsayable': An Introduction to Women's Autobiography," in *Gender Studies: New Directions in Feminist Criticism*, ed. Judith Spector (Bowling Green, 1986), 224. . . .

33 Lumpkin, *Making of a Southerner*; 111–47, esp. 130.

34 Ibid., 115; Katharine Du Pre Lumpkin, "Plans for Work," [1943–1944], Lumpkin Papers; Katharine Du Pre Lumpkin interview by Jacquelyn Hall, Aug. 4, 1974, transcript, 66, Southern Oral History Program Collection, SCH. . . .

35 Lumpkin, *Making of a Southerner*, 117–20.

36 Ibid., 121. See also newsclip, Nov. 13, 1906, 8, 10 (in Hall's possession).

37 Lumpkin, *Making of a Southerner*, 122–24, 184.

38 Ibid., 124–25, 136–37.

39 Ibid., 126.

40 Ibid., 185; Glenn, "Bitterroot"; Grace Lumpkin, "Annette Caroline Morris [Lumpkin]," in Lumpkin, "Lumpkin." . . . .

41 Lumpkin, *Making of a Southerner*; 123, 185–86.

42 Ibid., 127–28.

43 For contrasting views of the relationship between commemoration and critical inquiry, see Hutton, *History as an Art of Memory*; and Gordon, review of *History as an Art of Memory* by Hutton. Katharine's insistence on the contingent, social nature of her transformation had the political purpose of persuading white southerners that change was integral to southern history, not imposed from without. She was also adopting a trope of (white) women's autobiography: the attribution of success or personal transformation to "providential circumstance." See Sandra M. Gilbert and Susan Gubar, *No Man's Land? The Place of the Woman Writer in the Twentieth Century*, vol. I: *The War of Words* (New Haven, 1988), 66–67. . . .

44 Lumpkin, undated, handwritten note left in her personal copy of *The Making of a Southerner* . . .; Lumpkin, *Making of a Southerner*; 131–32, 151–73, 180–86; Lumpkin, *Emancipation of Angelina Grimké*, 3–5, 14–16, esp. 5; "Testimony of Angelina Grimké Weld," in *American Slavery as It Is: Testimony of a Thousand Witnesses*, ed. Theodore Dwight Weld (1839; New York, 1969), 52–57; Lumpkin interview, 7. In *The Making of a Southerner*; Katharine referred to the cook's abuser as "the white master of the house." Like Angelina, who, Katharine noted, wrote about her brother's rages anonymously, Katharine could not bring herself to name her father directly.

45 Lumpkin, *Making of a Southerner*; 151–186, esp. 182.

46 Lumpkin interview, 24; Lumpkin, *Making of a Southerner*; 203 . . . .; On the significance of this relationship with Dorothy Wolff Douglas, see Jacquelyn Dowd Hall, "Open Secrets: Memory, Imagination, and the Refashioning of Southern Identity," *American Quarterly*, 50 (March 1998), 110–24.

47 For Katharine's denial that racial mores were immutable, see Lumpkin, *Making of a Southerner*; 203–4. For how assumptions of agency enable memoir, see Connerton, *How Societies Remember*, 19.

48 Franklin D. Roosevelt characterized the South in these terms; see David L. Carlton and Peter A. Coclanis, eds., *Confronting Southern Poverty in the Great Depression: "The Report on Economic Conditions of the South" with Related Documents* (Boston, 1996), 42. Katharine Du Pre Lumpkin, *The South in Progress* (New York, 1940).

49 Lumpkin, "Lecture to a General Audience," 3; Lumpkin, "Lecture to Prof. Harlow's Class," 13; Myra Page, review of *The Making of a Southerner* by Katharine Du Pre Lumpkin and *The Way of the South* by Howard Odum, *Science and Society*, 12 (Spring 1948), 276–78, esp. 276.

50 Lumpkin, *Making of a Southerner* 235–36, 239; Modleski, *Feminism without Women*, 46.

51 Studs Terkel, *Hard Times: An Oral History of the Great Depression* (New York, 1970), 17. . . .

52 The metaphor of the "master's tools" appears in Audre Lorde, "Age, Race, Class, and Sex: Women Redefining Difference," in *Words of Fire: An Anthology of African-American Feminist Thought*, ed. Beverly Guy-Sheftall (New York, 1995), 291.

53 For contributions by feminist historians to the surge of first-person writing, see Carol Ascher, Louise DeSalvo, and Sara Ruddick, eds., *Between Women: Biographers, Novelists, Critics, Teachers and Artists Write about Their Work on Women* (Boston, 1984); and Sara Alpern et al., eds., *The Challenge of Feminist Biography: Writing the Lives of Modern American Women* (Urbana, 1992). For works of historians who have placed their own memories in the histories

they write, by speaking in the first-person singular or by making readers aware of their struggles with evidence and interpretation, see, for example, Robert A. Rosenstone, *Mirror in the Shrine: American Encounters with Meiji Japan* (Cambridge, Mass., 1988); Laurel Thatcher Ulrich, *A Midwife's Tale: The Life of Martha Ballard Based on Her Diary, 1786–1812* (New York, 1990); William S. McFeely, *Sapelo's People: A Long Walk into Freedom* (New York, 1994); Nell Irvin Painter, *Sojourner Truth: A Life, A Symbol* (New York, 1996); Simon Schama, *Landscape and Memory* (New York, 1995). . . . On the debates over the *I* in the text, see Robert Rosenstone, Bryant Simon, and Moshe Sluhovsky, "Experiments in Narrating Histories: A Workshop," *Perspectives, 32* (Sept. 1994), 7–10.

54 On African American countermemories and histories, see Genevieve Fabre and Robert O'Meally, eds., *History and Memory in African-American Culture* (New York, 1994); David W. Blight, " 'For Something beyond the Battlefield': Frederick Douglass and the Memory of the Civil War," *Journal of American History*, 75 (March 1989), 1156–78; Spencie Love, *One Blood: the Death and Resurrection of Charles R. Drew* (Chapel Hill, 1996); and August Meier and Elliott Rudwick, *Black History and the Historical Profession, 1915–80* (Urbana, 1986).

55 See Alon Confino, "Collective Memory and Cultural History: Problems of Method," *American Historical Review*, 102 (Dec. 1997), 1386–1403.

56 "Robert Penn Warren," *Vanity Fair* April 1985, 45; Love, *One Blood*, 8 . . .

11

"YOU DON'T HAVE TO RIDE JIM CROW"

CORE and the 1947 Journey of Reconciliation

Raymond Arsenault

Raymond Arsenault's essay on the 1947 Journey of Reconciliation recounts the story of an important precedent for a key moment in the mass Civil Rights Movement of the 1960s. In the background of the Journey was the decision of Irene Morgan, a young African-American woman from Maryland on her way back from a family visit in Virginia, to defy Virginia's segregation statutes as they applied to interstate busses. When she was arrested and convicted in 1944, she appealed the conviction, and eventually the Supreme Court ruled, in Morgan vs. Commonwealth of Virginia *(1946), that Virginia's law requiring segregation on interstate transportation violated the Constitution's interstate commerce clause. However, the effect of the ruling was largely negated when southern officials pressed bus and railroad companies to continue to segregate passengers on the basis of "private" company policy.*

In response, a young organization called the Congress on Racial Equality (CORE) decided to challenge bus segregation with direct action. Led by Bayard Rustin and James Peck—who, like the activists in Patricia Sullivan's essay in this volume, had been deeply involved in radical politics throughout the 1930s and 1940s—CORE organized a bus trip during which eight whites and eight African Americans traveled together through the upper South, refusing to sit in the areas reserved for "their" race. Although the immediate results of the Journey were quite limited, fourteen years later CORE (including some of the same activists) would organize the "Freedom Rides" of 1961 that played a major role in galvanizing the mass movement for Civil Rights during the 1960s.

* * *

In the fall of 1946, the NAACP's disengagement from the fading, unresolved controversy over the *Morgan* decision created an opening for the radical wing of the civil rights movement. Though no one realized it at the time, this opening represented an important turning point in the history of the modern American freedom struggle. When the NAACP fell by the wayside, a small but determined group of radical activists seized the opportunity to take the desegregation struggle out of the courts and into the streets. Inspired by an international tradition of nonviolent direct action, this response to segregationist intransigence transcended the cautious legal realism of the NAACP. In the short run, as we shall see, their efforts to breathe life into the *Morgan* decision failed, but in the long run their use of direct action in the late 1940s planted the seeds of an idea that bore remarkable fruit a decade and a half later. Although called a "Journey of Reconciliation," this nonviolent foray into the world of Jim Crow represented the first formal "freedom ride."

To most Americans, then and now, the pioneer freedom riders were obscure figures, men and women who lived and labored outside the spotlight of celebrity and notoriety. During the immediate postwar era, the radical wing of the civil rights struggle was small, predominantly white, and fragmented among several organizations. Concentrated in New York, Chicago, and several other large northern cities, the radicals included followers of Mohandas Gandhi, Christian socialists, labor and peace activists, Quaker pacifists, Communists, and a varied assortment of left-wing intellectuals. Though ideologically diverse, they shared a commitment to militant agitation aimed at bringing about fundamental and even revolutionary change. Like Gandhi, who was in the final stages of demonstrating the power of nonviolent resistance in India, they dreamed of a world liberated from the scourges of racial prejudice, class oppression, and colonialism. Open to a variety of provocative tactics—economic boycotts, picketing, protest marches, sit-ins, and other forms of direct action—they operated on the radical fringe of American politics. With perhaps a few thousand adherents, the radical approach constituted something less than a mass movement at this point, but the social and political turmoil of the Great Depression and World War II had produced a vanguard of activists passionately committed to widening the scope and accelerating the pace of the struggle for civil and human rights.

In 1946 the most active members of this radical vanguard were affiliated with two interrelated organizations, the Congress of Racial Equality (CORE) and its parent organization, the Fellowship of Reconciliation (FOR). It was within these groups that the idea of the Freedom Ride was born. Founded in Chicago in 1942, CORE drew inspiration from the wartime stirrings of decolonization in Africa and Asia and from the recent success of nonviolent mass resistance in Gandhi's

India. But it also drew upon a somewhat older tradition of nonviolent protest nurtured by FOR.[1]

Founded in 1914 at an international gathering of Christian pacifists, FOR maintained a steady course of dissent through war and peace. During the 1920s and 1930s, the American branch of FOR included some of the nation's leading social justice advocates, including radical economist Scott Nearing, Socialist leader Norman Thomas, American Civil Liberties Union founder Roger Baldwin, and eminent theologians such as Reinhold Niebuhr, Harry Emerson Fosdick, and Howard Thurman. Representing the interests of such a diverse group was never easy, but with the approach of World War II the organization found it increasingly difficult to satisfy both radical pacifists, who insisted on an absolutist commitment to nonviolence, and pragmatic pacifists, who acknowledged the necessity of waging war against totalitarian oppression. In 1940 the selection of an absolutist, A. J. Muste, as executive director drove most of the pragmatists out of the FOR, leaving the American branch with a small but dedicated core of radical activists. A former Dutch Reformed and Congregationalist minister who passed through Trotskyism and militant trade unionism before embracing radical pacifism and Gandhianism, Muste turned the American FOR into a vanguard of social change. . . . Muste believed that American society needed a radical overhaul, especially in the area of race relations, and he welcomed the creation of CORE as a natural extension of FOR's reform program. Muste's prescriptive model was not for everyone, even in faithful pacifist circles, but his impassioned calls for engagement and sacrifice drew a number of remarkable individuals into the FOR/CORE orbit. During the early 1940s, the FOR national office in New York became the nerve center of American Gandhianism. Crammed into a small building on upper Broadway, near Columbia University, the FOR staff of twelve shared ideas, plans, and soaring dreams of social justice. Young, well educated, and impoverished—most made less than twenty dollars a week—they lived and worked in the subterranean fringe of American life.[2]

Among the FOR/CORE stalwarts were . . . Bayard Rustin [and] James Peck. . . . A founding member of CORE and the co-secretary of FOR'S Race and Industrial Department, Rustin—along with co-secretary George Houser—organized and led the Journey of Reconciliation of 1947 and later served as an adviser to Martin Luther King Jr. during and after the Montgomery Bus Boycott of 1955–56. . . . [P]erhaps more than anyone else, Rustin was the intellectual godfather of the Freedom Rider movement. Peck, a radical journalist who acted as CORE'S chief publicist, was the only person to participate in both the Journey of Reconciliation and the 1961 Freedom Rides. Severely beaten by Klansmen in Alabama in May 1961, he later authored a revealing memoir of his experiences as a Freedom Rider.... [These] activists provided a critical link between the nonviolent civil rights initiatives of the 1940s and the full-blown movement of the 1960s, [and] each in his own way exerted a powerful influence on the development of nonviolence in the United States. Their personal stories reveal a great deal about the origins and context of the Freedom Rides and about the hidden history of the civil rights struggle—especially the complex connections between North and South, black and white, liberalism and radicalism, and religious and secular motivation.[3]

Born in 1912 in West Chester, Pennsylvania, [Rustin] was the child of Florence Rustin, an unwed teenager, and Archie Hopkins, an itinerant black laborer who barely acknowledged his son's existence. Adopted by Florence's parents, Julia and Janifer Rustin, young Bayard was raised by an extended family of grandparents, aunts, and uncles who collectively eked out a living by cooking and catering for the local Quaker gentry. Julia Rustin was a member of the local Quaker meeting before joining her husband's African Methodist Episcopal Church following their marriage in 1891. And she remained a Quaker "at Heart," naming her grandson for Bayard Taylor, a celebrated mid-nineteenth-century Quaker leader. A woman of substance and deep moral conviction, Julia was the most important influence in Bayard's upbringing and the primary source of the pacifist doctrines that would anchor his lifelong commitment to nonviolence. Indulged as the favorite child of the Rustin clan, he gained a reputation as a brilliant student and gifted singer and musician, first as one of a handful of black students at West Chester High School, where he also excelled as a track and football star, and later at all-black Wilberforce University in Ohio, where he studied history and literature and toured as the lead soloist of the Wilberforce Quartet. Despite these accomplishments, he eventually ran afoul of the Wilberforce administration by challenging the school's compulsory ROTC program and engaging in homosexual activity (he reportedly fell in love with the son of the university president). Expelled in December 1933, he returned to Pennsylvania and enrolled at Cheyney State Teachers College the following fall.

At Cheyney, where he remained for three years, Rustin gained a reputation as a multitalented student leader, distinguishing himself as a singer, a keen student of philosophy, and a committed peace activist. When Cheyney's president, Leslie Pinckney Hill, a devout black Quaker, invited the American Friends Service Committee (AFSC) to hold an international peace institute on the campus in the spring of 1937, Rustin was a willing and eager participant. Inspired by the dedicated pacifists who attended the institute and already primed for social action by his family and religious background, he soon accepted a position as a "peace volunteer" with the AFSC's Emergency Peace

Campaign (EPC). During an EPC training session, he received further inspiration from Muriel Lester, a noted British pacifist and Gandhi protege. After listening to Lester's eloquent plea for pacifism and nonviolent struggle, he threw himself into the peace campaign with an uncommon zeal that would later become his trademark. . . .

[In the fall of 1937,] propelled by a growing disenchantment with southeastern Pennsylvania's political and cultural scene and by a second scandalous (and interracial) homosexual incident, he moved northward to the alluring uncertainties of metropolitan Harlem, the unofficial capital of black America. Cast adrift from the relatively secure world of college life and facing the vagaries of the Great Depression, Rustin embarked on a remarkable odyssey of survival and discovery that propelled him through a labyrinth of radical politics and bohemian culture. Along the way he became a professional singer, a dedicated Communist, and an uncloseted homosexual. During the late 1930s he sang backup for Josh White and Huddie "Ledbelly" Ledbetter, worked as a recruiter for the Young Communist League (YCL), preached revolution and brotherhood on countless street corners, and even squeezed in a few classes at City College, all the while gaining a reputation as one of Harlem's most colorful characters. In early 1941, the YCL asked Rustin to organize a campaign against segregation in the American armed forces, but later in the year, following the unexpected German attack on the Soviet Union, YCL leaders ordered him to cancel the campaign in the interest of Allied military solidarity. With this apparent shift away from agitation for racial and social justice, Rustin became deeply disillusioned with the Communist Party. "You can all go to hell," he told his New York comrades. "I see the Communist movement is only interested in what happens in Russia. You don't give a damn about Negroes." In June 1941 he left the Communist fold for good and transferred his allegiance to A. Philip Randolph, the legendary black Socialist and labor leader who was then planning a mass march on Washington, D.C., to protest the Roosevelt administration's refusal to guarantee equal employment opportunities for black and white defense workers. Randolph appointed Rustin the youth organizer for the march, but the two men soon had a serious falling out. After Roosevelt responded to Randolph's threatened march with an executive order creating a Fair Employment Practices Committee (FEPC), Randolph agreed to call off the march. But many of his young supporters, including Rustin, thought the protest march should continue as planned. . . . Consequently, in the fall of 1941, he accepted a staff position with A. J. Muste's Fellowship of Reconciliation.

As FOR youth secretary, Rustin returned to the pacifist track he had followed as an EPC volunteer, immersing himself in the writings and teachings of Gandhi and pledging his loyalty to nonviolence, not just as a strategy for change but as a way of life. Muste encouraged and nurtured Rustin's determination to apply Gandhian precepts to the African American struggle for racial equality, and in the spring of 1942 the two men joined forces with other FOR activists to found the Committee (later "Congress") of Racial Equality. "Certainly the Negro possesses qualities essential for nonviolent direct action," Rustin wrote prophetically in October 1942. "He has long since learned to endure suffering. He can admit his own share of guilt and has to be pushed hard to become bitter. . . . He is creative and has learned to adjust himself to conditions easily. But above all he possesses a rich religious heritage and today finds the church the center of his life."[4]

As a CORE stalwart, Rustin participated in a number of nonviolent protests, including an impromptu refusal to move to the back of a bus during a trip from Louisville to Nashville in the early summer of 1942. This particular episode earned him a roadside beating at the hands of the Nashville police, who later hauled him off to jail. A month after the incident, Rustin offered the readers of the FOR journal *Fellowship* a somewhat whimsical description of his arrest:

> I was put into the back seat of the police car, between two policemen. Two others sat in front. During the thirteen-mile ride to town they called me every conceivable name and said anything they could think of to incite me to violence. . . . When we reached Nashville, a number of policemen were lined up on both sides of the hallway down which I had to pass on my way to the captain's office. They tossed me from one to another like a volleyball. . . . Finally the captain said, "Come here, nigger." I walked directly to him, "What can I do for you?" I asked. "Nigger," he said menacingly, "you're supposed to be scared when you come in here!" "I am fortified by the truth, justice and Christ," I said. "There's no need for me to fear." He was flabbergasted and, for a time, completely at a loss for words. Finally he said to another officer, "I believe the nigger's crazy!"

In the end, the timely intervention of a sympathetic white bystander . . . and the restraint of a coolheaded assistant district attorney . . . kept Rustin out of jail, reinforcing his suspicion that even the white South could be redeemed through nonviolent struggle.[5]

. . . . in 1943 [Rustin] rejected the traditional Quaker compromise of alternative service in an army hospital. Convicted of draft evasion, he spent the next twenty-eight months in federal prison. For nearly two years he was imprisoned at the Ashland, Ohio, penitentiary, where he waged spirited if futile campaigns against everything from the censorship of reading materials to racial segregation. In August 1945 a final effort to desegregate the prison dining hall led to solitary confinement, but soon thereafter he and several other pacifist malcontents were transferred to a federal facility in Lewisburg, Pennsylvania. Following his release from Lewisburg in June 1946, Rustin returned to New York to accept an appointment as co-secretary (with George Houser) of FOR'S Race and Industrial Department, a position he promptly turned into a roving ambassadorship of Gandhian nonviolence. Though physically weak and emaciated, he took to the road, preaching the gospel of nonviolent direct action to anyone who would listen. As biographer Jervis Anderson has noted, during the critical postwar year of 1946 Rustin "functioned as a one-man civil disobedience movement in his travels across the United States. He occupied 'white only' railroad compartments; sat in at 'white only' hotels; and refused to budge unless he was forcibly ejected." All of this reinforced his dual reputation as a fearless activist and a Gandhian sage. He was both irrepressible and imaginative; and no one who knew him well was surprised when he, along with Houser, came up with the provocative idea of an interracial bus ride through the Jim Crow South. After the Journey of Reconciliation proposal was hatched, Rustin acted as a relentless advocate, eventually winning over or at least wearing down those who thought the plan was too dangerous. Without his involvement, the Journey—and perhaps even the Freedom Rides of 1960s—would never have taken place.[6]

Jim Peck followed a somewhat different path to the Journey of Reconciliation. Three years younger than Rustin, he grew up in one of Manhattan's most prosperous households. The son of Samuel Peck, a wealthy clothing wholesaler (who died when Peck was eleven years old), he spent the early years of the Great Depression at Choate, a tony prep school in Wallingford, Connecticut. Despite his family's conversion from Judaism to Episcopalianism, Peck was a social outsider at Choate, which used a strict quota system to limit the number of religious and ethnic minorities on campus. The primary factor separating him from his fellow students was not religion or ethnicity, however. Politically precocious, he cultivated a reputation as an independent thinker who espoused idealistic political doctrines and preferred the company of bookish intellectuals. In the fall of 1933 he enrolled at Harvard, where he honed his skills as a writer while assuming the role of a campus radical. At Harvard he missed few opportunities to challenge the social and political conventions of the Ivy League elite, and he shocked his classmates by showing up at the freshman dance with a black date. This particular act of defiance was directed not only at "the soberly dressed Boston matrons on the sidelines" who "stared at us, whispered, and then stared again" but also at his own mother, who "referred to Negroes as 'coons' " and "frequently remarked that she would never hire one as a servant because 'they are dirty and they steal.' " By the end of his freshman year he was a pariah, and his alienation from his family and the American establishment was complete. Dropping out of school, he immigrated to Paris, where he lived as an avant-garde expatriate for two years. Set against a backdrop of authoritarian ascendancy, his years in Europe deepened his commitment to activism and social justice. In the late 1930s a severe case of wanderlust and a desire to identify with the working class led to a series of jobs as a merchant seaman, an experience that eventually propelled him into the turbulent world of radical unionism. His years at sea also reinforced his commitment to civil rights. "Living and working aboard ships with interracial crews," he later recalled, "strengthened my beliefs in equality."

Returning to the United States in 1938, Peck helped to organize the National Maritime Union, which made good use of his skills as a writer and publicist. During these years he also became a friend and follower of Roger Baldwin, the strong-willed founder of the American Civil Liberties Union. Baldwin encouraged him to become involved in a number of social justice organizations, including the War Resisters League (WRL), and helped him find work with a trade union news syndicate. By the end of the decade, Peck was an avowed pacifist who spent much of his time publicizing the activities of the WRL. Like Rustin, he refused to submit to the draft, and in 1942 he was imprisoned for his defiance. He spent almost three years in the federal prison in Danbury, Connecticut, where he helped to organize a work strike that led to the desegregation of the prison mess hall. After his release in 1945, he rededicated himself to pacifism and militant trade unionism, offering his services to a number of progressive organizations. For a time he devoted most of his energies to the WRL and to editing the *Workers Defense League News Bulletin*, but in late 1946 he became increasingly absorbed with the race issue, especially after discovering and joining CORE. Recent events had convinced him that the struggle for racial equality was an essential precondition for the social transformation of American society, and CORE'S direct-action philosophy provided him with a means of acting upon his convictions. With the zeal of a new recruit, he embraced the idea of the Journey of Reconciliation, which would be his first venture as a CORE volunteer.[7]*

The plan for an interracial bus ride through the Jim Crow South grew out of a series of discussions between Bayard Rustin and George

---

* A section on James Farmer, who helped found CORE but was not involved in the 1947 Journey of Reconciliation, has been omitted—ed.

Houser held during the summer of 1946. Like Rustin, Houser was a northerner with little firsthand experience in the South [and a pacifist]. . . . Convicted of draft evasion, he served a year in federal prison. Following Houser's release in the fall of 1941, Muste hired him to run FOR's Chicago office. During the early days of CORE, he . . . developed [a close] relationship with Rustin, whom he came to admire greatly. Later, as the newly appointed co-secretaries of FOR's Race and Industrial Department and as members of CORE's executive committee, the two young friends were eager to boost CORE's profile by demonstrating the utility of nonviolent direct action.[8]

For Rustin and Houser, the timing of the *Morgan* decision and the ensuing controversy over compliance and enforcement could not have been better. During its first four years, CORE had operated as "a loose federation of local groups which were united mostly by their aim of tackling discrimination by a particular method—nonviolent direct action." Because "this put emphasis almost completely on local issues and organization," Houser recalled many years later, "it was difficult to get a sense of a national movement or to develop a national strategy. One of the results of this really was that it was almost impossible for CORE to raise funds to establish itself as a separate entity." In addition to enhancing CORE's national stature and autonomy, a project like the Journey of Reconciliation promised to provide "an entering wedge for CORE into the South." As Houser explained, "We had no local groups in the South and it wasn't easy to organize them at this point, especially with the two words 'racial equality' in our name. Those were fighting words in the South. But with a definite project around which to rally, we felt there was a possibility of opening up an area seemingly out of reach." Rustin and Houser were confident that the issue of Jim Crow transit—which "touched virtually every black person, was demeaning in its effect and a source of frequent conflict"—represented a perfect target for CORE's first national project. Even if the project failed to desegregate interstate buses, "challenging discrimination in transportation, by striking a raw nerve, would get public attention."[9]

During the summer . . . the idea of a CORE-sponsored freedom ride became a frequent topic of conversation among CORE stalwarts in New York. In July the idea received an unexpected boost from Wilson Head, a courageous black World War II veteran who undertook his own freedom ride from Atlanta to Washington, D.C. Traveling on the Greyhound line and insisting on his right to sit in the front of the bus, he braved angry drivers, enraged passengers, and menacing police officers—one of whom threatened to shoot him during a brief detention in Chapel Hill, North Carolina. But somehow Head managed to make it to Washington without injury or formal arrest, a feat which suggested that testing compliance in the South might not be such a crazy notion after all. By the time CORE's executive committee met in Cleveland in mid-September, Rustin and Houser had developed a full-scale plan for the ride. After a lengthy discussion of the risks and dangers of a southern foray, the committee endorsed the idea and authorized Rustin and Houser to seek approval and funding from FOR. With a little coaxing, the FOR staff soon embraced the plan, although Muste insisted that the ride be a joint project of FOR and CORE.[10]

Over the next few months, FOR's Race and Industrial Department worked out the details, adding an educational component and ultimately limiting the scope of the ride to the Upper South. The revised plan called for "a racially mixed deputation of lecturers" who would speak at various points along the route, giving "some purpose to the trip outside of simple tests and experimentation with techniques." The riders would not only test compliance with the *Morgan* decision but also spread the gospel of nonviolence to at least part of the South. The original plan involved a region-wide journey from Washington, D.C., to New Orleans, Louisiana, but after several of CORE's southern contacts warned that an interracial journey through the Deep South would provoke "wholesale violence," Rustin and Houser reluctantly agreed to restrict the ride to the more moderate Upper South. "The deep South may be touched later," they explained, "depending on what comes out of this first experience." After much debate, they also agreed that all of the riders would be men, acknowledging that "mixing the races and sexes would possibly exacerbate an already volatile situation." This decision was a grave disappointment to several women—including Ella Baker and Paula Murray—who had been actively involved in planning the trip. . . . But their plaintive protests against paternalistic condescension fell on deaf ears. Less controversially, Rustin and Houser also came up with an official name for the project—the Journey of Reconciliation. This redemptive phrase pleased Muste and lent an air of moral authority to the project.[11]

For reasons of safety and to ensure that the compliance tests would be valid, CORE leaders did not seek any advance publicity for the Journey, but within the confines of the movement they quietly spread the word that CORE was about to invade the South. The proposed ride received enthusiastic endorsements from a number of black leaders . . . and from several organizations, including the Fellowship of Southern Churchmen, an interracial group of liberal southern clergymen. The one organization that expressly refused to endorse the ride was, predictably, the NAACP [whose attorneys had been seemingly stymied by the new strategy of "private" segregation].[12]

In mid-November, [Thurgood] Marshall and the NAACP legal brain trust held a two-day strategy meeting in New York to address the challenge of privatized segregation. No firm solution emerged from the meeting, but the attorneys did reach a consensus that CORE'S proposal for an interracial ride through the South was a very bad idea. The last thing the NAACP needed at this point, or so its leaders believed, was a provocative diversion led by a bunch of impractical agitators. A week later Marshall went public with the NAACP's opposition to direct action. Speaking in New Orleans on the topic "The Next Twenty Years toward Freedom for the Negro in America," he criticized "well-meaning radical groups in New York" who were planning to use Gandhian tactics to breach the wall of racial segregation. Predicting a needless catastrophe, he insisted that a "disobedience movement on the part of Negroes and their white allies, if employed in the South, would result in wholesale slaughter with no good achieved." He did not mention FOR or CORE by name, nor did he divulge any details about the impending Journey of Reconciliation, but his words, which were reprinted in the *New York Times*, sent a clear warning to Muste, Rustin, and Houser. Since the Journey would inevitably lead to multiple arrests, everyone involved knew that at some point CORE would require the assistance and cooperation of NAACP-affiliated attorneys, so Marshall's words could not be taken lightly. The leaders of FOR and CORE were in no position to challenge the supremacy of the NAACP, but after some hesitation they realized that Marshall's pointed critique could not go unanswered.[13]

The response, written by Rustin and published in the *Louisiana Weekly* in early January 1947, was a sharp rebuke to Marshall and a rallying cry for the nonviolent movement:

I am sure that Marshall is either ill-informed on the principles and techniques of non-violence or ignorant of the processes of social change. Unjust social laws and patterns do not change because supreme courts deliver just opinions. One need merely observe the continued practices of jim crow in interstate travel six months after the Supreme Court's decision to see the necessity of resistance. Social progress comes from struggle; all freedom demands a price.... I cannot believe that Thurgood Marshall thinks that such a program would lead to wholesale slaughter.... But if anyone at this date in history believes that the "white problem," which is one of privilege, can be settled without some violence, he is mistaken and fails to realize the ends to which man can be driven to hold on to what they consider privileges. This is why Negroes and whites who participate in direct action must pledge themselves to nonviolence in word and deed. For in this way alone can the inevitable violence be reduced to a minimum. The simple truth is this: unless we find non-violent methods which can be used by the rank-and-file who more and more tend to resist, they will more and more resort to violence. . . .[14]

Rustin's provocative and prophetic manifesto failed to soften Marshall's opposition to direct action, but it did help to convince Marshall and NAACP executive director Walter White that CORE was determined to follow through with the Journey of Reconciliation, with or without their cooperation. CORE leaders had already announced that the two-week Journey would begin on April 9, and there was no turning back for activists like Rustin and Houser who believed that the time for resolute action had arrived. For them, all the signs—including Harry Truman's unexpected decision, in December 1946, to create a President's Committee on Civil Rights—suggested that the movement for racial justice had reached a crossroads. It was time to turn ideas into action, to demonstrate the power of nonviolence as Gandhi and others were already doing in India.[15]

With this in mind, Rustin and Houser left New York in mid-January on a scouting expedition through the Upper South states of Virginia, North Carolina, Tennessee, and Kentucky. During three weeks of reconnaissance they followed the route of the coming Journey, scrupulously obeying the laws and customs of Jim Crow transit so as to avoid arrest. At each stop along the route, they met with local civil rights and community leaders who helped to arrange housing, lecture and rally facilities, and possible legal representation for the riders to come. Some dismissed the interracial duo as an odd and misguided pair of outside agitators, but most did what they could to help. In several communities, Rustin and Houser encountered the "other" NAACP: the restless branch leaders and youth council volunteers (and even some black attorneys) who were eager to take the struggle beyond the courtroom. After Rustin returned to New York in late January, Houser traveled alone to Tennessee and Kentucky, where he continued to be impressed with the untapped potential of the black South. In the end the four-state scouting trip produced a briefcase full of commitments from church leaders and state and local NAACP officials, a harvest that pushed Marshall and his colleagues toward a grudging acceptance of the coming Journey's legitimacy. Soon Spot Robinson, Charles Houston, and even Marshall himself were offering "helpful suggestions" and promising to provide CORE with legal backup if and when the riders were arrested. Most national NAACP leaders still considered the Journey a foolhardy venture, but as its start drew near there was a noticeable closing of the ranks, a feeling of solidarity that provided the riders with a reassuring measure of legal and institutional protection. As Houser put it, with the promise of southern support and with the NAACP more or less on board, "we felt our group of participants would not be isolated victims as they challenged the local and state laws."[16]

Even so, the Journey remained a dangerous prospect, and finding sixteen qualified and dependable volunteers who had the time and money to spend two weeks on the road was not easy. The organizers' determination to enlist riders who had already demonstrated a commitment to nonviolent direct action narrowed the field and forced CORE to draw upon its own staff and other seasoned veterans of FOR and CORE campaigns. When it proved impossible to find a full complement of volunteers who could commit themselves to the entire Journey, Rustin and Houser reluctantly allowed the riders to come and go as personal circumstances dictated. In the end, less than half of the riders completed the entire trip.[17]

Despite these complications, the sixteen volunteers who traveled to Washington in early April to undergo two days of training and orientation represented a broad range of nonviolent activists. There were eight whites and eight blacks and an interesting mix of secular and religious backgrounds. In addition to Houser, the white volunteers included Jim Peck; Homer Jack, a Unitarian minister and founding member of CORE who headed the Chicago Council against Racial and Religious Discrimination; Worth Randle, a CORE stalwart and biologist from Cincinnati; Igal Roodenko, a peace activist from upstate New York; Joseph Felmet, a conscientious objector from Asheville, North Carolina, representing the Southern Workers Defense League; and two FOR-affiliated Methodist ministers from North Carolina, Ernest Bromley and Louis Adams. The black volunteers included Rustin; Dennis Banks, a jazz musician from Chicago; Conrad Lynn, a civil rights attorney from New York City; Eugene Stanley, an agronomy student at North Carolina A&T College in Greensboro; William Worthy, a radical journalist affiliated with the New York Council for a Permanent FEPC; and three CORE activists from Cincinnati—law student Andrew Johnson, pacifist lecturer Wallace Nelson, and social worker Nathan Wright.[18]

Most of the volunteers were young men still in their twenties; several were barely out of their teens. Rustin, at age thirty-five, was the oldest. Nearly all, despite their youth, had some experience with direct action, but with the exception of Rustin's impromptu freedom ride in 1942, none of this experience had been gained in the Jim Crow South. No member of the group had ever been involved in a direct-action campaign quite like the Journey of Reconciliation, and only the North Carolinians had spent more than a few weeks in the South.

Faced with so many unknowns and the challenge of taking an untried corps of volunteers into the heart of darkness, Rustin and

Houser fashioned an intensive orientation program. Meeting at FOR'S Washington Fellowship House, nine of the riders participated in a series of seminars that "taught not only the principles but the practices of nonviolence in specific situations that would arise aboard the buses." Using techniques pioneered by FOR peace activists and CORE chapters, the seminars addressed expected problems by staging dramatic role-playing sessions. "What if the bus driver insulted you? What if you were actually assaulted? What if the police threatened you? These and many other questions were resolved through socio-drama in which participants would act the roles of bus drivers, hysterical segregationists, police—and you. Whether the roles had been acted correctly and whether you had done the right thing was then discussed. . . .," Jim Peck recalled. Two days of this regimen left the riders exhausted but better prepared for the challenges to come.[19]

Leaving little to chance, Rustin and Houser also provided each rider with a detailed list of instructions. Later reprinted in a pamphlet entitled "You Don't Have to Ride Jim Crow," the instructions made it clear that the task at hand was not, strictly speaking, civil disobedience but rather establishing "the fact that the word of the U.S. Supreme Court is law":

WHEN TRAVELING BY BUS WITH A TICKET FROM A POINT IN ONE STATE TO A POINT IN ANOTHER STATE:

1. If you are a Negro, sit in a front seat. If you are a white, sit in a rear seat.
2. If the driver asks you to move, tell him calmly and courteously, "as an interstate passenger I have a right to sit anywhere in this bus. This is the law as laid down by the United States Supreme Court."
3. If the driver summons the police and repeats his order in their presence, tell him exactly what you told the driver when he first asked you to move.
4. If the police ask you to "come along" without putting you under arrest, tell him you will not go until you are put under arrest. Police have often used the tactic of frightening a person into getting off the bus without making an arrest, keeping him until the bus has left and then just leaving him standing by the empty roadside. In such a case this person has no redress.
5. If the police put you under arrest, go with them peacefully. At the police station, phone the nearest headquarters of the National Association of the Advancement of Colored People, or one of their lawyers. They will assist you.
6. If you have money with you, you can get out on bail immediately.

It will probably be either $25 or $50. If you don't have bail, antidiscrimination organizations will help raise it for you.

7. If you happen to be arrested, the delay in your journey will only be a few hours. The value or your action in breaking down Jim Crow will be too great to be measured.[20]

Additional instructions assigned specific functions to individuals or subgroups of riders and distinguished between designated testers and observers. "Just which individual sat where on each lap of our trip," Peck recalled, "would be planned at meetings of the group on the eve of departure. A few were to act as observers. They necessarily had to sit in a segregated manner. So did whoever was designated to handle bail in the event of arrest. The roles shifted on each lap of the Journey. It was important that all sixteen not be arrested simultaneously and the trip thus halted." Throughout the training sessions, Rustin and Houser reiterated that Jim Crow could not be vanquished by courage alone; careful organization, tight discipline, and strict adherence to nonviolence were also essential. . . .[21]

When the nine riders gathered at the Greyhound and Trailways station in downtown Washington on the morning of April 9 for the beginning of the Journey, the predominant mood was anxious but upbeat. As the riders boarded the buses, the only members of the press on hand were Ollie Stewart of the *Baltimore Afro-American* and Lem Graves of the *Pittsburgh Courier*, two black journalists who had agreed to accompany the riders during the first week. Joking with the reporters, Rustin, as always, set a jovial tone that helped to relieve the worst tensions for the moment. But there was also a general air of confidence that belied the dangers ahead. Sitting on the bus prior to departure, Peck thought to himself that "it would not be too long until Greyhound and Trailways would 'give up segregation practices' in the South." Years later, following the Freedom Rides of 1961, he would look back on this early and unwarranted optimism with a jaundiced eye, but during the first stage of the Journey his hopes seemed justified.[22]

The ride from Washington to Richmond was uneventful for both groups of riders, and no one challenged their legal right to sit anywhere they pleased. For a few minutes, Rustin even sat in the seat directly behind the Greyhound driver. Most gratifying was the decision by several regular passengers to sit outside the section designated for their race. Everyone, including drivers, seemed to take desegregated transit in stride, confirming a CORE report that claimed the Jim Crow line had broken down in northern Virginia in recent months. "Today any trouble is unlikely until you get south of Richmond," the report concluded. "So many persons have insisted upon their rights and fought their cases successfully, that today courts in the northern

Virginia area are not handing down guilty verdicts in which Jim Crow state laws are violated by interstate passengers." At the end of the first day, the CORE riders celebrated their initial success at a mass meeting held at the Leigh Avenue Baptist Church, and prior to their departure for Petersburg the following morning Wally Nelson delivered a moving speech on nonviolence during a chapel service at all-black Virginia Union College. At the church the enthusiasm for desegregation among local blacks was palpable, suggesting that at least some southern blacks were more militant than the riders had been led to believe. But the mood was decidedly different among the predominantly middle-class students at Virginia Union, who exhibited an attitude of detachment and denial. During a question-and-answer session, it became clear that many of the students were "unwilling to admit that they had suffered discrimination in transportation." As Conrad Lynn, who joined the Journey in Richmond, observed, the students simply "pretended that racial oppression did not exist for them."[23]

The prospects for white compliance and black militancy were less promising on the second leg of the Journey. But even in southern Virginia, where most judges and law enforcement officials had yet to acknowledge the *Morgan* decision, the riders encountered little resistance. During the short stint from Richmond to Petersburg there were no incidents other than a warning from a black passenger who remarked that although black protesters like Nelson and Lynn might get away with sitting in the front of the bus in Virginia, things would get tougher farther South. "Some bus drivers are crazy," he insisted, "and the farther South you go, the crazier they get." As if to prove the point, Rustin had a run-in with a segregationist Greyhound driver the following morning. Ten miles south of Petersburg, the driver ordered the black activist, who was seated next to Peck, to the back of the bus. After Rustin politely but firmly refused to move, the driver vowed to take care of the situation once the bus reached North Carolina. At Oxford the driver called the local police, but after several minutes of interrogation the officer in charge declined to make an arrest. During the wait most of the black passengers seemed sympathetic to Rustin's actions, but a black schoolteacher boarding the bus at Oxford scolded him for needlessly causing a forty-five-minute delay. "Please move. Don't do this," he pleaded. "You'll reach your destination either in front or in back. What difference does it make?" This would not be the last time the CORE riders would hear this kind of accommodationist rhetoric.[24]

While Rustin was dealing with the Greyhound driver's outrage, a more serious incident occurred on the Trailways bus. Before the bus left the Petersburg station, the driver informed Lynn that he could not remain in the front section reserved for whites. Lynn did his best to explain the implications of the *Morgan* decision, but the driver—unaccustomed to dealing with black lawyers—"countered that he was in the employ of the bus company, not the Supreme Court, and that he followed the company rules about segregation." The unflappable New Yorker's refusal to move led to his arrest on a charge of disorderly conduct, but only after the local magistrate talked with the bus company's attorney in Richmond. During a two-hour delay, several of the CORE riders conducted a spirited but largely futile campaign to drum up support among the regular passengers. A white navy man in uniform grumbled that Lynn's behavior merited a response from the Ku Klux Klan, and an incredulous black porter (who reminded Houser of a fawning Uncle Tom character in Richard Wright's *Black Boy*) challenged Lynn's sanity. "What's the matter with him? He's crazy. Where does he think he is?" the porter demanded, adding, "We know how to deal with him. We ought to drag him off." As a menacing crowd gathered around the bus, Lynn feared that he might be beaten up or even killed, especially after the porter screamed: "Let's take the nigger off! We don't want him down here!" But in the end he managed to escape the vigilantism of both races. Released on a $25 bail bond, he soon rejoined his comrades in Raleigh, where a large crowd of black students from St. Augustine's College gathered to hear Nelson and Roodenko hold forth on the promise of nonviolent struggle. Thanks to Lynn's composure, a relieved Nelson told the crowd, the Journey had experienced its first arrest without disrupting the spirit of nonviolence.[25]

New challenges awaited the riders in Durham, where three members of the Trailways group—Rustin, Peck, and Johnson—were arrested on the morning of April 12. While Rustin and Johnson were being hauled off for ignoring the station superintendent's order to move to the black section of the bus, Peck informed the police: "If you arrest them, you'll have to arrest me, too, for I'm going to sit in the rear." The arresting officers promptly obliged him and carted all three off to jail. When Joe Felmet and local NAACP attorney C. Jerry Gates showed up at the jail a half hour later to secure their release, the charges were dropped, but a conversation with the Trailways superintendent revealed that there was more trouble ahead. "We know all about this," the superintendent declared. "Greyhound is letting them ride. But we are not." Even more disturbing was the effort by a number of local black leaders to pressure Gates and the Durham NAACP to shun the riders as unwelcome outside agitators. A rally in support of the Journey drew an expectedly large crowd, and the local branch of the NAACP refused to abandon the riders, but the rift within Durham's black community reminded the riders that white segregationists were not the only obstruction to the movement for racial equality.[26]

The next stop was Chapel Hill, the home of the University of North

Carolina (UNC). Here, for the first time, the CORE riders would depend on the hospitality of white southerners. Their host was Rev. Charles M. Jones, the courageous pastor of a Presbyterian congregation that included UNC president Frank Porter Graham . . . and several other outspoken liberals. A native Tennessean, Jones was a member of the Fellowship of Southern Churchmen, a former member of FOR'S national council, and a leading figure among Chapel Hill's white civil rights advocates. Despite the efforts of Jones and others, life in this small college town remained segregated, but there were signs that the local color line was beginning to fade. Earlier in the year, the black singer Dorothy Maynor had performed before a racially integrated audience on campus, and Jones's church had hosted an interracial union meeting sponsored by the Congress of Industrial Organizations (CIO). These and other breaches of segregationist orthodoxy signaled a rising tolerance in the university community, but they also stoked the fires of reaction among local defenders of Jim Crow. By the time the CORE riders arrived, the town's most militant segregationists were primed and ready for a confrontation that would serve warning that Chapel Hill, despite the influence of the university and its liberal president, was still a white man's country.[27]

The riders' first few hours in Chapel Hill seemed to confirm the town's reputation as an outpost of racial moderation. Jones and several church elders welcomed them at the station, and a Saturday-night meeting with students and faculty at the university went off without a hitch. On Sunday morning most of the riders, including several blacks, attended services at Jones's church and later met with a delegation representing the Fellowship of Southern Churchmen. At this point there was no hint of trouble, and the interracial nature of the gatherings, as Houser later recalled, seemed natural "in the liberal setting of this college town." As the riders boarded a Trailways bus for the next leg, they could only hope that things would continue to go as smoothly in Greensboro, where a Sunday-night mass meeting was scheduled. Since there was no Greyhound run from Chapel Hill to Greensboro, the riders divided into two groups and purchased two blocs of tickets on Trailways buses scheduled to leave three hours apart.[28]

Five of the riders—Johnson, Felmet, Peck, Rustin, and Roodenko—boarded the first bus just after lunch, but they never made it out of the station. As soon as Felmet and Johnson sat down in adjoining seats near the front of the bus, the driver ordered Johnson to the "colored" section in the rear. The two riders explained that they "were traveling together to meet speaking engagements in Greensboro and other points south" and "that they were inter-state passengers . . . 'covered' by the Irene Morgan decision." Unmoved, the driver walked to the nearby police station to arrange for their arrest. While he was gone, Rustin and Roodenko engaged several of the passengers in conversation, creating an "open forum" which revealed that many of the passengers supported Felmet and Johnson's protest. When the driver later passed out waiver cards that the bus company used to absolve itself from liability, one woman balked, declaring, "You don't want me to sign one of those. I am a damn Yankee, and I think this is an outrage." Shaking her hand, Roodenko exclaimed: "Well, there are two damn Yankees on the bus!" By this time, Felmet and Johnson had been carted off to the police station, and Peck had followed them to the station to arrange bail. But the driver soon discovered that he had two more protesters to deal with. Encouraged by the sympathetic reaction among the regular passengers, Rustin and Roodenko moved to the seat vacated by the arrested riders, which prompted a second round of arrests. Having already paid $50 each for Felmet and Johnson's release, Peck called Houser, who was still at Jones's parsonage, to bring down another $100 to get Rustin and Roodenko out of jail.[29]

While the four men waited for Houser and Jones to arrive with the bail money, Peck shuttled back and forth from the police station, checking on his colleagues' bags and trying to keep tabs on the situation at the bus station. By this point the bus had been delayed almost two hours, and it was obvious to everyone at the scene that a group of "outside agitators" had provoked an incident. One bystander, a white cab driver, vowed, "They'll never get a bus out of here tonight," and a few minutes later Peck found himself surrounded by five angry cab drivers as he crossed the street. Snarling "Coming down here to stir up the niggers," one of the drivers punched Peck in the side of the head. When Peck refused to retaliate and simply asked, "What's the matter?" the man gave him "a perplexed look and started to walk away awkwardly." Two men, a black professor from North Carolina A&T College and a local white minister, urged the driver to leave Peck alone, but they were told to mind their own business. Thinking that the two sympathizers were part of the CORE group, the cab drivers rushed toward them menacingly, but after learning that the two men were North Carolinians who just happened to be at the station they let them go. Returning to the police station, Peck warned Jones and Houser that trouble was brewing.[30]

After surveying the situation, Jones concluded that the riders would have to travel to Greensboro by car. Once bond had been arranged for the arrested riders, the CORE group piled into Jones's car and headed to the parsonage for a brief stop before leaving town. Unfortunately, two cabs filled with irate whites sped after them. Peck recalled the harrowing scene: "We succeeded in getting to Reverend Jones' home before them. When we got inside and looked out the window, we saw two of the drivers getting out with big sticks. Others started to pick up rocks by the roadside. Then, two of the drivers, apparently scared, motioned to the others to stop. They drove away. But a few minutes later Reverend Jones, who since the CIO meeting in his church had been marked as a 'nigger lover,' received an anonymous phone call. 'Get the niggers out of town by midnight or we'll burn down your house,' threatened a quivering voice." Determined to get the riders out of Chapel Hill before nightfall, Jones rounded up three university students willing to drive the group to Greensboro and also called the police, who reluctantly agreed to provide an escort to the county line.[31]

As soon as the riders left, Jones took his wife and two children to a friend's house for protection, a precaution that was proved warranted by subsequent events. When Jones returned home Sunday evening accompanied by a friend, Hilton Seals, he found a crowd of angry white protesters in his front yard. The two men tried to ignore the crowd's taunts, but as they walked to the door Seals was struck with a rock. On Monday morning, Jones received a second anonymous call threatening him with death. Later in the day several cab drivers milling around the bus station attacked Martin Walker, a disabled white war veteran and university student, after he was seen "talking to a Negro woman," and a second university student, Ray Sylvester, "was knocked unconscious by a cab driver for 'being too liberal.' " During the next few days Jones received additional death threats by mail, and several anonymous calls threatened his church, prompting an emergency meeting of the congregation. When they learned of the threats, several UNC students volunteered to guard Jones's home and church, but this gesture proved unnecessary, thanks in part to UNC president Frank Graham's forceful consultation with the local police. By the end of the week the wave of intimidation had subsided, even though the controversy surrounding the incident at the bus station continued to simmer.[32]

Speaking to an overflow crowd at the university's Memorial Hall four days after the arrests, Jones defended the Journey of Reconciliation as the work of true Christians who had made "a thorough and exhaustive study of law as related to transportation in order that Christians and others might understand the law and practice it." But several students in the audience criticized the Journey's provocative tactics. "When you consider the general attitudes and practices in the South," one student insisted, "it is stupid to raise a point which can bring only friction, a crusade of going about and raising such questions cannot be merely trying to bring about reconciliation. It has as its end the creation of dissensions not here before. I cannot but damn all connected with bringing a group here merely to stir up dissension." Unmoved, Jones continued to speak out on behalf of CORE and the struggle for racial justice. For most of the Chapel Hill community, the restoration of an uneasy truce between "university liberals" and the local segregationist majority represented an acceptable resolution of the crisis. . . .[33]

In the wake of the Chapel Hill incident, the CORE riders were apprehensive about the remaining ten days of the Journey. But whatever doubts they may have had about the wisdom of continuing the trip disappeared during a rousing mass meeting in Greensboro on Sunday evening. At the Shiloh Baptist Church . . . the congregation's emotional embrace reminded them of why they had come south seeking justice. "The church was crowded to capacity and an atmosphere of excitement prevailed," Peck recalled in 1962. "Word had spread about what had happened to us and why we were late. . . . After the usual invocation, hymn-singing, scripture-reading, and prayer, Rustin, who is a particularly talented speaker, told our story. He interrupted it only to get one or another of us to rise and tell about a specific incident or experience. Then he continued. When he finished, the people in the crowded church came forward to shake the hands and congratulate us. A number of women had tears in their eyes. A few shook my hand more than once."[34]

The mass meeting in Greensboro was the emotional high point of the Journey. For most of the riders, the last ten days on the road represented little more than a long anticlimax. There were, however, a few tense moments—and a few surprises—as the riders wound their way through the mountains of western North Carolina, Tennessee, Kentucky, and Virginia. No two bus drivers—and no two groups of passengers—were quite the same. On the leg from Greensboro to Winston-Salem, a white passenger from South Carolina expressed his disgust that no one had removed Lynn from a front seat. "In my state," he declared, "he would either move or be killed." The following day, during a Greyhound run from Winston-Salem to Statesville, Nelson occupied a front seat without incident. After the riders transferred to a Trailways bus in Statesville, however, the driver ordered him to the rear. The driver relented when Nelson explained that he was an interstate passenger protected by the *Morgan* decision, but this did not satisfy several white passengers, including a soldier who demanded to know why Nelson had not been moved or arrested. "If you want to do something about this," the driver responded, "don't blame this man [Nelson]; kill those bastards up in Washington." Following several stops north of Asheville, the white section of the bus became so crowded that two white women had to stand in the aisle. When they asked why Nelson had not been forced to give up his seat, the driver cited the *Morgan* decision. Although the women later moved to the Jim Crow section in the back, the atmosphere on the bus remained tense. "It was a relief to reach Asheville," Houser recalled many years later.[35]

Asheville was the hometown of Joe Felmet, the young Southern Workers Defense League organizer who had been arrested in Chapel Hill, and several of the riders spent the night at his parents' house. This did not please at least one neighbor, who shouted "How're your nigger friends this morning?" as Felmet and the other riders left for the station. After the riders boarded a Trailways bus headed for Knoxville, Tennessee, a white woman complained to the driver that Dennis Banks, a black musician from Chicago who had just joined the Journey, was sitting in the whites-only section. When Banks, who was sitting next to Peck, politely refused to comply with the driver's order to move, the police were summoned. Twenty minutes of haggling over the law ensued before Banks was finally arrested. The police also arrested Peck, but only after he moved to the Jim Crow section and insisted that he be treated the same as his black traveling companion.

Brought before Judge Sam Cathey, a blind and notoriously hard-edge Asheville politician, the two defendants created a sensation by hiring Curtiss Todd to represent them in court. Neither Cathey nor the local prosecutor had ever heard of the *Morgan* decision, and they had to borrow Todd's copy of the decision during the trial. An NAACP-affiliated attorney from Winston-Salem, Todd was the first black lawyer ever to practice in an Asheville courtroom. Despite this breach of local racial etiquette, Judge Cathey—who reminded the defendants that "We pride ourselves on our race relations here"—made sure that other shibboleths of Jim Crow justice remained in force. "In the courtroom where we were tried," Peck later declared, "I saw the most fantastic extreme of segregation in my experience—Jim Crow bibles. Along the edges of one Bible had been printed in large letters the words 'white.' Along the page edges of the other Bible was the word 'colored.' When a white person swore in he simply raised his right hand while the clerk held the Bible. When a Negro swore in, he had to raise his right hand while holding the colored Bible in his left hand. The white clerk could not touch the colored Bible."[36]

The Jim Crow ethos did not prevent the two defendants from receiving the same sentence—thirty days on the road gang, the maximum under North Carolina law. During a long night in the white section of the city jail, Peck discovered that many of his fellow inmates bore a special animus toward white agitators from the North. "Defending the niggers?" one oversized man bellowed, moving toward the rail-thin activist with his fists clenched. "They should have given you thirty years." Bracing for a blow, Peck blurted out: "I was just traveling with my friend and I happened to believe that men are equal." After an awkward silence, another inmate, playing the role of peacemaker, interjected: "Well, it's too bad that all men can't get along together, but they can't." With this puzzling statement, the mood shifted and the inmates decided to leave Peck alone. Banks had less trouble among the black inmates, some of whom regarded him as a hero. But both riders were relieved when Todd arrived with the required $800 bail bond a few hours later.[37]

While Peck and Banks were detained in Asheville, the rest of the riders went on to Knoxville, where they welcomed three new riders— Homer Jack, Nathan Wright, and Bill Worthy. A seasoned veteran of Chicago direct-action campaigns, Jack could hardly wait to join the Journey, but he found the "taut morale" of his CORE colleagues a bit unnerving. "The whites were beginning to know the terror that many Negroes have to live with all the days of their lives," he noted. "All members of the party were dead tired, not only from the constant tenseness, but also from participating in many meetings and conferences at every stop."[38]

Jack himself soon experienced the emotional highs and lows of direct action in the Jim Crow South. After a full day of interracial meetings in Knoxville, he and Wright tested compliance on the night Greyhound run to Nashville. With Houser serving as the designated observer, they sat in adjoining seats four rows behind the driver. "Slowly heads began to turn around and within five minutes the driver asked Wright to go to the back of the bus," Jack recalled. "Wright answered, 'I prefer to sit here.' I said I and Wright were friends, that we were riding together, that we could legally do so because of the *Morgan* decision. The bus driver pleaded, 'Wouldn't you like to move?' We said we would like to stay where we were. The driver left the bus, apparently to talk to bus officials and police. After much ogling by passengers and bus employees ... the driver finally reappeared and started the bus, without any more words to us." So far so good, Jack thought to himself, but as the bus left the outskirts of Knoxville he started to worry that "the hard part of the Journey was still ahead." Unaccustomed to the isolation of the rural South, he began to conjure up images of impending doom. "Ours was the first night test of the entire Journey," he later noted. "The southern night, to Northerners at least, is full of vigilante justice and the lynch rope from pine trees if not palms. We wondered whether ... the bus company—or one of its more militant employees—would telephone ahead for a road block and vigilantes to greet us in one of the Tennessee mountain towns. Neither of us slept a moment that night. We just watched the road." When nothing of this sort actually happened, Jack felt more than a little foolish, concluding that the South, or at least Tennessee, was less benighted than he had been led to believe. "The reaction of the passengers on the trip was not one of evident anger," he observed, "and certainly not of violence. It was first surprise, then astonishment, and even tittering. On that bus, anyway, there was only apathy, certainly no eager leadership in preserving the ways of the Old South."

In Nashville, Jack and Wright—having arrived "early in the morning, exhausted, relieved, and with a bit of exhilaration of the adventure"—regaled several college classes with tales of nonviolent struggle. But at the end of the day, just before midnight, they resumed their journey of discovery, boarding a train for Louisville. This was "the first train test" attempted by the CORE riders, and no one knew quite what to expect. When a conductor spied Jack and Wright sitting in adjoining reserved seats in a whites-only coach, he collected their tickets without comment. But he soon returned, whispering to Jack: "He's your prisoner, isn't he?" After Jack responded "no," the incredulous conductor ordered Wright to "go back to the Jim Crow coach." Wright refused, citing *Morgan*, which prompted the conductor to mutter "that he never had had to face this situation before and that if we were riding back in Alabama he wouldn't have to face it: the passengers would throw us both out the window." Despite this bluster, the conductor did not follow through with his threat to have them arrested when the train stopped in Bowling Green, and Wright remained in the white coach all the way to Louisville.[39]

A second team of riders traveled from Knoxville to Louisville by Greyhound, and they too escaped arrest. Worthy and Roodenko shared a seat in the front of the bus, and no one commented on the arrangement until they reached the small town of Corbin, a hundred miles north of Knoxville. When the young black journalist refused to move to the back, the driver called the police and "hinted that there would be violence from the crowd if Worthy did not move." However, the driver and the local police relented after one of the white passengers, a woman from Tennessee, defended Worthy's legal right to sit where he pleased. Once again there was hard evidence that at least some white southerners were willing to accept desegregated transit.[40]

Several of the riders, including Jack and Wright, left the Journey in Louisville on April 19, but approximately half participated in the final four days of testing as three small groups of riders converged on Washington. Although most of these concluding bus and train trips were uneventful, there were two arrests in western Virginia—Nelson in Amherst and Banks in Culpepper. In both cases, the drivers and law enforcement officers involved evidenced confusion about the law and some reluctance to follow through with actual arrests, suggesting that Virginia officials were still trying to sort out the implications of *Morgan*. And, despite the arrests, the behavior of several bystanders indicated that race relations in Virginia were changing. In Culpepper, one courageous black woman who sold bus tickets at a local concession stand boarded the bus and offered to help Banks in any way she could, and two local whites spoke out on Banks's behalf. "If I had been you I would have fought them before letting them take me off the bus," one of them told Banks as the young musician calmly went off to jail.[41]

For the riders, the return to Washington on April 23 brought a sense of relief—and a measure of pride in their perseverance. But, to their dismay, there was no public event to mark the conclusion of their remarkable collective experience. "At the end of our Journey," Peck recalled in 1962, "there were no reporters flocking around us to ask whether it had been worth it or whether we would do it again—as they did after the Freedom Ride fourteen years later. If there had been, most of would have answered yes." The Journey's official balance sheet, as reported by CORE, listed twenty-six tests of compliance, twelve arrests, and only one act of violent resistance. But the project's accomplishments drew little attention from the mainstream press in the spring of 1947. Even among white reporters interested in racial matters, the Journey could not compete with the unfolding drama of Jackie Robinson's first few weeks in a Brooklyn Dodger uniform.[42]

In the black press the Journey fared much better, especially in the columns of the two black reporters who accompanied the riders during the first week of the trip. Ollie Stewart of the *Baltimore Afro-American*, who witnessed the confrontation in Chapel Hill and the mass meeting in Greensboro, hailed the Journey as a watershed event. He wrote in late April:

> For my part, I am glad to have had even a small part of the project—even that of an observer. History was definitely made. White and colored persons, when the whole thing was explained to them as they sat in their seats on several occasions, will never forget what they heard (or saw). The white couple who went to the very back seat and sat between colored passengers, the white marine who slept while a colored woman sat beside him, the white Southern girl who, when her mother wouldn't take a seat in the rear, exclaimed "I do not care, I'm tired"—all these people now have an awareness of the problem. The Journey of Reconciliation, with whites and colored traveling and sleeping and eating together, to my way of thinking, made the solution of segregation seem far more simple than it ever had before. I heard one man refer to the group as pioneers. I think he had something there. They wrote a new page in the history of America.[43]

In the weeks and months following the Journey, several riders published reports on their experiences. Rustin and Houser—in CORE'S official report, *We Challenged Jim Crow*—offered both a day-by-day narrative and general commentary on what the Journey had revealed. "The one word which most universally describes the attitude of police, of passengers, and of the Negro and white bus riders is 'confusion,' " they concluded. "Persons taking part in the psychological struggle in the buses and trains either did not know of the *Morgan* decision or, if they did, possessed no clear understanding of it." And yet there were clear indications that the confusion could be alleviated. "Much was gained when someone in our group took the lead in discussion with bus drivers or train conductors and when police appeared," they reported, adding: "As the trip progressed it became evident that the police and the bus drivers were learning about the Irene Morgan decision as word of the 'test cases' was passed from city to city and from driver to driver." To Rustin and Houser, the Journey demonstrated "the need for incidents as 'teaching techniques.' " "It is our belief that without direct action on the part of groups and individuals, the Jim Crow pattern in the South cannot be broken," they insisted. "We are equally certain that such action must be nonviolent." Homer Jack, writing in the Unitarian magazine *Common Ground*, offered a similar assessment. "What, finally, did the Journey of Reconciliation accomplish?" he asked. He answered: "It showed progressive Americans that the *Morgan* decision must be implemented by constant 'testing'— in the spirit of goodwill—and by subsequent law enforcement. The Journey helped implement the decision at least by spreading knowledge of it to bus drivers and some law-enforcement officers (both policemen and judges) in the upper South. The Journey also showed whites and Negroes living in that area that the *Morgan* decision could be enforced without disastrous results, if the proper psychological and legal techniques were used. The Journey gave these techniques—and accompanying inspiration—to thousands of whites and Negroes in the South."[44]*

. . . . [A]s the decade drew to a close it was all too obvious that the Journey of Reconciliation's primary objective remained unfulfilled. While the first freedom ride had demonstrated the viability of nonviolent direct action in the upper South, it had not precipitated wholesale desegregation or even protest on a mass scale. With few exceptions, company rules and social inertia still kept the races apart on interstate buses and trains; and no one, other than a few die-hard optimists, expected the situation to change anytime soon. As it had done so many times in the past, the shape-shifting monster known as Jim Crow had adapted to changing legal and political realities without sacrificing the

---

* A section on the trials of four of the riders in Chapel Hill has been omitted—ed.

cold heart of racial discrimination. Irene Morgan, like so many brave souls before her, would have to wait a little longer for the year of jubilee.[45]

NOTES

1 . . . . [A] number of monographs discuss the activities of individual activists and specific [Civil Rights] organizations. See especially August Meier and Elliott Rudwick, *CORE: A Study in the Civil Rights Movement* (Urbana, Ill. 1975), 3–40; Jervis Anderson, *Bayard Rustin: Troubles I've Seen* (New York, 1997), 3–149; Daniel Levine, *Bayard Rustin and the Civil Rights Movement* (New Brunswick, 2000); Jervis Anderson, *A. Philip Randolph: A Biographical Portrait* (New York:, 1973); Paula E. Pfeffer, *A. Phillip Randolph: Pioneer of the Civil Rights Movement* (Baton Rouge, 1990); Jo Ann O. Robinson, *Abraham Went Out: A Biography of A. J. Muste* (Philadelphia, 1981), 109–37. . . .; John Egerton, *Speak Now Against the Day: The Generations before the Civil Rights Movement in the South* (New York, 1994).

2 Robinson, *Abraham Went Out*, 3–118; Meier and Rudwick, *CORE*, 4–34; Anderson, *Bayard Rustin*, 61–77, 81–110; James Farmer, *Lay Bare the Heart: An Autobiography of the Civil Rights Movement* (New York, 1989, 70–161. . . .

3 Anderson, *Bayard Rustin*, 114–24, 183–96, 224–35; Bayard Rustin, *Down the Line: The Collected Writings of Bayard Rustin* (Chicago, 1971), ix–61 . . .; James Peck, *Freedom Ride* (New York, 1962); Farmer, *Lay Bare the Heart*, 2–32, 101–16, 165–66, 195–221; Meier and Rudwick, *CORE*, 4–19, 131–417.

4 Anderson, *Bayard Rustin*, 6–95; Levine, *Rustin and the Civil Rights Movement*, 7–29; Charles Moritz, ed., *Current Biography Yearbook, 1967*, (New York, 1967), 360; Taylor Branch, *Parting the Waters: America in the King Years, 1954–1963* (New York, 1988), 168–71; Adam Fairclough, *To Redeem the Soul of America: The Southern Christian Leadership Conference and Martin Luther King, Jr.* (Athens, Ga., 1987), 23–24; Robinson, *Abraham Went Out*, 111; Anderson, *A. Philip Randolph*, 249–74, 275 (first quote), 280–81, 378–80; Pfeffer, *A. Phillip Randolph*, 51–90; . . . Bayard Rustin, "The Negro and Non-Violence," *Fellowship* 8 (October 1942): 166–67 (second quote); Rustin, *Down the Line*, ix–xv, 11. . . .

5 Rustin, *Down the Line*, 6–7; Levine, *Rustin and the Civil Rights Movement*, 32–33. . . .

6 Anderson, *Bayard Rustin*, 96–110, quote on 111; Levine, *Rustin and the Civil Rights Movement*, 27–28, 34–51; Moritz, *Current Biography Yearbook, 1967*, 360–61; Rustin, *Down the Line*, ix–x, 5–52; Branch, *Parting the Waters*, 171–72; Fairclough, *To Redeem the Soul of America*, 24; Robinson, *Abraham Went Out*, 111–17; Viorst, *Fire in the Streets*, 208–10; Pfeffer, *A. Philip Randolph*, 62, 142, 150–68; Meier and Rudwick, *CORE*, 12–20, 34–50, 57, 64.

7 *New York Times*, July 13, 1993 (obituary); James Peck, *Underdogs vs. Upperdogs* (Canterbury, N.J., 1969); Peck, *Freedom Ride*, 15–38, quotes on 39; Meier and Rudwick, *CORE*, 35; James Peck, interview by James Mosby Jr., February 19, 1970, Ralph Bunche Oral History Collection, Moorland-Spingarn Research Center, Howard University, Washington, D.C.; Nancy L. Roberts, *American Peace Writers, Editors, and Periodicals: A Dictionary* (Westport, Conn., 1991), 221–22.

8 Houser interview; George M. Houser, "A Personal Retrospective on the 1947 Journey of Reconciliation," paper given at Bluffton College, September 1, 1992, typescript, box 1, Congress of Racial Equality Collection [here-

after cited as CORE Collection], Swarthmore College Peace Collection, Swarthmore College, Swarthmore, Pennsylvania; George M. Houser, " 'Thy Brother's Blood': Reminiscences of World War II," *Christian Century*, August 16, 1995, 774; Meier and Rudwick, *CORE*, 5–6, 16–21, 29, 34.

9 Houser, "A Personal Retrospective," 3–4.

10 On Wilson Head's freedom ride, see John A. Salmond, *"My Mind Set on Freedom": A History of the Civil Rights Movement, 1954–1968*, (Chicago, 1997), 3–4, 87, 149; Houser interview; Houser, "A Personal Retrospective," 2–6; Anderson, *Bayard Rustin*, 114–16;. . . .

11 Houser, "A Personal Retrospective," 5–6 (quotes); George M. Houser and Bayard Rustin, "Memorandum Number 2: BLS and Train Travel in the South," box 20, Fellowship of Reconciliation Papers, Swarthmore College (hereafter FOR Papers); Peck, *Freedom Ride*, 16; Meier and Rudwick, *CORE*, 34. . . .

12 Robert L. Carter to Daniel E. Byrd, June 12, 1946, George Houser to Marian Perry, October 9, 1946, W. A. C. Hughes to Thurgood Marshall, July 8, 1946, Robert L. Carter, Memos to Walter White, July 26, September 26, 1946, all in box II-B 190, Papers of the NAACP, Library of Congress (hereafter NAACP Papers); *Baltimore Afro-American*, June 26, July 6 and 27, November 2, 1946; *Los Angeles Tribune*, September 21, 1946; *Kansas City Plaindealer*, September 20, 1946; *Chicago Defender*, August 17, November 30, 1946;. . . . Houser, "A Personal Retrospective," 6–8; Catherine Barnes A., *Journey from Jim Crow: The Desegregation of Southern Transit* (New York, 1983), 52–53, 62–63; Mark V. Tushnet, *Making Civil Rights Law: Thurgood Marshall and the Supreme Court, 1935–1961* (New York, 1994), 74–76; Peck, *Freedom Ride*, 17; Meier and Rudwick, *CORE*, 34–35; Anderson, *Bayard Rustin*, 114–15. . . .

13 Thurgood Marshall to Dear Sir [members of NAACP Legal Committee], November 6, 1946, box 11-H 190, NAACP Papers; *New York Times*, November 23, 1946 (quote); Anderson, *Bayard Rustin*, 114–15.

14 Bayard Rustin, "Our Guest Column: Beyond the Courts," *Louisiana Weekly*, January 4, 1947; Anderson, *Bayard Rustin*, 115–16.

15 On Truman and the President's Committee on Civil Rights, see John Hope Franklin, "A Half-Century of Presidential Race Initiatives: Some Reflections," *Journal of Supreme Court History* 24 (1999): 227–30; William C. Berman, *The Politics of Civil Rights in the Truman Administration* (Columbus, Oh., 1970). . . .

16 Peck, *Freedom Ride*, 17; Houser, "A Personal Ketrospective," 6–7 (quote). . . .

17 Houser, "A Personal Retrospective," 7–8; Rustin and Houser, "Memorandum Number 2."

18 Rustin, *Down the Line*, 13–14; Houser, "A Personal Retrospective," 7–8; Meier and Rudwick, *CORE, 35*; Anderson, *Bayard Rustin*, 116.

19 Peck, *Freedom Ride*, 15–16 (quotes); Houser, "A Personal Retrospective," 8; Anderson, *Bayard Rustin*, 116; Meier and Rudwick, *CORE*, 35–36.

20 Bayard Rustin and George Houser, "You Don't Have to Ride Jim Crow" (Washington, D.C., 1947). Copy in reel 25, CORE Papers, microfilm edition (Washington, D.C.:)

21 Peck, *Freedom Ride*, 16.

22 Ibid., 18 (quote); "Log-Journey of Reconciliation," April 9–23, 1947, typescript, box 51, Bayard Rustin Files, FOR Papers. . . .

23 "Log—Journey of Reconciliation," 1–2; Rustin and Houser, "You Don't Have to Ride Jim Crow," 1 (quote); Rustin, *Down the Line*, 14; Houser, "A Personal Retrospective," 9–10; Peck, *Freedom Ride*, 18; Anderson, *Bayard Rustin*, 117; Conrad Lynn, *There Is a Fountain* (Westport, Conn, 1979), 109 (quote).

24 "Log—Journey of Reconciliation," 2; Rustin and Houser, "You Don't Have to Ride Jim Crow," 1; Houser, "A Personal Retrospective," 10 (quote); Rustin, *Down the Line*, 14–15, 16 (quote).

25 Rustin, *Down the Line*, 15 (first and second quotes); "Log—Journey of Reconciliation," 2–4; Houser, "A Personal Retrospective," 10–11; Anderson, *Bayard Rustin*, 117; Lynn, *There Is a Fountain*, 109–10, 111 (third quote).

26 Rustin, *Down the Line*, 16–17 (quotes); "Log-Journey of Reconciliation," 5–6; Peck, *Freedom Ride*, 18–20; Houser, "A Personal Retrospective," 11–12.

27 "Log—Journey of Reconciliation," 6–7; Houser, "A Personal Retrospective," 12–14; Houser interview; Peck, *Freedom Ride*, 20–21; Anderson, *Bayard Rustin*, 118; Egerton, *Speak Now*, 422–23, 556–59. The "George Houser Scrapbook–Journey of Reconciliation 1947" (FOR Papers) contains numerous clippings on the Chapel Hill incident. . . . On Frank Porter Graham, see Warren Ashby, *Frank Porter Graham: A Southern Liberal* (Winston-Salem, N.C., 1980).

28 Houser, "A Personal Retrospective," 12 (quote); Peck, *Freedom Ride*, 20–21; *Pittsburgh Courier*, April 19, 1947.

29 "Log—Journey of Reconciliation," 6 (quotes), 7; Houser interview; Peck, *Freedom Ride*, 21–22; Rustin, *Down the Line*, 17; Anderson, *Bayard Rustin*, 18; *New York Times*, April 14, 1947.

30 Rustin, *Down the Line*, 17 (first quote); Peck, *Freedom Ride*, 21 (second and third quotes); Houser interview; "Log–Journey of Reconciliation," 7; *Pittsburgh Courier*, April 19, 1947. The North Carolina A & T professor was Eugene Stanley.

31 Peck, *Freedom Ride*, 22 (quotes), 23; "Log—Journey of Reconciliation," 7; Rustin, *Down the Line*, 17; *Pittsburgh Courier;* April 19, 1947. . . .

32 Peck, *Freedom Ride*, 23; *New York Times*, April 14, 1947; *Greensboro Daily News*, April 17, 1947 (first quote); *Chicago Defender;* May 3, 1947 (second quote).

33 *Greensboro Daily News*, April 18, 1947 (quotes); *Carolina Times*, April 26, 1947. . . . Conservative editors and reporters in North Carolina often printed diatribes against Jones. See, e.g., the editorial in the *Charlotte Textile Times*, April 15, 1947 (typescript copy in "George Houser Scrapbook-Journey of Reconciliation 1947"), ... See Ashby, *Frank Porter Graham*, 305–9; "Deplore Secrecy in the Jones Case," *Christian Century*, March 4, 1953, 245; "Presbyterian U.S. Commission Fires Chapel Hill Pastor," *Christian Century*, March 18, 1953, 319–20; and "Pastor vs. Presbytery," *Time*, February 23, 1953, 53.

34 Peck, *Freedom Ride*, 23.

35 Rustin, *Down the Line*, 18 (first and second quotes); "Log—Journey of Reconciliation," 8; Houser, "A Personal Retrospective," 14, 15 (third quotes).

36 Peck, *Freedom Ride*, 24–26 (quotes); Rustin, *Down the Line*, 18; Houser, "A Personal Retrospective," 16; *Asheville Citizen*, April 19, 1947; *Pittsburgh Courier*, April 26, 1947; *Baltimore Afro-American*, April 26, 1947; James Peck, "Not So Deep Are the Roots," *Crisis*, September 1947, 274. On Felmet, see the Joe Felmet Papers, Southern Historical Collection, University of North Carolina, Chapel Hill; for the FBI files on Felmet see the Journey of Reconciliation folder, box 20, FOR Papers.

37 Peck, *Freedom Ride*, 26 (quotes); Rustin, *Down the Line*, 18; Curtiss Todd to Thurgood Marshall, April 19, 1947, Robert L. Carter to Curtiss Todd, April 23, 1947, box 11-B 184, NAACP Papers.

38 Homer A. Jack, "Journey of Reconciliation," *Common Ground*, Autumn 1947,

22, 23 (quote); Houser, "A Personal Retrospective," 14–15; Houser inter-view, 66. Jack, "Journey of Reconciliation," 23–24 (quotes); Rustin, *Down the Line*, 19; Houser, "A Personal Retrospective," 15–16.

39 Jack, "Journey of Reconciliation," 23–24; Rustin, *Down the Line*, 19; Houser, "A Personal Retrospective," 15–16.

40 Rustin, *Down the Line*, 19; Houser, "A Personal Retrospective," 15–16.

41 Jack, "Journey of Reconciliation," 24; Rustin, *Down the Line*, 19–21; Houser, "A Personal Retrospective," 16–17; Houser interview; Peck, "Not So Deep Are the Roots," 273, 274 (quote); *Lynchburg News*, April 23–24, 2 8, 1947; *Lynchburg Advance*, April 29, 1947. . . .

42 Peck, *Freedom Ride*, 27 (quote); "Log—Journey of Reconciliation," 11; Rustin, *Down the Line*, 14. For a sampling of the press reaction to the Journey of Reconciliation, see "George Houser Scrapbook-Journey of Reconciliation 1947." . . . .

43 *Baltimore Afro-American*, April 26, 1947.

44 Rustin, *Down the Line*, 22–25; Jack, "Journey of Reconciliation," 26.

45 Houser, "A Personal Retrospective," 17–21; Peck, *Freedom Ride*, 27; Bayard Rustin, "From Freedom Ride to Ballot Box: The Changing Strategies of Black Struggle," typescript of lecture delivered as part of the William Radner Lecture Series, Columbia University, October 9–11, 1973, 31, reel 18, Bayard Rustin Papers; Anderson, *Bayard Rustin*, 123; Meier and Rudwick, *CORE*, 38–39; Barnes, *Journey from Jim Crow*, 60–65; Levine, *Rustin and the Civil Rights Movement*, 64–67.

12

BOMBINGHAM

Glenn T. Eskew

Birmingham, Alabama, became a famous—or infamous—site of Civil Rights activism during the campaign for desegregation headed by Martin Luther King, Jr., in 1963. In this selection, taken from his study of Birmingham in the era of Civil Rights, Glenn T. Eskew shows that the roots of the 1963 movement went back to the generation of the 1940s.

Although in the 1930s, Birmingham, like much of the South, experienced a surge of radical challenges to the status quo, after World War II that opposition became largely quiescent. Birmingham's small black middle class "articulated a class consciousness comparable to that of the city's white elite"; while they sometimes pressed the white establishment for improvements in black neighborhoods, their work for change was confined to improvements within the southern doctrine of "separate but equal." The local branch of the National Association for the Advancement of Colored People, for example, was largely moribund, and economically successful African Americans were focused on maximizing their opportunities within the confines of white supremacy.

In the late 1940s, however, members of this middle class were thwarted when they attempted to buy homes in areas on the edge of white neighborhoods. Even though they tried to follow the rules of segregated zoning, their attempts were met, literally, with dynamite, and their defenses of their rights as property owners were dismissed or ignored by the white elite. While at first black citizens simply wanted decent treatment in a segregated society, white violence led them to turn against segregation itself, laying a foundation for the later movements of the 1960s.

* * *

The dynamite blast that shattered the house of Sam Matthews on August 18, 1947, marked the first in a series of racially motivated bombings brought on by the postwar transformation of Birmingham, Alabama. Although racial attacks occurred in other southern cities, the frequency and number—some fifty dynamitings between 1947 and

1965—made Birmingham an exception and gave rise to the sobriquet "Bombingham." At first, the victims of the bombings were African Americans who had responded to a postwar shortage of adequate black housing by moving onto the fringes of white neighborhoods. In time, civil rights integrationists became the targets of the attacks. White vigilantes saw their acts of terrorism as a defense of white supremacy. African Americans responded to the dynamitings by defending black property rights. The traditional Negro leadership class had sought a solution within the confines Jim Crow, but the failure of white political leaders to address the housing shortage drove black home owners to challenge the color line through a legal battle over Birmingham's unconstitutional racial zoning ordinance. An analysis of residential bombings in postwar Birmingham reveals the evolution of black protest from a request for separate but equal services to a demand for an end to segregation.[1]

Two decades of depression and world war had given way to a postwar boom that allowed residents to focus on domestic needs; yet for families wanting to leave congested neighborhoods, the shortage of houses and land for expansion in "Negro" areas created a desperate situation. Birmingham enforced illegal zoning laws that restricted black access to housing. The adoption of a general zoning code in 1915 and its revision into a comprehensive zoning ordinance in 1926 initiated a process of prohibiting African Americans from living in certain areas of Birmingham, a spatial manifestation of white supremacy. Despite the U.S. Supreme Court's 1917 decision against residential segregation, the author of the Birmingham ordinance confidently explained in 1933 that the zoning had been "quite acceptable to both races since adoption." In the postwar period, however, an acute lack of housing altered the black middle class's accommodation to the zoning arrangement in Birmingham. A group of black property owners who had been denied access to their new houses or land because of the racial zoning ordinance appealed to the NAACP for assistance in early 1946. The black attorney for the local NAACP branch, Arthur Shores, took on the fight.[2]

The highly contested area of North Smithfield in the Graymont subdivision of Birmingham became a battleground over the city's zoning ordinance. The lower-status white section of North Smithfield—an older residential neighborhood near Legion Field approximately five blocks square—was surrounded on three sides by the black section anchored around the Smithfield Court Housing Project for Negroes. The case of Alice P. Allen illustrated the transition of North Smithfield's white area to black. Mrs. Allen was an employee at Colored Methodist Episcopal (CME) Church-affiliated Miles College. In 1946 she had bought a house on Eleventh Avenue with the understanding that the tract was properly zoned "Negro." The realtor had listed the house in the newspaper for sale to white people but after finding no takers sold it to Mrs. Allen. White neighbors pressured her not to move in, and vigilantes broke out the windows. The city refused to allow her to occupy the house, so she rented it to white people and hired Arthur Shores to file suit against Birmingham's zoning law. Rather than defend the ordinance at that time, the city rezoned the lot in question and allowed her to move into the house. Prospective black neighbors up the street were less fortunate.[3]

Forty-three-year-old Sam Matthews . . . in 1946 bought a lot for a new house on the outskirts of North Smithfield . . . from a white realtor, William R. Coleman. In anticipation of the land being rezoned "Negro," Coleman had purchased nearly fifty lots for resale to black home builders. He had checked with the city commission, city engine and zoning commission to confirm his understanding that the land would be rezoned. He then sold the property to Matthews and several others. Before the commission acted, however, members of the Graymont College Hill Civic Association protested the rezoning. White people living in the area feared not only a perceived decline in property values but also the possible integration of school districts if black people moved into neighborhood. Coleman attended a meeting of the neighborhood group in the McCoy Memorial Church where angry white members confronted the developer. J. E. Monteith sat in the audience that night and later accosted the real estate agent. Monteith asked Coleman if he intended to sell any other lots to African Americans. When Coleman said yes, Monteith responded: "We ain't going to stand for that at all. . . . You sold that lot down there to that negro knowing it was zoned for white people." As Coleman turned to leave, Monteith seethed: "You'd better get going now. If you don't we are going to wait on you." Coleman swore out a "breach of the peace" warrant against Monteith.[4]

Believing the land properly zoned "Negro," Matthews applied for and received a building permit from H. E. Hagood, the city building inspector, after which he constructed a six-room frame house at 120 Eleventh Court North. Once it was completed, Matthews returned to Hagood seeking an occupancy permit. When the inspector denied the request, Matthews contacted Shores, who filed a suit against Birmingham's zoning law. Members of the black community contributed to the legal costs, with churches taking up money to finance the case. On July 31, 1947, Judge Clarence Mullins of the U.S. district court ruled the ordinance unconstitutional. Night riders painted a skull-and-crossbones threat on the house to warn Matthews not to move in. Then on August 18 around 10:45 P.M. vigilantes detonated six sticks of dynamite in the living room of the vacant house, destroying the structure. By this time Matthews had tried to rent or sell the house to white people but had found no takers because of its close proximity to other black-owned houses. With the blast demolishing his uninsured $3,700 investment, Matthews wanted to drop the "whole thing and hoped that he would never have to go into court."[5]

Police did not bother to investigate the bombing until after Shores and Matthews had filed a report of the crime the next morning. Detectives delayed taking statements for several days. The all-around resistance reflected the police department's support for the white-sanctioned vigilante violence. One suspect, J. E. Monteith, worked in the plant department of the Southern Bell Company and lived a block and a half from Matthews's house. He told officers that the explosion woke him up but that he rolled over and returned to sleep. A longtime resident of his community, Monteith explained that "he was not in favor of solving the case." The court dropped the "breach of the peace" charge against him. Likewise, detectives closed the Matthews case after their investigation "failed to reveal sufficient evidence to make an arrest." For three decades similar words appeared at the bottom of Birmingham Police Department case reports on unsolved bombings in the city.[6]

Angela Y. Davis was a young black girl growing up on "the hill" when the dynamitings began. In 1948 her parents had moved out of the Smithfield Court Housing Project for Negroes and into a large white gabled house on the "colored" side of Center Street. She remembered the Monteiths as "an elderly couple across the street" on the "white" side who "sat on their porch all the time, their eyes heavy with belligerence." As Angela grew older and as more black children moved to "the hill," she joined them in summertime games of hide-and-seek that quickly developed into challenges "to go up on the Montees' porch" and ring the doorbell. "The old woman or old man came out, trying to figure out what was going on. When they finally caught on to our game, even though they could seldom find us, they stood on the porch screaming, 'You little niggers better leave us alone!' "[7]

In addition to William R. Coleman and the white Coleman-Kendrick Real Estate Company, the black Hollins and Shores Real Estate Company, headed by Arthur Shores, aggressively bought houses formerly owned by white people for resale to black people in the North Smithfield area. Shores's firm negotiated the sale of the Eleventh Avenue, West, house of B. S. Brown, a white man, to African Americans Johnnie and Emily Madison in October 1948. Brown assured the anxious couple that "there would no objection to Negroes in this neighborhood." Madison closed the deal February 1, 1949, and began repairing and redecorating the house. . . . Visiting the house after dark one night, the Madisons discovered a pile of old window shades burning in the backyard. Emily Madison said: "Johnnie, I don't like this. Why would anyone set this on fire?" The next week, on March 24, 1949, Johnnie Madison worked on the house until 10:30 P.M. Two hours later vigilantes placed dynamite under the floor of a rear bedroom on the corner of the house and lit the fuse. The explosion—one of three that night—demolished the structure. Similar blasts destroyed two other houses just up the street, both recently purchased by Bishop S. L. Green of the African Methodist Episcopal (AME) Church.[8]

. . . . The three blasts in March 1949 occurred just over the hill from the explosion that destroyed the Matthews house in July 1947. The Graymont-College Hills Civic Association demanded that the city commission enforce the zoning laws and stop the transition of the neighborhood from white to black. Association members Monteith, John J. Gould, and Sam L. Chesnut were questioned by detectives but revealed nothing to officers. All had been contacted by Coleman, Shores, and other realtors about selling their houses. An employee of the post office, Gould had lived in his house for forty-five years and "had never had any trouble with any Negroes" until the last year, when they had been moving into his immediate neighborhood. Chesnut felt the same way. Having lived in North Smithfield since 1908, he refused to leave, turning down one outlandish offer for his house by asking the inquiring man whom he intended to sell to. To the realtor's "it doesn't matter, does it?" Chesnut had replied, "It does to me."[9]

On the night of the bombing, Chesnut said he was called back to work as paymaster at the Alabama Power Company. From 11:00 P.M. to 1:00 A.M.—the hours of vigilante action, with the bombings at 12:30 A.M.—he reportedly attended to his business and then checked out. Although company watchmen confirmed that Chesnut had been at the plant, officials could not verify what he was doing. Neither could Chesnut recall a suspicious incident that, according to his white neighbor C. E. Henderson, had happened the day before. Henderson said he had received a call from an unidentified man who explained that he "was familiar with the situation that the neighborhood was having with the negroes." Several minutes later the caller drove up the alley in a black car and stopped where Henderson and Chesnut were talking in the back yard. Again the man refused to identify himself, but he asked Henderson to get in the car and show him houses bought by Negroes in areas zoned "white." Henderson complied, and Chesnut denied ever seeing the man or the car. The afternoon before the bombings Henderson received another call notifying him that someone was "going to burn some wood on the hill that night." Apparently the vigilantes notified members of the white community in advance their actions.[10]

Two black women renting a house from Shores on Center Street called a "good deal of activity" that night as cars circled the hill after dark. The women reported that between eleven and midnight two black automobiles containing white men parked bumper to bumper across the street from the house. Then mysteriously they drove away. Moments after the explosions, a black cab driver turned the corner and startled another parked car that took off at great speed. The cabbie gave police a car tag number, but nothing came of the report, apparently because the police were assisting the vigilantes. The Reverend O. C. Bickerstaff of the AME Church witnessed a police car with its parking lights on, poised as if guarding the intersection of Tenth Avenue and Center Street minutes after and just blocks from the explosions. Bickerstaff testified that as he drove past the patrol car, "another police car came by the first and blinked its lights." Rumors circulated about police involvement in the bombings.[11]

As detectives ended their unsuccessful investigation and white ministers collected donations from middle-class churches to rebuild the bombed houses, white vigilantes threatened black people wanting to move into the disputed area of North Smithfield. On May 21, 1949, William German, a black insurance salesman from Florida, was warned not to occupy the house he had bought at 1100 Center Street North. Robert E. Chambliss, a city employee who identified himself as a Klansman, stopped German, pointed to the shattered remains of Bishop Green's property, and said: "If you move in, that is liable to happen to you." Willie German listened to Chambliss and vacated the premises. Mayor W. Cooper Green suspended Chambliss—who worked in the city's auto repair shop—for ten days because of his comments. Robert E. "Dynamite Bob" Chambliss would later be convicted for the bombing of the Sixteenth Street Baptist Church that killed four black girls in September 1963.[12]

To limit black access to housing and thus halt the bombings, the city commissioners proposed the creation of a buffer zone that would separate the black and white neighborhoods of Smithfield. Arthur Shores demanded an opportunity to speak against the city commission's proposal, and at the May 1949 hearing he denounced the plan by detailing the unconstitutionality of the buffer idea.

On July 1, 1949, the Reverend Milton Curry Jr. put his furniture in the house at 1100 Center Street North. Birmingham building inspector H. E. Hagood refused to issue an occupancy permit, but Shores advised Curry to stand firm, for "he was within his rights in moving into the house and was willing and determined to remain there." Nevertheless, Curry rented the house to another black man, B. W. Henderson.[13] Again vigilantes struck. On July 28, 1949, Henderson carried to Shores's legal office a bomb that had failed to go off. He found the three sticks of dynamite wrapped in a newspaper near the chimney of his house. Having no faith in the local police force, Shores immediately contacted the Federal Bureau of Investigation (FBI). U.S. district attorney John D. Hill had sent the FBI to Birmingham on May 31, 1949, to investigate the unsolved bombings. Reflecting the federal agency's defense of the racial status quo, a duplicitous FBI agent informed Shores that "this evidence did not fit in with their theory and for him to turn it over to the municipal police. . . ."[14]

As the only practicing black attorney in Alabama for nearly twenty years, Shores had anticipated the lack of cooperation from the local police, but he had expected more from the federal government. A native of Birmingham, Arthur Davis Shores was born on September 25, 1904. He attended Parker High School and worked his way through Talladega College, graduating in 1927. While employed as principal at Dunbar High School in Bessemer, he completed through correspondence the LL.B. degree from the University of Kansas. Shores opened his law practice in 1937 and won his first of many NAACP-supported cases in July 1939, when he prosecuted a white Birmingham officer charged with police brutality against a black man. . . . When the Jefferson County Board of Registrars refused to enfranchise African Americans seeking the vote in a drive that summer, Shores filed suit against the board and appealed unsuccessfully when he lost in the lower courts. In 1941 he defended a black man demoted by the railroad because of his race. Shores and Charles Hamilton Houston of the NAACP Legal Defense and Educational Fund, Inc., argued the case, *Steele v. Louisville and Nashville Railroad Company et al.*, before the U.S. Supreme Court in 1944. The court's ruling prohibited discrimination against nonunion workers, in this case predominantly black employees. Like other lone black attorneys elsewhere in the South, Shores represented the legal interests of the NAACP on the local level. His law practice, real estate interests, and directorship of a black-owned bank placed him among the elite of Birmingham's black middle class. Short and stocky, above the crisp suit and polished attire a warm face often smiled, slightly turning up the tips of a distinctive mustache. His controlled posture underscored a shrewd mind and determined will. His measured approach to Birmingham's crisis in black housing contrasted sharply with the illogical antics of the city's white politicians.[15]

During the first week of August 1949, the Birmingham City Commission confronted the shortage of housing by discussing the racial zoning ordinance. Commissioner of Public Improvements James W. "Jimmy" Morgan called the city's zoning ordinance unconstitutional because of its requirement for racial separation. The next week, Commissioner of Public Safety T. Eugene "Bull" Connor surprised Morgan and Mayor W. Cooper Green with a new ordinance, 709-F, designed to circumvent the previous problem of racial zoning. Connor bragged that "the best legal minds in the state" had prepared the measure and given it to him that morning. The new law put police power behind the enforcement of residential segregation by making it a misdemeanor for whites to move into black or blacks to move into white areas "generally and historically recognized at the time" as racially specific neighborhoods. Connor later confessed that his mentor, former state senator and TCI attorney James A. Simpson, had written the ordinance.[16]

As Simpson explained in a letter to City Attorney James H. Willis, the new ordinance had nothing to do with zoning and everything to do with the separate-but-equal logic behind other segregation laws. Simpson drafted the measure to ward off "amalgamation." He argued: "If you let the situation disintegrate and negroes continue to infiltrate white areas and whites infiltrate negro areas so that your lines of demarcation become broken down, you are in for disorders and bloodshed and our ancient and excellent plan of life here in Alabama is gone." Simpson offered the city free legal advice on the matter.[17]

In announcing the new ordinance, Bull Connor accused Arthur Shores of creating the zoning conflict in North Smithfield: "It is impossible to compromise with Shores who is putting money above his race." Connor passionately added: "I tell you we're going to have bloodshed in this town as sure as you're sitting here. The white people are not going to stand for it." What these white people would not tolerate according to Connor was the selling of houses to black people. The police commissioner promised, "Pass this law and the first one who moves in, white or Negro, I guarantee you Connor's men will put him in the jug." Connor believed that the new ordinance would survive the Supreme Court and that his legal friends would "take it there at no charge if necessary."[18]

Circumventing Birmingham's unconstitutional racial zoning ordinance did not solve the shortage of adequate black housing, as Commissioner Morgan recognized by asking: "Where are those Negroes going to live and build? Almost fifty percent of our people are colored. So much of our area is zoned for white." Morgan spoke a simple truth. The *Birmingham World,* which had commended Morgan for his "courageous" stand when he called the zoning law unconstitutional the week before, otherwise chastised the commissioners for their insensitivity. The newspaper charged: "Negro citizens are bottled in the slums and restricted to the blighted areas . . . [they] . . . are zoned near the railroad tracks, near the over-flowing creeks, near the shops." In housing, as in everything else in Birmingham, black people suffered severe discrimination.[19]*

* A section describing the severe shortage of decent housing for Birmingham's black residents has been omitted—ed.

Most African Americans lived in congested neighborhoods surrounded by white residences that precluded expansion. The controversy over North Smithfield began as a natural outgrowth of overcrowding when black people living nearby sought access to the area as white people moved to the suburbs. The African Americans bought the old housing stock in a logical progression of their segregated neighborhood. They had no alternative, as the city zoned only three small areas "Negro" residential that could accommodate less than one-third of Birmingham's black population. These in-town neighborhoods housed Birmingham's black middle class of professionals, with on average 90 percent of the houses owner-occupied. The residents maintained their dwellings and paid property taxes. Nevertheless, the city neglected the neighborhoods by not paving roads, putting in streetlights, or extending public transportation to the area. Although contractors developed black subdivisions such as Honeysuckle Hill, the white builders failed to recognize the purchasing power of some African Americans by building small, inexpensive houses that few middle-class black people wanted. Consequently, the black elite moved into North Smithfield and the formerly white middle-class area of Graymont where substantial houses, street lights, and paved roads already existed. The other two-thirds of black Birmingham lived in congested industrial areas or flood plains that lacked basic public services. Consistent with racial zoning ordinances, these black neighborhoods developed as industrial suburbs or satellite communities. . . .[20]

The postwar shortage of black housing resulted from a lack of land properly although unconstitutionally zoned "Negro" for the expansion of black neighborhoods. While Commissioner Morgan attempted to address the problem, Bull Connor made it a point to care less about the needs of the city's black citizens, perhaps out of a desire to see Birmingham's black population decrease. Connor found an ally in the zoning board, which resisted adding new land to black communities and which rezoned as "white" some land already owned by African Americans. As a result, many black neighborhoods were decreasing in size, a problem exacerbated by slum clearance and urban renewal. During 1948 and 1949 alone, African Americans lost 1,200 dwellings, with little provision made for new structures as public housing units absorbed only a fraction of those displaced. . . . The increasing urban population, severe postwar shortage of adequate housing, and baby boom combined to create a crisis in black housing.[21]

Desperate to escape the congested ghetto, African Americans readily bought white-owned houses, although generally in areas they believed had been rezoned "Negro." In their bid for adequate housing they challenged the color line. They bought property on the edges of formerly white neighborhoods near black communities. As white people moved out, black people moved in, usually block by block in an orderly manner. The transition afforded the unscrupulous an opportunity to buy low and sell high, but occasionally both races profited. Having acquired adequate housing, these new black home owners defended their rights in property from attacks by white vigilantes.[22]

Three nights after the city commission adopted Simpson's ordinance to authorize the police department to enforce racial zoning, explosions rocked the city, but this time, as the blasts lit up the night sky, the black community fought back. Around 10:00 P.M. on August 12, 1949, B. W. Henderson, the black man living at 1100 Center Street North foiled one bombing attempt when a white man who had stepped out of a car realized "the Negroes are watching us." The vigilante climbed back in and then drove off, but Henderson followed, trying to get down the tag number. The suspicious car met two others near the Smithfield Project. Henderson returned home to warn his friends of the threat. Neighbors and ministers joined family members on the porch of the Reverend. B. DeYampert's house in a show of strength. Several were armed. Around midnight, a black Buick slowly drove down Center Street, coming to a complete stop in front of DeYampert's house. The front passenger door opened and the car light turned on, revealing several white men inside the vehicle. After a passenger threw something at the house, shots were fired at the car by those gathered on the porch. Once the charge ignited, sound and smoke filled the front yard. Seconds later, another explosion occurred at Henderson's house two doors away. Neither bomb reached its target, but both blew huge craters in the yard. . . . As the vigilantes drove off into the night, hundreds of outraged African Americans swarmed over "Dynamite Hill."[23]

When the blast occurred, five-year-old Angela Davis was washing out white shoelaces for her Sunday shoes in preparation for church the next morning. Suddenly, "an explosion a hundred times louder than the loudest, most frightening thunderclap I had ever heard shook our house. Medecine bottles fell off the shelves, shattering all around me. The floor seemed to slip away from my feet as I raced into the kitchen and my frightened mother's arms." Outside, "crowds of angry Black people came up the hill and stood on 'our' side, staring at the bombed-out ruins of the Deyaberts' [sic] house. Far into the night they spoke of death, of white hatred, death, white people, and more death. But of their own fear they said nothing. Apparently it did not exist, for Black families continued to move in. The bombings were such a constant response that soon our neighborhood became known as Dynamite Hill."[24]

The local chapter of the NAACP fired off a telegram to Mayor Green demanding "day and night police protection for the Negro home dwellers in Smithfield." The NAACP reminded the commissioners that detectives had yet to solve any of the six bombings. Commissioner Morgan released a statement to the newspapers expressing his regret and reiterating "that some land should be made available to our colored citizens to construct homes." In protest of the bombings, two thousand African Americans gathered on the lawn at the Smithfield Court Housing Project on August 17, 1949. Various black middle-class organizations sponsored the mass meeting to vent community frustrations. The audience adopted resolutions that criticized Bull Connor's comment that he could not "protect the lives and property" of African Americans who lived in the disputed area and condemned the city commission's "questionable and illegal means to ram down the throats of law abiding citizens the unconstitutional compromise zoning plan of an opposing group."[25]

The black protest crowd at Smithfield Court praised the courage of Arthur Shores and identified him as representing the "combined thinking of Negro leadership and fellowship" in Birmingham. Shores emerged as a spokesman for desegregation. Yet, along with his peers in the traditional Negro leadership class, Shores also accommodated Jim Crow paternalism when accommodation suited his interests. The willingness of black leaders such as Shores to negotiate and compromise with white leaders reflected their ability to broker agreements within the confines of segregation. Such racial diplomacy in the city was set forth first by the Reverend Dr. William Rufus Pettiford as the new century began.[26]

Through racial uplift and self-segregation, Pettiford articulated the ideology of the traditional Negro leadership class in Birmingham. He pastored the socially prominent Sixteenth Street Baptist Church, the city's oldest black congregation, and he headed the Alabama Penny Savings Bank, a black institution. Pettiford joined other black businessmen in advocating economic self-help and racial solidarity while accepting an accommodationist ideology articulated best by Booker T. Washington. In 1899 Pettiford headed a black delegation that petitioned the city to finance a Negro industrial school. He succeeded in part by convincing the white school board president of the need for what later became Parker High School. Pettiford demonstrated the practice of petitioning white leaders for public services while accepting Jim Crow, a pragmatic choice between discrimination and outright exclusion simultaneously made by black leaders in other southern cities. Birmingham's traditional Negro leadership class followed this pattern of protest through the activities of the NAACP and other organizations.[27]

Although small, the local black elite articulated a class consciousness comparable to that of the city's white elite. Birmingham had few

Negro colleges, as opposed to other southern metropolises such as Atlanta and Nashville, a fact that contributed to the limited number of university-educated African Americans living in the area. Only two schools, Miles College of the CME Church and Daniel Payne College of the AME Church, operated in Birmingham; nevertheless, both provided cultural and political leadership within the black community. A handful of black businessmen catering to a Negro clientele had organized a chapter of the National Negro Business League, but it folded for lack of support. Lawyers, doctors, and dentists operated out of offices in the Pythian Temple on Eighteenth Street and the Colored Masonic Temple on Fourth Avenue North. Both buildings demarcated the black business district and provided settings for social activities. Greek fraternities, such as Alpha Phi Alpha and Omega Psi Phi, and women's groups, such as Periclean Club, Imperial Club and Links, Inc., offered outlets for the black bourgeoisie, and this class comprised the core membership of the NAACP. As a result, many African Americans viewed the organization as elitist. The NAACP's penchant for bureaucracy and its inactivity on behalf of Birmingham's common black folk further alienated the black working class.[28]

During the early years of the Great Depression, Communist Party (CP) operatives moved into Birmingham to organize the black masses. Although opposed by the NAACP, the CP quickly spread as a grassroots movement among the black working poor and unemployed. The efforts of the International Labor Defense (ILD) on behalf of the Scottsboro Boys and the initial failure of the NAACP to participate in this case contributed to the popularity of the CP and thus provided a mass-based challenge to the traditional Negro leadership class in Birmingham. In addition, the depression limited black involvement in the NAACP, which saw its local membership decline to an all-time low of only six paid members in 1931. To reverse the decline, the national NAACP endorsed the ILD in order to gain mass support. In contrast, the CP's decision to foster a popular front among its members, the black middle class, and white liberals had the effect of curtailing independent leadership from the black working class. When the ILD disbanded in 1937, the CP encouraged its activists to join the NAACP, whose roster likewise expanded to 750, the largest number since the 1920s. By the 1940s thousands of African Americans belonged to the Birmingham branch.[29]

In the aftermath of World War II, black activists working within a biracial popular front attempted to revive the liberal reform movement of the 1930s. In Birmingham, the Southern Negro Youth Congress (SNYC), an organization for the black masses that had ties to the NAACP and the CP, directed a voting rights campaign for returning veterans. In late January 1946 about one hundred black servicemen in uniform marched in double file formation to the Jefferson County Courthouse to present their discharge papers and register to vote. County officials rejected a majority of the applicants for failing to adequately "interpret the U.S. Constitution," a favorite trick used by white authorities to prevent black enfranchisement in Alabama. Louis E. Burnham of the SNYC and the Reverends J. L. Ware and John W. Goodgame created a Citizens Veterans' Committee to file an appeal in circuit court on behalf of the failed registrants and to gain support from the Veterans Administration for job training and other benefits available under the G.I. Bill of Rights.[30]

Responding to the SNYC-led initiative, Emory O. Jackson, editor of the black biweekly *Birmingham World* and secretary of the local NAACP chapter, began a campaign to finance the legal fight for the black veteran vote. Like all good newspaper editors, Jackson could be obstinate. Born in Buena Vista, Georgia, in 1908, Emory Overton Jackson moved with his parents to the Enon Ridge neighborhood of Birmingham in 1919. He matriculated at Morehouse College in Atlanta and there exhibited a sensitivity to discrimination. Working on the *Maroon Tiger*, the undergraduate Jackson protested the "Faculty Men" and "Boys" labeling of campus rest room facilities and succeeded in convincing the administration at the prestigious college to drop the designations. Graduating from Morehouse in 1932, Jackson accepted a teaching post, first in Dothan, Alabama, and then at Westfield High, in Jefferson County.... The *Birmingham World* hired Jackson as managing editor in 1943 after he completed service in World War II. In his column "The Tip Off," Jackson demonstrated a crusading spirit akin to that of the old-fashioned newspaper editor. Despite his numerous associations—memberships in many of the Negro civic and fraternal organizations in the city—he remained an independent voice within the black community. His brusque style alienated other members of the traditional Negro leadership class, and, regardless of their views, he consistently demanded an end to Jim Crow and full civil rights for African Americans.[31]

After police shot to death black ex-Marine Timothy Hood for allegedly moving the color bar that maintained segregated seating on the streetcar and for fighting with the conductor, twelve hundred African Americans marched in protest. Publicity on behalf of the veterans' campaign appeared in the *World*, with guest editorials telling the former servicemen that "this battle is not to be waged with bullets, it is to be waged with ballots." In his "Tip Off" column, Jackson warned of the difficulties applicants faced and gave the correct answers to questions asked by registrars. Nonetheless, the veterans' registration effort stalled. This earlier movement for civil rights collapsed when local white resistance combined with national red-baiting, when Bull Connor shut down the SNYC during a political rally for Henry Wallce [presidential candidate of the left-wing Progressive Party] in 1948. The black veterans' movement never achieved its potential in Birmingham, and Jackson never recovered from the lost opportunity.[32]

Membership in the local NAACP declined rapidly with the collapse of popular front and the increase in racial hostility expressed by Dixiecrats and the other white people. Participation in the Birmingham branch dropped from more than 7,000 in 1947, to . . . 1,554 in 1951. Infighting among factions within the local chapter hindered a registration drive designed to halt the downturn. Assisted by the national office, the membership campaign revealed the inner workings of the Birmingham branch.[33]

A rift developed between Jackson and local NAACP branch leadership. A majority of the executive committee that determined local strategy had decided to hold a "Miss NAACP Contest" to attract new interest in the organization. As branch secretary, Jackson opposed the plan to award monetary prizes to the beauty pageant contestants as inconsistent with NAACP policy. The rift became public during the NAACP membership drive headed by committee chairman and funeral home operator W. E. Shortridge. Shortridge authorized the brothers of Alpha Phi Alpha fraternity to conduct the membership drive, and Jackson—an Omega—denounced the plan as elitist. In the pages of the *World*, Jackson called on "the humble people to have a showdown with its high leadership." He accused Shortridge and others of supporting activities antithetical to NAACP policy, in particular participating in a private effort to pressure the city for a "Negro" golf course. Finally, in April 1952 a disgusted Jackson resigned as secretary of the Birmingham branch of the NAACP. He referred to "a shocking and disgraceful departure from NAACP principles" and declared: "The Branch no longer represents the crusading spirit which brought me to it several years ago. It has allowed certain members to corrupt its program and to advocate courses of action and procedures which are in contradiction, hostility, and opposition to the methods, philosophy and aims of the NAACP."[34]

. . . . Jackson had lost the crusading spirit. As he wrote a friend during Autherine Lucy's desegregation attempt at the University of Alabama, "When the 'Lucy Case' is settled one way or the other I plan to remove myself from the front-line scene. All of my life has been spent in the interest of the other fellow. I want to be able to read, relax, and retire. Retirement is merely a withdrawal [sic] from battle, not a cessation from earning a living."[35]

A lack of interest within the black community and the inept leadership of president W. C. Patton limited the effectiveness of the NAACP's Birmingham branch. Despite "Miss NAACP Contests," the local organization continued to deteriorate. While the traditional Negro leadership class dominated the NAACP through the service of Patton, the Reverend Ware, and attorneys Shores, Peter Hall, and Orzell Billingsley, other more activist members such as Mrs. Lucinda B. Robey, W. E. Shortridge, and later the Reverend Fred L. Shuttlesworth struggled to generate interest in the NAACP among the black masses.[36]

Limited in mass appeal, the NAACP provided the only organized and consistent black protest in Birmingham during the postwar years. The association defended black property rights by condemning the racial bombings and police brutality, adopting resolutions against the building of a sewage treatment plant in a black neighborhood, and filing suit to stop slum clearance projects that targeted black-owned homes. Quick to pass a petition in protest of any white provocation, the local branch proved equally willing to negotiate with white leaders behind closed doors. Such conferences occasionally produced results that contradicted the national organization's stated goals. The Freedom Train incident of 1947 demonstrated the inconsistency in objectives between the local and national organizations.[37]

In a bid to bolster patriotic feelings during the emerging Cold War, the U.S. government entrusted its most valuable documents—the Declaration of Independence, the Constitution, the Bill of Rights, the Emancipation Proclamation—to the American Heritage Foundation for a train tour of the forty-eight states in the fall of 1947. Planners picked Birmingham as a stop, and local people prepared for the public display. When national organizers balked at the decision to segregate viewers in Memphis, Birmingham officials scrambled to cover up similar arrangements. Dr. Ernest W. Taggart of the NAACP and other Negro leaders had compromised with city commissioners on a Jim Crow strategy that would allow Bull Connor to enforce the city's segregation laws during the viewing of the national treasures. Apparently NAACP executive director Walter White got wind of the idea and decided to make hay out of southern discrimination, for the national office pressured the American Heritage Foundation to cancel the Birmingham stop unless total integration occurred. The local branch quickly altered its prior agreement and parroted national policy. Defending segregation, Birmingham's leaders canceled the stop and thus prevented citizens from seeing the documents that attested to their liberties. The Freedom Train incident demonstrated the duplicity of the traditional Negro leadership class. As the African American steelworker Hosea Hudson recalled about the NAACP but in a different context: "They still didn't want to rock the boat, make they good [white] friends mad. The [black] leadership was still trying to make deals."[38]

More often than not, the traditional Negro leadership class quietly worked with white leaders to achieve its goals without the interference of the NAACP. . . .

The struggle to convince the city commission to construct a Negro golf course epitomized the strategy of patient negotiations for segregated services used by the traditional Negro leadership class. Representing the black bourgeoisie in the Magic City Golf Club, Dr. E. W. Taggart petitioned the city park and recreation board to buy land near the Negro neighborhood of Powderly Heights for the proposed facility. The sportsmen had an important ally in that Mayor Green supported their request. As he explained to Charles W. Hall of the Birmingham Country Club, "We feel we must go ahead on the proposition before it is too late and the courts rule that they can play on the white golf course." Green compared the project to the recently designed facility at Vestavia Hills Country Club, and he saw the undertaking through to completion. In appreciation of his hard work, the black elite joined the city in naming the nine holes the Coopergreen Park and Golf Course.[39]

As in the negotiations for the "Negro" golf course, an increased demand for Jim Crow public services led to a rise in black activism. In the postwar years, municipal leaders authorized a general increase in government-sponsored programs and public utilities to meet the needs of urban expansion. Black protest emerged as a rejection of continued exclusion and as a desire for access to the new public services within the context of separate but equal. With the civil rights movement this activism developed into a black demand for equal access as consumers and equal opportunity for jobs.

From its founding, Birmingham's park and recreation facilities inadequately met the needs of its black and white population. When developers laid out the city, they set aside only three small areas a few blocks long for public use: Capitol (renamed Woodrow Wilson and then Charles Linn) Park, East (renamed Marconi) Park, and West (renamed Kelly Ingram) Park. Progressive Mayor George B. Ward increased the acreage under city control, but the random expansion remained slow and marked by discrimination. Birmingham spent less per capita on parks and recreation than any other major southern city.[40]

A political consciousness among the black masses developed around the issue of public parks. Groups such as the Interdenominational Recreational Council of 1941 organized petitions requesting that the city commission construct "proper parks, playgrounds and recreational centers" in order "to decrease and possibly eliminate entirely juvenile delinquency." Using the black church as its base, the Interdenominational Recreational Council collected hundreds of signatures involving everyday people in the protest. Adopting similar methods, Negro neighborhood associations such as the South Elyton Civic League, the Enon Ridge Civic League, and the Civic League of Zion City corresponded with city commissioners requesting creational facilities and other Jim Crow neighborhood improvements.[41]

Although aware of the needs of its black citizens, the city continued to treat the requests paternalistically, giving little thought to the opinions or desires of the black community. When Emory O. Jackson headed a movement to rename the Colored Memorial Park on the southside after Julius Ellsberry, a black man killed at Pearl Harbor and the first casualty from Birmingham in World War II, just as the white Kelly Ingram was the first victim of World War I and had a park named after him, the city commission not only refused to entertain the request, but also Mayor Green accused Jackson of doing "more harm to the negro park cause here than anything that has happened . . . in the last ten years." Despite not acknowledging the hero, the city continued to create segregated parks throughout the 1950s and early 1960s, in some instances merely redefining as "Negro" formerly "white" facilities.[42]

The issue of Jim Crow library services compared to that of the parks. Again, Birmingham woefully neglected the needs of its black and white patrons. Although white citizens constructed a magnificent central facility in the latter 1920s, the system of branch libraries—several of them financed through the Carnegie Foundation—remained inadequate. In response to a subscription drive by African Americans, officials located a "Negro" library, the Booker T. Washington branch, in the Colored Masonic Temple in 1918 and added a smaller collection at Slossfield in 1940.[43]

The need for a central "Negro" library became more pressing during a debate over a bond issue in 1953. Library officials believed that in order "to preserve our Southern tradition of segregation, it is essential that the facilities provided for Negro citizens immediately be made more nearly on the same level as those provided the white citizens." Members of the traditional Negro leadership class responded to the plans within the context of accommodation. The Reverend Luke Beard, pastor of the Sixteenth Street Baptist Church, wrote to thank the board for taking this "great step forward in the general progress of Birmingham." The local NAACP commended the city commission for placing African Americans on an advisory committee to the library board and hoped that "in the not too distant future" black citizens would serve on the board itself. When the city considered the construction of a new building for the "white" branch in Ensley, the Negro Ensley Civic League petitioned the city to convert the old facility into a "Negro" branch. Thus as with the parks, so too with the libraries, a rising black demand for Jim Crow municipal facilities and the federal threat of desegregation convinced Birmingham to provide more—albeit unequal —public services to the black community at the same time it increased operations for white citizens.[44]

Unlike Atlanta, where an expanding black electorate convinced city officials to increase public services to the black community, Birmingham's black community wielded no political influence. Only 456 of the more than 28,000 registered voters in Jefferson County in 1935 were black. Holding the franchise became a sign of status within Birmingham's black community. In 1938 Hosea Hudson and several other radicals organized the Right To Vote Club to get the black masses registered. The effort immediately clashed with the traditional Negro leadership class's control over the Negro ballot.[45]

Hudson recalled a meeting with the elitist Jefferson County Negro Democratic League, directed by conservatives D. L. White and Henry Harris, at which they attempted to convince the democratic Right To Vote Club to merge with their organization. According to Hudson, white city leaders responded to Communist Party agitation in 1933 by supporting the incorporation of the Jefferson County Negro Democratic League under the leadership of White and Harris and working out an arrangement with the Jefferson County Board of Registrars that approved Negro voters recommended by the league. As White explained to the upstart Hudson, the white registrars had told the Negro conservatives: "We only going qualify those that you all will recommend, send down or bring down. Your friends, we'll qualify them. But don't send everybody down. Don't bring no common nigras, and don't bring over fifty a year."[46]

The Right To Vote Club remained independent of the traditional Negro leadership class and succeeded in getting many of its members registered before disbanding in 1940. Anywhere from 878 to 3,000 African Americans were registered by 1940. Just over a decade later, in 1952, the number had inched up to 3,650. . . .[47]

Reflecting its conservatism and bureaucratic tendencies, Birmingham's traditional Negro leadership class formed two local groups that addressed the issue of voter qualification and participation in the political system. The Jefferson County Progressive Democratic Council endorsed candidates for office as the "oldest partisan political organization among Negroes in Birmingham." Attorney Arthur D. Shores served as president. Similar to other groups across the state, the Jefferson County Progressive Democratic Council worked to register black voters. An effort to assist such groups culminated in the 1951 formation of the Alabama State Coordinating Council for Registration and Voting, headed by W. C. Patton. Through its voter education program the council sponsored speakers at meetings designed to inculcate values of good citizenship within the black community. Both Jefferson County Progressive Democratic Council and the Alabama State Coordinating Association for Registration and Voting appealed to an elite group of Negro citizens and never took root among the African American masses. Consequently, the organizations achieved little, although both attracted white opposition as did the activities of the NAACP.[48]

Although willing to compromise on other black requests for segregated municipal services, with the housing crisis the city stood firm in its refusal to provide more land zoned "Negro," as demonstrated in the Monk case. Like so many other black people who moved into the disputed area of North Smithfield, Mary Means Monk had attempted to work out the zoning problem with the authorities according to Jim Crow custom. She purchased a vacant lot at 950 Center Street in June 1949. City building inspector H. E. Hagood delayed granting a building permit because of Commissioner Morgan's absence but encouraged her to clear off the land and start construction. When Morgan returned, he explained that the zoning committee had discussed the situation and had failed to act but that she should continue working on the house. Monk's contractor laid the foundation but stopped building when he needed the approval of the city inspector before putting in the plumbing. She returned to Morgan, who told her to get Shores to call him, for "he would direct him in some way that he probably could get the city to give a building permit" to Monk. Shores filed suit against the city, demanding permission to complete the house.[49]

City attorney Willis defended residential segregation in Birmingham by citing the new ordinance that put police power behind zoning enforcement, which therefore prohibited Monk from erecting a house in an area "generally and historically recognized . . . for occupancy by members of the white race." On September 28, 1949, Shores amended Monk's case to include fourteen other people. . . . Shores filed the class action suit against the city of Birmingham, calling the racial zoning ordinances unconstitutional. Recognizing the likelihood of just such a ruling, Willis began to backslide. He met with the Graymont College Hills Civic Association in a futile attempt to convince the white residents to allow the rezoning of some land along Center Street to "Negro" in order to have the case dismissed and thus protect racial zoning in the rest of the city. The association discussed Willis's plan at its November 1, 1949, meeting and voted "100 percent against any change of the Center Street zoning line." Furthermore, the members adopted a resolution requesting that the city hire additional counsel to defend the ordinances in court.[50]

Responding to its white constituency's desire for a legal battle, the city commission obtained the assistance of Klansman, Dixiecrat, and all-around race baiter Horace C. Wilkinson. Bull Connor's prediction that the "best legal minds in the state" would defend the racial zoning ordinances for free proved false, for the city commission secured Wilkinson's services by paying a fee of $5,000 plus an additional $1,000 for local legal assistance. On November 14, 1949, Wilkinson informed Willis that the $1,500 allotted for research in Washington, D.C., would have to be increased to $2,500. For a city government renowned for its frugality, paying such exorbitant legal fees for what was generally recognized as a lost cause suggested racial politics. The city commission financed the Monk case as a symbolic gesture to assure the shopkeepers, steelworkers, plant managers, clerks, firemen, and other members of Birmingham's white lower middle class that segregation would be upheld.[51]

When *City of Birmingham v. Monk* reached federal court on December 13, 1949, Judge Clarence Mullins forcefully declared as unconstitutional Birmingham's racial zoning ordinances. Wilkinson filed an appeal in January 1950. Not everyone agreed with the city commission's decision to continue the case. The broker George B. Alexander defended Judge Mullins's ruling but blamed the problem on "people of the ilk and breed of the negro lawyer, Arthur Shores." Others were more forthright. Mrs. R. D. DeLaure wrote Mayor Green to say that the Ku Klux Klan "ought to get Shores." Although vigilantes avoided the attorney, they were far from silent.[52]

Having elite white "friends" did not protect Dr. and Mrs. Joel A. Boykin from the bombers who dynamited their new house on April 13, 1950. Back in 1948 Boykin, a black dentist, had drafted plans for a $10,000 house and office to be constructed on a "white" buffer lot he owned in a block otherwise zoned "Negro." Previous efforts to build on city-approved land had failed, so Boykin appealed to the zoning board of adjustment to get the tract rezoned. Ten white neighbors protested his application at the hearing, and the board turned down the request. Boykin contacted his white attorney, the prominent realtor Sidney W. Smyer, who interceded on his behalf. Despite Smyer's pleading, the zoning board stood firm. Nevertheless, Boykin hired a black contractor and built the structure on Twelfth Terrace North, some five blocks from Smithfield.[53]

The explosion at the Boykin house rattled black and white residents of this western section of Birmingham, all of whom agreed that "what happened shouldn't have occurred." Right after the blast, a black neighbor, Lubirta Jones, ran outside to rescue her little dog, Lady, as pieces of rock rained down. She told a reporter: "We are colored and have lived in our house here for almost two years. We'd like to keep living here in peace." Fellow black dentist Dr. J. J. Thompson expressed little sympathy: "Those folks were warned before they started that house. And I know from experience that when a Negro gets a warning, he'd better heed it." . . . . An elderly white woman who lived nearby, Mrs. Jack Guest, explained that she had no complaints about her African American neighbors and added, "It was a mighty nice house they blew up."[54]

Vigilantes struck another house ten days later. Night riders destroyed the two-story frame structure a 1100 Center Street in North Smithfield shortly after eight o'clock on April 22, 1950, when a dynamite bomb exploded, caving in the front porch, splintering timbers, and shattering windows. Three people, including a three-month-old baby, miraculously emerged from the debris. Down the street when the explosion occurred, the owner raced to the rubble of his house: "Isn't it a shame?" a hysterical Henderson asked a reporter. "It's awful. It's ridiculous that this could happen in a civilized country. I should have known it, because I was down to Dr. Boykin's after they blew up his house." Then Henderson recalled: "Just last Monday, a group of white fellows walked by and gave this house the eye. I watched them from the window and heard one of them say, 'This one will be next.' "[55]

The April 1950 spate of bombings finally elicited a response from the local press. The *Birmingham News*, in a strongly worded and reproachful editorial, spoke to the vigilantes: "The men who performed the deed are cowards. They must be found. The city's police declare they are active in trying to find the criminals. In other previous bombings not one arrest has ever been made." After returning to an earlier argument that deplored the threat to property, the *News* concluded, "The time has come when action is demanded and when excuses no longer will satisfy anyone." Likewise, the *Birmingham Age-Herald* criticized the inaction of the police department and called for state and federal forces to help "apprehend these law violators." The *Birmingham Post* offered a five-hundred-dollar reward for information leading to the arrest of the perpetrators. "The bombings have got to stop," the newspaper implored.[56]

Amid the society news and announcements of corporate transfers printed in the *Shades Valley Sun*, the column of the anonymous "Button Gwinnett" condemned the dynamiting and demanded the "preservation of law and order." Recognizing Smithfield as "properly a place for Negroes," the opinion called for a "voluntary agreement between the races for demarcation of the sections of the city where they are to live" as the best way to maintain "reasonable lines of separation." Using a pseudonym, Charles F. Zukoski wrote the column for the weekly that serviced the affluent enclaves of Homewood, Mountain Brook, and Vestavia Hills. He hoped to impress Birmingham's elite who lived over the mountain.[57]

. . . . [T]he Button Gwinnett columns enabled Zukoski to articulate the emerging opinions of a racial liberal in the postwar era. As he wrote in

October 1948, "Change is inevitable and will either be an orderly and self-imposed one or a violent and destructive assault from without." He struggled to convince others of the need for orderly change. Zukoski never wavered from his conservative demand for Negro civil rights, but he consistently denied writing the columns for the *Sun* because he believed that his supervisors at the bank would view the ideas as "radical if not downright heresy." Espousing a northeastern establishment approach to solving problems, Zukoski and his Button Gwinnett columns presented an alternative voice for hidebound Birmingham.[58]

Despite assurances from police chief C. Floyd Eddins that "We're going to keep right on top of this thing until we find out who did it," law enforcement officers made little headway in their investigation of Birmingham's eighth unsolved racial bombing. Police did question Robert E. Chambliss about the explosion but "uncovered no new leads." Fired by the city after his 1949 indictment by a grand jury for "flogging while masked," Klansman Chambliss was tried and acquitted of the charge in March 1950. Governor James E. Folsom sent two state investigators to assist the four city detectives and three sheriff's deputies already probing the explosions.[59]

In October 1950 the U.S. court of appeals heard Horace Wilkinson's defense of Birmingham's racial zoning ordinances. Thurgood Marshall of the NAACP's Legal Defense and Educational Fund, Inc., joined Arthur Shores and Peter A. Hall in presenting Monk's case. On December 19, 1950, the Fifth Circuit upheld Judge Mullins's lower court ruling in *City of Birmingham v. Monk*. The decision found zoning ordinances 1604, 160 and 709-F in violation of the Fourteenth Amendment and enjoined Birmingham from enforcing them. On December 20 the city complied with the court's ruling and allowed Mary Monk to occupy her home. The next evening, vigilantes dynamited the house.[60]

The bombing followed the pattern of those that had preceded it. Believing her ordeal over, Monk had moved into the house located at 950 Center Street North in Smithfield. A friend helping her clean the kitchen witnessed two suspicious men standing at the back of the lot staring at the house. Uneasy and afraid that bombers might strike, she left on the outside light on the night of December 21. Around 10:30 P.M., as Monk turned down the bed in the front room, she heard a thud on the screen porch. Fearing the worst, she turned and ran, reaching the hallway when the charge ignited. The blast nearly reduced her house to rubble. Black neighbors saw speeding cars leaving the scene. During the police interrogation that followed, detectives tried to bait Monk by inquiring whether she thought the "communist" NAACP or those "people up in Washington" should meddle in Birmingham's racial affairs. Probably in all honesty, she replied, "The city should work it out ... the people in Birmingham ought to work it out themselves, since they are the ones that live here."[61]

Monk spoke from the perspective of a black schoolteacher seeking adequate housing. Indeed, her case symbolized the struggle of Birmingham's black middle class reluctantly forcing an issue—the unconstitutionality of the city's racial zoning laws—because of the obstinacy of city commissioners who refused to approve new land for black neighborhoods. The resistance of white people had escalated the crisis in black housing into a conflict over segregation. The decision of Monk, Shores, and Gaston to fight a legal challenge to Birmingham's segregated zoning ordinance reflected a transitional period in black protest that occurred in the years preceding the civil rights movement. Originally a defense of black property rights, the postwar protest evolved from a request for segregated municipal services to a demand for desegregation. With the emergence of the Alabama Christian Movement for Human Rights led by the Reverend Fred L. Shuttlesworth, the transition in black protest was completed, for the new organization used nonviolent direct action to achieve integration. When Shuttlesworth survived the dynamiting of his own house in 1956, his reputation as a charismatic civil rights activist increased tenfold.

After the Monk bombing, the racially motivated vigilante violence continued. Supporting the status quo in race relations, the police department scuttled its investigations while the fire department stood by and watched firebombed buildings burn down. One student of Birmingham's racial zoning troubles concluded in 1951 that Bull Connor and the police department were "part of this violent scheme to prevent Negroes from enjoying those rights and privileges granted them by the Constitution of the United States." The testimony of a city detective corroborated his theory. Angela Davis claimed that "Connor would announce on the radio that a 'nigger family' had moved in on the white side of the street. His prediction 'There will be bloodshed tonight' would be followed by a bombing. So common were the bombings on Dynamite Hill that the horror of them diminished." Yet the effect of the terrorism was extensive. As the years passed and hostilities increased, outside opinion of Birmingham deteriorated. The unsolved bombings earned Birmingham the sobriquet "Bombingham" and an international reputation as a city plagued by racial turmoil.[62]

NOTES

1 There is lacking in the literature a thorough examination of the racially motivated residential bombings in the South and their relationship to the

civil rights movement. For an overview of southern cities and their varied responses to race reform in the period see Elizabeth Jacoway and David R. Colburn, eds., *Southern Businessmen and Desegregation.*

2 Oliver W. Leavy, "Zoning Ordinances in Relation to Segregated Negro Housing in Birmingham, Alabama" (M. A. Thesis, Indiana University, 1951), 7–10 . . .; Carl V. Harris, *Political Power in Birmingham, 1871–1921* (Knoxville, 1977), 188, 215–16; Marjorie Longenecker White, *Downtown Birmingham: Architectural and Historical Walking Tour Guide* (Birmingham, 1980), 57, 111–15; "Report of the Birmingham Zoning Commission," June 21, 1926, and John H. Adams, chairman, zoning commission, to T. E Weiss, June 4, 1933 (quotation), box 7, file 9, Jones Papers, Birmingham Public Library Department of Archives and Manuscripts [BPLDAM]. . . . In *Buchanan v. Warley* (1917), the U.S. Supreme Court ruled the racial zoning ordinances of Louisville, Kentucky, unconstitutional.

3 Zoning map of North Smithfield, box 6, file 4B, Police Surveillance Papers [PSP], BPLDAM; Leavy, "Zoning Ordinances," 26–28. . . .

4 E. B. Lewis to Chief C. Floyd Eddins, August 20, 1947, box 7, file 24, PSP.

5 *Birmingham News* [*BN*], August 1, 1947; *Birmingham World* [*BW*], August 22, 1947: *Birmingham Age-Herald* [*BA-H*], August 20, (quotation), condemning the nighttime work of "culprits, vandals and other sneakers"; Willie Lee Patterson, September 6, 1947, and "State Bureau of Investigation and Identification Report" of W. H. Lee, September 25, 1947, box 7, file 24, PSP. . . .

6 Report of W. H. Lee, September 25, 1947, box 7, file 24, PSP; Leavy, "Zoning Ordinances," 32.

7 Angela Y. Davis, *An Autobiography* (1974; repr. New York, 1988), 77–78, 95–96. . . .

8 Statements of John J. Gould, April 7, 1949, and Detective P. E. McMahan et al. to Chief Eddins, report on "Bombing of Three Unoccupied Dwellings," March 26, 1949, box 6, file 4A, PSP.

9 Statements of H. G. Hicks and his wife, April 21, 1949, J. E. Monteith, April 7, 1949, John J. Gould. April 7, 1949, and Sam L. Chesnut, April 21, 1949, box 6, file 4A, PSP.

10 Statements of Sam L. Chesnut, April 21, 1949, Watchmen T. J. Dusenberry Jr., Joseph F. Bass, May 29, 1949, and Supervisor C. A. Bingham, July 19, 1949, of the Alabama Power Co., and C. E. Henderson, April 18, 1949, box 6, file 4A, ibid.

11 Statements of Mary Atkins and Annie Sims, April 7, 1949, George Smith, April 14, 1949, and Rev. O. C. Bickerstaff, July 5, 1949, box 6, file 4; Report of Paul E. McMahan to Chief C. F. Eddins, May 21, 1949, box 6, file 4B, all in ibid.

12 *BA-H*, May 2, 1949; statement of Robert E. Chambliss, May 23, 1949, box 6, file 4A, PSP; Leavy, "Zoning Ordinances," 36; Frank Sikora, *Until Justice Rolls Down: The Birmingham Church Bombing Case* (Tuscaloosa, Al., 1991), 153–54.

13 E. O. Jackson to W. Cooper Green, May 7, and Green to Jackson, May 9, 1949, box 9, file 19, W. Cooper Green Papers, BPLDAM; Leavy, "Zoning Ordinances," 37–40; Statement of Rev. Milton Curry, June 9, 1949, box 6, file 4A, PSP; NAACP statement in support of Curry, June 3, 1949, box 4, file 26, Green Papers.

14 Statement of Arthur D. Shores, August 9, 1949, box 6, file 4A, PSP (police corroborated the FBI's actions by calling agent Payton Norvell); Leavy, "Zoning Ordinances," 37.

15 Cochran, "Arthur Davis Shores"; *BN*, September 18, 1977; Robert J. Norrell, "Labor at the Ballot Box: Alabama Politics from the New Deal to the Dixiecrat Movement," *Journal of Southern History*, 57 (May 1991), 224–25; Howell Raines, *My Soul Is Rested: Movement Days in the Deep South Remembered* (repr. New York, 1978), 384–87. . . .

16 *BW*, August 12, 1949; copy of August 9, 1949 ordinance, box 6, file 4B, PSP.

17 James H. Willis to James A. Simpson, August 16, and Simpson to Willis, August 18, 1949, box 9, file 24, Green Papers.

18 *BN*, August 9, 1949. The new ordinance, No. 709-F, joined ordinances 1604 and 1605 in the *General Code of . . . Birmingham*, 639–41.

19 *BN*, August 9, 1949; BW, August 12, 1949.

20 Bobby M. Wilson, "Black Housing Opportunities in Birmingham, Alabama," *Southeastern Geographer*, 17 (1977), 49–57; Robert A. Thompson, Hylan Lewis, and Davis McEntire, "Atlanta and Birmingham: A Comparative Study in Negro Housing," *Studies* (1960), 57–58, 62. For a contemporary black discussion of housing in Birmingham see Geraldine Moore, *Behind the Ebony Mask* (Birmingham, 1961), 34–38 and Leavy, "Zoning Ordinances," 73–82. . . .

21 In contrast to Birmingham, Atlanta worked out a biracial solution to its housing crisis. . . . Clarence N. Stone, *Regime Politics: Governing Atlanta, 1946–1988* (Lawrence, Ks., 1989); *BN*, August 9, 1949; Leavy, "Zoning Ordinances," 54.

22 For a helpful discussion on race relations during the transition of a neighborhood from white to black see Gunnar Myrdal, *An American Dilemma: The Negro Problem and Modern Democracy* (New York, 1944), 622–27. For a historical account that explores the unscrupulous and exploitative potential of residential racial change and that considers the human stories involved see W. Edward Orser, *Blockbusting in Baltimore: The Edmondson Village Story* (Lexington, Ky., 1994).

23 Statements of Rev. E. B. DeYampert, August 16, B. W. Henderson, August 22, John J. Gould, August 15, Johnnie Brooks, August 17, Rev. J. H. Coleman, August 23, H. V. Early to Chief C. F. Eddins, August 13, demolition expert D. Petrig, August 16, 1949, and DeYampert, box 6, file 4A, PSP. . . .

24 Davis. *Autobiography*, 78–79. DeYampert had moved onto the "white" side of Center Street next door to the Monteiths.

25 J. J. Green of the NAACP to Cooper Green, August 13, 1949, James W. Morgan's Press Release, August 13, box 4, file 26, and the August 17 resolutions, box 10, file 9, Green Papers. The flier "Negroes' Homes Bombed Again!!" listed the following black sponsors: the Birmingham Business League, Property Owners Protective Association, Progressive Democratic Association, Interdenominational Ministerial Alliance, Birmingham-Jefferson County Housewives League, Birmingham Emancipation Association, and Social Workers Council, box 6, file 4B, PSP.

26 August 17, 1949, "Resolution," box 10, file 9, Green Papers; Daniel C. Thompson, *The Negro Leadership Class* (Englewood Cliffs, N.J., 1963). Thompson argued that three different types of black leaders existed: Uncle Toms, who petitioned white leaders for services within the rubric of separate but equal; racial diplomats, who proposed biracial negotiations to achieve concessions within a segregated framework, and race men, who rejected compromises that maintained segregation. Louis E. Lomax, *The Negro Revolt* (New York, 1963), described only two types of Negro leaders those who worked within the system and those who rejected outright segregation. As

Lomax noted, "The sit-ins marked the end of the great era of the traditional Negro leadership class, a half century of fiercely guarded glory" (138–39). The subtle distinctions Thompson drew between Uncle Toms and racial diplomats are collapsed in this analysis of Birmingham to conform to Lomax's description of a traditional Negro leadership class challenged by the new race men.

27 W. R. Pettiford, "How to Help the Negro to Help Himself," in *Twentieth-Century Negro Literature* (Atlanta, 1902), 468–72; Birmingfind [Robert J. Norrell], *The Other Side: Birmingham's Black Community* (Birmingham, n.d.); Arthur Harold Parker, *A Dream That Came True: The Autobiography of Arthur Harold Parker* (Birmingham, 1932); Carl V. Harris, "Stability and Change in Discrimination against Black Public Schools: Birmingham, Alabama, 1871–1931," *Journal of Southern History*, 51 (Aug. 1985), 396, 403–4. . . .

28 The size of the black middle class in a city influenced local race relations, as demonstrated by Robert J. Norrell, *Reaping the Whirlwind: The Civil Rights Movement in Tuskegee* (New York, 1985), and William H. Chafe, *Civilities* and *Civil Rights: Greensboro, North Carolina, and the Black Struggle for Freedom* (New York, 1980), but, as Chafe recognized, the traditional Negro leadership class participated in civilities without gaining civil rights for the larger black community. . . . On Birmingham's black middle class see Geraldine Moore, *Behind the Ebony Mask*, 52–54, 63–66, 114–23.

29 The seminal work on Communist Party activities in Birmingham is Robin D. G. Kelley, *Hammer and Hoe: Alabama Communists during the Great Depression* (Chapel Hill, 1990); see esp. 78–91,134. . . . The standard account of the Scottsboro Boys remains Dan T. Carter, *Scottsboro: A Tragedy of the American South* (Baton Rouge, 1979). . . .

30 *Chicago Defender*, February 2, 1946; *BW*, February 5, 22, 1946; Johnetta Richards, "The Southern Negro Youth Congress: A History" (Ph.D. diss., University of Cincinnati, 1987); SNYC programs of the 1940 and 1948 All-Southern Negro Youth Conferences held in Birmingham, private collection of James and Esther Jackson, New York City, copies in author's possession.

31 Emory O. Jackson to Gloster B. Current, June 12, NAACP Papers, BPLDAM. Current approved the idea. See Current to Jackson, September 17, 1951, ibid.; *Pittsburgh Courier*, September 27, 1975, file 70.1.3.1.4, and Jackson to Lerone Bennett, n.d., file 70.1.1.1.1, Jackson Papers, BPLDAM; and Edward A. Jones, *A Candle in the Dark: A History of Morehouse College* (Valley Forge, 1967), 291. . . .

32 *BW*, February 12, 15, 22, March 3, 1946. . . .

33 On NAACP membership statistics see Gloster B. Current to L. Pearl Mitchell, March 14, 1952, W. C. Patton to "NAACP Leader," May 29, 1951, Emory O. Jackson to Current, February 11, 1952, NAACP Papers. For an analysis of the Alabama NAACP that notes a decline in the postwar activism of the Birmingham chapter see Dorothy Autrey, "The National Association for the Advancement of Colored People in Alabama, 1913–1952," (Ph.D. diss., Notre Dame University, 1985).

34 Emory O. Jackson to W. E. Shortridge, April 8, Jackson to Rev. R. L. Alford, April 11, 1952, NAACP Papers. Jackson apparently returned to office only to resign again in October. See Jackson to Dr. J. King Chandler III, October 4, 1952, ibid.; *BP-H*. April 24, 1952, and *BW*, March 21, 1952.

35 Emory O. Jackson to Anne C. Rutledge, February 23, 1956, Jackson Papers.

36 The national NAACP office had selected Birmingham as its southeastern headquarters and stationed Mrs. Ruby Hurley in the city as regional

secretary. On the branch's membership problems see Hurley's "Report to the Executive Board," April 27, 1953, NAACP Papers. . . .

37 Emory O. Jackson to W. D. Kendrick, president of the Jefferson County Commission, March 26, 1951, and I. King Chandler III to Rev. R. L. Alford, February 26, 1951, NAACP Papers; *BP-H*, January 15, 1953; *BN*, July 24, 1953. For an analysis of the federal policy and the NAACP's defense of black property see Christopher MacGregor Scribner, "The Housing Act of 1949: Birmingham as a Test Case," (M.A. Thesis, Vanderbilt University, 1992).

38 "The American Heritage Program: A Plan to Raise the Level of Active Citizenship in Our Country," telegrams of Thomas D'A. Brophy to W. Cooper Green. December 16. Green to Brophy, December 17, 1947, Hayes King [a black man] to Green, n.d., Green to King, December 17, 1947, with the note "Your people have endorsed this plan," NAACP's "Citizens Committee Statement," box 7, file 15, Green Papers. . . .

39 Dr. E. W. Taggart to James Downey Jr., February 11, Green to Taggart, February 12, King Sparks Jr., superintendent of parks, to Green, February 15, and Green to Charles W. Hall, February 28, 1952 (quotation), box 10, file 10, Green Papers; Green to Sparks, April 17, Sparks to Green, May 27, and Emory O. Jackson to Sparks, August 16, 1952, box 19, file 22, Morgan Papers, BPLDAM. . . .

40 Robert Weldon Cooper, *Metropolitan County: A Survey of Government in the Birmingham Area* (Birmingham, 1949), 70–76; Edward Shannon LaMonte, *George B. Ward Birmingham's Urban Statesman* (Birmingham, 1974), 16; Olmstead report, box 11, file 7, Green Papers; Harris, *Political Power*, 167. . . .

41 Interdenominational Recreational Council petitions (box 11, file 12, Green Papers), a signed by members of the traditional Negro leadership class including . . . Jackson, Taggart. The civic leagues coordinated their efforts through the Alabama State Federation of Colored Civic Leagues. See "Declaration of Incorporation," January 19, 1933, box 4, file 3 Jones Papers, BPLDAM; Rufus Jones to W. Cooper Green, May 31, 1943, box 11, file 12, Green Papers; J. J. Ryles to J.W. Morgan, April 27, 1953, box 19, file 23, C. L. Burns to Morgan, January 21, 1952, box 20, file 24, Morgan Papers. . . .

42 Program, "First Annual Celebration of the Colored Memorial Park," May 31, 1943, Emory O. Jackson to W. Cooper Green, July 22, Jackson to R. S. Marshall, September 2; Green to Jackson, September 11, 1942, box 11, file 12, Green Papers. . . .

43 Cooper, *Metropolitan County*, 77–82; LaMonte, *Ward*, 44; Harris, *Political Power*, 167; R. Paul Huffstutler, president library board, to W. Cooper Green, September 19, 1952, box 6, file 22, Morgan Papers.

44 For a description of library services for African Americans and the building of the new Negro branch see Davis, *Autobiography*, 97; Paul R. Huffstutler to the City Commission, September 17, 1953, box 6, file 22 (first quotation), Rev. Luke Beard to Emily Miller Danton, director of the library, March 28, 1952, box 5, file 5, "Preliminary Committee" (undated list of black library advisers), E. A. Carter to Morgan, October 7, November 18, 1953 (second quotation), D. Scurlark, Ensley Civic League president, to Morgan and Morgan to Scurlark, November 20, 1954, box 5, file 6, Morgan Papers. . . .

45 Martin, Hartsfeld, 68, 99–101; L. B. Cooper, chairman, Jefferson County Board of Registrars, to state senator James A. Simpson, May 14, 1935, Simpson Papers, Alabama Department of Archives and History (black voting statistics for 1935). . . . Hosea Hudson quoted Emory Jackson as saying that

less than 500 black people could vote when the Right To Vote Club organized at the instigation of Joseph Gelders in 1938; Nell Irvin Painter, *Narrative of Hosea Hudson: His Life as a Negro Communist in the South* (Cambridge, Mass., 1979), 268, 381 n4.

46 Painter, *Narrative of Hosea Hudson*, 264 (quotation); Ralph J. Bunche, *The Political Status of the Negro in the Age of FDR*, ed. by Dewey Grantham (Chicago, 1973), 478–80.

47 Estimates vary on the number of registered black voters in Jefferson County. . . . The steady increase in registered black voters [to 1952 and beyond] appears accurate . . .

48 Bunche, *Political Status of the Negro*, 253–58; Moore, *Behind the Ebony Mask*, 202–3 (quotation); Ray Hugh MacNair, "Social Distance Among Kin Organizations: Civil Rights Networks in Cleveland and Birmingham" (Ph.D. diss., University of Michigan, 1970), 101–5. Shores at one time headed an organization called the Alabama Progressive Democratic Association, which endorsed Robert Lindbergh in 1953 for the position of police commissioner: see "Open Letter of the Alabama Progressive Democratic Association," box 11, file 27, Morgan Papers.

49 Statement of Mary Means Monk, January 8, 1951, box 7, file 35, PSP.

50 James H. Willis to James A. Simpson, August 16, 1949, J. R. Gardner Jr. to W. Cooper Green, November 2, 1949, and Green to Gardner, November 12, 1949, box 9, file 20, Green Papers. . . .

51 Horace C. Wilkinson to James H. Willis, November 14, 1949, box 9, file 24, Green Papers; see also Glenn Feldman, *From Demagogue to Dixiecrat: Horace Wilkinson and the Politics of Race* (Lanham, Md., 1995), 165. . . .

52 Horace C. Wilkinson to James H. Willis, December 28, 1949, box 9, file 24, George B. Alexander to W. Cooper Green, December 14, and Mrs. R. D. DeLaure to Green, December 15, 1949, box 9, file 20. Green Papers; Leavy, "Zoning Ordinances," 45–47.

53 George R. Byrum Jr., chairman, zoning board of adjustment, to James W. Morgan, November 19, and Sidney W. Smyer to Cooper Green, November 16, 1948, box 4, file 26, Green Papers.

54 *Birmingham Post* [*BP*], April 24, 1950.

55 United Press wire service newspaper clipping, April 22, 1950, with note attached: "This looks bad your honor. The whole USA saw this"; box 4, file 26, Green Papers; *BA-H*, April 24, 1950.

56 *BN*, August 23, 1949, April 15, 1950; *BA-H*, April 25, 1950 (see also editorial cartoon on April 15); *BP*, April 24, 1950. Foreign newspapers also reported the racial bombings; see undated and unidentified British clipping "This Is Dynamite Town!" box 4, file 26, Green Papers.

57 "Button Gwinnett Says: Disgrace in Smithfield," *Shades Valley Sun*, May 4, 1950.

58 Charles Frederick Zukoski, Jr., "A Life Story," manuscript, BPLDAM, 190–92, 330–32. . . . [After numerous complaints, Zukowski's employer, the First National Bank, demanded that Zukoski either stop writing the opinions or resign. The Button Gwinnett series ceased after December 12, 1957. Nevertheless, Zukoski's outspoken support for race reform persuaded the bank to offer him early retirement in June 1962.]

59 *BP*, April 24, 1950, and undated and unidentified clipping, "Man is Freed after Quiz in Bomb Probe," box 4, file 26, Green Papers.

60 Horace C. Wilkinson to Cooper Green, October 18, 1950, box 9, file 24, Green Papers; *City of Birmingham v. Monk*. . . .

61 Statements of Mary Means Monk, January 10, and Monroe Monk, January 11, Birmingham Police Department preliminary Investigation report, January 10, 1951, box 7, file 35, PSP.

62 Leavy, "Zoning Ordinances," 48; Davis, *Autobiography*, 95. Leavy concludes and the police were involved in the bombings, a charge confirmed by the testimony Henry Darnell in *BN*, January 28, 1953. . . .

13

SEX, SEGREGATION, AND THE SACRED AFTER *BROWN*

Jane Dailey

Jane Dailey examines the "long Civil Rights Movement" from the perspective of its white segregationist opponents. While it is well known that religious conviction played a central role in motivating and justifying the work of activists such as Martin Luther King, Jr., Dailey argues that historians have failed to appreciate the degree to which segregationists, too, founded their stance on biblical justification. The Civil Rights Movement should be seen, she writes, not as a battle between "true" and "false" religious beliefs, but as "a religious conflict over orthodoxy between two strongly held Christian traditions."

Here, Dailey focuses on the anti-integrationist belief that marriage and pro-creation between men and women of different "races" was a violation of God's law as revealed in the Bible. For many white Christians, she writes, "the Brown *decision raised practical moral and theological issues." Both ministers and lay people appealed to the Bible when they opposed school integration on the grounds that it would open the door to miscegenation. Dailey traces this religious opposition far back in southern history: to theological arguments in support of segregation in the late nineteenth century and, before that, in support of racial slavery.*

* * *

Asked to explain the victories of the civil rights movement, activists have often replied, "God was on our side." Martin Luther King Jr., for example, portrayed himself and his cause as divinely sanctioned, positioning segregationists clearly across the fence. "We have the strange feeling down in Montgomery that in our struggle we have cosmic companionship," King revealed during the bus boycott in 1956. "We feel that the universe is on the side of right and righteousness. That is what keeps us going." King did not simply consider segregation unconstitutional; he considered it a sin, and its Christian champions, heretics. Speaking of the boycott in another context, King portrayed segregationists as wayward Christians who, like the Prodigal Son, "have strayed away to some far country of sin and evil."[1]

Many white supporters of black civil rights felt the same way. The director of religious life at the University of Mississippi and Methodist minister Will Campbell believed that racism was a "heresy" infecting white southern Protestantism. Integrationist Christians, referring time and again to the Apostle Paul's notion of the church as the body of Christ (Ephesians 4), denounced their segregationist brethren for poisoning and polluting that body. "The Church is first of all the body of Christ, and in that Body we are one, not races or clans," declared another white Mississippi Methodist minister. King agreed: The "church is the Body of Christ. So when the church is true to its nature it knows neither division nor disunity. I am disturbed about what you [segregationists] are doing to the Body of Christ." The "beloved community," as King explained on another occasion, had to be integrated because "segregation is a blatant denial of the unity which we all have in Jesus Christ."[2] Segregation, in other words, was a theological as well as a social and political fallacy.

On the whole, American historians have subscribed to King's version of the sacred history of the civil rights movement. Most books written about the struggle for racial equality emphasize the central role that religion played in articulating the challenge that the civil rights movement offered to the existing order of segregation. There are good reasons for this: as Aldon D. Morris noted in *The Origins of the Civil Rights Movement*, black churches were the "institutional center" of the African American freedom struggle. Historians have noted respectfully the deep religious faith of many civil rights leaders and supporters and the influence of religious language and ideals on the movement. Although more recent scholarship has broadened both the organizational and ideological genealogy of the civil rights movement, even those historians who qualify the influence of the black church on the movement recognize the importance of the religiosity of black and white southerners in structuring their views in favor of civil rights.[3]

The religiosity of anti-integrationists has not fared so well in the scholarly literature. Some of the historians most engaged with the religious beliefs of civil rights activists have, almost in the same breath, denigrated the religious faith of segregationists. For example, David Chappell, who sees black Christian faith in the prophetic tradition as the key to the success of the civil rights movement, downplays the theological beliefs of white southerners and considers religious segregationists dupes at best. While in recent years a number of scholars have written sensitively about what Paul Harvey calls the "theology of segregationism" and Bill Leonard has dubbed "a theology for racism," few have treated segregationist ideas about religion with the care that has been devoted to proslavery ideology and thinkers. Harvey, Leonard, Charles Marsh, Wayne Flynt, and Andrew Michael Manis are among the few historians who have reckoned seriously with the substance of segregationists' religious beliefs.[4]

In their response to the arguments of King and others, Christian segregationists entered an argument as old as the Church itself: In what ways could and should the world of the flesh be made like the world of the spirit? Taking the tack that normative Christians have taken since the second century, anti-integrationists pitted the pastoral Paul, providing guidelines for the day-to-day administration of Christian communities, against the eschatological Paul, proclaiming the impending end of time and the irrelevance of life in the flesh. There are distinctions on earth (different languages, races, sexes), segregationists argued; these distinctions are created by God; and, although humans can all become one in spirit through conversion to Jesus, and although once the Messiah comes all earthly distinctions will pass away, in this world and in this flesh earthly distinctions are real—and Christians should not rebel against them. In his May 30, 1954, sermon, "Integration or Segregation?"—which was reprinted widely in newspapers and circulated in pamphlet form—Rev. James F. Burks of Bayview Baptist Church in Norfolk, Virginia, rebutted the efforts of integrationists to cloak themselves in Christian righteousness. "The spiritual 'oneness' of believers in the Lord Jesus Christ actually and ethically has nothing to do" with the issue of segregation, Burks explained. Spiritual kinship differs from physical kinship, just as the spiritual and secular worlds differ. "If integration of races is based upon the contention that men are all 'one in Christ,' then the foundation is not secure. The idea of 'Universal Fatherhood of God and Brotherhood of Man' is MAN's concoction and contradicts the Word of God," Burks charged. "Those who are 'one in Christ' are such through a spiritual union and certainly not physical." Citing Deuteronomy 32:8 and Paul in Acts 17:26 on the division of peoples, Burks insisted that, from a theological perspective,

> We are interested—finally and absolutely—in what the Word of God teaches about the races of men. . . . The Word of God is the surest and only infallible source of our facts of Ethnology, and when man sets aside the plain teachings of this Blessed Book and disregards the boundary lines God Himself has drawn, man assumes a prerogative that belongs to God alone.

Citing Paul's pastoral letters once again, Burks warned, "The Anti-Christ will consummate this [rebellious] attitude by opposing and exalting Himself above God."[5]

This article explores how religion served as a vessel for one particular language crucial to racial segregation in the South: the language of miscegenation. It was through sex that racial segregation in the South moved from being a local social practice to a part of the divine plan for the world. It was thus through sex that segregation assumed, for the believing Christian, cosmological significance. Focusing on the theological arguments wielded by segregation's champions reveals how deeply interwoven Christian theology was in the segregationist ideology that supported the discriminatory world of Jim Crow. It also demonstrates that religion played a central role in articulating not only the challenge that the civil rights movement offered Jim Crow but the *resistance* to that challenge.

Placed in context, white southern reactions to the civil rights movement—in particular, to the Supreme Court's decision in *Brown v. Board of Education* on May 17, 1954—represented a religious conflict over orthodoxy between two strongly held Christian traditions. For the historian (as opposed to the believer), orthodoxy is the product, not of revelation, but of conflict, in which the victory of one interpretation over another is historically produced rather than divinely ordained. Historians of the civil rights era tend to pass over this conflict and, ignoring or condemning the testimony of the many who believed that segregation was "the commandment and law of God," award the palm of orthodoxy to the color-blind, universalist theology of Martin Luther King's beloved community.[6]

When we do this we participate in what was perhaps the most lasting triumph of the civil rights movement: its successful appropriation of Christian dogma. At the same time, we miss the titanic struggle waged by participants on both sides of the conflict to harness the immense power of the divine to their cause. Viewing the civil rights movement as in part an argument about competing claims to Christian orthodoxy will help us better understand the arguments made by both sides of this struggle and the strategic actions they took.

We will begin where segregationist Christians began: with the Bible. When civil rights supporters quoted the Apostle Paul's argument in Acts 17:26 that "From one single stock [God] ... created the whole human race so that they could occupy the entire earth," segregationists responded by reciting the second half of the verse, in which the God who created all men "decreed how long each nation should flourish and what the boundaries of its territory should be." Reliance on this particular Bible verse freed segregationists from the discredited separate creations theory (polygenesis) cited by proslavery advocates a century earlier. It also meant that the Biblical defense of segregation could exist side-by-side with contemporary anthropology cited by Christian supporters of integration.[7]

But segregation did not stand on Paul alone. Turning to their Bibles, anti-integrationists found many narratives to support a segregated world. White ministers and laymen across the South offered a biblically based history of the world that accounted for all of the significant tragedies of human history, from the Fall and the Flood through the Holocaust, in terms of race relations. Binding the narrative together and linking the catastrophes of the past with the integrated apocalypse to come was the chief sin in the service of the anti-Christ: miscegenation. The notion that the sin committed in the Garden of Eden was sexual in nature stretches back centuries. By the Middle Ages, rabbinical readings of the Fall commonly considered the serpent a male, since it lusted after Eve. Proslavery apologists in the nineteenth century favored a variant of this theory in which Eve was tempted, not by a snake, but by a pre-Adamite black man (even, in an 1843 version, a "Negro gardener"). Needless to say, more than an apple was on offer. Most southern Christians rejected as heretical the notion that Negroes were created before Adam (and were, therefore, soulless beasts incapable of salvation), but several influential postemancipation writers persisted in arguing precisely this point. Buckner H. Payne, a Nashville publisher and clergyman who wrote under the pseudonym Ariel, insisted in 1867 that the tempter in the garden was a talking beast—a black man—and his interactions with Eve the first cause of the Fall. Writing at the height of Radical Reconstruction, Ariel concluded his argument by reminding his readers that "a man can not commit so great an offense against his race, against his country, against his God, in any other way, as to give his daughter in marriage to a negro—a *beast*—or to take one of their females for his wife." Should America fail to heed his warning, Ariel predicted disaster: "The states or people that favor this equality and amalgamation of the white and black races, *God will exterminate*."[8]

Although rebutted at the time and later, Ariel's argument remained current through the middle of the twentieth century, buttressed along the way by such widely read books as Charles Carroll's *The Negro a Beast* (1900) and *The Tempter of Eve* (1902), both of which considered miscegenation the greatest of sins. Denounced for its acceptance of separate creations, *The Negro a Beast* was nonetheless enormously influential. Recalling the door-to-door sales campaign that brought the book to the notice of whites across the South, a historian of religion lamented in 1909 that "during the opening years of the twentieth century it has become the Scripture of tens of thousands of poor whites, and its doctrine is maintained with an appalling stubbornness and persistence." In this tradition, miscegenation—or, more commonly, amalgamation or mongrelization—was the original sin, the root of all corruption in humankind.[9]

The expulsion from Paradise did not solve the problem of miscegenation. By the time of Noah race mixing was so prevalent that, in the words of one civil rights–era pamphleteer, "God destroyed *'all flesh'* in that part of the world for that one sin. Only Noah was *'perfect in his generation'* . . . so God saved him and his family to rebuild the Adamic Race." That perfection did not last long, however; according to some traditions, the cursed son of Ham, already doomed to a life of servitude, mixed his blood with "pre-Adamite negroes" in the Land of Nod. Again and again God's wrath is aroused by the sin of miscegenation, and the people feel the awful weight of his punishment: Sodom and Gomorrah were destroyed for this sin, as was the Tower of Babel, where, in a failed effort to protect racial purity, God dispersed the peoples across the globe. King Solomon, "reputed to be the wisest of men, with a kingdom of matchless splendor and wealth was ruined as a direct result of his marrying women of many different races," and the "physical mixing of races" that occurred between the Israelites and the Egyptians who accompanied Moses into the wilderness "resulted in social and spiritual weakness," leading God to sentence the Exodus generation to die before reaching the Promised Land. For evidence that the God of Noah remained as adamantly opposed to racial mixing as ever, white southern believers could look back a mere fifteen years to the Holocaust. The liquidation of six million people was caused, D. B. Red explained in his pamphlet *Race Mixing a Religious Fraud* (c. 1959), by the sexual "mingling" of the Jews, who suffered what Red represents as God's final solution to the miscegenation problem: "Totally destroy the people involved." Here, surely, was proof that segregation was "divine law, enacted for the defense of society and civilization."[10]

Narratives such as these had two key pedagogical aims: to make the case for segregation as divine law, and to warn that transgression of this law would inevitably be followed by divine punishment. In the 1950s and 1960s this punishment was imagined to be directed at the nation (in the form of the Communist partisans of the anti-Christ) and at local communities and congregations. Referring to the fate of Sodom and Gomorrah, Carey Daniel, pastor of the First Baptist Church of West Dallas, Texas (and active in his region's White Citizens' Council), explained, "Anyone familiar with the Biblical history of those cities during that period can readily understand why we here in the South are determined to maintain segregation." Rev. James F. Burks of Norfolk was more explicit. As he lectured shortly after the *Brown* decision was announced,

> Spurning and rejecting the plain Truth of the Word of God has always resulted in the Judgment of God. Man, in overstepping

the boundary lines God has drawn, has taken another step in the direction of inviting the Judgment of Almighty God. This step of racial integration is but another stepping stone toward the gross immorality and lawlessness that will be characteristic of the last days, just preceding the Return of the Lord Jesus Christ.

If this happened, it would be the fault of no one but white southern Christians themselves, for did not the Bible make clear, as Mississippi senator Theodore G. Bilbo warned, that "miscegenation and amalgamation are sins of man in direct defiance with the will of God?"[11]

Racial extremists such as Bilbo were not the only people who believed this. The 1955 opinion of Henry Louttit, Episcopal bishop of South Florida, that only a few "sincere but deluded folk" would use scripture to back up their belief in segregation turned out to be optimistic. The argument that God was against sexual integration was articulated across a broad spectrum of education and respectability, by senators and Ku Klux Klansmen, by housewives, sorority sisters, and Rotarians, and, not least of all, by mainstream Protestant clergymen. Dr. W. M. Caskey, a professor at Mississippi College (the state's leading Baptist institution), explained in 1960, "We . . . believe with Governor [Ross] Barnett, that our Southern segregation way is the Christian way. . . . [W]e believe that this Bible teaches that Thou wast the original segregationist." Segregationist ministers who believed that the Bible "gave clear guidance on the integration-segregation issue" were prominent in the crowds surrounding Central High School in Little Rock, Arkansas, in 1957. Editorialists and congregations elsewhere spoke out as well. "In integrating the races in schools, we foster miscegenation, thereby changing God's plan and destroying His handiwork," resolved the Cameron Baptist Church in Cameron, South Carolina. David M. Gardner, writing in the *Baptist Standard*, agreed: "God created and established the color line in the races, and evidently meant for it to remain. Therefore, we have no right to try and eradicate it."[12]

As absurd as the argument for divine segregation may appear to today's readers, it had great power in its day. Evidence of the political and social power of these ideas is everywhere—in legal decisions, in personal correspondence, in sermons and pamphlets and speeches and newspapers. Organizations acted on these assumptions; in 1958 the Daughters of the American Revolution (DAR) denounced interracial marriage and resolved that "racial integrity" was a "fundamental Christian principle." Judges even incorporated these theological positions into legal decisions. Upholding segregation in a 1955 ruling, the Florida Supreme Court preferred its own reading of the Bible to that of the bishop of South Florida. "When God created man," the Florida justices explained, "He allotted each race to his own continent according to color, Europe to the white man, Asia to the yellow man, Africa to the black man, and America to the red man." A decade later in Virginia, federal circuit court judge Leon A. Bazile also appealed to divine sanction, in the case that would soon form the basis for the Supreme Court's 1967 ruling in *Loving v. Virginia* that antimiscegenation laws violated the Fourteenth Amendment. According to Bazile,

> Almighty God created the races white, black, yellow, malay and red, and he placed them on separate continents. And but for the interference with his arrangement there would be no cause for such marriages. The fact that he separated the races shows that he did not intend for the races to mix.[13]

More than most sources, Bazile's ruling in *Loving v. Commonwealth* provides a clear example of the importance of the sexual and theological nexus in the civil rights struggle. That nexus—visible to anyone who looked beneath the surface of southern race relations—burst into the open in May 1954.

Like the chief executives of the other southern states, Virginia governor Thomas B. Stanley spent the spring of 1954 wrestling with the issue of state compliance with the *Brown* decision. Eager to communicate with their governor on this topic, hundreds of Virginians wrote to express their opinions about the Supreme Court ruling. Most who wrote objected to integration. The most common argument of the dissenters was theological: integration encouraged miscegenation, which contradicted divine Word.[14]

On the face of things, this response seems surprising: the *Brown* decision, limited as it was to desegregation of public schools, looked to be about anything but sex and marriage. This impression was the result of a deliberate strategy on the part of *Brown*'s architects, both within the National Association for the Advancement of Colored People (NAACP) and on the Supreme Court, which went to considerable trouble to limit the decision's language to public education alone. Nor did the decision claim that statutory considerations of race or color were impermissible in arenas other than public education. In addition, the justices who backed *Brown* explicitly refused to rule on the constitutionality of antimiscegenation laws. The Court ducked a chance to evaluate restrictive marriage laws in 1955, a decision that was widely derided. A decade later, Felix Frankfurter's law clerk Alexander Bickel justified the Court's reluctance to rule on another interracial marriage case by insisting that the issue was "hardly of central importance in the civil rights struggle." But the justices knew better: they avoided ruling on miscegenation not because it was unimportant, but because it was too hot to handle. As Justice John Marshall Harlan II put the matter in a 1955 note to his colleagues during the controversy over *Brown*, "One bombshell at a time is enough."[15]

In avoiding the issue of miscegenation, the Warren court was following the NAACP strategy of attacking segregation first from its extremities. Certainly both the Court and the NAACP recognized that restrictions on sex and marriage lay at the heart of Jim Crow. When the *Brown* decision was announced in May 1954, sex and marriage between those defined at law as white and those defined as nonwhite were prohibited in twenty-seven states—and had been, with a few brief exceptions during Reconstruction, for the previous three hundred years. State antimiscegenation laws underpinned the edifice of racial segregation and discrimination in America, a fact advertised by students of southern social relations since the 1920s. Gunnar Myrdal canonized this position in 1944 when he announced in *An American Dilemma* that sex was "the principle around which the whole structure of segregation of the Negroes ... [was] organized."[16]

Black southerners did not need Gunnar Myrdal to explain that sexual control was central to both the ideology and the practice of white supremacy. Early black rights organizations, including the NAACP, set their sights on restrictive marriage laws. As a practical issue, however, the risks of addressing the sexual question outpaced the advantages. By 1940 the NAACP's new Legal Defense and Educational Fund (LDEF) had crafted a strategy of attacking Jim Crow from the outside in, through lawsuits focused on higher education and discriminatory voting practices such as the white primary. Sex was the last thing the association wanted to talk about. But it was a topic that simply would not go away. Whether they fought for integrated public education at the graduate or primary level, civil rights groups opened themselves to the charge that they favored interracial sex and marriage. When he recalled the NAACP "s successful campaign to get George W. McLaurin admitted to the graduate school of the University of Oklahoma in 1948, Thurgood Marshall (then heading the LDEF) noted that his strategy revolved in good measure around defusing whites" fears of racial mixing. "We had eight people who had applied and who were eligible to be plaintiffs, but we deliberately picked Professor McLaurin," Marshall explained, "because he was sixty-eight years old and we didn't think he was going to marry or intermarry. . . . They could not bring that one up on us, anyhow."[17]

Everyone connected with the school cases that became known collectively as *Brown v. Board of Education* understood how vital it was that they not be linked with sex. Despite the precautions of both the NAACP and the Warren court, however, the *Brown* decision was interpreted by a large and vocal segment of white southerners in explicitly sexual terms. "The first reaction to the Supreme Court's decision was almost psychotic," Mark Ethridge, editor of the *Louisville Courier-Journal*, recalled. In a typical editorial comment, the *Jackson Daily News* in Mississippi denounced the school decision as "the first step, or an opening wedge, toward mixed marriages, miscegenation, and the mongrelization of the human race." Walter C. Givhan, an Alabama state senator, interpreted the *Brown* decision the same way. "What is the real purpose of this? To open the bedroom doors of our white women to Negro men." Numerous letters sent to southern governors struck the same theme. In a letter to Georgia governor Herman E. Talmadge (who was on record arguing that "God himself segregated the races" and who would continue to assert that "segregation is not inconsistent with Christianity"), William A. Robinson Jr. worried about the future. "Of course, we may abolish the public schools," Robinson wrote, "but when the NAACP procures from an obliging Court, as seems quite likely in the near future, a ruling adverse to our marriage restrictions, we cannot meet that issue by abolishing marriage." Georgia's state attorney general, Eugene Cook, agreed with this line of reasoning and took it a step further, predicting "an amalgamation stampede" should the Court rule against state antimiscegenation laws. *Racial Facts*, a popular pamphlet, made the same point in a way any southern gardener could understand, warning of "Negroid blood like the jungle, steadily and completely swallowing up everything."[18]

It was within this highly charged sexual context that the battle for divine sanction between supporters and opponents of desegregation took place. While white southern opponents of *Brown* were making dire predictions of syphilis in the schools, southern moderates and reformers leapt to take the moral high ground. With southern newspapers and politicians almost unanimously opposed to the Supreme Court decision, *Brown*'s supporters turned to the white churches. The relative silence of white ministers on the race issue through 1954 may have encouraged moderates to try to co-opt the church. Mississippi's Hodding Carter—who had won the Pulitzer Prize in 1946 for a series of antilynching editorials—made a claim for religious authority and linked Christianity to democracy when he wrote in the *Delta Democrat-Times* that "the Court could not have made a different decision in the light of democratic and Christian principles and against the background of today." A group of thirty-seven college students and counselors attending the Southeastern Regional Methodist Student Conference in Virginia made the same rhetorical move in a letter to Gov. Thomas Stanley. The *Brown* decision, the students and counselors explained, was "in keeping with the spirit of democracy and Christianity and should not be side-stepped in any way." Methodist youth in North

Carolina took a similar tack when they resolved in August 1954 at the annual Methodist Youth Fellowship that "segregation is un-Christian" and voted to present resolutions urging support of the *Brown* decision. Black southerners also tried to tie the *Brown* decision to Christian ideals. The National Baptist Convention (the leading forum of black Baptists) announced that on May 17, 1954, "the Social Gospel of Jesus received its endorsement by the Highest Court of the nation." Other African Americans reacted less reverently. The boxer Joe Louis, who had wandered into the office of *Ebony* magazine as editors there heard the news, smiled broadly and said, "Tell me, did Herman Talmadge drop dead?"[19]

Civil rights supporters understood immediately the importance of having God—and his spokesmen—on their side. "If the ministers speak out bravely, quietly, persuasively they can give direction to the feelings of millions of white southerners who don't know what to do or where to turn," wrote the liberal author Lillian Smith from her home in Georgia. Although Smith was hardly representative of either southern Protestantism or white southern thought more generally, her hopes were not entirely unfounded: there is evidence that white Christian consciences were strained by many aspects of segregation. Certainly many southern religious leaders, especially those connected with seminaries or foreign mission work, questioned segregation long before 1954. In June 1954—just two weeks after the announcement of the *Brown* decision—the ten thousand messengers of the Southern Baptist Convention (SBC) endorsed the Supreme Court's decision, proclaiming it "in harmony with the constitutional guarantee of equal freedom to all citizens, and with the Christian principles of equal justice and love for all men." The governing boards of the National Council of Churches of Christ in the U.S.A. (NCC), the World Council of Churches, and the Synagogue Council of America all passed resolutions praising the decision. The Catholics, Methodists, and Presbyterians also followed suit, although not without first addressing the trump argument: the Southern Presbyterian General Assembly accompanied its support for school integration with the assurance that interracial marriage would not follow.[20]

The proclamations of the national church organizations were useful to supporters of black civil rights. George E. Nabb Jr., a Virginia minister, lectured his governor that in trying to circumvent the *Brown* decision Virginia was ignoring "the expressed wishes of the four, largest religious bodies in our State." But these organizations—especially the SBC's progressive Christian Life Commission, which authored the denomination's official response to *Brown*—were not necessarily representative of the masses of white Christian Protestants or of the clergy. (As one white southerner remarked of the messengers to Robert Penn Warren,

"They were just a little bit exalted. When they got back with the home folks a lot of 'em wondered how they did it.") For every Protestant minister who declared that the *Brown* decision "showed the hand of God in it," there were others who saw the diabolical machinations of the Kremlin instead and who denounced "pinkos in the pulpit" for their support of integration. Douglas Hudgins, pastor of the enormously powerful First Baptist Church of Jackson, Mississippi, was one of the few messengers to object to the report recommending support of the *Brown* decision. But he was surely not the only Baptist minister to preach the Sunday after the convention on the local autonomy of churches. Pastor of a congregation studded with state leaders, Hudgins almost never preached on contemporary events. Now he took the opportunity to remind his flock of the congregational autonomy at the heart of Baptist associational life. Decisions taken by the Southern Baptist Convention had no binding authority on local churches, he insisted. Furthermore, he explained, the Supreme Court decision was "a purely civic matter" and thus an inappropriate topic for the Christian Life Commission in the first place. In this Hudgins echoed SBC president J. W. Storer, who endorsed the *Brown* decision on civic rather than theological grounds. Repudiating the religious arguments of his organization's Christian Life Commission, Storer argued that Baptists should obey the Supreme Court decision because "We 'Render to Caesar the things that are Caesar's, and to God the things that are God's.' "[21]

Public schools belonged to Caesar. Racial purity belonged to God. In *Brown*'s wake, many white southern Christian leaders tried to find a way to obey both the law of man and that of God and at the same time chart a middle course between massive resistance and capitulation to the theology of the emerging civil rights movement. Worried about the sexual and theological implications of the *Brown* decision and anxious about schism, in 1956 the Episcopal Church's National Council backtracked on its belief, expressed just a year earlier, that desegregation was "the will of God." Replacing this explicitly theological justification for desegregation with a civic concern for justice, the Episcopalians substituted "free access to institutions" for the goal of "integration"—a loaded term that suggested intermarriage, from which "the majority of church leaders still shrank." In 1957 an interdenominational group of Atlanta clergymen published a statement that disavowed support for racial amalgamation but declared that "as Americans and Christians we have an obligation to obey the law." The *Alabama Baptist*'s Leon Macon went further, arguing that "When we violate a law we hurt man and grieve God." Liberal clergymen in Little Rock during the integration crisis there in September 1957 took the same tack, insisting that good Christians could disagree about segregation but not about upholding the law.[22]

But what were good Christians to do when the law of the land contradicted God's holy word? The more recent historiography of the *Brown* decision has noted the way that white southerners framed their anger at school integration in terms of sexual danger. What has slipped under the radar is the theological articulation of that worry. The *Brown* decision raised practical moral and theological issues for many southern white Christians. While liberal Presbyterians worried that "the courts have shown more sympathy toward the Negro than has the church" and admonished it to "strive to keep apace of its Master or become bereft of his spirit," segregationist Christians suspected that the state was following not the Master, but his principal challenger. Like Norfolk's Rev. James F. Burks, who argued that "modern-day Christianity has substituted a social Gospel for the Blood-purchased Gospel of Christ," many white southerners considered the *Brown* decision at direct odds with God's moral codes. Angry about the desegregation decision and the support liberal clergy had given it, W. L. Trotten Sr. of North Carolina complained that "we the people . . . are being forced to disobey the laws of our GOD who created us." Insisting that "God is the author of segregation," Elmer M. Ramsey of Miami charged the Supreme Court with "exceed[ing] its authority" by interfering with divine law.[23]

This argument, it is important to note, was not about school integration per se; it was about its consequences, which segregationists considered to be interracial sex and marriage, leading to race corruption. The most common line of argument among the hundreds of letters that Virginia governor Thomas B. Stanley received in the weeks following the *Brown* decision insisted that school integration led inevitably to intermarriage, which violated God's plans for the universe. Written largely by women, the letters to Governor Stanley parallel the correspondence received by other southern governors in the weeks following the school decision. Mrs. Jesse L. West confessed that she had "never felt so strongly about anything before" and thus was compelled to write her governor even though she could not "phrase fancy statements." Mrs. West supported equal education for black Virginians ("they should have good, clean schools, buses to ride there, etc."), but she drew the line at integration, which she believed was a sin.

> Having attended my beloved little county church from infancy I believe I know the fundamentals of the teachings of God's Holy Word. . . . [N]owhere can I find anything to convince me that God intended us living together as one big family in schools, churches and other public places.

Mrs. G. P. Smith agreed. "My strong religious conviction tells me that

God does not require this of us. He made us different and put us separate on His good earth." Should schools be integrated, she warned, "In less than ten years we will face the problem of intermarriage." Mr. and Mrs. J. W. Layne stated straightforwardly that "integrated schools will lead to interracial marriage" and signed off with a benediction: "May the Lord direct you and others in doing what we believe to be right."[24]

Divine gubernatorial guidance was essential, these correspondents believed, because in integrating its public schools the nation was teetering on the brink of damnation. Fretting that "God's word is being made away with and people is believing in their selves and forgetting God," Mrs. R. E. Martin warned Governor Stanley that "the wicked shall be turned into hell, and all the Nations that forget God." Mrs. Henry Winter Davis was more explicit on the link between integration and hell.

> We consider this non segregation business comes directly from Satan, that old deceiver, the devil, to destroy *all peace in America forevermore!* . . . That is his business—to destroy all good. He whispered to that California man in [the] Supreme Court that it would be an advantage to abolish segregation—while one of our own statesmen would have known the danger, which is worse than any menace ever to threaten America . . . as it is in our *very midst, an every day menace.*[25]

As the civil rights movement left the courts and entered the streets, the struggle for cultural legitimacy became fiercer. Ministers often found themselves in the cross hairs on the segregation question, as congregants attempted to counteract the influence of clergymen in civic affairs and to capture the power of Christian righteousness for segregation. "It seems to me that there is a feeling among the clergy that you cannot be a Christian and oppose the integration of the negro and white races in our public schools," wrote R. D. Cook to Governor Stanley in June 1954. "I am sorry that I cannot see it their way." Pitting his own expertise against his pastor's, Cook continued, "Although I may not be as good a Christian as I should be, I have belonged to the Board of Deacons in my church for a number of years and am now superintendent of the Sunday school." Then he got to the point:

> I believe that the integration of the races in our public schools will result in intermarriage of the negro and white races, and I am sure that the NAACP will next try to have the law repealed prohibiting intermarriage of the two races. I believe that the Lord would have made us all one color if he had intended that we be one race.

Cook's neighbor J. D. Jones wrote a similar letter:

> I know you have seen a lot about what the preachers have had
> to say about it [the *Brown* decision], but I do not believe that
> they are representing their congregations at all. . . . I have been
> a Baptist for forty years and have been a Deacon in my church
> for thirty odd years, and I know that our congregation is very
> much opposed to doing away with segregation in the public
> schools.

Local feeling on ministerial misrepresentation could run high. "The
ministers of our country have been among the foremost advocates of
this movement [to comply with *Brown*] and have falsely misrepre-
sented their churches as being of the same opinion," wrote Mrs. James
Irving Beale. "They have passed resolutions at conventions where the
delegates probably feel they would be most unchristlike to disagree
and yet I do not know of a single instance where the minister has
asked a vote in his individual church. He knows full well it would not
support his opinion."[26]

Generalizations across denominational boundaries are treacherous,
but on the whole ministers seem to have been more likely to support
desegregation than their congregations were. Ministers who challenged
their congregations on the segregation issue often found themselves
without a pulpit. Thomas Thrasher, rector of the Church of the Ascen-
sion in Montgomery, was forced out for talking too much about human
brotherhood. As an Episcopalian and thus answerable to a bishop
and not simply to a local congregation, Thrasher perhaps thought he
had greater freedom of speech. He found no ally in Rt. Rev. Charles
Carpenter of Selma, however, who failed to use his episcopal authority
to come to Thrasher's aid. Often presented in anticlerical terms as a
clash between "pulpit and pew," the theological struggle over the
rightness of desegregation spilled over into the sacristy, as Thrasher's
case indicates. As one representative of the progressive Southern
Regional Council—which kept statistics on integrationist ministers run
out of their churches—noted wryly, "In the South we have a new class
of DPs—displaced parsons." Given these internal dynamics, is it any
wonder that, as one civil rights worker complained, trying to fire
up the white church was like "trying to strike a match on a wet
windowpane"?[27]

Parishioners were not the only critics of the clergy. In April 1956 the
Citizens' Council complained that

> many ministers of the Gospel and laymen are telling us that
> integration is the word of God. . . . Many others, equally

devout and, one is to assume, equally prayerful in their search for Divine guidance, have received no word from the Throne of Grace that public school integration is God's wish.

Admitting that there was ample biblical justification to support notions of the brotherhood of man and the equality of all men in God's sight, the official publication of the White Citizens' Council maintained, nonetheless, that "It does not follow that God intended the different races of men to intermarry." It was this prospect of miscegenation that accounted for "the strong opposition of thousands of devout Christians to public school integration." Civil rights supporters, meanwhile, attacked the root argument and interpreted the more extreme manifestations of this strong opposition of whites to integration as evidence of their irreligion. Referring to the bombing of four churches associated with the Montgomery bus boycott, Martin Luther King painted die-hard white supremacists as heathens and tried to narrow the ground Christian segregationists could occupy: "What manner of men are these, men whose pagan impulses drive them to bomb ministers and desecrate the House of the Lord?"[28]

It is not uncommon for accusations of heresy to strengthen resolve. After *Brown*, Christian laymen and many ministers clashed with their denominational bodies and with each other and articulated what Paul Harvey calls "a newly self-conscious theology of segregationism." Here again worries about sexuality—specifically, intermarriage—blended with theological concerns. Informed that their position was unChristian by their denominational leaders and in many instances by the coming generation in the form of youth conference declarations, segregationists fought back. In North Carolina, the Quarterly Conference of the Newton Grove Methodist Charge wrote a resolution that upheld segregation as God's law and criticized the "impractical idealists within our churches" who dared to speak for the whole church. Integration, Newton Grove warned, could but lead to "the intermarrying of the races, which we believe to be contrary to the very ordinance of God." Asked to implement his church's official policy to desegregate denominational schools, the response of a Baltimore attorney (an alumnus of two denominational schools and a trustee of three) reveals the theological, and not just social and political, stakes involved in desegregation:

When the Church steps forward as the champion of evil causes—as has happened in the long course of history—there is nothing left to Christians but to cry out at whatever peril to themselves, as their Lord cried out against the hierarchy of his day, which crucified him.... Where in particular do

Christian churchmen get the idea that there is anything sinful in segregation?

Other churches criticized their national bodies implicitly through the publication of church resolutions that stressed the biblical defense of segregation. Quoting the Apostle Paul's proclamation in Acts 17:26, South Carolina's Summerton Baptist Church resolved in October 1957 that integration was wrong because

> (1). God made men of different races and ordained the basic difference between races; (2). Race has a purpose in the Divine plan, each race having a unique purpose and a distinctive mission in God's plan; (3). God meant for people of different races to maintain their race purity and racial identity and seek the highest development of their racial group. God has determined "the bounds of their habitation."[29]

The desire to have God on their side also motivated secular organizations dedicated to the maintenance of segregation. The minutes for the Jackson, Mississippi, chapter of Americans for the Preservation of the White Race reveal an absorbing preoccupation with determining God's will on segregation. In between voting to inscribe "If God be for us who can be against us" on their organizational letterhead and erecting highway billboards denouncing Martin Luther King as a Communist, this all-male association listened to an astonishing number of guest lectures dedicated to "The Bible and Segregation" and "The Scripture and How It Applies to Present Problems." Far from "sens[ing] the limitations of the Bible," as the historian David Chappell has charged, religious segregationists grounded their defense of segregation firmly in their reading of that holy text and pitted their own interpretations of it against their more liberal co-religionists.[30]*

Recognizing the religious dynamics of the conflict between segregationists and integrationists not as ungodly versus godly, but as a yet-undecided struggle for the crown of orthodoxy helps us understand the reaction to the *Brown* decision ... and much of the shape that the civil rights movement took—in terms both of the strategic decisions of its leaders and of the strategies of resistance adopted by its opponents. It also helps contextualize more recent history. As anticipated in many reactions to *Brown*, sexualized Christian theology remains a way of

---

* A section on anti-miscegenationist religious concerns about sex during the Selma-to-Mongomery march in 1965 has been omitted—ed.

championing segregation. At the congregational level, the debate has raged over the issue of integrated churches—a question that was raised only after the mid-1950s, when many white Protestant churches adopted closed-door policies in response to the civil rights movement. This problem gained national attention in 1976 when the deacons of Plains Baptist Church, the home church of Democratic presidential candidate Jimmy Carter of Georgia, enforced its closed-door policy against Rev. Clennon King and three other African Americans. The specter haunting Baptists wrangling over integrated churches was a familiar one: miscegenation. In 1971, the Baptist Sunday School Board revised 140,000 copies of *Becoming*, its quarterly magazine for teenagers, because an article supporting open churches was accompanied by a photograph of an African American boy talking to two white girls.[31]

More important than the way Christian theology continues to buttress segregationist views within the church has been the effort to use the constitutional protection of religion to expand the social sphere in which segregation could remain. The main battleground here has been private religious schools. In 1979 (against the counsel of the Christian Life Commission, still sounding from the wilderness), the Southern Baptist Convention adopted by an overwhelming margin a resolution that opposed a federal proposal to deny tax-exempt status to private schools that discriminated on the basis of race. While the SBC resolved, the federal government sued. Its target was well chosen: Bob Jones University in South Carolina, which until the spring of 2000 prohibited interracial dating among its students. Founded in 1927, Bob Jones excluded black students until 1971. Revealing a deep concern about interracial marriage, from 1971 to 1975 the university accepted a small number of black students who were already married to other African Americans. In 1975 the university began to accept unmarried black students but prohibited interracial dating and marriage, insisting that "God has separated people for His own purpose."[32]

Because of this policy, in 1976 the Internal Revenue Service stripped the university of its tax-exempt status, arguing that federally supported institutions could not advocate views "contrary to established public policy" even if those views were grounded in religious belief. In 1983 the Supreme Court upheld this decision in *Bob Jones University v. United States*. In this important ruling, the Court failed to grant constitutional protection to the expansion of religious privacy into other associational areas. At the same time, however, the Court recognized that some Americans might "engage in racial discrimination on the basis of sincerely-held religious beliefs." White supremacists and other defenders of segregation have not been shy about embracing such beliefs, especially if such a move gains them the protection of the religion clause of the First Amendment and the Fourteenth Amendment's "zone of privacy." In 1984, Mississippi senator Trent Lott insisted that the main issue in the Bob Jones case was "not a racial question, but a religious question. And yet the Internal Revenue Service is going in, making a determination of that school's tax-deductible status, based on a religious belief."[33]

If religion has been and continues to be so important to those arguing in favor of segregation as well as to those resisting it, why have modern historians preferred to study scientific racism or white supremacist politics and ignored this more widespread and deeply held set of beliefs? Perhaps the answer lies in a scholarly inclination to take the historical teleology of secularization so seriously as to distort our own idea of what is important. Religion ends up being seen as an archaic vestige, at most a rhetorical plaything of ideologues in the modern age (as indeed it sometimes is), and not as a coherent cosmology capable of providing modern people with an all-encompassing model of social relations. Such an outlook overlooks the "suppleness" of American religion and underplays its importance in modern America.[34]

An equally important reason for continued scholarly indifference to the religious roots of white resistance to black civil rights has to do with what can only be seen as the victory of the theology of the beloved community. For many scholars otherwise uninterested in seeing religion as a meaningful part of public life in post-World War II America, "true" Christianity has become synonymous with the vision of Martin Luther King and other Christian integrationists. In a recent issue of the *New Yorker*, Louis Menand argued,

> It was King's genius to see that in the matter of racial equality the teachings of the Christian Bible are on all fours with the promise of the Constitution and its amendments. With one brilliant stroke, he transformed what had been a legal struggle into a spiritual one, and lost nothing in the bargain.[35]

King certainly lost nothing in this bargain. But those scholars who treat uncritically King's Christianity as "orthodox" or "true" not only lose a great deal of historical and theological complexity, they also miss most of the real drama in the monumental conflict between the integrationist Christian theology of liberation and its venerable counterpart, the theology of segregation.

NOTES

1 David L. Chappell, *A Stone of Hope: Prophetic Religion and the Death of Jim Crow* (Chapel Hill, 2004), 4. Clayborne Carson, ed., *The Papers of Martin Luther King Jr.* (4 vols., Berkeley, 1992–), III, 306. King on the Prodigal Son

quoted in Ralph E. Luker, "Kingdom of God and Beloved Community in the Thought of Martin Luther King Jr.," in *The Role of Ideas in the Civil Rights Movement*, ed. Ted Ownby (Jackson, 2002), 44.

2 Will Campbell quoted in *New York Times*, July 14, 1958. "Body of Christ" from *Student Voice* (Tougaloo College Student Movement paper), April 1964, folder 3, box 3, Ed King Collection (Special Collections, J. D. Williams Library, University of Mississippi, Oxford) [WLUM]. King quoted in Charles Marsh, "The Civil Rights Movement as Theological Drama," in *Role of Ideas in the Civil Rights Movement*, ed. Ownby, 30.

3 Aldon D. Morris, *The Origins of the Civil Rights Movement: Black Communities Organizing for Change* (New York, 1984), 4. For a nuanced argument of the importance of religion to the movement, see Charles M. Payne, *I've Got the Light of Freedom: The Organizing Tradition and the Mississippi Freedom Struggle* (Berkeley, 1995), 257; for a qualification of its influence, see Adam Fairclough, *To Redeem the Soul of America: The Southern Christian Leadership Conference and Martin Luther King Jr.* (Athens, Ga., 1987), 9. . . .

4 Chappell refers to the "strained arguments segregationists used to justify segregation on religious grounds," in Chappell, *Stone of Hope*, 3; see also . . . Chappell, "Religious Ideas of the Segregationists," *Journal of American Studies*, 32 (no. 2, 1998), 253. Paul Harvey, "Religion, Race, and the Right in the Baptist South, 1945–1990" (manuscript in Jane Dailey's possession), 5; Bill J. Leonard, "A Theology for Racism: Southern Fundamentalists and the Civil Rights Movement," in *Southern Landscapes*, ed. Tony Badger, Walter Edgar, and Jan Nordby Gretlunds (Tübingen, 1996), 165–81. Wayne Flynt also refers to "segregationist theology": Wayne Flynt, *Alabama Baptists: Southern Baptists in the Heart of Dixie* (Tuscaloosa, 1998), 458. . . . While there was a broad and growing split on the race question between national denominational leaders and seminaries, on the one hand, and southern laypersons and many clergy, on the other, to denote segregationist theology as "folk" theology is to miss the crucial point that, as Flynt writes with regard to the Baptists (by far the largest southern Protestant denomination), "lay people charted the course on race relations. Laymen shaped the Baptist response to race from the *Brown* decision forward": Flynt, *Alabama Baptists*, 465. Andrew Michael Manis presents the civil rights movement in the South as an internal dispute among Baptists . . .; see Andrew Michael Manis, *Southern Civil Religions in Conflict: Black and White Baptists and Civil Rights, 1954–1957* (Athens, Ga., 1987). . . .

5 Rev. James F. Burks, "Integration or Segregation?" May 30, 1954, typescript, folder 1, box 100, General Correspondence, Executive Papers, Gov. Thomas B. Stanley (1954–1958) (Library of Virginia, Richmond). Deuteronomy 32:8: "When the Most High gave the nations their inheritance, when he divided the sons of men, he fixed their bounds," *Jerusalem Bible* (1966); Acts 17:26: "From one single stock he not only created the whole human race so that they could occupy the entire earth, but he decreed how long each nation should flourish and what the boundaries of its territory should be," *ibid.* Burks's warning referred to II Thessalonians 2:3–4.

6 Pastor of Highland Baptist Church of Montgomery quoted in Neil R. McMillan, *The Citizens' Council: Organized Resistance to the Second Reconstruction, 1954–64* (Urbana, 1971), 174.

7 Some Christian apologists for segregation used the curse of Ham argument; see, for example, G. T. Gillespie Sr., *A Christian View of Segregation* (Greenwood, Miss., 1954). My evidence suggests, however, that most Christian

segregationists referred more easily to the bounds of habitation argument. On the curse of Ham, see Sparks, *Religion in Mississippi*, 229. . . .

8 The biblical narrative is Genesis 3:1–7. Henry Ansgar Kelly, "The Metamorphosis of the Eden Serpent during the Middle Ages and Renaissance," *Viator*, 2 (1971), 301–28. The "Negro gardener" argument is from Samuel A. Cartwright, quoted in George M. Fredrickson, *The Black Image in the White Mind: The Debate on Afro-American Character and Destiny, 1817–1914* (Middletown, 1987), 87–88. Ariel [Buckner H. Payne], *The Negro: What Is His Ethnological Status?* (1867), in John David Smith, *The "Ariel" Controversy: Religion and "The Negro Problem"* (New York, 1993), 45, 48. . . .

9 Charles Carroll, *The Negro a Beast* (St. Louis, 1900); Charles Carroll, *The Tempter of Eve* (St. Louis, 1902). . . . H. Paul Douglass, *Christian Reconstruction in the South* (Boston, 1909), 114. On the longevity of proslavery arguments, including religious arguments, and their applicability in the Jim Crow era, see Smith, *Old Creed for the New South*, 286.

10 Early Van Deventer, *Perfection of the Races* [1954] (pamphlet), folder 1, box 100, General Correspondence, Stanley Executive Papers; Burks, "Integration or Segregation?"; D. B. Red, *Race Mixing a Religious Fraud* [c. 1959], box 2, Wm. D. McCain Papers (McCain Archives and Special Collections, Cook Library, University of Southern Mississippi, Hattiesburg). *Laurel* [Miss.] *Leader Call* quoted in Charles Marsh, *God's Long Summer: Stories of Faith and Civil Rights* (Princeton, 1997), 93. The biblical narratives being discussed are in Genesis 6–9, 18, 11; 1 Kings 11; Exodus.

11 Numerous pamphlets and private letters consider integration and miscegenation a Communist plot. . . . Carey Daniel, "God the Original Segregationist," quoted in McMillan, *Citizens' Council*, 175. Burks, "Integration or Segregation?" Theodore G. Bilbo, *Take Your Choice: Separation or Mongrelization* (Poplarville, Miss., 1947), 109.

12 Henry Louttit quoted in Gardiner H. Shattuck Jr., *Episcopalians and Race: Civil War to Civil Rights* (Lexington, 2000), 68; W. M. Caskey quoted in Randy J. Sparks, *Religion in Mississippi* (Jackson, 2001), 231. Ministers at Little Rock in Ernest Q. Campbell and Thomas F. Pettigrew, *Christians in Racial Crisis: A Study of Little Rock's Ministry* (Washington, 1959), 51. Cameron Baptist Church quoted in Mark Newman, *Getting Right with God: Southern Baptists and Desegregation, 1945–1995* (Tuscaloosa, 2001), 51; David M. Gardner quoted *ibid.*, 50.

13 Daughters of the American Revolution quoted in flyer "Racial Integrity," p. 2 n. 15, #3551, E. A. Holt Papers (Southern Historical Collection, University of North Carolina). *Florida ex rel. Hawkins v. Board of Control* . . . quoted in David L. Chappell, *Inside Agitators: White Southerners in the Civil Rights Movement* (Baltimore, 1994), 91. *Loving v. Commonwealth* (1965) (Record No. 6163), 15.

14 For the letters to Gov. Thomas B. Stanley, see boxes 100 and 101, General Correspondence, Stanley Executive Papers.

15 On the reluctance of the Court to tackle the miscegenation issue while *Brown II* was pending, see interview of Philip Elman by Norman Silber, "The Solicitor General's Office, Justice Frankfurter, and Civil Rights Litigation, 1946–1960: An Oral History," *Harvard Law Review*, 100 (Feb. 1987), 846. On reaction to the 1955 antimiscegenation case (*Naim v. Naim*, 350 U.S. 891), see Gerald Gunther, "The Subtle Vices of the 'Passive Virtues'—A Comment on the Principle and Expediency in Judicial Review," *Columbia Law Review*, 1 (1964), 11. Alexander M. Bickel, "Integrated Cohabitation," *New Republic*,

May 30, 1964, p. 4. . . . Memorandum from Justice John Marshall Harlan II quoted in Rachel F. Moran, *Interracial Intimacy: The Regulation of Race and Romance* (Chicago, 2001), 91.

16 On the history of antimiscegenation laws in America, see Peter Wallenstein, *Tell the Court I Love My Wife: Race, Marriage, and Law—An American History* (New York, 2002); Moran, *Interracial Intimacy*; Peggy Pascoe, "Miscegenation Law, Court Cases, and Ideologies of 'Race' in Twentieth-Century America," *Journal of American History*, 83 (June 1996), 44–69; and Walter Wadlington, "The *Loving* Case: Virginia's Anti-Miscegenation Statute in Historical Perspective," *Virginia Law Review*, 52 (1966), 1189–1223. Gunnar Myrdal, *An American Dilemma: The Negro Problem and Modern Democracy* (New York, 1944), 587.

17 For the NAACP position on intermarriage, see the correspondence between Walter White, Alfred Lewis (secretary of the Boston branch), and Florence H. Luscomb, June 1–6, 1938, folder 247, box 11, Florence Hope Luscomb Papers (Schlesinger Library, Radcliffe Institute for Advanced Study, Cambridge, Mass.). Thurgood Marshall quoted in Richard Kluger, *Simple Justice: The History of Brown v. Board of Education and Black America's Struggle for Equality* (New York, 1975), 266. On the NAACP's attempts to avoid cases involving sex offenses, see Jack Greenberg, *Crusaders in the Courts: How a Dedicated Band of Lawyers Fought for the Civil Rights Revolution* (New York, 1994), 102.

18 Mark Ethridge, "A Call to the South," *Nieman Reports*, 13 (April 1959), 9. *Jackson Daily News* quoted in Stephen J. Whitfield, *A Death in the Delta: The Story of Emmett Till* (Baltimore, 1988), 9. Walter C. Givhan quoted in Melissa Fay Green, *The Temple Bombing* (Reading, Mass., 1996), 148. Herman E. Talmadge quoted in Stephen G. N. Tuck, *Beyond Atlanta: The Struggle for Racial Equality in Georgia, 1940–1980* (Athens, Ga., 2001), 77; Talmadge quoted in *Ebony*, 12 (April 1957), 78; William A. Robinson Jr. to Talmadge, May 25, 1954 (copied to Thomas B. Stanley), in folder 2, box 100, General Correspondence, Stanley Executive Papers. Eugene Cook quoted in Green, *Temple Bombing*, 149. *Racial Facts* (1964) quoted in Marsh, *God's Long Summer*, 84.

19 Of the thirty largest daily newspapers in the South, all were hostile to the *Brown* decision except for a dozen in the border states; see David R. Davies, *The Press and Race: Mississippi Journalists Confront the Movement* (Jackson, 2001), 9. Keith Miller's survey of homiletic collections reveals few sermons concerned with race issues prior to the Montgomery bus boycott; see Keith Miller, *Voice of Deliverance: The Language of Martin Luther King Jr. and its Sources* (New York, 1992), 53. Hodding Carter quoted in Tony Badger, "The Crisis of Southern Liberalism, 1946–65," in *The Making of Martin Luther King and the Civil Rights Movement*, ed. Brian Ward and Tony Badger (New York, 1996), 69. Southeastern Regional Methodist Student Conference (37 signatures) to Stanley, June 11, 1954, folder 1, box 100, General Correspondence, Stanley Executive Papers. For the North Carolina Methodist conference, see *Raleigh News and Observer*, Aug. 21, 1954, p. 1. National Baptist Convention announcement quoted in Manis, *Southern Civil Religions in Conflict*, 61. Joe Louis quoted in "Backstage," *Ebony*, 9 (Aug. 1954), 14.

20 Lillian Smith quoted in Pete Daniel, *Lost Revolutions: The South in the 1950s* (Chapel Hill, 2000), 182. A complaint representative of the concerns of those funding foreign missions was that "the practice of legal segregation on the basis of race weakens our Christian witness at home and abroad and lays a

roadblock across the path of our missionaries": Editor's Page, *Alabama Baptist*, Nov. 4, 1954. On the governing boards, see Michael B. Friedland, *Lift Up Your Voice like a Trumpet: White Clergy and the Civil Rights and Antiwar Movements, 1954–1973* (Chapel Hill, 1998), 18–19. Joel L. Alvis Jr., *Religion and Race: Southern Presbyterians, 1946–1983* (Tuscaloosa, 1994), 57–58.

21 Rev. George E. Naff Jr., Coeburn Methodist Church, to Stanley, July 1, 1954, folder 1, box 101, General Correspondence, Stanley Executive Papers. Robert Penn Warren, *Segregation: The Inner Conflict in the South* (New York, 1956), 57. . . . "Hand of God," quoted in Daniel, *Lost Revolutions*, 184; "Pinkos in the Pulpit," *Citizens' Council*, Dec. 1956, quoted in David L. Chappell, "A Stone of Hope: Prophetic Faith, Liberalism, and the Death of Jim Crow," *Journal of the Historical Society*, 3 (March 2003), 152. Douglas Hudgins quoted in Marsh, *God's Long Summer*, 100–1. J. W. Storer quoted in Newman, *Getting Right with God*, 23. . . . King objected to this interpretation; he insisted that Christians must embrace the civil rights movement on theological and moral grounds as well as civic ones. See Martin Luther King, "Letter from Birmingham City Jail" (1963), in *A Testament of Hope: The Essential Writings of Martin Luther King Jr.*, ed. James Melvin Washington (San Francisco, 1986), 289–302.

22 Shattuck, *Episcopalians and Race*, 79–80. Statement of Atlanta clergymen quoted in Newman, *Getting Right with God*, 45. Editor's Page, *Alabama Baptist*, Feb. 10, 1955. Campbell and Pettigrew, *Christians in Racial Crisis*, 100.

23 . . . [For the] historiographical consensus on the sexualization of school desegregation; see James T. Patterson, Brown v. Board of Education: *A Civil Rights Milestone and Its Troubled Legacy* (New York, 2001), 86–117. Special issue, "The Church and Segregation," *Presbyterian Outlook*, May 3, 1954, folder 1, box 100, General Correspondence, Stanley Executive Papers. Burks, "Integration or Segregation?" W. L. Trotten Sr. to Stanley, June 8, 1954, folder 1, box 100, General Correspondence, Stanley Executive Papers; Elmer M. Ramsey to Stanley, June 7, 1954, *ibid*.

24 Mrs. Jesse L. West to Stanley, June 3, 1954, folder 1, box 100, General Correspondence, Stanley Executive Papers; Mrs. G. P. Smith to Stanley, June 8, 1954, *ibid.*; Mr. and Mrs. J. W. Layne to Stanley, June 8, 1954, *ibid.* . . .

25 Mrs. R. E. Martin to Stanley, May 27, 1954, folder 1, box 100, General Correspondence, Stanley Executive Papers; Mrs. Henry Winter Davis to Stanley, June 10, 1954, *ibid*.

26 R. D. Cook to Stanley, June 3, 1954, folder 2, *ibid.*; J. D. Jones to Stanley, May 28, 1954, folder 1, *ibid.*; Mrs. James Irving Beale to Stanley, June 8, 1954, *ibid*.

27 On Thrasher and more broadly on the Episcopal Church and desegregation, see Shattuck, *Episcopalians and Race*, 77. "Pulpit and Pew," chapter title in Chappell, *Stone of Hope*. Regional council official quoted in Reed Sarratt, *The Ordeal of Desegregation: The First Decade* (New York, 1966), 276. Marshall Frady, "God and Man in the South," *Atlantic Monthly*, 219 (Jan. 1967), 38.

28 *Citizens' Council*, 1 (April 1956), in folder 19, box 1, Ed King Collection. King in *Ebony*, 12 (April 1957), 120. . . .

29 Harvey, "Religion, Race, and the Right in the Baptist South," 5. For youth conference delegations, see, for example, Resolution of Methodist Youth from Eastern North Carolina, as reported in *Raleigh News and Observer*, Aug. 21, 1954. "Resolution Adopted on December 12 by the Quarterly Conference of the Newton Grove Charge and Wesley Circuit," Dec. 12, 1954, 1953–54 file, Nell Battle Lewis Collection, PS 255.40 (North Carolina State Archives, Raleigh). Lawyer quoted in Thomas F. Pettigrew, "Our

Caste-Ridden Protestant Campuses," *Christianity and Crisis: Race in America*, 21 (May 29, 1961), 88–91, in folder 3, box 3, Ed King Collection. The denomination was probably the Episcopalians. Summerton Baptist Church resolution quoted in Newman, *Getting Right with God*, 53. On Episcopalians see Shattuck, *Episcopalians and Race*, 68; on southern Baptists see Newman, *Getting Right with God*, 41; overall, see Chappell, "Stone of Hope," 151.

30 Minutes, 1964–1966, box 1, Americans for the Preservation of the White Race Collection (WLUM). Chappell, "Religious Ideas of the Segregationists," 249.

31 On *Becoming*, see Newman, *Getting Right with God*, 33. Considerable scholarly work on the integration of southern churches will have to be undertaken before it becomes possible to make more than speculative assertions about this debate. But it is clear at least that both sides recognized sacred space as a crucial frontier in the desegregation battle, and both sides made theological arguments in favor of their conflicting positions. . . .

32 A recent analysis of federal data on private school enrollments by the Civil Rights Project at Harvard University found that private religious schools are more racially segregated than public ones: "Study Finds Parochial Schools Segregated along Racial Lines," *New York Times*, Aug. 30, 2002, A18. Admissions Office of Bob Jones University to James Landrith, Aug. 31, 1998, in *The Multiracial Activist* http://www.multiracial.com/letters/bobjonesuniversity.html > (Dec. 11, 2003); . . . .

33 *Bob Jones University v. United States*, 461 U.S. 574, 602 (1983). Trent Lott interview in *Southern Partisan* (Fall 1984), 47.

34 Jon Butler, "Jack-in-the-Box Faith: The Religion Problem in Modern American History," *Journal of American History*, 90 (March 2004), 1357–78, esp. 1359.

35 Louis Menand, "Moses in Alabama," *New Yorker*, Sept. 8, 2003, p. 31.

INDEX